ORIGINS OF MODERNISM
VOL. 7

KEEPING THE VICTORIAN HOUSE

GARLAND REFERENCE LIBRARY
OF THE HUMANITIES
VOL. 1818

ORIGINS OF MODERNISM:
GARLAND STUDIES IN BRITISH LITERATURE

TODD K. BENDER
Series Editor

KEEPING THE VICTORIAN HOUSE

A Collection of Essays

edited by

Vanessa D. Dickerson

GARLAND PUBLISHING, Inc.
New York & London / 1995

Library of Congress Cataloging-in-Publication Data

Keeping the Victorian house : a collection of essays /
edited by Vanessa D. Dickerson.
      p.   cm. — (Garland reference library of the hu-
manities ; vol. 1818. Origins of modernism ; vol. 7)
    Includes bibliographical references.
    ISBN 0–8153–1575–9
    1. Domestic fiction, English—History and criti-
cism.   2. Literature and society—Great Britain—History—19th century.   3. Women and literature—Great
Britain—History—19th century.   4. English fiction—
19th century—History and criticism.   5. Home economics in literature.   6. Dwellings in literature.   7.
Family in literature.   8. Home in literature.   I.
Dickerson, Vanessa D., 1955–   . II. Series: Garland
reference library of the humanities ; vol. 1818.   III.
Series: Garland reference library of the humanities.
Origins of modernism ; vol. 7.
PR878.D65K44   1995
820.9'355—dc20   94–30414
                                                   CIP

Printed on acid-free, 250-year-life paper
Manufactured in the United States of America

To Yanna, for keeping me

Contents

**Part Two: A Woman's Work Is Never Done:
Women's Work and Domestic Space**

Series Editor's Preface

The Modernist Movement, characterized by the works of T.S. Eliot, James Joyce, Virginia Woolf, William Faulkner, and writers of similar stature, dominated Anglo-American literature for some fifty years following World War I. By the time the United States emerged from its military involvement in Indo-China in the 1970s, the Modernist Movement had disintegrated into Post-Modernism. High Modernism's most proud claim was that it would "make it new," that it represented a radical and sudden break with previous cultural traditions. We now see this claim to be false. Nowhere is Modernism more derivative than in its claim to radical novelty. The Modernist "revolution" of the twentieth century is best seen as the culmination of ideology developing in the late nineteenth century. This series of books is devoted to the study of the origins of Modernism in the half-century between the Franco-Prussian War and the First World War, from the death of Dickens to the roaring twenties and the Lost Generation.

As drama is the center of the literature of the Elizabethan Age, so criticism is the focus of the Modernist Age. Modernist writers worked in an environment of university and school curricula more introspective, self-conscious, and cannibalistic than ever before. How did the philosophical and pedagogical system supporting Modernism develop? What part does feminism play in the struggle for literary domination? How do changing systems of patronage and the economy of literature influence Modernism as a vastly expanded reading public is eventually augmented by cinema, radio, and television as consumers of literature? Do the roots of cultural pluralism within English literature recede back to the Victorian era? When

English is used as the vehicle for expression of American, Canadian, Australian, or Indian culture; or for Afro-American, Hispano-American, Asian-American, or Amero-Indian culture, where do the origins of this eclectic pluralism lie?

We believe that there are two important groups of writers essential to the development of Modernism: (1) Gerard Manley Hopkins and the circle of his correspondents (Robert Bridges, Coventry Patmore, Canon Richard Watson Dixon, and related figures) and (2) the circle of writers surrounding Joseph Conrad (Ford Madox Ford, Henry James, Stephen Crane, and others). We especially encourage the further study of these two groups as foundation stones for the Modernist Movement, but there are many other sources important to its development.

Todd K. Bender
University of Wisconsin

Acknowledgments

I would like to thank the Faculty Development Committee and the Office of the Academic Dean at Rhodes College for providing me with the time and money to shape and complete this project. Frank Fennell also gets a big "thank you" for some very timely advice. I am grateful to Todd K. Bender who took the time to read the manuscript and see its merits. Finally I want to acknowledge the invaluable assistance of Charles Wilkinson who helped me make this manuscript presentable, who helped me get this manuscript to press.

Housekeeping and Housekept Angels

House and home are part of an ongoing natural phenomenon: all animals have habitats. The houses in which human beings dwell, however, accrue so much more significance when one acknowledges how "divisions of spaces and social formations are intimately associated," how space once it is "bounded and shaped . . . is no longer merely a neutral background: it exerts its own influence."[1] In fact, as one of the most significant structurings of space, the house constitutes not only a natural but also a social, cultural, political, economic and, according to Gaston Bachelard, a poetic phenomenon.[2] The very houses people build may in turn speak, as Shirley Arderner, citing E.T. Hall, says of space; the house can and does shape and define life.

Up until the onset of industrialism, the concept of house and home had mainly evoked ideas of shelter, protection, rest, even economic subsistence and enterprise, as the agrarian and pre-industrial household was a work site where men, women, and children got their living. The house allowed for and accommodated more traffic and movement since it encompassed closed and private personal space as well as open and public work space. But with the advent of the Industrial Revolution, labor for wages, and the attendant export especially of work with textile and clothing manufacture from the home to the factories, there was a shrinkage in the house as a "theatre of action."[3]

And yet, the house had never so powerfully, explicitly, and strictly defined society as it would in nineteenth-century Britain. It was during this period that the Victorians, harkening back to the idea of natural habitats, would further limit the house as a theatre of action by re-inventing the home as woman's natural or appropriate place: she belonged in the house be-

cause biology put her there. Even today, a writer like Sally
Gearhart concedes that "Finally biology for sure is destiny in this
sense, that as women we *are* what the patriarchy has labelled us:
vessels, containers, receptacles, carriers, shelters, houses, nurtur-
ers, incubators, holders, enfolders, listeners."[4] Vanguard for the
"patriarchal doctrine of the separate spheres,"[5] the Victorian
house, privatized and compartmentalized as it was, no longer or
so obviously constituted a multipurpose or multivalent space. It
was increasingly a space defined by an interiority it shared with
the female. Oddly enough this interiority, though ostensibly valued, was still based in negation and separation and ultimately
associated with subordination if not out-and-out inferiority: the
home was "other," a narrow and colonized female space that existed in opposition to and in support of the master space, that
place outside the home where the business of making a living
took place, where livings were earned instead of consumed. As
such, the Victorian home proved one of the first configurations
of space in a capitalist society into what Daphne Spain in her excellent study of gendered spaces refers to as "masculine centers
of production and feminine suburbs of reproduction."[6]

During the Victorian Age one of the most powerful and
notable registers of woman's sphere was the phrase Coventry
Patmore made current with his poem about the ideal woman
and wife, "The Angel in the House" (1854-1856). Describing Patmore's tribute to the "connubial sacrament" as "overdrawn,"
Marlene Springer admits that the angel in the house, who figures
in the poem as one "saintly, submissive" and, by virtue of her
love, an "indispensable civilizing power"—this one angelic
Honoria "was taken to be on the whole a realistic possibility.
Many Victorians tried to be, or to have, Honoria; the book [*The
Angel in the House*] sold a quarter of a million copies before Patmore's death in 1896."[7] The troping of the Victorian woman as
angel proved as much a subtle depreciation as it was an elevation of woman's position. Taking as it gives, prescribing as it describes, undercutting even as it aggrandizes, the concept of the
angel in the house is double-edged and consequently troubling.
What, after all, are the semantic and spatial implications of removing an angel from heaven and stationing that being in a
household? A being so positioned brings to mind notions of

blessings and of an earthly paradise; nevertheless, these pleasant associations are upon reflection quickly attended by thoughts of dislocation, displacement, and confinement, if not concealment, exile, and banishment. In other words, the terms "angel" and "house" problematize each other. To call woman an angel was to deify her as a being with special spiritual powers; however, to relegate the angelic woman to the house was in fact to fix her at the center of a dwelling increasingly bounded and marked by "gates, drives, hedges and walls,"[8] to limit, moreover, her access to exterior expanses, and to abstract and thereby dismiss her powers in realms where men expressed themselves and wielded material-based power. The expression "angel in the house" cloaked a spatial arrangement that, as Spain convincingly argues, "reinforced status differences between men and women." The angel experienced in fact a debilitating segregation. Assigned to the home, women were effectively barred from acquiring the knowledge that secured "male advantages." Dwellings, schools, and workplaces, again according to Spain's study, "form barriers to woman's acquisition of knowledge by assigning women and men to different gendered spaces. Masculine spaces . . . contain socially valued knowledge of theology, law, and medicine, while feminine spaces (such as the home) contain devalued knowledge of child care, cooking, and cleaning."[9] The segregation of the Victorian woman was, then, insidious. Her discretion, her ability to "soften and attract,"[10] to comfort, quieten, and morally sway were lauded and cherished above and beyond any demonic energies she might betray by acting outside the bounds of the domestic circle into which she was charmed.[11]

Within the walls of the house, the true woman could spiritualize space. That is, she could enhance "the maternal features of the house" which, like woman's body, is the place where "Life begins well, it begins enclosed, protected, all warm in the bosom of the house." Cultivating and enhancing these features of the house, even reinscribing them in her very body, the Victorian woman could lend viability to what French phenomenologist Gaston Bouchelard calls "the soul of the house," the house which after all "constitutes a body of images that give mankind proofs or illusions of stability." By fostering life, love, stability, the angelic woman would create if not a sacred space then at least a place apart from the flux of that arena which more than any other during the Victorian era lay "outside the being of the house, a circumstance in which the hostility of men and of the universe accumulates"[12]—the marketplace. As Linda C. Hunt writes in *A Woman's Portion* (1988), her study of ideology and culture in the British female novel: "In the mind of society the female character had become an alternative to the marketplace values which threatened to obliterate the aesthetic, moral, and emotional dimensions of life. For this reason, even those intellectuals who repudiated conventional Christianity and embraced advanced ideas were often unable to extricate themselves from the mythology of true womanhood."[13]

Interestingly enough, it requires only a little more effort to conceive how the house in turn could spiritualize the woman. For in spite of Ruskin's assurance that the true wife carries the home round her wherever she is, the etherealized female needed to be housed; that is, she wanted an office for her agency, she needed a home base.[14] The importance of this requisite becomes clear when one considers the Victorian woman's relation to "organized religion [here the Protestant Church, which] often reinforce[d] women's lower status.[15] As Coon, Haldane, and Sommer point out in their introduction to *That Gentle Strength* (1990), ". . . although Protestantism gave women positive secular roles (as wives and mothers) its rejection of monastic piety made holding any unique spiritual office problematic. There was no specific institutional place wherein women could express spirituality." There was however the home where angels dared to tread. Coon, Haldane, and Sommers also recognize this locus of women's spiritual agency when they observe, "More than in any other period, Victorian women and men agreed that women were the more spiritual sex. But because their spiritual role was based in the home, they could not exercise public authority."[16] Spiritualization has its limitations, it would seem, especially when domesticated. Recently, however, Nina Auerbach, commenting on the relation of the angel to Christianity, has shrewdly suggested that the spiritualized, if not de-politicized woman in the house was not as passive as she initially appears. "This apparently quiescent figure [the angel in the house]," writes Auerbach, "is an implicit revolt against the patriarchal imagery of official Christianity, suggesting less a passive with-drawal from life than an active displacement of male religious icons. In their elevation of the female angel, men we dismiss too easily as reactionary were part of a broader surge towards the establishment of a new mythos."[17] Men could resuscitate their empirically belabored and expiring religion through the women-folk, through the cults of domesticity and of true womanhood.

Be this as it may, the fact remains that for every angel in the house there was a God on the premises too. That is to say, though the Victorian angel presided over the house, even here, final and real authority rested with the male who was head of the family. Whether "the husband . . . father, or in his absence, brother, brother-in-law, or eldest son," the male was, Davidoff and Hall confirm, "the civil as well as religious representative. He exemplified external authority and the Fatherhood of God; and he usually controlled economic resources."[18] H.L. Beales colorfully and more forcefully declares of the Victorian man around the house, "Every Englishman's home was his castle. In its sanctities and privacy a man might escape from the trials of the outer world and be safe from its prying eyes. The family was indeed a kind of estate, like, say, the British Empire, and subject like it to the benevolent despotism of its lord and master. For it *had* a lord and master, and his ways were expected to be authori-tarian."[19] The home that was the *donnée* of the female, was also the preserve of the male.

Architecturally, the house, especially the Victorian country house, reflected a particular if not fastidious concern for the needs of the male for space within the domestic arena. "The ideal Victorian home," for example, "contained a drawing room for ladies and smoking and billiard rooms for gentlemen; the 'growlery' was the husband's retreat from domesticity."[20] Com-menting on how "both geography and architecture" increasingly "marked" the separation of spheres, Janet Wolff effectively quotes Mark Girouard's *The Victorian Country Home* (1979), making it clear that the Victorian male occupied special areas in the house:

> The design of the new houses themselves usually accorded
> well with the ideology of separate spheres. With regard to
> the middle-class elite, Mark Girouard argues that agree-

ment by 1850 about what a 'gentleman's house' should be like included the requirements that 'it should provide decent quarters for servants. It should protect the womanliness of women and encourage the manliness of men.' As well as an extremely complex and often impractical arrangement of rooms, so that children, servants, mothers, and fathers should only coincide at approved times and in approved places, Victorian houses also contained 'an increasingly large and sacrosanct male domain', whose nucleus was the billiard room. The domain often expanded to include the smoking room and the gun room, and sometimes an adjoining dressing room and study.[21]

These spatial boundaries between men and women within the home helped to maintain even here "the unequal status of women."[22]

The ideal Victorian home may have been socially, culturally, and mythically associated with the female but it was legally and financially under the auspices of the male. For though the house was set apart from the marketplace, "it had to provide more than just a haven for family withdrawal for the home was also a stage for social ritual and outward manifestation of status in the community."[23] In other words, the house could serve as a showplace for the male's successful activities in the marketplace. The money he earned helped create and sustain the domestic quarters that were a retreat from the commercialization of public life. The house, then, was not merely some quasi-heaven through which woman floated. It was, especially for the wealthy and also the middle classes, a possession, a piece of real estate usually owned by the male who legally did pretty much the same by his wife; that is, he practically owned her too, since she lived, according to the law of coverture, only in him. As John Stuart Mill recognized, the woman unable to hold property was "the actual bond-servant of her husband:" "she can acquire no property but for him; the instant it becomes hers, even if by inheritance, it becomes *ipso facto* his."[24] Though it was Shakespeare's crafty Petruchio who, set upon taming his shrewish Kate, declared that "she [among the other things] is my house,"[25] it was the Victorians who sought most avidly to ensure the male's position as head of the house even as they standardized the equation between the angelic female and the male-owned house. The Victorian woman more than any other female before or after her was in the house, of the house, the very house itself. More specifically, the angel in the house tended to be in the patriarchal house, "within his house, as ruled by her," as Ruskin, that most influential artistic and social critic of the age, declared.[26]

This is not to say that men's investment in the hearth and home was strictly financial and legal or that all men dictatorily occupied domestic space. Davidoff and Hall point out that though some men as head of household "exercised their power in a direct and domineering manner," there were those who were intensely involved with their families and took "a loving interest in their children's lives." Elsewhere in *Family Fortunes* (1987), Davidoff and Hall contend that "men also took an active part in setting up the home . . . they often planned and maintained the garden, or at least the masculine sections of it. Men were responsible for buying certain items: wine, books, pictures, musical instruments and wheeled vehicles. They accompanied their wives to buy furniture and carpets, while both men and women painted and papered rooms." Still the daily business of homemaking fell to women who "were mainly responsible for creating and maintaining the house, its contents and its human constitutents."[27] Victorian women kept the father's house.

Being in the father's house could prove an attractive proposition, especially to the dispossessed and the homeless. One of the nineteenth century's most enduring works, Mary Shelley's *Frankenstein* (1818) strongly suggests that the father's house was indeed a desirable place to be. The monster in the novel, driven from pillar to post, quickly comes to recognize the allure of the house.[28] The creature is enthralled when it gets its first good look at a human habitation: "This was a new sight to me, and I examined the structure with great curiosity . . . I was enchanted by the appearance of the hut; here the snow and rain could not penetrate; the ground was dry; and it presented to me then as exquisite and divine a retreat as Pandemonium appeared to the demons of hell after their sufferings in the lake of fire." The creature is even more appreciative when it happens upon a community of houses: "I arrived at a village. How miraculous did this appear! The huts, the neater cottages, and stately houses engaged my admiration by turns."[29] Parentless, lonely, solitary, hounded, and despised, the monster not only understands the physical, but also witnesses the social, communal, humanistic benefits that can radiate from the house when it takes asylum in a hovel adjacent to the cottage of the French-speaking De Laceys. As the creature observes the cottagers and Safie, the foreign female who joins them, it not only acquires language, but also gains a sense of how the house and home might legitimize it or at least be the compass of familial relations it hopes to establish with the De Laceys, a connection it has already begun to establish with the Arabian Safie who shares its foreigness and its need to learn the language of the cottagers. Subsequently, the monster tries to ingratiate itself with the De Laceys by becoming their guardian angel and contributing to the upkeep of the household: it secretly gathers food for the kitchen stores and fuel for the family hearth. When the feminized creature[30] finally begs the blind father De Lacey to be let into the house, it expresses its most ardent desire not only to be, like Safie and Agatha, protected, but also to experience intimacy and to partake of the domesticity from which it has been excluded. From where the creature stands or, more precisely, crouches, the father's house looks like a warm, loving, educational space.

This same wondrous space, however, could sorely confine, as a later novel, Emily Brontë's *Wuthering Heights* (1847), suggests. When Catherine Earnshaw marries Edgar Linton, she gains admittance to and sway over Thrushcross Grange, a type of the decent, lovely, ideal Victorian home. Unlike the monster in Shelley's novel, Brontë's female protagonist finds that the hearth of the stately house she comes to live in is too warm a space, is in fact a furnace that suffocates her. She burns to be free of the heavenly Thrushcross Grange: "Oh, I am burning! I wish I were out of doors— . . . I'm sure I should be myself were I once among the heather on those hills . . . Open the window again wide. . . ." Whereas the monster, who longs for a human identity, pleads to get in, Catherine, who at one point looks into a mirror to discover that she has lost her identity, pleads to get out. She rejects the idea of serving as the angel at Thrushcross Grange. Though she is later identified as a spirit in the novel and literally becomes a ghost that presides over and haunts her childhood home, Catherine is no angel. "Hard to guide any way but her own," she is an intractable moorland spirit that seeks to get back to the indecent and savage Wuthering Heights which, as its name suggests, is a house more akin to the landscape, to the asylum Mary Shelley's monster finds in the hovel, than to the civilized, Victorian Thrushcross Grange.[31] Brontë hereby suggests that for the woman who has a mind of her own the conventional and ideal abode of the angel can mean oppression, isolation, pallor, and death rather than freedom, breath, color, community, and life. Whereas Shelley's creature finds in the house and in housekeeping potential empowerment and affirmation, Brontë's Catherine finds, to borrow philosopher Mary Daly's expression, a "blockage of her powers," a "blockage of participation in Be-ing."[32]

The essays in this volume demonstrate how Victorian women took up various positions along a continuum that ranged from the desire of Shelley's creature for the power and acceptance it associated with the house to the rejection of Brontë's heroine of the immobility and powerlessness she ultimately experienced there. More specifically the essays in this volume explore the nature of the Victorian woman's domestic relations by centering in the one activity that most informed her place in what was often the father's house: housekeeping. Playing on the density of meaning in the concept of keeping house, especially as these are manifested in the nineteenth-century British novel, the twelve essays here focus on what women did physically, socially, artistically, and economically to tend, use, own, even transcend the home and its contents. The traditional cooking, cleaning, sewing, decorating, budgeting, and the managing of servants that contributed to the physical maintenance of the house and establishment of a home, then, are a subject of the essays; however, the ideas presented here go beyond Ann Oakley's sociological studies of housewifery. To keep house, these essays posit, was also to keep bodies, spirits, souls. To keep house was not only to cook, clean, and nurse, but also to regulate and police, to draw, paint, and write, to hold, own, save, and consume. Housekeeping meant not only keeping but also being kept, trapped, confined, sweated. Yet housekeeping could also mean empowerment and freedom. It was perhaps the most demanding, complicated, and impossible function woman (even today's woman) has ever had to perform. The essays in this edition determine how writers, especially novelists, both male and female, used housekeeping to construct, reconstruct, represent, and inscribe the female self and condition.

The book is comprised of two sections, the first of which focuses on how domestic space is gendered space. Examining as they do women and masculine hegemony, the six essays in "In My Father's House, or In Search of a Home of Her Own" show how "she who makes the bed" does not necessarily or usually own the bed.[33] To put it another way, the essays in the first half of the book reveal the omnipresence of man even in matriarchal territory, as womanspace, whether under the aegis of the father or set up in spite of or outside of it, remains within the domain of patriarchy. Thus, in the first essay, "Housekeeping and Hegemony," Martin A. Danahay looks at Dickens's Esther Summerson and finds her strikingly positioned in the father's Bleak House. At the behest, desire, and will of the patriarch, Esther is allotted a bunch of keys which enable her not only literally to secure the conserves and preserves of the family's material possessions, but also figuratively to keep the hearth as well as the minds of the children. Linked with male professionals in the novel who also seek to protect the family, Esther, Danahay argues, polices the home; nevertheless, her "self enforced labor" or, I would add, Foucaultian self-regulation, is not valued as highly as the efforts of the male professionals because it is limited to the domestic space. Standing in opposition to Danahay's, the next essay is not about the angel who upholds the status quo in either the name of or for the plot of the father. Instead, in "Stitching Repentance, Sewing Rebellion" Deborah Denenholz Morse finds in Elizabeth Gaskell's stories about the Victorian seamstress and the prostitute "a subversive text that aligns all Victorian women against the narrative of the father." The mother's moral but forgiving narrative displaces the father's harsh authoritarian narrative, making the forgiveness, if not the rescue of the prostitute—that woman who "has fallen out of the father's house"—possible or desirable. According to Morse, in seeking to align the angelic woman or mother inside the home with the seamstress and the fallen women who are outside the home, Gaskell critiques the "strictures of gender roles."

In her essay, "God's House, Women's Place," Laura Fasick too writes about women beyond the hegemonic awning, but with a twist. Fasick's essay spotlights old maids that—unlike either Esther who works for the father or the Libbies and Ruths of Gaskell's texts which replace the paternal narrative with a maternal one— set up houses of their own by using the Father's house. As Fasick puts it, these odd women demonstrate how "Victorian religion although patriarchal itself and embedded in a patriarchal society, could also become an opening through which women could locate themselves outside of masculine territory." With her focus on a devotion to the heavenly instead of any earthly fathers, the spinster could justify not only her own "alternative" space, but also her attention to herself.

Julia M. Gergits in "Women Artists at Home" also examines women who make a place outside of masculine territory, setting up homes of their own where their creativity can flourish, while Sandra Kumamoto Stanley's essay looks at the phenomenon of female acquisition, the female's desire to, if not actually own the home, then the objects in it. Like the fallen women of Deborah Morse's essay and the spinsters of Laura Fasick's, the females who are the subject of Gergit's essay also create alternative spaces because they are also in some sense dispossessed. The female characters in the fiction of Brontë, Collins, Dickens and Eliot are artists, exceptional women, according to Gergits, endowed with both the intelligence and the talent to defy or escape the father's house and make and possess by their own efforts and sometimes with the help of others a space of their own. Stanley's essay is not so much about women who make homes for themselves or own homes as it is about what Dickens in *Our Mutual Friend* would probably call portable property. In James's *The Spoils of Poynton* women compete for the possession of things within the house and in doing so, according to Stanley, reveal a desire James ultimately represents as reprehensible if not unangelic. Women who had themselves been for most of the nineteenth century commodities were not supposed to seek or acquire property for to do so was unbecoming, undecorous, undomestic.[34]

Eileen Connell concludes this section by directing our attention to what is undoubtedly one of the most effective, because apparently innocuous, vehicles of patriarchal ideology and hegemony—the Victorian fairy tale. In her essay, Connell, antici-pating other essays in the volume that set gender and class more squarely before us, shows how not only gender but also class and race shaped Victorian domesticity. In "Playing House," she reveals how Frances H. Burnett in *Sara Crewe* takes the very fairy tale that was meant to romanticize the idea of keeping house for the father and gives us glimpses of "social and racial oppression within the domestic sphere." The fairy tales that literarily social-ized Victorian girls as housekeepers for the father could also displace the hidden story of the colonized servant who made middle-class domesticity possible and comfortable.

The second half of the volume, "A Woman's Work Is Never Done: Women's Work and Domestic Spaces," groups es-says specifically and mainly about women's activities in the home and the valuation of those activities. As part of her house-keeping duties, a woman might, in addition to attending to the emotional and social needs of husband and children, haul wood or coal "up from a cellar or in from a yard," clean or stoke stoves, carry out ashes and clean soot or dust from the furniture, rooms, and windows, heat, cook, bake, or preserve food, make some items of clothing, boil clothes, "menstrual rags, diapers, and sheets before washing them," clean pots and dishes, empty and clean "chamber pots, water closets, and later toilets."[35] Of course, in addition to these physical labors there was also what Hilary Rose calls "peoplework," attending to the emotional and social needs of husband and children, for example.[36] Though the work women performed in the house was demanding and time-con-suming, it was not considered real work and was probably not what Thomas Carlyle had in mind when he exhorted Dilettante and Captain of Industry alike to acknowledge the nobleness and sacredness of work. Woman's naturalized, interiorized, and un-paid labor neither directly, nor immediately or notably affected the material progress the age experienced and prided itself upon. As Hilary Rose tells us, the housework and peoplework that women did effected little change and was predicated upon an experiential-based instead of the scientific-based knowledge that men, because of the educations they received, had and women didn't.[37] Even when women went outside the home to work, as the Victorian working-class woman did, the work they did was still underrated. A double dose of depreciation was the working-class woman's portion then, since she was still expected to keep house like an angel even if she spent long hours in a factory. As many of the essays in this volume, but particularly in this section make clear, class and even race impacted women's work, though the most obvious and powerful shaper of work was gender.

Work, this second half of the volume shows, meant a variety of things to and served a variety of purposes for the Victorian woman. As Jessica Gerard points out in her historical essay, "The Chatelaine," even the rich Victorian woman who was thought to have done precious little work in overseeing servants really performed managerially arduous duties which were necessary to the successful functioning of the estate. Gerard demonstrates that upper-class women who kept house were not frail, useless, but strong self-assured women. Their management of some of the "largest and most complex of domestic household[s] in nineteenth-century Britain" enhanced their esteem and lent them power. The chatelaine was able to employ not just domestic but administrative, economic, and political skills as she oversaw most of the inner workings of the "family seat," the home of past and future generations of the dynasty, "the power house."

A notch below the chatelaine was the middle-class woman who may have had one or two servants under her direction but who, unlike the chatelaine, had often to work beside her servants as she had a more direct hand in keeping the house. The next two articles focus on the middle-class woman in the Victorian home. One of the Victorian woman's contributions to the home that marked it as her space was the task of decorating the house, an activity that traditionally fell to woman. According to Thad Logan, the middle-class woman who not only maintained but also arranged the familial possessions was often involved in setting up a domestic decor to display the "paraphernalia of [the] gentility" which the chatelaine possessed and the middle-class homemaker desired. In "Decorating Domestic Space: Middle-Class Women and Victorian Interiors," Logan finds that decoration "serves many cultural and psychic purposes," asethetic expression being a notable one among these.

Food and its preparation likewise served a purpose, one more basic than decoration, since it involved literally the fuelling and refuelling of the family. The cooking and serving of food was and remains closely associated with and underscores woman's powers of nurturance. Yet, of all the facets of housekeeping, this activity is given little attention. Perhaps its close ties to woman's special ability to nurture, her exclusive ability to put child to breast, accounts for its derogation. As Spain has remarked, "Domestic information conveyed within the home is devalued, at least partially because it is possessed by women."[38] Food preparation and its connection to the kitchen which was historically and physically separated from the house may also account for the comparative neglect of this work carried out most by nineteenth-century women.[39] This aspect of women's work—serving and preparing food—gets treated in Monica Fennell and Francis Fennell's "Ladies, Loaf-Givers." Here, father and daughter find a "subtextual commentary" in the fiction of Charlotte Brontë and George Eliot centered in cooking and serving of food that enables these writers not only to represent the position of women in society, but also to explore the ways in which the woman as loaf-giver can at once be self-empowered and self-imperilled.

Maura Ives's essay addresses the limitations of women's work in the home which the period tended to define as "domestic, decorative, and dependent." Ives demonstrates that Brontë, who eschews references to working-class women, is yet ever aware of the separation of the productive masculine workplace and the home that is described "in terms of consumption rather than production." However, Ives finds that in Brontë's *Shirley* (1849) the devalued work of women, the work of sewing, for instance, though it could not rival the activity of men in the "industrial workplace," could provide women "an important means of expression and mark of affiliation" and even subvert the "hierarchical relationships established in the male workplace." Ives's essay on housework, mill work, and women's work is appropriately followed by Lynn M. Alexander's "Loss of the Domestic Idyll: Slop Workers in Victorian Fiction." In Alexander's essay the "industrial" workplace and the domestic workplace are met in both the millinery houses where women are able to perform a domestic task, that of sewing, outside the home and in the home where sewing done for the mill is carried out. The meeting of the industrial machine and the home do not prove felicitous, for as Alexander indicates, the women—specifically the very working-class women Brontë had begun, as Ives points out, to connect to middle-class women—these working-class women pay a high price. That price, Deborah Morse's essay emphasizes, is often moral. Lynn Alexander's essay aptly portrays the physical and the economic cost of merging one workplace with the other. As Alexander concludes, "Victorians were finally forced to admit that the ideal of domesticity held by the upper and middle classes was virtually impossible for working-class women, even those involved in a "domestic" occupation such as needlework." Alexander's essay not only drives home the fact that lower as well as middle and upper-class women aspired to the ideal of the angel in the house or the housekeeping angel, but also reminds us that this ideal was difficult to realize.

The last essay in the volume, Brian Shaffer's "Domestic Ironies," makes clear the power and pervasiveness of the mythic angel in the house, an ideal that was so dominant and persistent that by the turn of the century it got the attention of Joseph Conrad, who launches in *The Secret Agent* (1907) an attack on the Victorian idea of domesticity that ends in a critique of the New Woman. The secret of Conrad's *The Secret Agent*, Shaffer argues, is Winnie Verloc's effort to keep man by keeping house. In a world where "public and private values are alarmingly interanimating" and where marriage is an "exchange of domestic labor for the means of subsistence," Conrad's female protagonist imprisons herself with her housekeeping. Even when the Victorian woman becomes, as Winnie does, a New Woman, she continues to keep house for men, though she now does so as one who, Shaffer contends, degenerates into a "savage woman."

From the Victorian period to the twentieth century, whether a woman perceived the house to be her jail or her salvation, whether she owned a home or had been turned out of one, whether she was angelic, fallen, or savage, her identity, status, and being were powerfully determined by the concept of house and home. The house kept her just as surely as she was designated the one who ought to keep it. The connection between

woman and the house which the Victorians so fervently pro-
moted and Conrad so distinctly satirizes constitutes a legacy the
valuation of which still wavers in the balance. Domestic conster-
nation is especially evident in the Western world today when
more women than ever in this even more technologically-
advanced society work outside the home, when many families
unable to keep their houses are becoming homeless, and when
scholars, thinkers, and activists are becoming increasingly aware
of how issues of class and race are implicated in the relations of
the woman to the house. It is telling that in 1963, with the publication of *The Feminine Mystique*, Betty Friedan, who was not
speaking, as bell hooks pointed out, for the "masses of women
concerned about economic survival, ethnic and racial discrimina-
tion," who was not speaking for those who, like the creature in
Shelley's *Frankenstein*, suffered the hardships and evil of exclusion and longed to "shape their identities on the model of the
feminine mystique"[40]—it is telling that Betty Friedan, writing
about the role of the modern white middle-class woman in
America as housewife, could just as easily have been writing
about Catherine Linton and her nineteenth-century British
counterparts when she argued:

> It is urgent to understand how the very condition of being
> a housewife can create a sense of emptiness, non-existence,
> nothingness in women. There are aspects of the housewife
> role that make it almost impossible for a woman of adult
> intelligence to retain a sense of human identity, the firm
> core of self or "I" without which a human being, man or
> woman, is not truly alive. For women of ability, in Ameri-
> can today, I am convinced that there is something about
> the housewife state itself that is dangerous.[41]

Some twenty years later the futuristic female protagonist, the
handmaid in Canadian novelist Margaret Atwood's *The Handmaid's Tale* (1985), is still threatened by, is even more attuned to
the treacherous places in the house as she, firmly fixed in the
dystopia of "the doll's house [of] . . . Victorian prejudices,"[42] is
provoked to these thoughts about the word "household:"

> "*Household* : that is what we [females, handmaids] are. The
> Commander is the head of the household. The house is
> what he holds. To have and to hold, till death do us part.

The hold of a ship. Hollow.[43]

Questions that arose during the nineteeth century about woman's place and work in the domestic space still haunt modern women as social critics and novelists express anew concern about the ways in which the house can mediate woman's being. And so, the house the Victorians built proves, both for those wanting in as well as those wanting out, as yet inescapable.

Vanessa D. Dickerson

NOTES

1. Shirley Ardener, "Ground Rules and Social Maps for Women: An Introduction," in *Women and Space: Ground Rules and Social Maps*, ed. Shirley Ardener (New York: St. Martin's Press, 1981), 12. The second reference to Ardener's work in this paragraph is taken from page 12 of this text.

2. Gaston Bachelard, *The Poetics of Space*, trans. Maria Jolas (Boston: Beacon Press, 1969), xxxii-xxxiii.

3. Ardener, "Ground Rules," 12.

4. Sally Gearhart, "Womanpower: Energy Re-Sourcement," in Charlene Spretnak, ed., *The Politics of Women's Spirituality: Essays on the Rise of Spiritual Power Within the Feminist Movement* (New York: Anchor Books, 1982), 197.

5. Anne K. Mellor, ed., *Romanticism and Feminism* (Bloomington: Indiana University Press, 1988), 4.

6. Daphne Spain, *Gendered Spaces* (Chapel Hill, NC: University of North Carolina Press, 1992), 7.

7. Marlene Springer, "Angels and Other Women in Victorian Literature," in Marlene Springer, ed.,*What Manner of Woman: Essays in English and American Life and Literature* (New York: New York University Pess, 1977), 130, 131.

8. Leonore Davidoff and Catherine Hall, *Family Fortunes: Men and Women of the English Middle Class, 1780–1850* (Chicago: University of Chicago Press, 1987), 361.

9. Spain, *Gendered Spaces*, 3, 10–11.

10. I borrow this phrase from Mary Shelley's *Frankenstein; or, The Modern Prometheus* (New York: Signet, 1965), 37.

11. For a discussion of woman's demonic versus her angelic energies see Nina Auerbach's *Woman and the Demon: The Life of a Victorian Myth* (Cambridge: Harvard University Press, 1982).

12. Bachelard, *Poetics of Space*, 7, 17.

13. Linda C. Hunt, *A Woman's Portion: Ideology, Culture, and the British Female Novel Tradition* (New York: Garland, 1988), 5.

14. John Ruskin, *Sesame and Lilies*, in *Sesame and Lilies, The Two Paths, The King of the Golden River* (London: Dent, 1965), 60.

15. Spain, *Gendered Spaces*, 241.

16. Lynda L. Coon, Katherine J. Haldane, and Elisabeth W. Sommer, eds., *That Gentle Strength: Historical Perspectives on Women in Christianity* (Charlottesville, VA: University Press of Virginia, 1990), 7, 8.

17. Auerbach, *Woman and the Demon*, 73.

18. Davidoff and Hall, *Family Fortunes*, 329.

19. H.L. Beales, "The Victorian Family," in *Ideas and Beliefs of the Victorians: An Historic Revaluation of the Victorian Age* (London: Sylvan, 1949), 344.

20. Spain, *Gendered Spaces*, 12.

21. Janet Wolff, *Feminine Sentences: Essays on Women and Culture* (Berkeley: University of California Press, 1990), 15.

22. Spain, *Gendered Spaces*, 16.

23. Davidoff and Hall, *Family Fortunes*, 362.

24. John Stuart Mill, *The Subjection of Women* (Cambridge: MIT Press, 1970), 31.

25. William Shakespeare, *The Taming of the Shrew*, in *The Riverside Shakespeare*, ed. G. Blakemore Evans (Boston: Houghton Mifflin, 1974), 127.

26. Ruskin, *Sesame and Lilies*, 59.

27. Davidoff and Hall, *Family Fortunes*, 329, 387, 360.

28. After her elopement with the married Shelley, Mary, who had always striven to please her father William Godwin, earned his bitter disapproval. Her life with Percy Shelley, whom she, of course, eventually married, was one of virtual exile and constant financial

strain. See *The Endurance of Frankenstein: Essays on Mary Shelley's Novel*, George Levine and U.C. Knoepflmacher, eds. (Berkeley: University of California Press, 1974). See especially U.C. Knoepflmacher's essay in the volume, "Thoughts on the Aggression of Daughters," 88–119.

29. Shelley, *Frankenstein*, 101.

30. See my essay, "The Ghost of a Self: Female Identity in Mary Shelley's *Frankenstein*," in which I identify the monster with the women in the novel (*Journal of Popular Culture*, vol. 27 (Winter 1993): 79–92.

31. Emily Brontë, *Wuthering Heights*, ed. David Daiches (New York: Penguin, 1965), 163, 165. For a description of Thrushcross Grange see page 89 of this edition.

32. Mary Daly, *Pure Lust: Elemental Feminist Philosophy* (Boston: Beacon Press, 1984), 27, 36.

33. I am here indebted to my colleague, Elizabeth Kamhi, who contends that "she who makes the bed owns the bed."

34. See Lucy Irigaray's *This Sex Which Is Not One*, trans. Catherine Porter (Ithaca, New York: Cornell University Press, 1985), 172.

35. I take this information from *A History of Their Own: Women in Europe From Prehistory to the Present*, ed. Bonnie S. Anderson and Judith P. Zinsser, vol. 2 (New York: Harper and Row, 1988), 132–33.

36. Hilary Rose, "Women's Work: Women's Knowledge," in *What Is Feminism?* ed. Juliet Mitchell and Ann Oakley (New York: Pantheon Books, 1986), 168.

37. Rose, "Women's Work: Women's Knowledge," 162, 165.

38. Spain, *Gendered Spaces*, 235.

39. Davidoff and Hall observe that "segregating the mess and smell of food preparation from the social ritual of eating became an important hallmark of respectability and meant that the kitchen became ideally as remote as possible from the living rooms, no matter the cost in servants, or wife's time and labour"(383).

40. bell hooks, *Feminist Theory: from margin to center* (Boston: South End Press, 1984), 2.

41. Cited in hooks, *Feminist Theory*, 2.

42. hooks, *Feminist Theory*, 2.

43. Margaret Atwood, *The Handmaid's Tale* (New York: Fawcett Crest, 1985), 103.

PART ONE

In My Father's House;
or, In Search of a Home of Her Own

Housekeeping and Hegemony in Dickens's *Bleak House**

Martin A. Danahay

There has been much critical debate over the character of Esther Summerson in Dickens's *Bleak House*. This controversy has focussed on whether Esther Summerson is an "ambiguous" and "repugnant" figure, a "female paragon to whom Dickens felt so committed that he lost critical control over her creation," or a "subtle psychological portrait clear in its outlines and convincing in its details."[1] Sidestepping such psychologically based discussions of individual character, I propose a reading of the character of Esther Summerson in terms of her work in the novel. I will read Esther as a "sign of the feminine,"[2] a character who reveals the Victorian cultural construction of work along gender lines. Esther seems to have many roles in the novel; she cares for children, she organizes households, and she provides companionship for various male figures. All these roles can, however, be grouped under one term: housekeeper.

Since *Bleak House* ends with Esther's marriage, it does not represent Esther in the role of housewife, although "housekeeper" and "housewife" are obviously closely related terms; both participate in the nineteenth-century British cultural construction of the feminine in terms of domesticity. The ideology of women's natural domesticity, although present in previous centuries, was articulated most forcefully from the beginning of the nineteenth century on.[3] Ann Oakley in her tripartite history of the housewife denotes the period 1840–1914, within which *Bleak House* (1851–53) falls, as marking a "decline in the employment of women outside the home associated with the rising popularity of the belief in women's natural domesticity."[4] Although large numbers of women, especially working-class women, continued to work inside and outside the home, the expectation was that they be economically dependent and unproductive.[5]

Esther Summerson is a "keeper" of other people's houses and other people's children. She represents an intermediate stage in the development of the term housewife as we use it now. As Oakley points out, it was not until the "servant crisis" of the late nineteenth and early twentieth centuries when domestic help became less readily available that "the housewife and homeworker roles . . . merged."[6] Since one of Esther's main roles is organizing households and servants, she does not perform much of the daily manual labor in *Bleak House*. Her tasks are managerial. We do see in Esther Summerson, however, the same conjunction of the ideas of domestic labor and the socialization of children as in the concept "housewife." The two terms imply the same relationship between woman as mother and woman as domestic worker. Ann Oakley's definition of housewife reflects the conjunction of these aspects of the gender-specific role:

> A housewife is a woman: a housewife does housework . . .
> the synthesis of "house" and "wife" in a single term establishes the connections between womanhood, marriage, and the dwelling place of family groups. The role of housewife is a family role: it is a feminine role. Yet it is also a work role.[7]

As Oakley emphasizes, the term housewife denotes a particular form of work which, however, has an ambiguous status because it does not fit within the conventions of industrialized labor. Housekeepers work in the home, not in the factory, and they do not receive a direct wage for their work. Their labor is therefore not recognized as "work" in the same sense as male forms of industry. For instance, when in the census of 1851 the Registrar General acknowledged the existence of a large segment of the population of Britain who performed such work but were not paid for it, a "5th class" or category had to be invented to accommodate the data. In the 1851 census women were both confined to a class of their own, and separated from other forms of paid labor. The description of this new "5th class" emphasizes the different roles that women were acknowledged to play, but which did not fit the conventional categories of waged labor:

> The 5th class comprises large numbers of the population that have hitherto been held to have no occupation—but it requires no argument to prove that the *wife*, the *mother*, the *mistress*, of an *English family*—fills offices and discharges duties of no ordinary importance.[8]

Unable to unite the categories of wife, mother, mistress and work, the census must create a new class to accommodate women as people who do not have "occupations" but rather "duties." Unlike the occupation of lawyer or doctor, the duties of the housekeeper or housewife do not have status in and of themselves but only in so far as they help reproduce and maintain the Great British Family.

Feminist histories of housework have demonstrated how in pre-industrial households woman's work as housekeeper had prestige, and was directly related to the means of production, which was based in the extended family.[9] As factories replaced families as the sites of production from the late eighteenth century on, women's work became increasingly severed from direct market relations and devalued in consequence. The site of women's labor became a family increasingly defined in terms of consumption rather than production.[10] Thus the roles of mother, wife, and housekeeper in the 1851 census are all firmly circumscribed within the domestic sphere and are separated from "productive" wage labor. While the author of the Census may feel that the social value of these occupations needs no defense, he does not think that such services require payment.

As women continued to labor in the home, just as they had before industrialization, the labor they performed became progressively privatized and isolated from public forms of work such as being an operative in a factory. As the family became a center for the reproduction of labor rather than the production of material goods, women's work suffered a consequent loss in social prestige. A "gender hierarchy" of labor was created "whereby women's work was given a lower social and economic value than that of men."[11] This "hierarchy of labor" is reflected in

Dickens's novel by the status of Esther Summerson vis à vis the male professionals such as Dr. Woodcourt, the lawyer Tulkinghorn and Inspector Bucket. Esther's position is shown as subordinate to the prestige of these men. Her labor is not explicitly recognized as work in the same sense as the tasks performed by the male professionals. This lack of acknowledgment of Esther's labor results directly from the growing separation of women from work in the Victorian period. The ideology of "separate spheres," however, was not uniform or completely coherent. As Dickens's representation of Esther shows, there were conflicting and contradictory images circulating in the Victorian discourse on work.

Dickens inscribes Esther within a contradictory ideology. One prevalent Victorian image of women was the "leisured lady" who incarnated "the leisure most men could not afford to enjoy."[12] Upper- and middle-class women were not expected to work, because to be leisured was a marker of the wealth and success of their husbands.[13] They were therefore told to devote their energies to maintaining the household and organizing a few servants to carry out the physical labor in the home. So great was the separation of the notion of the lady from work that "'working ladies' was . . . a contradiction in terms."[14]

The association of women and leisure rather than work presented difficulties when Dickens tried to represent Esther in the role of housekeeper rather than a leisured lady. Dickens subscribes to a middle-class work ethic. Leisure in this ethic is seen as vice, industry as virtue. The "lady of leisure" in the novel, Lady Dedlock, is part of the corrupt and stagnant aristocracy of Chesney Wold. It is vital that Esther work in order to distinguish her from the corrupt world of aristocratic leisure, even if her labor is not explicitly acknowledged as work in the same sense as the tasks carried out by men.

Although Dickens represents Esther in terms of her work roles as housekeeper, he cannot portray her as a working woman in the sense of having a definite profession that would take her outside the home. For Esther to have a profession or an evangelical cause that took her outside the domestic sphere would threaten her femininity. Women at work "lose the grace of sex"[15] and become "loose" signifiers out of place. Thus "for Dickens, respectable women . . . simply do not perform professional work" so that "his representations of female professionals . . . are unambivalently hostile."[16] For Dickens a professional woman was by definition not "respectable."

By the time Dickens was writing *Bleak House* it was becoming increasingly difficult to join the feminine and work as various pieces of State legislation defined women and children as "protected persons" who must be separated from the rigors of certain kinds of labor. The Mines Act of 1842, for instance, prevented women from performing certain kinds of labor in the mines, and several different Factory Acts regulated the number of hours women and children could work. These Acts, according to Malos, "went along with attempts to restrict the field of employment for *all* women and especially all married women and mothers."[17] Not only does Dickens distinguish women from professional work, when he represents them as doing "good works" (i.e. unpaid acts of charity) he is critical also. As we shall see, Dickens's censure of women who neglect the home for the "good works" of evangelical and charitable causes is extreme.

Dickens therefore has Esther Summerson carry out a form of labor restricted completely to the domestic sphere and represents it in a way that does not acknowledge its status as work. Esther's work is seen as a natural extension of her biology, a genetic aptitude for looking after children and organizing domestic affairs that does not have to be learned because it is instinctive. Dickens in inscribing a maternal instinct in the character of Esther Summerson betrays the domestic ideology that Davidoff and Hall describe as asserting that "women, whether biological mothers or not, had a maternal instinct."[18] Dickens presents motherhood as an instinct to differentiate it from a trade or profession, which requires skills acquired through training or apprenticeship. Esther herself is therefore shown as unaware of how and why she does these things. Her narrative is peppered with gaps and elisions that denote the space of unconsciousness Dickens had to create to enable Esther both to work and not be damagingly aware that she is a "working woman."

These contradictions create the peculiar gaps in Esther Summerson's character that have so troubled critics. Rather than read these gaps as signs either of failed characterization or subtle psychological insight, I would read them as products of the Victorian gender hierarchy of labor in which women's work could not be acknowledged overtly. Dickens's difficulty in creating the character Esther Summerson points ultimately to contradictions in his own subject position as a male professional author attempting to represent a paragon of female subjectivity who both worked and was unaware that she did so. In the reading of the novel I present below, these gaps are a sign of a possible break in what Ann Oakley has termed the "circle of learnt deprivation and induced subjugation"[19] of women's enforced domesticity in that they point to fissures in the seemingly uniform surface of hegemony. The space of unconsciousness that Dickens had to create in Esther Summerson betrays the way in which he represses the alienating aspects of both her labor, and his own activity as a male professional writer.

The symbol of Esther's work in the novel is the key. It is a peculiar aspect of Esther's role in the novel that wherever she goes she is given keys. When she first enters Bleak House she is handed a basket of keys:

> A maid . . . brought a basket into my room, with two
> bunches of keys in it, all labelled.
> "For you, miss, if you please," said she.
> "For me?," said I.
> "The housekeeping keys, miss." [20]

Upon her arrival at Bleak House Esther is immediately cast in the role of housekeeper and given keys. She is initially surprised, but this surprise gives way immediately, and without any attempt at explanation on Dickens's part, to wonder at "the magnitude of my trust." This sequence is repeated when Esther goes in search of Necket's children and she is given a key by the landlady. No directions are given with the gift. On each occasion the giver of the key assumes that Esther will know what to do with it:

> I glanced at the key, and glanced at her; but she took it for
> granted that I knew what to do with it. As it could only be
> intended for the children's door, I came out without asking
> any more questions, and led the way up the dark
> stairs.[21]

Esther herself is portrayed as unaware of why people give her keys, but she inevitably ends up doing the right thing with them anyway. Her "maternal instinct" is shown in this case leading her to the correct door, and she takes the children into her protective custody. The key is obviously a very important symbol for women's work in Dickens's novels generally, not just in *Bleak House*.[22] For instance, in *Oliver Twist* when Fagin wishes to disguise Nancy as a suitable guardian for Oliver, he gives her two things: a basket, symbolizing her role as the purchaser of food for her fictitious family, and a large door key symbolizing her role as protector of the home's security and integrity. This, in Fagin's words, makes her look "more respectable" and ensures that her impersonation of Oliver's sister will be more credible.[23] The symbol of the key identifies both Esther and Nancy immediately as housekeepers and protectors of children, entitled to make a citizen's arrest of any vagrant and unprotected minors.

The symbol of the key also links Esther to the other male professionals in the novel who are entrusted with the duty of protecting the family, particularly the lawyer Tulkinghorn and the detective Inspector Bucket. Both men guard the secret of Lady Dedlock's adultery. Their protection of this secret is symbolized by the key. Tulkinghorn even has keys that unlock drawers that contain other keys. He "takes a small key from his pocket, unlocks a drawer in which there is another key, which unlocks a chest in which there is another, and so comes to the cellar-key."[24] Inspector Bucket owns a key to Tulkinghorn's office. Like Esther, these two characters use keys as part of their role in the novel as a means of gaining access to the domestic sphere. The key symbolizes their ability to enter and survey the domestic space of the family, and their guardianship of its material goods and secrets.

Children in *Bleak House* instinctively trust Esther as a mother figure, and it is part of the dark and terrible inversion of Esther's role that Nancy assumes the trappings of the home's guardian but in fact abducts Oliver in order to return him to Fagin's subterranean mafia, a family founded on crime not rectitude. Of course, in *Oliver Twist* Nancy is suitably punished for her impersonation, whereas Esther in *Bleak House* is rewarded with marriage and a home for her role in the novel. By the end of the novel Esther has discovered her metier, her chosen vocation as housekeeper and child minder.

In protecting children Esther assumes a role that French social historian Jacques Donzelot has termed "the policing of the family."[25] Donzelot reads the history of nineteenth-century institutions such as the hospital and juvenile court as signs of the increasing State surveillance of families, and describes an "alliance" arising between women and the State that allowed professionals such as social workers and doctors increased access to the family, especially working-class families. Children were defined as being "in danger" and therefore in need of protection by State institutions and full-time mothers. Women became increasingly important as the primary sources of protection and nurturance for children, and the guarantors of social stability in their socialization of children.

Corroborating Donzelot's assertion that children were represented as "in danger" and therefore needing to be rescued, Esther's work in *Bleak House* is partly to rescue and nurture children. Her labor as child minder is part of her training as housekeeper. The other part consists of the range of domestic skills needed to run a household. Donzelot characterizes domestic labor as taking the place of the dowry in nineteenth-century marriages, and asks "What might take the place of this starting capital that they (women) could no longer supply? . . . It would be their labor, their domestic labor, raised to the level of a trade."[26] Rather than use the word "trade," I would substitute the term "profession," and describe Esther Summerson's profession of housekeeper as providing her with the capital that makes her eligible for marriage. Esther is an orphan, with no family to provide her with a dowry. Her labor compensates for this lack. She brings her role as housekeeper to the domestic partnership of marriage. Like Esther, Agnes in *David Copperfield* contributes what Mary Poovey has termed "the dowry of her middle-class virtue and efficient house-keeping skills" to her marriage with Dr. Woodcourt.[27]

The housekeeper's primary role in *Bleak House* is the conservation or preservation of the family's material possessions. When Esther describes the domestic activities she and Caddy undertook at the Jellyby house, "keeping" is the most prominent aspect of her work as she labored at "contriving and cutting out, and repairing, and sewing, and saving, and doing the very best we could think of to make the most of her stock."[28] The emphasis in this description is upon small-scale conservation. The activity of housekeeping is fundamentally economic as it involves the saving and repairing of the family "stock." Whereas the male partner is involved in the production of capital outside the house, the woman's role is to preserve the property the two accumulate. Women's work roles were therefore defined as the preservation of capital accumulated by the male worker, rather than as productive labor in its own right.

Esther's duties within *Bleak House* are both managerial and social, as she summarizes her three weeks in the Jellyby household by saying "so, what with working and housekeeping, and lessons to Charley, and backgammon in the evening with my guardian, and duets with Ada, the three weeks slipped fast away." Esther is a manager of households as well as companion to Mr. Jarndyce. In her managerial role, she organizes and teaches servants. In one of the novel's most disturbing moments, Esther is "given" Charley Neckett as a maid. Charley announces that "If you please, miss, I'm a present to you, with Mr. Jarndyce's love. . . . And if you please miss . . . he thinks you'll like to teach me now and then."[29] As part of Esther's gradual socialization into her role she is given a personal servant, a marker of her class position. She will learn to "manage" servants by her supervision of Charley, although she is represented as the one giving the education. She assumes the role of mentor and teacher to Charley and the other lower-class servants under her control. Above both Esther and Charley, however, is the paternalist figure of Mr. Jarndyce, the benevolent despot who shuffles women around as extensions of his property. Although separated in terms of class, Charley and Esther are united in their gender position when at the end of the novel Mr. Jarndyce "gives" Esther to Dr. Woodcourt, just as he gave Charley to Esther.

Esther monitors the inventory of material goods in the household, and also presides over family meals, moving rapidly from one role to another. For instance, Dickens describes her first morning's work as housekeeper in a list of labors of Herculean proportions:

> Every part of the house was in such order, and everyone
> was so attentive to me, that I had no trouble with my two
> bunches of keys: though what with trying to remember the
> contents of each little store-room drawer, and cupboard;
> and what with making notes on a slate about jams, pickles
> and preserves, and bottles, and glass, and china and a
> great many other things; and what with generally being a
> methodical, old-maidish foolish little person; I was so
> busy that I could not believe it was breakfast-time when I
> heard the bell ring. Away I ran, however, and made tea, as
> I had already been installed into the responsibility of the
> teapot; and then, as they were all rather late, and nobody
> was down yet, I thought I would take a peep at the garden
> and get some knowledge of that too.[30]

This dizzying catalog of activities represents only Esther's early
morning schedule! While the rest of the household sleeps, she is
already hard at work surveying her new domain, which she
views with a proprietary pleasure. However, her activities here
are not described as labor, but rather as a hectic but enjoyable
romp. Work is redefined as pleasure, or in Nancy Armstrong's
terminology as "labor that is not labor."[31] She is also represented
in relentlessly self-deprecating terms, so that any suggestion of
skill or intelligence in the exercise of her duties is dismissed by
the diminutive epithets "little" and "foolish." Esther's work is
devalued by this technique of characterization.

When I refer to Esther Summerson's work as a
"profession" I intend to point out both its similarities to the work
of the male professionals, and underscore the differences. As
unpaid and undervalued labor, Esther's role is certainly not a
"profession" in many respects. However, in that her labor as
housekeeper defines her role in the novel, it also has points of
contact with the work of the male characters such as Tulkinghorn the lawyer, Woodcourt the doctor and Bucket the police
inspector.

It is important that Esther be unaware of the basis of her
professional prestige, and always slightly bemused when auto-
matically given keys, because a too self-conscious woman would
upset her role as supporter of the male professional provider. If
Esther were aware of her own power then Mr. Jarndyce or Dr.
Woodcourt would be in danger of becoming marginal figures

like Mr. Jellyby or Mr. Pardiggle, and the smooth functioning of the family would be endangered. It is part of Dickens's conservatism that he perceives an increased role for women in the work force as a threat to the power of the father. Esther, as a potential threat, must be carefully differentiated from the circle of female philanthropists in the book who are shown as destructive of their own households because their energies are directed outward toward society rather than inward into preserving the domestic sphere.

The circle of female philanthropists is composed of Mrs. Jellyby with her obsession with Africa, Mrs. Pardiggle the rapacious patroness and patronizer of the poor, and finally Miss Wisk the feminist, who makes particularly evident the reason for Dickens's disapproval of these women. Dickens ascribes to her anti-male sentiments when "Miss Wisk informed us . . . that the idea of woman's mission lying chiefly in the narrow sphere of Home was an outrageous slander on the part of Tyrant Man."[32] Dickens makes it easy for his Victorian readership to dismiss such remarks by having the speaker be a "miss" rather than a "Mrs.," a childless and husbandless woman whose major problem so far as Dickens is concerned is obviously that she is not married. Dickens suggests that the husbands of Mrs. Jellyby and Mrs. Pardiggle are weak and ineffectual and have let their women get out of hand. By concentrating on issues outside the home, all three women challenge the domestic division of labor along gender lines. Rather than policing their own families, these women go around stirring up trouble in spheres not appropriate to their stations. Mrs. Pardiggle, for instance, goes to visit the brickmakers with Esther and Ada and provides a model for how not to intervene in the lives of the working poor:

> Mrs. Pardiggle . . . pulled out a good book, as if it were a constable's staff, and took the whole family into custody. I mean into religious custody of course, but she really did it as if she were an inexorable moral Policeman carrying them all off to a station house.[33]

Mrs. Pardiggle's philanthropy is a "rapacious benevolence" that uses moral and evangelical language to justify its exercise of power over its working-class subjects. However, Dickens is not criticizing philanthropy itself here, but the way in which it is executed and the person carrying it out. The scene at the brickmaker's is unusual for a suppressed and barely concealed violence that is echoed in Mrs. Pardiggle's own family. Her children are described as "ferocious with discontent" and on the verge of revolution against the domestic order.[34] The problem here is that Mrs. Pardiggle is a woman, not a male professional like Dr. Woodcourt and Inspector Bucket, and that her intervention in the brickmaker's family is too obviously a police action, a direct and obvious enforcement of the law rather than a more subtle form of social control.[35]

The trouble with Mrs. Pardiggle's intervention, then, is that it was too obviously a policing action. As D.A. Miller points out in *The Novel and the Police, Bleak House* proposes a model of the hegemonic exercise of State power through its embodiment in the Chancery as something that "does not impose itself by physical coercion."[36] Its power is exerted through consent, or the apparently voluntary policing of the family by its own members. Rather than represent social control in terms of an overt police action, *Bleak House* relies upon a model of hegemony in which the State's subjects voluntarily assume their roles, as Miller makes clear in his description of Chancery's power when he states that "it relies on being voluntarily assumed by its subjects who, seduced by it, addicted to it, internalize the requirements for maintaining its hold."[37] One reason for Esther Summerson's lack of self-consciousness is that she must not be too aware of her role as an agent of the "social police." She must willingly, but unwittingly, internalize the requirements of her role in the State's "policing" of the family. One of the difficulties Dickens had in writing the book, as Miller points out, was to maintain the distinction between Chancery and the domestic space to which it is opposed. The family and the State come uncomfortably close to one another, especially in the conjunction of Esther and Inspector Bucket. Mrs. Pardiggle makes the congruence between woman as representative of the domestic "social police" and the law too obvious. Esther Summerson, by having a profession that circumscribes her role within the domestic sphere, embodies both the separation of the public body of the state and the private, domestic space of the family, and their congruence.

Esther comes closest to an overt "policing of the family" when she joins Inspector Bucket in the effort to track down her mother. This scene is a disturbing and ambiguous mixture of rescue and punishment. The chase exorcises the figure of Lady Dedlock as the "fallen woman" who represents the dark underside to Esther's domesticity. When she joins Inspector Bucket in tracking down her mother, Esther betrays her implication in the "policing" of the family and its secrets. Such an alliance comes dangerously close to naming the power relations between the state and the family, as D.A. Miller points out when he questions the separation of the domestic and the judicial by asserting that "All the ambiguities about the police serve to establish a radical uncertainty about the nature of private, familial space. . . . The police simultaneously produce and permeate . . . the space they leave to be "free."[38] The apparent autonomy of the family, its putative status as a refuge from the power relations embodied by the Chancery and the police force, is constantly in danger of being undermined. Mrs. Pardiggle's model of philanthropic intervention in the family is repudiated within the novel because it erodes this precarious boundary and too obviously invokes the police force.

Esther Summerson is a much more attractive figure because, as a former orphan, she apparently chooses to join the family, and internalizes its values without being aware of them. She voluntarily enters into matrimony at the end of the novel, the perfect good woman and housekeeper, a model wife for any professional man. Esther becomes for Dickens a paragon, the very embodiment of hegemony as the subject's willing submission to ideology. Esther, at the end of the novel, having been socialized into her role, becomes overtly a possession of the male professionals, as John Jarndyce says to Dr. Woodcourt: "Allen . . . take from me a willing gift, the best wife that man ever had."[39] The adjective "willing" here is ambiguous. At one level it is Jarndyce who is willingly giving away Esther. On another level it is Esther herself who is "willing," voluntarily entering into her new role as housewife, having perfected her skills as housekeeper. By the end of the novel Esther is ready to take her place as wife, housekeeper, and guardian of children in danger, having successfully internalized the values necessary to ensure the

smooth functioning of the family. It is, however, this internaliza-
tion of values that makes Esther Summerson a particularly striking representative of hegemony. Her role as housekeeper, a form
of work that is not work, involves her in a complex series of self-
denials and self-repressions. Housework in an industrialized society represents one of the most extreme forms of self-enforced
labor. There are apparently no bosses, no formal regulations, and
no explicit systems of sanctions to enforce housework:

> The compulsion to housework, then, is not economic or
> legal: it is moral and personal. And the housewife sees it in
> moral and personal terms. Hence her description of this
> structure of her oppression assumes querulous and com-
> plaining tones, the tones of a private neurosis to express a
> social fact.[40]

This description of housework by a group of women in the 1970s
illustrates how the illusion that housework is labor undertaken
voluntarily by the individual is perpetuated, when in fact it is labor that is as regulated by social codes of class and gender as any
other form of work. Domestic labor differs from other forms of
work only in the way in which it is viewed by its subjects as self-
imposed rather than mandated by wages. The apparent autonomy cited by the housewives in Ann Oakley's study of domestic
labor was a fiction in which "labor discipline appeared to them
as their own self-imposed schedule" when in fact it represented
an indirect reproduction of the routines of the factory.[41] Housework is therefore a particularly contradictory site of hegemony.
The subjects of domestic ideology are encouraged to view their
socially constructed labor as self-imposed and autonomous from
wage labor. It was as a reaction against this artificial separation
of women's work from other forms of paid labor that many
feminists in the 1970s called for a wage for housework.

Dickens's character Esther Summerson registers the "social
fact" of enforced domesticity in the lacunae of her narrative. At
the opposite extreme from the impersonal, authoritative and
masculine third-person narrative, her narrative can record events
only hesitatingly in personal terms. She records the effects of
hegemony in the form of personal neuroses, such as her habit of
jingling her basket of keys and saying to herself, "Esther, duty
my dear" as she reminds herself of her social role. Esther's pro-

fession is represented as "duty" rather than "occupation," a duty that she apparently imposes upon herself. The modesty tropes that Dickens uses to create the character of Esther Summerson correspond to her ideological position as a woman working within masculine terms, as a brief comment of D.A. Miller's underscores: "Like women's work, which is the external means to Esther's social regulation, the labors of modesty, its inner correlative, are never done.[42] This is, unfortunately, the only instance in *The Novel and the Police* where Miller acknowledges the role of gender in *Bleak House*. Miller here suggests very interestingly that a general hegemonic definition of women's labor in the Victorian period is played out in the character of Esther Summerson in terms of "modesty." Esther's continual self-effacement is a product of her position within the ideology of "women's work." Miller shows here the homology between the physical labor of "women's work" and its emotional counterpart. Mary Poovey has used the term "emotional labor" to characterize the social behavior expected of Victorian women. She has argued that for Victorian women their most important work "was increasingly represented as the emotional labor motivated by . . . maternal instinct."[43] In Esther's narrative Dickens represents this "emotional labor" as an internalized work ethic that reinforces a self-effacing and self-denying image of women. Dickens's portrayal of Esther does not subvert the Victorian representation of women's "emotional labor"; rather, as Suzanne Graver has argued, he "uses Esther's obliqueness not to subvert Victorian womanly ideals, but to celebrate a dutifully willed acceptance of them."[44]

Esther therefore apparently represents the complete inscription of women within "Victorian womanly ideals." As Graver goes on to point out, however, Dickens's attempt to write Esther's narrative in "a womanly way" opened up a field of questions that disturbed him deeply, and made *Bleak House* one of his most difficult novels to write.[45] Dickens found himself faced with irreconcilable contradictions in attempting this, however, in that his work as a professional writer bears close similarities to Esther's work as a housekeeper. In her analysis of *David Copperfield*, Mary Poovey suggests that Dickens carries out similar strategies of representation in portraying the labor of a housekeeper and of a professional writer:

> In both his representation of David's writing and Agnes's
> housekeeping . . . Dickens displaces the material details
> and the emotional strain of labor onto other episodes—
> thereby conveying the twin impressions that some kinds
> of work are less "degrading" and less alienating than oth-
> ers, and that some laborers are so selfless and skilled that
> to them work is simultaneously an expression of self and a
> gift to others.[46]

In other words, Dickens comes dangerously close in his representation of Esther's work to naming the contradictions in his
own position as a professional writer. Dickens carries out his labor in the home, labor that as "brain work" itself has an uneasy
relationship with the manual labor of the factory. Just as Dickens
represented Esther's work as "labor that is not labor," so he
views his own work as a writer as somehow more autonomous
and less alienated than other forms of work, especially working
in a blacking factory. Dickens's own position as a professional
writer is marked by contradictory ideologies, just as is Esther's
as a housekeeper. He finds his own subject position within the
Victorian gendered hierarchy of labor to be as problematic as
that of a woman performing domestic labor as a feminized form
of work:

> The contradiction for literary men who worked at home
> contributed to their fear of "effeminization" within a soci-
> ety that conflated "public" with masculine for the middle
> class and differentiated the competitive marketplace from
> the private "feminine" space of the home.[47]

Dickens's investment in the ideology of domesticity involved
him in the same set of contradictions around work and the home
as the site of leisure as he inscribed in Esther Summerson.
Although we apparently have in Dickens's portrayal of Esther
what Julia Swindells has termed "the professional writer in his
professional art idealizing the unprofessional woman," the case
is actually more complex than this because Dickens identifies
with Esther in interesting ways. Dickens himself is caught within
the same disabling dichotomies as the character Esther Summerson. He is caught in a set of dichotomies that Swindells
claims "a particular kind of masculine professionalism inscribes;
work and home, felt and thought, woman and man."[48] In writing

Bleak House, however, Dickens became dangerously aware of how such ideological distinctions were precarious fictions and what were represented as binary opposites were not in fact so very different from one another. Even though for Dickens "respectable" women did not work, Esther does indeed carry out. various forms of unacknowledged labor in the book. Her labor's ambiguous status reveals the contradictions in Dickens's own masculine professional ideology, contradictions that made him unable to recognize certain forms of work as work, including the work of a professional novel writer.

Dickens therefore represents his own awareness of the contradictions inherent in the Victorian division of labor along gender lines through his representation of women and their ambiguous relationship to wage labor. The contradictions in Esther's character bespeak the ruptures in Dickens's own professional identity, which was not as secure as it might at first seem. This is an aspect of the relationship between the "professional" male and the "unprofessional" female that Swindells does not consider in her otherwise excellent analysis; a man's relationship to the ideal of professional work could be fraught with contradictions similar to those of women, especially women fiction writers. The gender distinctions Dickens espouses overtly in *Bleak House* are subverted by his own uneasy awareness of the contradictions inherent in his own position, and the fissures in the hegemonic definition of work along gender lines.

Chris Vanden Bossche has described Dickens's position vis à vis his female characters particularly well. Characterizing Dickens's attempts to differentiate the domestic haven of the home from the competition of the marketplace as revealing his desire to represent his work as "unalienated labor," Vanden Bossche describes Dickens's relationship to his female characters in suggestive terms:

> The paradox of the work ethic, however, produces discontinuities within the role of the writer. Even as the writer himself enters the home, writers are represented in terms of the woman who crosses into the marketplace: the philanthropist and the prostitute.[49]

Vanden Bossche's analysis helps account for Dickens's vitriolic treatment of Miss Wisk or Mrs. Jellyby; both women threaten the distinction between the unalienated labor performed at home and the alienated labor of the factory by transgressing the gendered boundaries of private/public and work/home. Although Vanden Bossche claims that we as readers "ultimately find that the realms are interdependent and implicated within one another,"[50] Dickens overtly denies this fact. He attempts to represent women in ideal terms as separate from work. His vicarious identification with streetwalkers and other "wayward" women shows, however, how divided his loyalties on this score were.

Dickens's attempt to write "in a womanly way" in *Bleak House* involved him directly in questions of the gendered division of labor. The book raised troubling questions that exceeded Dickens's ability to answer. Although *Bleak House* ostensibly ends with Esther's marriage, the novel cannot come to a conclusion. *Bleak House* represents a fascinating counterpoint to *David Copperfield*. Poovey claims that in *David Copperfield*, "(masculine) gender is the constitutive feature of the subject."[51] In *Bleak House*, by contrast, Dickens attempted self-consciously to fashion a female subject, thereby initiating an implicit critique of the hegemonic definition of work along gender lines in the Victorian period. The novel enacts a dialectic between two voices, one the authorial, impersonal, public and masculine voice of the narrative, the other the hesitating, unauthorized voice of Esther Summerson.[52] The novel is thus riven by a division that it finally cannot overcome. The last voice in the novel is Esther's, not the authoritative, impersonal narrator, and rather than conclude her narrative she simply fades away:

> And don't you know that you are prettier than you ever were?

> I did not know that; I am not certain that I know it now. But I know that my dearest pets are very pretty, and that my darling is very beautiful, and that my husband is very handsome, and that my guardian has the brightest and most benevolent face that ever was seen; and that they can very well do without much beauty in me—even supposing—[53]

Given the ideological constraints in operation in his creation of Esther Summerson, Dickens has to end his novel with a statement of what Esther does *not* know, rather than what she has learned in the course of the narrative. She cannot look back over the novel and summarize its moral content because she is a space of willed unconsciousness rather than a character. She represents Dickens's repressed awareness of the deep contradictions in Victorian domestic ideology and its relationship to other forms of work in the Victorian period. By the end of the novel Esther has been differentiated from ideas of beauty and sexual attraction, from ideas of work, and from images of women who abandon their domestic duties for evangelical causes. There is not much Esther can be represented as knowing when all these areas of experience have been excluded. Dickens also cannot conclude the novel himself because this would entail his facing his own doubts and uncertainties about his own gender position and his insecure tenancy of his identity as a masculine professional author of novels who "worked" at home.

NOTES

I would like to thank Professors Mary Burgan and Vanessa D. Dickerson for reading and commenting extensively on an earlier version of this article.

* Originally published in *Studies in the Novel*, v. 23, Winter, 1991. Copyright 1991 by University of North Texas. Reprinted by permission of the publisher.

1. William Axton, "The Trouble with Esther," *Modern Language Quarterly* 25 (1965): 545; Alex Zwerdling, "Esther Summerson Rehabilitated," *PMLA* 88 (1973): 429. See also Carol A. Senf, "Bleak House: Dickens, Esther and the Androgynous Mind," *Victorian Newsletter* 64 (Fall 1983): 21–27; John P. Frazee, "The Character of Esther and the Narrative Structure of *Bleak House*," *Studies in the Novel* 17:3 (Fall 1985): 227–40; Joseph Sawicki, "'The Mere Truth won't do': Esther as Narrator in *Bleak House*," *Journal of Narrative Technique* 17:2 (1987): 211–228; Thomas Linehan, "Parallel Lives: The Past and Self-retribution in *Bleak House*," *Studies in the Novel* 20:2 (Summer 1988): 131–50.

2. See Griselda Pollock's chapter on "Woman as Sign in Pre-Raphaelite Art" for an explanation of this method of analysis. Griselda

Pollock, *Vision and Difference: Femininity, Feminism and Histories of Art* (New York: Routledge, 1988).

3. Helen I. Safa, in *Women's Work: Development and the Division of Labor by Gender*, ed. Eleanor Leacock and Helen I. Safa (South Hadley, MA: Bergin and Garvey, 1986),

4. Ann Oakley, *Woman's Work: The Housewife Past and Present* (New York: Pantheon Books, 1974), 34.

5. Oakley points out that the working classes adopted the middle-class model of the housewife toward the end of the nineteenth century (*Woman's Work*, 50).

6. Oakley, *Woman's Work*, 6.

7. Oakley, *Woman's Work*, 1.

8. Quoted in Leonore Davidoff and Catherine Hall, *Family Fortunes: Men and Women of the English Middle Class, 1780–1850* (Chicago: University of Chicago Press, 1987), 272.

9. Catherine Hall, "The History of the Housewife," in *The Politics of Housework*, ed. Ellen Malos (London: Allison and Busby, 1980); Leacock and Safa, eds., *Women's Work;* Harriet Bradley, *Men's Work, Women's Work: A Sociological History of the Sexual Division of Labour in Employment* (Cambridge: Polity Press, 1989).

10. Hall, "History of the Housewife," 52; Wanda Mingle, "The Industrial Revolution and the European Family: 'Childhood' as a Market for Family Labor," in Leacock and Safa, *Women's Work*, 17.

11. Elizabeth Roberts, *Women's Work, 1840–1940* (London: Macmillan Studies in Economic and Social History, 1988), 12.

12. Mary Poovey, *Uneven Developments: The Ideological Work of Gender in Mid-Victorian England* (Chicago: University of Chicago Press, 1988), 159.

13. Hall, "History of the Housewife," 55. This led to extremely ambivalent feelings on the part of men towards leisured women, as the Punch cartoon reprinted in Michael Hiley, *Victorian Working Women: Portraits from Life* (London: Gordon Fraser, 1988), 22–23, shows. For a sympathetic treatment of such ladies of leisure see M. Jeanne Peterson, *Family, Love and Work in the Lives of Victorian Gentlewomen* (Bloomington: Indiana University Press, 1989).

14. Lee Holcombe, *Victorian Ladies at Work: Middle-Class Working Women in England and Wales, 1850–1914* (Hamden, CT: Archon Books, 1973), 4.

15. Nancy Armstrong and Leonard Tennenhouse, "Gender and the Work of Words," *Cultural Critique* 13 (Fall 1989): 231.

16. Julia Swindells, *Victorian Writing and Working Women* (Minneapolis: University of Minnesota Press, 1985), 82.

17. Malos, *The Politics of Housework*, 17.

18. Davidoff and Hall, *Family Fortunes*, 335.

19. Oakley, *Woman's Work*, 240.

20. Charles Dickens, *Bleak House*, ed. Morton Dauwen Zabel (Boston: Riverside Press, 1956), 52.

21. Dickens, *Bleak House*, 158.

22. Chris Vanden Bossche, "Cookery, Not Rookery: Family and Class in *David Copperfield*," *Dickens Studies Annual* 15 (1986): 87–109. Vanden Bossche points out in the context of *David Copperfield* that Agnes's "actual work of housekeeping is disguised by descriptions of the basket of keys" (103). Mary Poovey in her analysis of *David Copperfield* has also remarked that Agnes's duties as housewife are "signified only by her basket of keys," and that we do not see her perform her work (*Uneven Developments*, 101). I would amend these two analyses by pointing out that in *Bleak House* we see Esther's labor both represented in the keys and described in some detail, but that it is not recognized as work.

23. Charles Dickens, *Oliver Twist* (London: Nonesuch, 1937), 90.

24. Dickens, *Bleak House*, 445.

25. Jacques Donzelot, *The Policing of Families*, trans. Robert Hurley (New York: Random House, 1979). While I find Donzelot's account of the increasing role of the State in the surveillance of nineteenth-century families persuasive, I do not subscribe to his misogynist premise that women were to blame for the penetration of the State into the family. Michele Barret and Mary MacIntosh have pointed out that "underlying *The Policing of Families* is a very familiar theme. The authoritarian patriarchal family is mourned, and women are blamed for the passing of this organic basis of social order." Michele Barret and Mary MacIntosh, *The Anti-Social Family* (Norfolk: Thetford Press, 1982), 104.

26. Donzelot, *The Policing of Families*, 35.

27. Poovey, *Uneven Developments*, 99.

28. Dickens, *Bleak House*, 317.

29. Dickens, *Bleak House*, 318, 255.

30. Dickens, *Bleak House*, 70.

31. Nancy Armstrong, *Desire and Domestic Fiction: A Political History of the Novel* (New York: Oxford University Press, 1987), 75.

32. Dickens, *Bleak House*, 321.

33. Dickens, *Bleak House*, 82.

34. Dickens, *Bleak House*, 77.

35. In his essay "'Social Police' and the Bureaucratic Elite: A Vision of Order in the Age of Reform," A.P. Donajgrodzki describes the "social police" as the product of an agenda that consisted not only of "legal systems, police forces and prisons, but of religion, morality, and of those factors which supported or propagated them—education, socially constructive leisure, even housing and public health." A.P. Donajgrodzki, ed., *Social Control in Nineteenth-Century Britain* (London: Croom Helm, 1977), 9.

36. D.A. Miller, *The Novel and the Police* (Berkeley: University of California Press, 1988), 61.

37. Miller, *Novel and the Police*, 61.

38. Miller, *Novel and the Police*, 80.

39. Dickens, *Bleak House*, 650.

40. Jan Williams, Hazel Twort and Ann Bachelli, "Women and the Family" in Malos, *Politics of Housework*, 115.

41. Judith Wittner, "Domestic Labor as Work Discipline," in Sarah Fenstermaker Berk, ed., *Women and Household Labor* (Beverly Hills: Sage, 1980), 232.

42. Miller, *Novel and the Police*, 101–102.

43. Poovey, *Uneven Developments*, 10.

44. Suzanne Graver, "Writing in a 'Womanly Way' and the Double Vision of *Bleak House*," *Dickens Quarterly* 4:1 (March 1987): 4.

45. Graver, "Writing in a 'Womanly Way,'" 13.

46. Poovey, *Uneven Developments*, 101.

47. Regenia Gagnier, "The Literary Standard, Working-Class Lifewriting, and Gender," *Textual Practice* 3, no. 1 (Spring 1989): 36–55.

48. Swindells, *Victorian Writing*, 84, 59.

49. Vanden Bossche, "Cookery, Not Rookery," 104.

50. Vanden Bossche, "Cookery, Not Rookery," 102.

51. Poovey, *Uneven Developments*, 90.

52. See Virginia Blain, "Double Vision and the Double Standard in *Bleak House:* A Feminist Perspective," in *Charles Dickens's "Bleak House,"*

ed. Harold Bloom (New York: Chelsea House, 1987); Christine Van Boheemen, *The Novel as Family Romance: Language, Gender and Authority from Fielding to Joyce* (Ithaca: Cornell University Press, 1987); and Robyn Warhol, *Gendered Interventions: Narrative Discourse in the Victorian Novel* (New Brunswick: Rutgers University Press, 1989).

53. Dickens, *Bleak House*, 665.

Stitching Repentance, Sewing Rebellion
Seamstresses and Fallen Women in Elizabeth Gaskell's Fiction

Deborah Denenholz Morse

The Victorian seamstress, as Helena Michie points out in *The Flesh Made Word,* occupied "so central a place in the Victorian conscience."[1] The public was informed of the atrocious conditions for Victorian needlewomen throughout the period by documents such as Edwin Chadwick's *Report on the Sanitary Condition of the Labouring Population of Great Britain* (1842), R.D. Grainger's parliamentary blue book, *The Second Report of the Children's Employment Commission of 1843,* Mayhew's 1849–50 *Morning Chronicle* articles, and late in the Victorian era, Charles Booth's *Life and Labour of All the People in London* (1889–1903). Along with the deep concern about the seamstress's terrible working conditions, there was a concomitant fear about her moral state. Ill-fed, cold, overworked, and lacking affectionate guardianship, the needlewoman, as several "social problem" novels depict her, was often in fact a fallen woman. In her 1859 lecture, "Woman's Right to Labor," Caroline Healey Dall lamented that "Practically, the command of society to the uneducated class is 'Marry, stitch, die, or do worse.'" As the authors of *The Woman Question* comment, Dall "reminded Americans in 1859 that prostitution was an ever-present alternative to starvation for Hood's poor seamstress. It paid better than stitching and might even offer a chance for social advancement for lower-class women: a prostitute might marry or save enough money to open a small business."[2]

No Victorian novelist focuses more centrally on the figure of the seamstress—and on the fallen woman—than Elizabeth Gaskell. In "The Three Eras of Libbie Marsh" (1847), Gaskell's heroine is a poor needlewoman who befriends a hardworking washerwoman and her crippled son.[3] In "Lizzie Leigh" (1850), Gaskell is concerned with a young farm girl who goes to the city, where she eventually falls into prostitution. In 1848, Gaskell tells the story of a young dressmaker in *Mary Barton,* her first novel, interweaving that tale with the tragedy of Mary's Chartist father, John, and factory relations between masters and men. In *Ruth* (1853), Gaskell's young country girl Ruth Hilton is forced into apprenticeship with a milliner in the city, and is seduced by a gentleman. In each of these stories, Gaskell's narrative—and moral—strategy consciously aligns the seamstress outside the Victorian home with the mother within it, and the fallen woman on the streets with the angel in the house.

In voicing the social protest against the seamstress's inhumane working conditions, Gaskell joined a formidable group of writers and social activists. Gaskell's charity work among the Manchester working classes made her keenly aware of the conditions of most segments of the working poor, and she was well informed about the controversy surrounding the plight of the Victorian seamstress. Charles Kingsley, F.D. Maurice, J.M. Ludlow, and other Christian Socialists, already organizing at the time of Mayhew's articles,[4] moved quickly in the meetings that resulted in the founding of the Working Tailors Association and the Needlewomen's Association.[5] Friedrich Engels would also turn his attention to the plight of the seamstresses in *The Condition of the Working Class in England* (1844), identifying them as young girls virtually enslaved:

> These establishments employ many young girls—there are said to be 15,000 in all—who have their meals and sleep on the premises. Since most of them are country girls they are held in a state of complete servitude by their employers. During the London season, which lasts for about four months every year, even the well-conducted establishments work fifteen hours a day. If they are exceptionally

busy, even eighteen hours a day may be worked. In most of the dressmaking workshops there are no fixed hours of labour at all during the London season and the girls never get more than six hours' sleep out of the twenty-four. Often they get only three or four hours' sleep and occasionally they get only two hours' sleep. The only limit to their labour is the physical impossibility of holding a needle any longer . . . in particular, the long hours of work and the lack of fresh air have tragic results as far as the health of these girls is concerned. Very often the eye complaints to which we have referred end in complete and incurable blindness. If a dressmaker or a milliner does retain sufficient eyesight to continue with her work, her brief and tragic career generally ends in tuberculosis.

The needlewomen, Engels continued, were "exploited just as cruelly as the dressmakers," although the needlewomen worked in their own homes. And shirtmakers were even worse off, earning "only 11/2 d. for sewing an ordinary shirt."[6]

Engels's painstaking description of the seamstresses' terrifying descent into ill health, blindness, and death is reiterated in the many visions of the seamstress that were produced in the early and mid-Victorian era.[7] In Thomas Hood's poem, "The Song of the Shirt" (1843), for example, the refrain echoes in poetic mode the reportorial prose of Engels: "Stitch—stitch—stitch,/ In poverty, hunger, and dirt,/ Sewing at once with a double thread,/ A Shroud as well as a shirt" (ll. 29–32). In turn, Hood's poem influenced others as the needlewoman was also—and perhaps most pervasively—imaged in art as the romanticized solitary seamstress, the shirtmaker of Hood's poem rather than one of Engels' group of dressmakers in a workshop. Richard Redgrave's *The Sempstress* (1844) was the earliest and most influential of this genre. In this incarnation, destitute but sacralized, the needlewoman was most palatable to middle-class sensibilities and the cult of sentimentality. As Lynn Alexander makes clear in a statement about Dickens's depictions of the seamstress, "His choice of the seamstress demonstrates his understanding that his audience—middle-and-upper-class women—could sympathize, perhaps empathize, while men in positions of power would not feel threatened by working-class women employed in a domestic activity and might be moved to effect a change."[8]

In their efforts to "effect a change," those concerned about the seamstress's condition tended to portray her less frequently in the workroom with other dressmakers, but rather, increasingly, in "situations which pointedly compare the maker with the wearer."[9] The most powerful and famous of this final group of images calculated to elicit both guilt and compassion is "The Haunted Lady, or The Ghost in the Looking-Glass," published in the July 4 1863 *Punch*.[10] In this cartoon, an upper-class woman, gorgeously arrayed in a new ball gown, looks at herself in the mirror, which reflects the image of the dying seamstress who has made the dress. The mistress of a sewing establishment, the ironically named Madame La Modeste, says to her beautifully gowned client in the caption: "We would not have disappointed Her Ladyship at any sacrifice, and the robe is finished a merveille." Wanda Neff substantiates this caricature of the mistress in *Victorian Working Women*, where she remarks that "dressmakers were more relentless toward the girls they hired than some of the most ignorant overlookers in Manchester factories."[11] Lynn Alexander tells us that despite Dickens's recognition of the seamstress' sentimental value, for Dickens "the seamstress was more than a means to an end . . . his constant return to the figure of the seamstress indicates that he never accepted the inevitability of the needleworker's hard life, and ending his series of portrayals with an image of horror rather than acceptance [in the 1860 *The Uncommercial Traveller* and the 1864 essay "The Point of the Needle"] suggests that he, like many Victorians, was always haunted by the Ghost in the Looking-glass."[12] The human cost of Victorian class-and-money defined demands for elaborate clothing on short notice, a demand met through the virtual slave labor of the seamstress, is addressed as well in texts such as Elizabeth Stone's *The Young Milliner* (1843); Charlotte Elizabeth Tonna's "Milliners and Dressmakers" (1843) and *The Wrongs of Woman* (1847); Camilla Toulmin's *The Orphan Milliners: A Story of the West End* (1844); Charles Kingsley's *Alton Locke, Tailor and Poet* (1850); Eliza Meteyard's *Lucy Dean: The Noble Needlewoman* (1850), as well as Gaskell's *Mary Barton* and *Ruth*.

In mid and High Victorian fiction, the fallen woman is often depicted as "stitching" her redemption for her sin, as in Margaret Oliphant's *Salem Chapel* (1863) or Gaskell's *Ruth*. The very different treatments of the seamstress/fallen woman are suggested by the alternative narratives of the fallen woman's history in these two novels. In Gaskell's *Ruth*, the seamstress who becomes a fallen woman eventually saves her upper-class seducer's life at the cost of her own. In Oliphant's novel, the fallen woman is an aristocrat assuming the role of seamstress as an act both of penance and disguise; the fallen Mrs. Hilyard, the "needlewoman of Back Grove Street,"[13] eventually rises up as female avenger and stabs the aristocratic seducer who wants to "sell" their beautiful daughter into a marriage that is virtual prostitution. While in Gaskell's *Ruth*, the lowly seamstress is ultimately a Christ figure, the repentant needlewoman in Oliphant's text becomes a Fury, avenging herself upon the male culture that has constructed her as fallen woman.

As Oliphant's novel indicates, Victorian fiction used the metaphor of sewing to express the emotional state not only of seamstresses and fallen women, but also women of the middle and upper classes, who stitched their rebellion against feminine gender roles. In Charlotte Brontë's *Villette* (1853), the schoolteacher Lucy Snowe sews the shroud of her "buried"self even more tightly closed, and in *Shirley* (1849), Caroline Helstone tries to repress her painful love for Robert Moore and her longing for meaningful work; both women stitch their submission and their angry rebellion against the prisonings of women's culturally-defined roles.[14] In Eliot's *The Mill on the Floss* (1860), Maggie Tulliver practices Thomas à Kempis's philosophy of patient submission by sewing, but eventually breaks out of her self-denial in her flight with Stephen Guest. She ultimately replaces stitching with rowing in her heroic rescue attempt of Tom. Since Victorian women of all social classes were taught to sew, there is an obvious subversiveness to these insistent portrayals of frustrated sewing women.[15] Through the depiction of the seamstress in all her guises, these novelists critique the strictures of their culture's gender roles. The figure of the seamstress allows Elizabeth Gaskell to focus more clearly than any other Victorian novelist, however, on linking the woman who rises to angelic heights of self-sacrifice and the fallen woman who is desecrated.

"The Three Eras of Libbie Marsh" (1847) opens with a spinster seamstress, Libbie Marsh, moving from her home because the people with whom she had shared a house are leaving Manchester: "Last November but one there was a flitting in our neighbourhood; hardly a flitting after all, for it was only a single person changing her place of abode." Libbie both goes out to sew and does plain sewing at her lodgings; society's perception of her negligible importance as a single working woman is indicated by the way in which her moving day is considered as "hardly a flitting after all." Libbie, unlike Esther or Mary in *Mary Barton*, is not a fallen or falling woman, and not a woman whose looks make it very likely that she will be the target of a seduction. She is, as the vocal factory workers' good-natured jokes make clear to her, a "very plain" woman.[16] Libbie is simply looking for someone to love, and enters the narrative on her moving day thinking "on the lonely creature she was in this wide world."[17]

During the course of the story, the orphaned Libbie resists the narrative of the father that separates mother and daughter. Libbie is the daughter of an abusive, drunken father who has killed her "darling baby" sister "in one of his bouts," and, as Libbie says, "in the long run it killed mother." In the course of the story, Libbie becomes a surrogate mother to Franky, a young crippled boy whose mother is the washerwoman Margaret Hall. Soon Franky has two maternal figures, as Libbie, "as eagerly as poor Margaret Hall, and with far more resources" tries to brighten Franky's life. Libbie first sees Franky while she sews at home; her solitude and loneliness make her particularly responsive to the painful sight of the crippled boy, who struggles daily with the wearying "heavy pulses of dull pain." Libbie Marsh's first era, "St. Valentine's Day," begins with her interest in and identification with both Franky's hardworking, apparently "termagant" mother, Margaret Hall, and the loving, patient Franky himself: "But when Libbie had plain sewing to do at her lodgings instead of going out to sew, she used to watch from her bed-room window for the time when the shadows opposite, by their mute gestures, told that the mother had returned to bend over her child." Libbie begins to emulate the Mother—both Margaret Hall and the mother Libbie herself remembers with such love: "And often in the night Libbie could not help rising gently from bed to see if the little arm was waving up and down, as was his accustomed habit when sleepless from pain."[18] The poor crippled Franky thus has two mothers rather than a father and mother. The working-class realignment of the patriarchal family subverts the middle-class cultural ideal. This feminized family significantly provides a nurturing home for the sick child that counters the violent masculine atmosphere in which Libbie was raised—and her sister killed.

The feminization of the family begins with the nature-named Libbie Marsh's gift of a canary to Franky (sold by the barber *Emanuel* Morris) after Libbie discovers the boy's delight in caring for flowers. Libbie performs this generous act in memory of her mother: "Many a year in the happy days of old had her mother delighted to surprise her with some little gift. . . . Since then, the 14th of February had been the dreariest day of all the year, because the most haunted by memory of departed happiness." Her gift is also a country tradition, kept alive by her mother from her "east of England" heritage, a part of the preindustrial past that Gaskell sees as life-giving in the harsh, unloving city. Libbie's decision to scrimp and save to buy Franky a bird to care for demonstrates her determination to move from daughter's role to mother's: "But now, this year, if she could not have the old gladness of heart herself, she would try and brighten the life of another." The delight that the child has in Libbie's gift in turn brings forth the maternal nature of Franky's mother who, Libbie witnesses, does "what, with all her tenderness, seemed rarely to have entered into her thoughts—she bent down, and kissed her boy in a mother's sympathy with the joy of her child."[19] St. Valentine's Day is of course the traditional day for sending gifts of love, especially to one's sweetheart, but Libbie's gift to Franky will begin an untraditional love relationship of mutual self-sacrifice between two workingwomen, a plain seamstress and a poor, overworked washerwoman. The fact that it is also Libbie's birthday marks not only her own selflessness, but also the birth of her most loving relationships since her mother and sister died.

The second "era" of the narrative constitutes a holy inter-
lude in which Gaskell aligns nature with the feminine. Libbie
and Margaret help Franky to the pinnacle of happiness when
they take him to Dunham Woods at the Whitsuntide holiday. It
is fitting that Whitsunday (Pentecost), the festival celebrating the
Descent of the Holy Spirit on the Apostles,[20] forms the backdrop
to the holiday scenes in the country. Gaskell—her own beloved
Knutsford no doubt in her mind—describes the sacred, soul-
deepening effect of the working people's excursion into
Wordsworthian Nature:

> . . . all so tender and kind; so softened, in fact, by the
> beauty of that earth; so unconsciously touched by the
> Spirit of Love which was the Creator of that lovely
> earth. . . . We have all of us one look, now and then, called
> up by some noble or loving thought, (our highest on
> earth), which will be our likeness in Heaven. I can catch
> the glance on many a face; the glancing light of the cloud
> of glory from Heaven, 'which is our home.'[21]

The tenderness and beauty of the love that helps the seamstress
and washerwoman create a home for the child is that same
"spirit of love" that wells up from the earth and reflects the glory
of that final home for which Franky will soon depart.

In fact, the final "era" of Libbie's story, "Michaelmas," details the seamstress' grief over Franky's death and the beginning
of her new life with Margaret Hall. Again, Gaskell perhaps invokes Michaelmas not only because it is a traditional day marking the end of rent term (quarter-day) and thus is a common
moving day, but because of its religious significance. Michaelmas (September 29) celebrates the feast of St. Michael, "the first
of the archangels, leader of the Hosts of Heaven who defeated
Lucifer when he revolted against God."[22] The spinster seamstress Libbie is implicitly compared with the "winged warrior"
who "rescues souls from Limbo and Hell and leads them to
Heaven." She is figured during the period of grief as a kind of
maternal presence for Margaret; Libbie literally restores the
washerwoman's senses at the funeral and then revives her will
to live by reminding the bereaved mother of the love Franky had
for Pete, the canary, who now must be cared for. There is a compelling scene in this final section of the story when Libbie reads

to the bereaved mother from the fourteenth chapter of St. John's Gospel, and the comfort that sacred text provides is defined in explicitly maternal terms: "The soul went home to its words of loving sympathy when weary and sorrowful, just as the little child seeks the tender comfort of its mother in all its griefs and cares."[23] This maternal image supplants the narrative of the abusive father in Libbie's story.

Thus, when Anne Dixon, the landlord's daughter, asks Libbie on the day of the funeral to be a bridesmaid at Anne's wedding to a man who is much like the needlewoman's drunken father, there is symbolic significance in Libbie's refusal. Instead of celebrating a marriage that will probably result in a home like that in which Libbie suffered, she chooses instead to form a household of two women, two "mothers," joined in the memory of "their" child, thereby celebrating the love her mother gave her in childhood. Libbie tries to explain to the uncomprehending Anne how she views her role as one of the "old maids, just looking round for the odd jobs God leaves in the world for such as old maids to do,—there's plenty of such work,—and there's the blessing of God on them as does it."[24] It is in particular impassioned speeches like Libbie's that Eva Figes has in mind when she observes that "as a writer Gaskell was unusual in making working-class characters speak for themselves."[25] Christine Krueger thoughtfully expands Figes' statement in her claim that "by investing the working-class voice with power, as More and Tonna had, Gaskell legitimates a marginal perspective. . . . Above all, it insists on the authority of female subjectivity."[26]

Libbie is the spokesperson for an ethic of caring that Gaskell clearly sees as the salvation of Victorian culture. Anne the bride-to-be has the name of a perfect mother in Christian lore, St. Anne, mother of the Virgin Mary, but it is Libbie the old maid—not the bride—who is the prototype of the ideal nurturer for Victorian society. Finally even Anne, on her wedding-day, recognizes something of Libbie's goodness and tells her: "Thou'rt a real good 'un, Libbie, and I'll keep your needle-book to my dying day, that I will." Libbie is significantly called "Elizabeth Marsh"[27] for the first time during this scene, as if her vision of her role in the world has sacralized her, given new maternal resonance to her name, the name both of the suffering mother St. Elizabeth and of Mary's kinswoman, mother to the forerunner of Christ, John the Baptist.

From beginning to end, the portrayal of the women's friendship marks Gaskell's attention to and respect for the lives of working women like Libbie and Margaret. Early on in the story, the washerwoman reciprocates Libbie's generosity with her own kindness: "... one evening, when Libbie was returning home with a bundle of work half as large as herself, as she dragged herself along through the heated street she was over-taken by Margaret Hall, her burden gently pulled from her, and her way home shortened, and her weary spirits soothed and cheered by the outpourings of Margaret's heart." At the end of the story, Margaret Hall, the "termagant," the "Tartar," the self-described "mad one, when I'm in a rage," has become the longed-for mother figure to Libbie: "Her dead mother could hardly have cared for her more tenderly than does the hard-featured washerwoman, not long ago so fierce and unwomanly."[28] As in the other texts I'll discuss, the new maternal narrative for the seamstress heroine—and for the culture—displaces the father's story.

Although in Gaskell's "Lizzie Leigh," Lizzie is not a seam-stress but a farm girl who is seduced when she goes to the city to work as a servant, her story is an important precursor to the treatments of the fallen woman in *Mary Barton* and *Ruth.* The woman who sews is the angelic keeper of the home, the pilgrim-named Susan Palmer, who raises the fallen Lizzie's illegitimate child. Susan works to earn her bread not as a needlewoman but as a schoolteacher of "very young children," an occupation that identifies her as a mother figure; however, Susan sews as a func-tion of her job. As one of her admiring neighbors in Manchester expresses it, "She'll bring her thimble wi' her, and mend up after the childer o' nights." Susan is the ideal Victorian angel, as this passage detailing Lizzie's brother Will's attraction to her exemplifies:

> She never spoke much; she was generally diligently at work; but when she moved, it was so noiselessly, and when she did speak, it was in so low and soft a voice, that silence, speech, motion, and stillness alike seemed to re-move her high above Will's reach into some saintly and

> inaccessible air of glory—high above his reach, even as she knew him! And, if she were made acquainted with the dark secret behind, of his sister's shame which was kept ever present to his mind by his mother's nightly search among the outcast and forsaken, would not Susan shrink away from him with loathing, as if he were tainted by the involuntary relationship? This was his dread . . . [29]

Susan's "silence, speech, motion, and stillness" define for Will the gulf between Susan and his sister, who as a fallen woman is also, ironically, silent (silenced) and still (stilled) in the world of the father. Will's "dread" that Susan will feel polluted by association with him or with his fallen sister is belied by the text's insistent association of the two women. Perhaps most significantly, Lizzie watches and chooses Susan as her daughter's surrogate mother, replacing her own care with Susan's, and making Susan a part of Lizzie's narrative of the fall. The association of the two women extends to others in the text as Susan, moreover, tells this story to Lizzie's mother, Anne Leigh, in response to Anne's tale of her daughter's fall. The context is significant, as Anne, wearing a "scarlet cloth cloak" that aligns her with the "scarlet" woman Lizzie,[30] first meets her granddaughter, Nanny, who is named for her, just before Susan begins her narration.

> One night, as I came home, I thought some woman was following me; I turned to look. The woman, before I could see her face (for she turned it to one side), offered me something. I held out my arms by instinct; she dropped a bundle into them, with a bursting sob that went straight to my heart. It was a baby. I looked round again; but the woman was gone. . . . There was a little packet of clothes—very few—and as if they were made out of its mother's gowns, for they were large patterns to buy for a baby.[31]

Because of "its mother's gowns" the grandchild is reunited with the grandmother for whom it is named, Anne Leigh; a note attached to the "bundle" given to Susan states "Call her Anne." The fact that Lizzie's mother and Lizzie's child bear the name of a perfect mother in Christian theology, the mother of the Virgin Mary, perhaps suggests the essential purity of Lizzie herself. In any event, mother and daughter are further linked as this Victorian Anne walks the streets as her fallen child has done, "with

never-wearying perseverance, till some light from shop or lamp
showed the cold strange face which was not her daughter's. . . . I
think they believed her to be crazy."[32] This scene foreshadows
the haunting, surreal passages narrating the Victorian an-
gel/daughter Esther Summerson's journey in search of her fallen
woman/mother Lady Dedlock in Dickens's *Bleak House* (1852–
53).[33] In both scenes, women who are clearly fallen—but are not
the searched for and beloved mother—are turned round on the
street and—in Dickens's text—fished out of the Thames,
"FOUND DROWNED."[34]

Although Esther's suspicion that the drowned woman is
her fallen mother proves unfounded, the iconography of the
drowned fallen woman resonates at this juncture of the novel.
Dickens perhaps had in mind works such as Thomas Hood's
"The Bridge of Sighs" (1844) and George F. Watts's "Found
Drowned" (1849). Lizzie's mother Anne is more fortunate in her
rescue efforts than Esther, who ultimately finds Lady Dedlock
dead at the pauper churchyard gates. Yet in both works, the text
argues for identification between mother and daughter, and with
all fallen women, all of whom are someone's daughters—and
many of whom are mothers. Moreover, the very title of the story,
"Lizzie Leigh," evokes both sacred Elizabeths, as well as echoing
the title of so many age-old ballads of women seduced and
abandoned, narratives which invariably are in sympathy with
the fallen woman. Gaskell, then, petitions for tolerance on both
biblical/religious and historical/literary grounds in the very
names she chooses for her story.

This tolerance is realized in the Victorian angel Susan,
whose generous, unjudgmental response to the strange fallen
woman, her infant child and her mother again evokes the forgiveness of the Gospels. Susan, who embodies the self-sacrifice
of Christ's example, opens her home in the symbolically named
Crown Street to the fallen woman's child, then to the suffering
grandmother, and finally, to the fallen mother herself. As Anne
Leigh tells her son Will, "'She's not one to harden her heart
against a mother's sorrow. . . . She's not one to judge and scorn
the sinner. She's too deep read in her New Testament for that. . . .
I did, I told her all! and she fell a-crying over my deep sorrow,
and the poor wench's sin. And then a light comed into her face,

trembling and quivering with some new glad thought. . . . That little Nanny is not her niece, she's our Lizzie's own child, my little grandchild.'" Although Will's first response is to recoil from identifying his holy figure Susan with his fallen sister and her illegitimate daughter—"'To think of Susan having to do with such a child!'"—Anne reminds him that "Susan, good and pure as the angels in heaven, yet, like them, full of hope and mercy, and one who like them, will rejoice over her as she repents." The mother's voice asserts its holy authority in this scene, in which Anne asks her son to receive his sister Lizzie again if she is ever found, and to love Lizzie's child: "I am your mother, and I dare to command you, because I know I am in the right, and that God is on my side."[35] Will quietly submits "in reverence at her words, and the solemn injunction which they conveyed," responding in "so subdued a voice that she was almost surprised at the sound, 'Mother, I will.'"[36]

The obedience Will gives to his mother defines his moral education in the true Christian spirit, embodied by the maternal spirit in this narrative. Mrs. Leigh's words are, as Christine Krueger states, a preachment, a legacy from the the evangelical tradition: "The prophetic role guaranteed to women by the evangelical mission enables Mrs. Leigh to appropriate privileged language on behalf of a fallen woman."[37] Will, the elder of two sons, is "like his father, stern, reserved, and scrupulously upright," we learn in the stark opening scene of the story, set during that father's deathbed forgiveness of his fallen daughter Lizzie, whom he has denied for the three years since her fall. He dies, significantly, on Christmas Day. Both his deathbed mercy to his daughter and the symbolic day of his death argue against the moral authority of his Old Testament judgement of the daughter's sin. James Leigh, we learn, has actively resisted the loving influence of the mother. As Anne tells Susan later in Manchester, "I had a daughter once, my heart's darling. Her father thought I made too much on her, and that she'd grow marred staying at home; so he said she mun go among strangers, and learn to rough it." Then, Anne goes on to relate, when Lizzie got into trouble, the urban father-surrogate, the master, "turned her into the street soon as he had heard of her condition—and she not seventeen!"[38] The moral outrage that Anne expresses is a trenchant critique of the patriarchal values which the rural and urban "fathers" share. In the case of the master of the house, Anne's anger is also a condemnation of the coldness of urban life, in which the father/master so patently fails to embody Christ's teachings.

Will's submission to his mother's authority is part of a process of feminizing him, of educating him into the Mother's moral world. Significantly, Will's new alliance to the mother links him to his much younger brother Tom, who "was gentle and delicate as a girl, both in appearance and character. He had always clung to his mother, and dreaded his father." Will has felt since Lizzie's disgrace that this "one event had made him old before his time; and had envied Tom the tears he had shed over poor, pretty, innocent, dead Lizzie. He thought about her sometimes, till he ground his teeth together, and could have struck her down in her shame."[39] The most disturbing part of Will's thoughts is his inadvertent acknowledgment that "dead" Lizzie is still alive—and that he would like to hurt her himself, that he in truth violently wishes she were dead.

It is this hardness of heart that eventually kills little Nanny, when Susan's own selfish, drunken father precipitates the accident by which the child dies.[40] Significantly, Nanny falls to her death in the home, hitting her head on the stone floor; symbolically, the father's responsibility in causing Nanny's hard mortal fall recalls the harshness of James Leigh casting Lizzie from the home, and the the factory owner's stony heart as he thrusts out the fallen, pregnant Lizzie. The women's maternal love opposes the father's hard-heartedness. Lizzie, the "shadow" outside the house, comes in to the house to see her dying child, and Susan's embrace joins angel and fallen woman, light and shadow: "The holy God had put courage into her heart, and her pure arms were round that guilty, wretched creature, and her tears were falling fast and warm upon her breast." The two mothers—the real mother and the surrogate mother—both blame themselves for the child's death. Lizzie says: "Oh, the murder is on my soul!" When the doctor accuses Lizzie of not taking care of her child, Susan says: "The little child slept with me; it was I that left her." Finally, the identification of the two mothers seems complete with Lizzie's quiet request, "May I have my own child to lie in my arms for a little while?" Susan prays over Lizzie, as Lizzie smiles and speaks to her dead child; Susan's fear that Lizzie "was going mad" harks back to the people on the street, who looked at Lizzie's mother Anne as she searched for her daughter and "believed her to be crazy."[41]

Lizzie's embrace of the dead child recalls not only Anne's first vision of Susan with the child, "her little niece in her arms, curled up with fond endearment against her breast," but also, inevitably, the Pietà, the final embrace of Mother and Child. When Anne comes to the house on Crown Street to see her fallen daughter, she too "hushed her on her breast; and lulled her as if she were a baby; and she grew still and quiet. . . . That night they lay in each other's arms; but Susan slept on the ground beside them."[42] As Margaret Homans notes in her fine analysis of "Lizzie Leigh" in *Bearing the Word:* "In this part of the story, there is general but not disturbing uncertainty as to who is daughter, who is mother, and of whom. Three mothers contemplate, in grief, the faces of two daughters, one who is dead, one who is 'like one dead.'"[43] All three mothers are part of a circle, whole in their passionate love and wild sorrow: the two "crazy" mothers, Lizzie and Anne, and Susan, the woman who comforts them both.

Susan and Will marry and live on the family farm, the sacred-sounding Upclose, restoring the Leigh family in this generation to wholeness, reconstituted in the authority of Christ and the maternal. Susan becomes Anne's "daughter" by marrying Will, and symbolically reincarnates the once innocent Lizzie by embodying her before her fall. She who has acted in loving sisterhood to the fallen woman becomes her sister-in-law. The sacred echoes of Susan's name give further resonance to this identification of Victorian angel and fallen woman. "Susan," from the Hebrew, means "lily," and suggests the purity of this young woman. The name also evokes the Apocryphal story of Susannah and the Elders, in which a pure young woman, accused of adultery because she will not submit to the lascivious gaze of the Fathers, is saved by Daniel. In identifying Susan with Lizzie, Gaskell implicitly defends the fallen woman's essential purity, blurring the figures of Pure and Fallen Woman.

The fallen Lizzie expiates her sin through service to others, coming "out of her seclusion whenever there's a shadow in any household. Many hearts bless Lizzie Leigh, but she—she prays always and ever for forgiveness—such forgiveness as may enable her to see her child once more." The mother Anne and daughter Lizzie continue to live a reclusive life together, dwelling again in the country nearby Upclose Farm, "in a cottage so secluded that, until you drop into the very hollow where it is placed, you do not see it." The other half of Lizzie's life of "shadow" is lived by the angelic Susan, "the bright one who brings sunshine to all. Children grow around her and call her blessed." Yet both women are "blessed" by others, and their final identification comes through Susan's daughter, whom she has named Nanny: "Her, Lizzie often takes to the sunny graveyard in the uplands, and while the little creature gathers the daisies, and makes chains, Lizzie sits by a little grave and weeps bitterly." This grave is not in the family churchyard, for "they dared not lay her by the stern grandfather in Milne Row churchyard, but they bore her to a lone moorland graveyard, where, long ago, the Quakers used to bury their dead. They laid her there on the sunny slope, where the earliest springflowers blow."[44] The sorrow of the past is not erased nor the remembrance of the hard lessons of the father, but the living Nanny is Lizzie's niece, her surrogate daughter, her companion. Perhaps Gaskell's vindication of the fallen woman, although it espoused full forgiveness, did not encompass full restoration in this world, the possibility of the fallen woman ending her expiatory period and reentering the world of sexuality and motherhood in her own person. However, through the bodies of other women with whom the fallen woman is identified, Gaskell writes a subversive text that aligns all Victorian women against the narrative of the father.

Mary Barton: A Tale of Manchester Life (1848) tells the story of a seamstress heroine whose romantic history is intertwined with that of her Chartist father John Barton's tragic story. Mary Barton, named for the much-beloved mother who dies in the third chapter of the novel, is apprenticed to a dressmaker in part because her father objects both to domestic service, which he views as "a species of slavery," and to factory work, which he rejects for Mary because in his view it has led to the probable sexual fall of Esther, his wife's sister. He swears that "my Mary shall never work in a factory, that I'm determined on."[45] Ironically, Mary's hard, monotonous life as a dressmaker makes her susceptible to the sexual advances of the millowner's handsome, dashing son Harry Carson, and she is nearly seduced as her Aunt Esther was.

In the context of both romantic and political plots of the novel, the activity of sewing and the lives of needlewomen are constructed and interpreted in a number of ways. There are in fact a number of scenes depicting seamstresses working: at Miss Simmonds's establishment, at Mary's home, and at Mary's friend Margaret Legh's home. The most poignant of these scenes associate the stitching woman with sympathy and caring. Thus, Mary's compassionate thoughts about a starving worker, Davenport, who dies of typhoid in a dank cellar, reveal her essential goodness. First she sits in the cellar with the grieving Mrs. Davenport; next she is sitting at Miss Simmonds's thinking of the mourning she will make for the widow. Stitching is depicted in this scene as an expression of compassion, even a creative effort, and a means through which even a poor seamstress can provide solace:

> And Mary forgot all purposed meeting with her gay lover, Harry Carson; forgot Mill Simmonds' errands, and her anger in the anxious desire to comfort the poor lone woman. . . . Mary had many a scolding from Miss Simmonds that day for her absence of mind. . . . She was too busy planning how her old black gown (her best when her mother died) might be spunged, and turned, and lengthened into something like decent mourning for the widow. And she went home at night (though it was very late, as a sort of retribution for her morning's negligence), she set to work at once, and was so busy, and so glad over her task, that she had, every now and then, to check herself in singing merry ditties, that she felt little accorded with the sewing on which she was engaged.

Mary's mothering of the widow Davenport and her unselfish gift of the mourning gown she wore at her own mother's death identify Mary's capacity for maternal love. This gift will be reciprocated in the renewed energy of Mrs. Davenport, who in turn helps Mrs. Wilson, Jem's mother, in her later sorrows. Mrs. Davenport is in fact present during the first part of the scene in which Mary goes to help Jane Wilson, impelled by "the old feeling which first bound Ruth to Naomi; the love they both held towards one object."[46] Mary sits all night with Jem's mother, like a mother at her child's bedside. In this scene, Gaskell portrays one of the most poignant expressions of maternal love and grief in the novel. As Margaret Homans recalls for us, Gaskell wrote *Mary Barton* in grief over both her first daughter, stillborn in 1836, and her only son, William, who died of scarlet fever in Wales in 1845, when he was ten months old.[47] When Mary thinks of the now widowed Jane Wilson's love for her only remaining child, Jem, who is accused of murder, the reader perhaps thinks of Gaskell's grief for her son: "what if in dreams (that land into which no sympathy nor love can penetrate with another, either to share its bliss or its agony,—that land whose scenes are unspeakable terrors, are hidden mysteries, are priceless treasures to one alone,—that land where alone I may see, while yet I tarry here, the sweet looks of my dead child),—what if, in the horrors of her dreams, her brain should go still more astray, and she should waken crazy with her visions, and the terrible reality that begot them?"[48]

The maternal narrative of Mary, Jane Wilson, and the Widow Davenport, the story of nurturance and love, is resisted by the harsh conditions of the workplace. The emphasis in Gaskell's portrayal of the dressmaking establishment itself is on the unwholesome moral atmosphere in which Mary sews. It is not so much a place of physical horrors, like those in Grainger's and Mayhew's reports, but a place of moral degradation. Mary is in truth often exhausted by her work, and she gets little to eat; at one point in the novel we are told that she fasts from noon dinner until midnight. However, the novel's focus is on the encouragement Mary is given in her flirtation with Carson, "a lover not beloved"; she is prodded by the young seamstress Sally Leadbitter, who copes with the boredom of endless stitching by pandering for other, more attractive girls in their love affairs.[49] As the thoughtful spinner Job Legh comments to Mary, "Yon's a bold, bad girl."[50] Her malicious hunger for vicarious pleasure is qualified by one saving grace: she cares lovingly for her invalid mother.

The grinding work of the seamstress and its concomitant terror of blindness are manifested powerfully in the novel. Margaret Legh, whose beautiful singing voice eventually brings her family out of poverty, is blinded by the sewing she must do to live and to help support her grandfather Job's one innocent indulgence, his "botanizing." One scene in particular, in which an exhausted Mary helps Margaret sew mourning for which she does not expect payment, illustrates the kindness and self-sacrifice of which these two working-class women are capable:

> 'Well, Margaret, you're right welcome as you know, and I'll sit down and help you with pleasure, though I was tired enough of sewing tonight at Miss Simmonds'. . . . '
> The weary sound of stitching was the only sound heard for a little while. . . .

> 'There's only one thing I dislike making black for, it does so hurt the eyes. . . . Mary! do you know I sometimes think I'm growing a little blind, and then what would become of grandfather and me? Oh, God help me, Lord help me!'

> She fell into an agony of tears, while Mary knelt by her, striving to soothe and to comfort her . . .

Despite the threat of personal blindness, Margaret assisted by Mary works to alleviate the distress of others without expecting compensation. It is significant as well that their work is in part motivated by knowledge that the widow, Mrs. Ogden, has "asked for credit at several places, saying her husband laid hands on every farthing he could get for drink."[51] Like Libbie Marsh, Mrs. Ogden has suffered from male excesses, male self-indulgence—perhaps, like Libbie, from male abuse.

As blindness is the terror behind Margaret's life as needlewoman, so falling out of the father's house as Esther has done is the danger for Mary. Esther, the fallen woman, is a resonant figure in the text. The perfection of the pastoral idyll in Green Heys Fields that opens the book is broken by the first spoken words of the novel, the question asked by John Barton's best friend George Wilson, "'Well, John, how goes it with you?' and, in a lower voice, he added, 'any news of Esther, yet?'" Mary's mother is crying over her fallen sister; as John explains to his friend, "'my wife spoiled her, it is true, for you see she was so much older than Esther she was more like a mother to her, doing everything for her.'" Throughout the story, Mary the daughter/falling woman is identified with Esther, the fallen woman who is both sister and "daughter" to Mary's mother. The death of the mother brings forth John Barton's wrath for the fallen sister whom he blames for the "shock to the system" that the doctor cites as the cause of her death: "His feelings toward Esther almost amounted to curses. It was she who had brought on all this sorrow. Her giddiness, her lightness of conduct, had wrought this woe. His previous thoughts about her had been tinged with wonder and pity, but now he hardened his heart against her forever." Later in the novel, when Esther is afraid Mary will succumb to young Carson's seduction, Esther reappears to warn Mary. She has now become the prostitute that John Barton prophesied she would be when he told George Wilson of his last words to Esther: "Says I, 'Esther, I see what you'll end at with your artificials, and your fly-away veils, and stopping out when honest women are in their beds; you'll be a street-walker, Esther, and then, don't you go to think I'll have you darken my door, though my wife is your sister.'"[52]

Mary's concern with dress—her longing to impress Margaret with her "pretty new blue merino, made tight to her throat, her little linen collar and linen cuffs"—and her flirtation with Harry Carson have already identified her with Esther and her "artificials, and . . . fly-away veils." However, Mary's blue and white dress also iconographically suggests the Virgin. It is significant, then, that the first vision Mary has of Esther identifies her with Mary's dead mother:

> So, without fear, without hesitation, she rose and unbarred the door. There, against the moonlight, stood a form, so closely resembling her dead mother, that Mary never doubted the identity, but exclaiming (as if she were a terrified child, secure of safety when near the protecting care of its parent)—
>
> 'Oh! mother! mother! You are come at last!'
>
> She threw herself, or rather fell into the trembling arms, of her long lost, unrecognized Aunt Esther.[53]

The identification of Esther with Mary's mother, who is also a Mary—and who also served as mother figure to Esther—creates a web of identification between daughter, mother, and fallen woman. All three women have biblical names with significant resonances as well of course: Mary as the perfect Mother; Esther as the queen who saved her people—but also as the successor to the fallen queen Vashti, rebel against her husband, King Ahaseurus, in his own house. The subversive result of this biblical allusiveness and blurring of identities is a questioning of the sharp distinctions that divide mother from fallen woman and fallen woman from the falling woman that Mary was before she rejected Harry Carson. Esther herself is a mother, and she notices with pain that Mary, "as she sat, bore a likeness to Esther's dead child. 'You are so like my little girl, Mary!' said Esther . . . recurring, with full heart, to the thought of the dead." In an earlier episode, Esther tells the tale of her illegitimate child, her own daughter Annie, to Jem, Mary's true love. She, unlike Mary, truly loved her seducer, and he seems to have cared for her as well, remaining with her for three years, a period that Esther describes as "three years of happiness. I suppose I ought not to have been happy, but I was." Esther's officer promises her marriage, but, as Esther tells Jem, "they all do."[54]

The errand that brings Esther to Mary—to John Barton's house—confirms this connection between the romantic and political plots of the novel.[55] Now Jem Wilson, listener to Esther's story of seduction, is being held for young Carson's murder. The murder was, however, committed not because of Jem's jealousy of Harry Carson, as is thought by the community, but because of class hatred. Harry has caricatured the starving workingmen as they meet with the masters, and the men afterwards draw lots to decide who will kill him. The murder, committed not by Mary's lover but by her father, John Barton, "belongs" to the political, not romantic, plot of the novel. In fact, however, the two plots are intertwined, inextricable. The class hatred that turns masters and men against one another is connected to the warped class and gender values that make Harry Carson feel that he can buy Mary's love, "feeling that at any price he must have her, only that he would obtain her as cheaply as he could."[56] Both exploitations are manifestations of

the corrupt values of the patriarchy, the need for spiritual
cleansing of the father's house.

It is significant that Esther, a keen sufferer in the house of
Victorian patriarchy—recently imprisoned for a month for
"disorderly vagrancy" after John Barton curses her and hurls her
away from him on the street—has detected evidence that the police have missed: a piece of paper on which she recognizes Jem
Wilson's handwriting. Her discovery constitutes the first step
towards releasing Mary's true love Jem from the patriarchal
house (here the courtroom and possibly the jail). The paper, as
Mary recognizes, is part of a valentine that she suspects Jem has
given her; at her father's request, she has copied upon it Samuel
Bamford's sad poem of working-class travail, "God help the
poor."[57] Ironically, John Barton has used Jem's valentine as
wadding for the gun he uses to kill Harry Carson. As Michael
Wheeler has explained, the police who pursue Jem follow the
"line of reasoning symbolically represented by the valentine
greeting" while "the motive of the actual murderer is symbolically represented in the Bamford poem written on the 'blank
half-sheet.'"[58]

The father's house must be transformed from the Old Testament place of Judgment that it has been to the New Testament
place of forgiveness. In the courtroom scene, when Mary testifies
for her beloved Jem Wilson, she is described as "more like the
well-known engraving from Guido's picture of 'Beatrice Cenci'
than anything else he could give me an idea of." Since Beatrice
released herself from the tortures of a tyrannical father by having
him killed, Mary's rebellion against the patriarchy represented
by a vengeful Mr. Carson might be inferred here. Will Wilson's
irreverence for the court's authority ("Will somebody with a wig
on please to ask him how much he can say for me?")[59] issues in
his evidence overturning the case against Jem. After the trial, Mr.
Carson encounters a little girl who forgives her tormentor; she
echoes Christ's words when she tells Carson that the boy "did
not know what he was doing."[60] Carson goes home to read the
Gospel and forgives his son's murderer, holding John Barton in
an embrace that recalls the Pietà.[61]

Part of John Barton's tragedy has been the hardening of his
heart in judgment of an entire class of people because of his great

suffering and loss, especially the death of his only son for lack of nourishing food when the child was ill. John Barton has always been a gentle if stern man, a loving, self-sacrificing person who identified with his mother, following her example as a child in stinting himself of food to provide for the younger children. As Patsy Stoneman points out, Barton as well as George Wilson (who supports his injured bride Jane "as tender as a mother"[62] during their wedding ceremony), Job Legh, and the other workingmen in the novel are feminized; they "performed from necessity the roles of child-rearing, sick-nursing, and housekeeping."[63] During the novel, John Barton moves further and further from his "feminized" self until he kills Harry Carson; the final scene of Barton's death, when Carson enacts the role of mother, portrays Barton—now symbolized as Christ/Child[64]—as the instrument through which Carson has come to realize the power of another ethic of love and forgiveness.[65] When we last hear of Carson in the novel, he has changed the harsh beliefs that led him to run his mill for profit only, whatever the human cost:

> ... the wish which lay nearest to his heart was that none might suffer from the cause from which he had suffered; that a perfect understanding, and complete confidence and love, might exist between masters and men; that the truth might be recognized that the interests of one were the interests of all; that hence it was most desirable to have educated workers, capable of judging, not mere machines of ignorant men; and to have them bound to their employers by the ties of respect and affection, not by mere money bargains alone; in short, to acknowledge the Spirit of Christ as the regulating law between both parties.

The Christian ethic of loving forgiveness is embodied by the father John Barton too, who before his poignant death must forgive Esther, his surrogate daughter. Like the mother Anne Leigh in "Lizzie Leigh," he searches for the fallen "daughter" on the streets, where she has been cast from the father's house. In particular, he repents his violence toward Esther when she first tries to warn him about Mary and Harry Carson, and he hurls the importunate woman against a lamp-post in his rage. The novel is concerned not only with the reconciliation of the working man John Barton with the master Carson, but also with the return of the prodigal son/fallen woman figure, Esther, and her reconciliation with her symbolic father, John Barton, in that father's final house, the grave: the murderer and the dead fallen woman are buried together at the novel's close:

> 'Has it been a dream then?' asked she wildly. Then with a habit, which came like instinct even in that awful dying hour, her hand sought for a locket which hung concealed in her bosom, and, finding that, she knew all was true which had befallen her, since last she lay an innocent girl on that bed.
>
> She fell back, and spoke word never more. She held the locket containing her child's hair still in her hand, and once or twice she kissed it with a long soft kiss. She cried feebly and sadly as long as she had any strength to cry, and then she died.
>
> They laid her in one grave with John Barton. And there they lie without name, or initial, or date. Only this verse is inscribed upon the stone which covers the remains of these two wanderers:
>
> Psalm ciii. v. 9.—'For He will not always chide, neither will He keep his anger for ever.'[66]

Esther is, significantly, depicted primarily as a mother in this scene, holding "the locket containing her child's hair"; her role as daughter, too, is recalled, when "last she lay an innocent girl on that bed." These identities as mother and daughter again suggest both Mary Bartons, mother and daughter, unfallen women, and serve as a kind of symbolic purification, in the sense that the identification of the fallen Lizzie Leigh with the Victorian angel Susan and the perfect mother Anne signifies purification. The "two wanderers," murderer and fallen woman—unnamed, ungendered, one Being in Christ—share a final home in the biblical promise of forgiveness that is inscribed on their tombstone in lieu of their names.

Yet finally, the house of English patriarchal culture is escaped entirely when Jem and Mary emigrate to Canada after he loses his job as engineer at Duncombe's foundry—despite his patented inventions—in the aftermath of the trial. They have a baby boy, symbolically named Johnnie after Mary's father. Will

Wilson and Margaret Legh (who has regained her sight), accompanied by old Job Legh, are on the eve of emigrating to join them. All the symbolism of the ending points to a New World order, a "world elsewhere"[67] is envisioned. The last words of the novel, "Dear Job Legh, " spoken by Mary, invoke the patience and faith not only of the biblical Job but also of this kind, learned workingman, whose tale of raising his granddaughter Margaret—child of his beloved daughter of the same name—is a compelling story within *Mary Barton*.

Job is the new, feminized father—but not on English soil, which is not yet ready for this new vision of working-class heroism embodied by John Barton, Jem, Will, and Job, in their different ways. Jem's traditional male heroism has been proven in the raging mill fire, in which he saved his father and another worker in a dramatic rescue; at the end of the novel, Jem is playing peek-a-boo with Johnnie. Will is a bold spirit, an adventurous sailor who now will begin a family with the quiet, plain Margaret Legh, whose beautiful singing voice has awakened some middle-class audiences to working-class sorrows. And Job will continue his work as "wizard" naturalist, "trying to pick up a few Canadian insects," his expertise largely unappreciated by any except his family and friends—and Gaskell herself: "Such are the tastes and pursuits of some of the thoughtful, little understood, working men of Manchester." When Mary needs strength before she leaves on her desperate errand to seek Will Wilson so that he can provide an alibi for Jem, Job "bent down and blessed her, as if she had been a child of his own. To Mary the old man's blessing came like words of power." Job's model of male nurturance is echoed not only in John Barton's and George Wilson's nursing of the dying Davenport in the typhoid-ridden cellar, but even in minor characters in the novel: while Mary is searching for Will, an old boatman cares for her: "Once she opened her eyes heavily, and dimly saw the old, grey, rough boatman (who had stood out the most obstinately for the full fare) covering her with his thick pea-jacket. He had taken it off on purpose, and was doing it tenderly in his way. . . ."[68]

Ultimately however, the novel rejects even as it meliorates English industrial society. While Carson works to better relations between masters and men, the hero and heroine of the novel go

back in time to an agrarian world by going out to Canada.
Gaskell has constructed the country (Nature) throughout the
novel as not only feminine but specifically maternal. Old Alice
Wilson, aunt and surrogate mother to Will, is from the country;
she uses the knowledge of herbs she learned there in her girlhood to heal working people in the city. Long ago, in her girlhood, Alice left her mother to go to the city; as she gets old,
"Alice knew that before long she should go to that mother." The
scene of her death is figured as a return to her mother and sister
and to the Nature she loved as a girl: "Alice lay . . . totally absorbed in recollections of the days of her girlhood. . . . Still she
talked of green fields, and still she spoke to the long-dead
mother and sister. . . ."[69]

There is, finally, a subversive message running counter to
the conciliatory official narration of this "novel with a purpose"
that suggests that Mary and Jem and their kind cannot wait for a
transformed English society. The New World of Canada—a land
in which a poor needlewoman like Margaret Legh will use her
rekindled sight—might be perceived in Romantic terms as Co-
leridge's apocalyptic "new earth and new heaven," a vision of
the transfigured world. And in the New World, there is no suggestion that Mary Barton the wife and mother, once a seamstress,
will ever stitch or starve again.

Ruth more clearly than *Mary Barton* focuses on the story of
a Victorian fallen woman, one of Engels' country girls who becomes a seamstress in the city.[70] Gaskell's account—founded on
the real experiences of a young girl named Pasley whom Gaskell
and Dickens helped to emigrate[71]—is a significant response to
her culture's stereotypes of fallen women as somehow different
from other women, as flawed characters who are inherently
weak or bad.[72] As Rosemarie Bodenheimer states: "Ruth's story
is designed to make her suffer for her past, yet the act of expo-
sure challenges conventional images of the fallen woman as a
separate and tainted being who carries the threat of sin."[73]
Ruth's path back to the innocence of her childhood Eden and
"upward" to Heaven and her virtual transformation into a secular saint embody the contradictions in Gaskell's vindication of
the fallen woman: her fall is placed in the context of Ruth's personal history, but Ruth must still spend the rest of her life expiat-

ing her sin until she is at last purified. Ruth's need to atone is, seemingly, in tension with her innocence; she is always a pure woman, like her fictional sister Tess.

Ruth Hilton's fall in fact issues from a lack of loving care after her parents die, from her natural longing for love and intimacy. Ruth spends her childhood with affectionate parents on their farm, Milham Grange; she recurs to this time in memory as perfect and secure, a pastoral idyll.[74] Ruth has been loved by her mother in particular, but she, "a delicate and fine lady," a poor curate's daughter, is not physically strong; presumably after Ruth's birth Mrs. Hilton "fell into a delicate state of health." When Ruth is twelve, just on the eve of womanhood and before she has been told about the facts of life, her mother dies suddenly: "They found her lying on her accustomed sofa."[75] This mother of "strong sense and lively faculty of hope," despite her physical weakness, has in fact been the moral strength of the family, which has been beset by "calamities" and "worldly misfortunes" from which Ruth has apparently been protected. Yet there is surely an underlying suggestion in the text—the illness following birth, the mother's death as Ruth enters puberty, the elided discussion of sexual relations—that the mother rejects female sexuality. In *Mary Barton*, the narrator tells us that Mary was "unconscious of the fact, that she was far superior in sense and spirit to the mother she mourned."[76] Ruth too will idolize in memory a mother who ultimately is not her equal even in maternal skills, a mother who is not in truth sufficiently immersed in the world of experience truly to warn the daughter about the world's evils. In *Ruth*, although Gaskell finds it difficult overtly to criticize the mother, it is clear that Mrs. Hilton's moral superiority is in truth undermined by her retreat to her "accustomed sofa." Ruth's painful experience will serve her much better in protecting her own child Leonard from Bellingham's evil influence when, much later on the sands of Abermouth, she denies her corrupt former lover any authority over their son.

The perfect security Ruth has felt throughout childhood dissolves when Mrs. Hilton dies. The father neglects his duty to his daughter, who is compelled to coax him to take some interest in life, even to walk with her. Although Mr. Hilton is "still a hale-looking elderly man, and his bodily health appeared as

good as ever," he abdicates all responsibilities to his household
and seems through sheer inertia to decline into death: "He sat for
hours in his easy chair, looking into the fire, not moving, nor
speaking unless it was absolutely necessary to answer repeated
questions." The power of the father, as embodied by Mr. Hilton,
seems to be merely static image, which is strangely evoked in
Ruth's memory when, in the company of Bellingham, her gentleman seducer, she sees a spiderweb across the front entrance of
the house at Milham Grange: "The sight of this conveyed a sense
of desolation to Ruth's heart; she thought it was possible the
state entrance had never been used since her father's dead body
had been borne forth, and without speaking a word, she turned
abruptly away, and went round the house to another door."
When Ruth's father dies, Ruth finds his house invaded: "The
creditors were the chief people who appeared to take any interest in the affairs; and it seemed strange to Ruth to see people,
whom she scarcely knew, examining and touching all that she
had been accustomed to consider as precious and sacred." Her
father has appointed "the person of most consequence amongst
those whom he did know" as Ruth's guardian; rather than a
kind, interested paternal figure, this "sensitive, hard-headed
man of the world" apprentices fifteen-year-old Ruth to the harsh
dressmaker Mrs. Mason.[77]

In contrast, Ruth's allegiance to the memory of her mother
is signified by her name, the name of the faithful biblical daugh-
ter-in-law to Naomi. The sacred Word is identified with Ruth's
mother as well; when the cold and hungry Ruth is left alone on
Sundays at the dressmaker's establishment, she tries to read her
Bible, "and to think the old holy thoughts which had been her
childish meditations at her mother's knee." All her life, Ruth will
long to recreate this mother-daughter relation. When Ruth revis-
its the Grange with Bellingham, Gaskell evokes the strength of
this filial bond through Ruth's fervent emotions: "There, the
bleak look of what had once been full of peace and mother's
love, struck cold on her heart. She uttered a cry, and threw herself down on the sofa, hiding her face in her hands, while her
frame quivered with her repressed sobs." Symbolically, in contrast to the image of the spiderweb associated with the father's
dead body and the father's house, the mother's holy image is as-

sociated with flowers still blooming long after Ruth's departure from the farm; on her return, "she ran, with her eyes streaming with tears, round the garden, tearing off in a passion of love whole boughs of favourite China and damask roses, late flowering against the casement-window of what had been her mother's room."[78]

Mrs. Mason is an exploiter rather than a maternal surrogate. She casts Ruth out from her house with excoriating words when she finds the young dressmaker walking with Bellingham: "Don't attempt to show your face at my house again after this conduct." As the narrator comments, "It would have been a better and more Christian thing, if she had kept up the character of her girls by tender vigilance and maternal care." Amid the harsh conditions of unmitigated toil and little sleep at the millinery establishment, Ruth does temporarily find a mother figure in the kind, ailing seamstress Jenny Wood, to whom Ruth tells her dreams of her dead mother. However, soon after Ruth meets Bellingham, the consumptive Jenny, with her "warning voice and gentle wisdom," is taken away by her own mother who has come to nurse her. The mother's presence is figured as nearly sacred to the other young milliners: "Then a pale, gentle-looking woman was seen moving softly about; and it was whispered that this was the mother come to nurse her child. Everybody liked her, she was so sweet-looking, and gave so little trouble, and seemed so patient, and so thankful for any inquiries about her daughter. . . ."[79]

When Jenny leaves her, Ruth is without even spiritual kin. She is ripe for the entreaties of Bellingham, who has been struck with her natural, queenly beauty at the ball where she is sent to mend dresses for the ladies. Three failed fathers are evoked in this scene: Ruth is, symbolically, still in her old black mourning for her father when she encounters this new father-lover figure, who will eventually seduce and abandon her; she wears the old dress because her surrogate father, the unpaternal guardian her father chose for her, has refused Ruth money even to buy a shawl for the cold weather, so she dares not write for a new dress. At the ball, the charming Bellingham offers her a white camellia, which suggests not only her naturalness in contrast to Bellingham's "artificial" dance partner, but also symbolizes her purity. She dreams that "he presented flower after flower to her in that baseless morning dream."[80] Ruth's dreams have been discussed by Patsy Stoneman, who reads them as evidences of the repressed subtext of Ruth's sexual desire: "The disruptive factor is female sexuality, which cannot be acknowledged in the ideological surface of the novel, but is repressed, emerging as a subtext of imagery and dreams."[81] The flowers are also connectives to the maternalized pastoral world that Ruth identifies with her country childhood, a world in which she loved Nature so much, as she tells Jenny, that "I have many a time run up the lane all the way to the mill, just to see the icicles hang on the great wheel, and when I was once out, I could hardly find it in my heart to come in, even to mother, sitting by the fire;—even to mother."[82]

Ruth's longing for kindred and for her country past is assuaged by Bellingham, who takes her on long country walks and asks her to "tell me everything, Ruth, as you would to a brother": "almost insensibly Jenny's place in Ruth's heart was filled up; there was someone who listened with tender interest to all her little revelations; who questioned her about her early days of happiness . . ." He is also figured as a kind of hero of romance as well as a preserver of family, when he saves little Tom from drowning, an act that the falling Ruth, "dizzy and sick with emotion," perceives as "the most heroic deed of daring": ". . . a horse galloping through the water in which she was standing. Passed her like lightning—down in the stream, swimming along with the current—a stooping rider—an outstretched, grasping arm—a little life redeemed, and a child saved to those who loved it!" To the desperately lonely Ruth with her "loving disposition," Bellingham manages to appear glamorous, courtly, and brotherly simultaneously.[83]

Bellingham in his turn is attracted to Ruth because of her innocent beauty, finding "something bewitching in the union of the grace and loveliness of womanhood with naiveté, simplicity, and innocence of an intelligent child." He senses something natural, even primitive in her nature, and feels that "it would be an exquisite delight to attract and tame her wildness, just as he had often allured and tamed the timid fawns in his mother's park." While Bellingham responds more to the innocence that his experience eroticizes, and to the erotics of mastery in taming

Ruth's natural wildness, Ruth herself is a Romantic figure, "innocent and snow pure," who is at one with Nature. In her walks with Bellingham before her fall, she "almost forgot the presence of Bellingham—in her delight at the new tender beauty of an early spring day in February." Ruth expresses the ache for her maternalized childhood in a Romantic longing for Nature in the city. The first time that we see Ruth, she is compared to an imprisoned bird. She is allowed a brief respite from sewing a ball dress; while the other seamstresses stretch or eat or sleep, Ruth "sprang to the large old window, and pressed against it as a bird presses and gazed into the quiet moonlight night. . . . Ruth's eyes filled with tears, and she stood quite still, dreaming of the days that were gone." It is the Nature-named Jenny Wood, significantly, who touches her with motherly care at this point and encourages her to eat. She is the only nurturing figure Ruth will find in this place of constant, exhausting work. When Bellingham at last takes her out of the city to the country home of her childhood, Ruth "wound in and out in natural, graceful, wavy lines between the luxuriant and overgrown shrubs, which were fragrant with a leafy smell of spring growth; she went on, careless of watching eyes, indeed unconscious, for the time, of their existence."[84]

It is this very country innocence that prevents Ruth from understanding the city language of seduction that Bellingham speaks after Mrs. Mason condemns her.[85] While the Manchester-bred, working-class Mary Barton does finally understand the "plain English" of Harry Carson's offers of love : "'I thought we could be happy enough without marriage.' (Deep sank those words into Mary's heart.),"[86] Ruth does not comprehend Bellingham's insistence on succouring her in her distress. She "little imagined the infinite consequences" of acquiescing to Bellingham's proposal: "The thought of being with him was all and everything." Yet Ruth almost abandons her seducer when she recalls her country home as a possible refuge. Gaskell evokes the remembrance of Milham Grange, the beloved mother, and the faithful old servant Thomas—who has earlier in the day pronounced a biblical warning in which he identifies Bellingham as the devil—one final time before Ruth's fall. As Ruth waits for Bellingham at the inn, she is reminded of her old home by the fragrance of the sweetbriar, and she "had instantly before her eyes the little garden beneath the window of her mother's room, and the old man leaning on his stick . . ."[87] Significantly, another aroma, the masculine scent of the innkeeper's tobacco, recalls Ruth to her present state and her lack of money to pay for her cup of tea, and she waits passively for Bellingham to return.

Despite her fall, Ruth's relation to nature seems un-changed, as a number of critics have noted.[88] A year after Bellingham sweeps Ruth away to London, she figures as a prelapsarian Eve or as Prosperpine before her abduction and "fall" in this beautiful scene in the Wales woods; Bellingham, a Satan or Hades figure, decks her white dress with white water-lilies symbolizing her innocent sexuality:

She knew that she was beautiful; but that seemed abstract, and removed from herself. Her existence was in feeling, and thinking, and loving.

> Down in that green hollow they were quite in harmony. Her beauty was all that Mr. Bellingham cared for, and it was supreme. It was all he recognised of her, and he was proud of it. She stood in her white dress against the trees which grew around; her face was flushed into a brilliancy of colour which resembled that of a rose in June; the great heavy white flowers drooped on either side of her beauti-ful head, and if her brown hair was a little disordered, the very disorder only seemed to add a grace. She pleased him more by looking so lovely than by all her tender endeav-ours to fall in with his varying humour.[89]

Ruth's psychological fall has actually occured just before this scene, with the recognition of her social role as fallen woman. Ruth is hit and scolded by a little boy, who tells his nurse that "she's not a lady! . . . She's a bad naughty girl—mamma said so, she did; and she shan't kiss our baby." Gaskell creates a scene which in microcosm gives Ruth "the sense she was just beginning to entertain of the estimation in which she was henceforward to be held."[90] The male child hurts and then condemns her, and she is not allowed contact with the innocent baby, a girl. The return to the edenic woods is only a brief respite from Ruth's new self-consciousness. When Bellingham becomes ill, the complete selfishness he has demonstrated all along is encouraged by his mother, who subscribes to patriarchal society's attitudes towards seduction: i.e., that the woman is guilty of "entrapping into vice" and should be sent to a penitentiary. [91]

Gaskell reinstates the maternal narrative after Bellingham abandons Ruth, and she is rescued from despairing suicide by the Reverend Thurstan Benson, a crippled Dissenting minister. Benson's deformity signifies him as outside of culturally-defined roles of masculine power and sexuality and aligns him with other marginalized figures in the text: women—even fallen women—and the poor. Like the hunchbacked Philip Wakem in Eliot's *The Mill on the Floss*, Benson is explicitly associated with the feminine and the maternal. When Benson tries to give the abandoned Ruth comfort—"'Oh, my God! for Christ's sake, pity her!'—his pitiful look, or his words, reminded her of the childish days when she knelt at her mother's knee." Significantly, he later invokes the name of the mother in order to prevent Ruth from committing suicide: "In your mother's name, whether she be dead or alive, I command you to stay here until I am able to speak to you."[92] He also solicits the maternal instincts of Ruth herself, when he literally falls on the rocky common as he tries to overtake her, and she returns to help him. His literal fall, too, identifies him with the fallen Ruth, and signals Gaskell's theme that all mankind is fallen and in need of succor. Since he is figured as Christ-like in his self-sacrifice, Benson's fall seems a "fortunate fall," in that it brings about Ruth's redemption.

From the perspective of another kind of narrative, the fairy tale, Benson can be seen as an alternative Prince Charming in a story in which the conventional prince abandons the damsel in distress rather than marrying her and making her happy ever after. Benson is identified by Bellingham as no gentleman, but "Riquet-with-the-Tuft," the Perrault dwarf, because of his hunchback. Perrault's dwarf triumphs in the fairytale despite his ugliness; Shelston tells us in the notes to *Ruth* that "he has the power of endowing the woman he loves with wit and intelligence. He falls in love with a beautiful but unintelligent woman who marries him in spite of his ugliness: she becomes intelligent, he handsome." Following the fairy tale narrative, Ruth intuitively recognizes Benson's spiritual beauty and nobility, expressed in his face, which Ruth insists is "very singular; quite beautiful!"[93] In his turn, Benson instructs Ruth, drawing out her thoughtful intelligence.

In Ruth's new life in the feminized Benson household, Benson's sister Faith gives her the name of Mrs. Denbigh, Faith's own mother's name. Gaskell thus identifies this "gentle mother, from whom Thurstan Benson derived so much of his character" with the fallen woman as well. Faith also bestows her grandmother's wedding-ring on Ruth, a further connection with the maternal. Ruth associates the Benson household with her own "gentle, blessed mother, who had made her childhood's home holy ground." The Benson household is explicitly juxtaposed to that of the Bradshaws, a patriarchal home in which only the letter of the law is observed and all protest against the father's authority is condemned. The mother in this household is reduced to a "subdued, scared-looking little lady" who nevertheless rises up in rebellion at last to forgive and protect her son Richard from the father's harshness.[94] The "respectable" Richard forges legal documents—a signally masculine crime of business and the law—to pay off debts incurred through speculation, a wildness expressing resistance to the rigid authoritarian rule of his father. Mr. Bradshaw, a tradesman and pillar of Benson's church, first admires Ruth's seeming feminine docility and meekness, employing her as governess to his girls. Later, when he discovers Ruth's past, Bradshaw violently excoriates her in the presence of his tempestuous eldest daughter Jemima.

In *The Gypsy-Bachelor of Manchester*, Felicia Bonaparte analyzes Jemima as Ruth's "daemonic double."[95] Certainly, we might consider the rebellious Jemima—who witnesses for Ruth's purity and resists her own father's unjust authority—as an unconventional exemplar for Victorian womanhood. The identification of the sexually pure daughter Jemima with the fallen woman Ruth is a doubling that I have discussed in "Lizzie Leigh" and *Mary Barton* as well. Ruth, although she is identified with Jemima's purity, is never permitted through her own body to have the passionate sexual life of a real woman once she has been awakened to her sin, unlike Hardy's later Tess. Her alterego, Jemima, is eventually allowed to marry the man she loves, her father's business partner Mr. Farquhar, a man who is for a time attracted to Ruth's meekness. Ruth's life after her fall will

be devoid of sexual passion, as is Lizzie Leigh's (once she is rescued from prostitution), or Emily's in *David Copperfield* or the
fallen Mrs. Hilyard's in Oliphant's *Salem Chapel.* Jemima "lives
out" Ruth's role as wife and mother after Ruth's death, providing maternal protection to Ruth's son Leonard. This pattern recalls yet significantly alters how the story "Lizzie Leigh" figures
the fallen woman in relation to motherhood. In that text, Susan's
surrogate mothering of the first Nanny, Lizzie's illegitimate
child, is like Jemima's nurturing of the illegitimate Leonard;
Susan's biological mothering of the second, legitimate Nanny is
allowed to her—as to Jemima—because they are not fallen, and
their bodies do not stand in need of purification. And yet, the
observation that Jemima is "mother" to Leonard recognizes the
liminal space between legitimacy and illegitimacy, as Lizzie's
mothering of the second Nanny, Susan's daughter, does as well.

As Jemima takes on the role of Mother, Ruth is allowed at
last to once again be the Faithful Daughter in her deathbed
scene. Critics tend to disagree about the significance of Ruth's
mental return to girlhood in this scene. Coral Lansbury argues
that "the little seamstress, betrayed and abandoned by her lover,
is destined to become a heroine in the eyes of society, mourned
after her death like a saint. The compassionate irony of the work
is that Ruth is no brighter at the end of the work than at the beginning—the child who once went astray dies singing like a
child."[96] Felicia Bonaparte contends that "for Ruth and Gaskell,
reality lies in the passionate life. And this is the life Ruth dies to
enter . . . in her mind she has returned to her daemonic self in
Wales."[97] It seems to me that Gaskell's intent in Ruth's deathbed
scene is misinterpreted. Ruth's final purification is effected in
this scene, in which she returns to the mother for whom she has
ached all her life: "Her open, unconscious eyes . . . all they told
was of a sweet, childlike insanity within. . . . They had never
heard her sing; indeed the simple art which her mother had
taught her, had died, with her early joyousness, at that dear
mother's death."[98] The only other time that Ruth sings is during
an apparent domestic idyll with the Bensons, when she "kept up
a low brooding song, such as she remembered her mother
singing long ago."[99] In this scene Ruth reinforces her role and
duty as mother after refusing Mr. Bellingham's offer of marriage

because of her responsibility for Leonard's spiritual welfare. What *is* contradictory and disturbing is the erasure of the maternal narrative and the entire history of Ruth's fallenness and redemption; Gaskell's final portrayal is of a "purified" daughter when Ruth has *always* been depicted as pure[100]—and when she has, moreover, expiated her sin through tremendous suffering and self-sacrifice: Ruth "never looked at anyone with the slightest glimpse of memory or intelligence in her face; no, not even at Leonard."[101] There is an intended purification of Ruth's sin which, finally, entails an erasure of her sexual history, of the time after girlhood with the mother.

Surely Gaskell intends that God be interpreted as Mother. As Felicia Bonaparte points out, "This image of God as a tender mother is unusual in Christianity, but it is very common in Gaskell."[102] There is a sense too that Ruth's return to the mother is the closure of the Romantic circle, the return to Eden, the time before her Fall. The loss the reader must feel despite these intentions is in the refutation of all social roles—friend, surrogate daughter, mother, nurse—through which Ruth has come to her heroic death. Gaskell's art can be understood more readily perhaps if one comprehends that Jemima takes on these social roles, becomes Mother to Leonard, with the intimation that her little Rosa will perhaps marry Leonard someday and complete the identification of Jemima with Ruth, of pure daughter and fallen woman. Jemima, named for one of the three inheriting daughters of Job—as Faith Benson points out to Ruth[103]—inherits Ruth's future history as it might be in a transformed, feminized culture of tolerance.

In the important scene in which Jemima defends Ruth, she aligns herself with this fallen woman, attesting to her purity: "Father, I will speak. I will not keep silence. I will bear witness to Ruth." Jemima's brave words resonate in a text in which Bellingham has said to the falling seamstress: "You make me too happy by your silence, Ruth." The daughter speaks in the father's house in defense of the fallen woman, but Ruth is still cast out: "He absolutely took her by the shoulders and turned her by force out of the room . . . He held the street door open wide; and said, between his teeth, 'If ever you, or your bastard, darken this door again, I will have you both turned out by the police.'" Only at the story's close does Bradshaw reverse his judgment, stung to remorse by his own son's crime and subsequent near-fatal accident, by the report of Ruth's saintliness during the cholera epidemic and resultant death from nursing Bellingham, and by Benson's eulogy for Ruth. In this sermon, to which Bradshaw and the entire community of the sacred-named Eccleston listen, Benson discards the eulogy he has written and simply reads from Revelations, asserting Ruth's place by the throne of God, as one of those who have "'washed their robes, and made them white in the blood of the lamb.'" Human words will not suffice to commemorate Ruth's life and death; only the Word of God, the promise of the Gospels, is equal to her Christ-like self-sacrifice. Indeed, after Ruth's heroic nursing during the epidemic, the community virtually canonizes the fallen woman. As one of the town's poor says of Ruth in Leonard's hearing, "She will be in the light of God's countenance when you and I will be standing afar off."[104] In her progress toward perfect redemption, Ruth becomes not only saint but savior figure to her community. The fallen woman is ultimately not the destroyer of the father's house, as she is figured by the unconverted Mr. Bradshaws of Victorian society, but the savior of her culture.

To effect this reconstruction of patriarchal Victorian culture, Gaskell insists on a reinterpretation of the Bible itself, an interpretation that emphasizes the Gospel message of forgiveness for all, including fallen women and illegitimate children. Coral Lansbury states that "Gaskell . . . concealed her subversive opinions of society in a traditional mode made inoffensive by constant biblical reference."[105] Gaskell's many biblical allusions in *Ruth* serve to identify Ruth with her faithful biblical namesake, as well as with Mary Magdalene, Saul's concubine Rizpah (both magdalen and heroic mother), the Prodigal Son, the Madonna, and ultimately, as Jenn Morey asserts, "the narrative finally implies a connection even between Ruth and Jesus Christ."[106] Gaskell's feminist reinscription of the Bible questions patriarchal interpretation, and thus the authority of Victorian patriarchy.

In the final scene of the novel, the former arbiter of this judgmental reading of Scripture, Mr. Bradshaw, now chastened and weeping, carries the mourning Leonard across the threshold of Thurston Benson's home, that other, feminized household: "The first time, for years, that he had entered Mr. Benson's house, he came leading and comforting her son—and, for a moment, he could not speak to his old friend, for the sympathy which choked up his voice, and filled his eyes with tears." The tears that both Bradshaw and Leonard cry for Ruth identify this father with the illegitimate son and his fallen mother.[107] There is an intentional echo again in Gaskell's fiction of the Pietà, yet in this instance the Son is alive, although he has "a wild look of agony."[108] Bradshaw, like Carson in *Mary Barton*, is at last maternalized, an icon of the Mother with her Child. The home which he enters is the imagined ideal house of Victorian culture, in which both fathers and mothers nurture—and forgive. It is a house in which a starving needlewoman—and even a wretched fallen woman—might find succor.

NOTES

1.   Helena Michie, *The Flesh Made Word: Female Figures and Women's Bodies* (Oxford: Oxford University Press, 1987), 56.

2.   Elizabeth Helsinger, Robin Sheets, and William Veeder, *The Woman Question*, vol. 2 (Chicago: University of Chicago Press, 1986), 150.

3.   There is biographical background to Gaskell's frequent use of crippled characters as moral touchstones. The Rev. Thurstan Benson in *Ruth* and Nest Gwynn in "The Well of Pen Morfa" are examples of this figuration. After her mother's death when she was thirteen months old, Gaskell was then adopted by her maternal cousin Mary Anne Lumb (after whom Gaskell named her eldest daughter), who was crippled when, as an infant, she jumped out of her nurse's arms "on seeing her mother approach the house" (Winifred Gérin, *Elizabeth Gaskell* (Oxford: Oxford University Press, 1980), 8.

4. Gertrude Himmelfarb, *The Idea of Poverty: England in the Early Industrial Age* (New York: Knopf, 1984), 353.

5. Indeed, even before this, the terrible conditions of London's tailors and needlewomen had instigated Lord Ashley to form a Milliners' and Dressmakers' Association, which *Fraser's Magazine* spoke of approvingly in the November 1849 issue (Himmelfarb, *Idea of Poverty*, 354). Mayhew's articles put the number of needlewomen at 31,000; the horrors they exposed instigated Charles Kingsley's "immediate response" (Elizabeth A. Cripps, Introduction to Charles Kingsley, *Alton Locke: Tailor and Poet* [Oxford: Oxford University Press, 1983]), an exposé of the conditions of London tailors in his 1850 pamphlet "Cheap Clothes and Nasty." E.P. Thompson states in *The Making of the English Working Class* (New York: Vintage, 1966) that "dressmaking—a notoriously sweated trade—was largely done by needlewomen (often country or small-town immigrants) in shops contracted by large establishments" (258).

6. Friedrich Engels, *The Condition of the Working Class in England*, trans. and ed. W.O. Henderson and W.H. Chaloner (Stanford: Stanford University Press, 1968), 237–38.

7. T.J. Edelstein's important article on the Victorian seamstress, "They Sang the Song of the Shirt: The Visual Iconology of the Seamstress," *Victorian Studies* 23 No. 2 (Winter 1980): 183–211, tells us that the popularity of Thomas Hood's poem, published anonymously in the December 1843 *Punch*, influenced the depiction of the seamstress not only in later poems, fiction, and articles, but also in engravings, poems, wall paintings, articles, and cartoons.

8. Lynn Alexander, "Following the Thread: Dickens and the Seamstress," *The Victorian Newsletter*, No. 80 (Fall 1991): 7.

9. Edelstein, "They Sang the Song of the Shirt," 85.

10. Joseph Kestner suggests in *Protest and Reform: The British Social Narrative by Women, 1827–1867* (Madison: University of Wisconsin Press, 1985) that a passage from Elizabeth Stone's *The Young Milliner* might "have been the inspiration for the well-known *Punch* cartoon of 'The Haunted Lady, or 'The Ghost in the Looking-Glass'" (87).

11. Wanda Neff, *Victorian Working Women: An Historical and Literary Study of Women in British Industries and Professions, 1832–1850* (New York: AMS Press, 1966), 136.

12. Alexander, "Following the Thread," 7.

13. Margaret Oliphant, *Salem Chapel* (New York: Penguin, 1986), 432.

14. Robert Southey's letter advising Charlotte Brontë to abjure literary endeavors as unwomanly—"Literature *cannot* and *ought* not to be the business of a woman's life"—elicited this response in Brontë: "I have endeavoured not only attentively to observe all the duties a woman ought to fulfil, but to feel deeply interested in them. I don't always succeed, for sometimes when I'm teaching or sewing I would rather be reading or writing; but I try to deny myself; and my father's approbation amply rewarded me for the privation" (qtd. in Elizabeth Gaskell, *The Life of Charlotte Brontë* [New York: Penguin, 1985], 175).

15. See Sandra Gilbert and Susan Gubar, *The Madwoman in the Attic: The Woman Writer and the Nineteenth-Century Literary Imagination* (New Haven: Yale University Press, 1979), for a good discussion of the sewing metaphor, especially 520–26 and 638–42.

16. Elizabeth Gaskell, "The Three Eras of Libbie Marsh," in *Elizabeth Gaskell: Four Short Stories* (London: Pandora Press, 1983), 23, 24.

17. This line echoes that of the child David Copperfield, who mourns when he is told that his mother is dead: "I had already broken out in a desolate cry, and felt an orphan in the wide world" (Dickens, *David Copperfield* [London: Penguin, 1985], 176). Interestingly, this chapter, chapter nine, is entitled "I Have a Memorable Birthday," a title resembling the St. Valentine's birthday that marks the first stage of Libbie's spiritual recovery.

18. Gaskell, "Three Eras of Libbie Marsh," 43, 32, 26.

19. Gaskell, "Three Eras of Libbie Marsh," 28, 30.

20. J.C.J. Metford, *Dictionary of Christian Lore and Legend* (London: Thames and Hudson, 1983), 195.

21. Gaskell, "Three Eras of Libbie Marsh," 39.

22. Metford, *Dictionary of Christian Lore and Legend*, 174.

23. Gaskell, "Three Eras of Libbie Marsh," 41.

24. Gaskell, "Three Eras of Libbie Marsh," 44.

25. Eva Figes, *Sex and Subterfuge: Women Writers to 1850* (New York: Persea Press, 1982), 155.

26. Christine Krueger, *The Reader's Repentance: Women Preachers, Women Writers, and Nineteenth-Century Social Discourse* (Chicago: University of Chicago Press, 1992), 155; 164–65.

27. Gaskell, "Three Eras of Libbie Marsh," 46.

28. Gaskell, "Three Eras of Libbie Marsh," 32, 45, 47.

29. Elizabeth Gaskell, "Lizzie Leigh," in *Lizzie Leigh and Other Tales* (Freeport, NY: Books for Libraries Press, 1972), 18, 25, 19.

30. Gaskell uses the image of a scarlet cloak to identify the pure country girl Sylvia with the sailor's prostitute "Newcastle Bess" in *Sylvia's Lovers* as well. Both women weep for joy as the ship *Alcestis* approaches Monkshaven with long-departed sailors on board, including Charles Kinraid, who will be Sylvia's great passion.

31. Gaskell, "Lizzie Leigh," 28.

32. Gaskell, "Lizzie Leigh," 29, 16.

33. The scene of the mother looking for the face of the fallen daughter also recalls a scene in DeQuincey's *Confessions of an English Opium-Eater*, when DeQuincey looks in vain for the fallen Ann of Oxford Street, peering into the faces of the women on the street.

34. "Against the mouldering wall by which they stood, there was a bill, on which I could discern the words, . . . And still it was like the horror of a dream. A man yet dark and muddy . . . whispered with Mr. Bucket, who went away with him down some slippery steps—as if to look at something secret that he had to show. They came back, wiping their hands upon their coats, after turning over something wet; but thank God it was not what I feared!" (Dickens, *Bleak House*, ch. 57).

35. Gaskell, "Lizzie Leigh," 34, 35.

36. There is, for readers of *Jane Eyre*, published three years before "Lizzie Leigh" but written ten years afterwards, a resonant echo of Jane's reply to the maternal moon's warning, "Daughter, flee temptation," to which Jane answers, "Mother, I will." It is provocative that Gaskell, who was Charlotte Brontë's friend (and first biographer, in *The Life of Charlotte Brontë* [1857]) uses precisely the same response to evoke the idea of hearkening to the maternal.

37. Krueger, *Reader's Repentance*, 169.

38. Gaskell, "Lizzie Leigh," 26.

39. Gaskell, "Lizzie Leigh," 10, 13.

40. In Margaret Homans's fine reading of this story in *Bearing the Word: Language and Female Experience in Nineteenth-Century Women's Writing* (Chicago and London: University of Chicago Press, 1986), she explains that Lizzie's and Nanny's falls "can be described in exactly the same words: the daughter falls because the love between mother and daughter is in conflict with, and is finally sacrificed to, the father's wishes. . . . Thus, like her own mother, Nanny falls into the gap created by the conflict between the mother's love for her daughter and her obli-

gations to the father's authority" (230). Felicia Bonaparte, in *The Gypsy-Bachelor of Manchester: The Life of Mrs. Gaskell's Demon* (Charlottesville: University Press of Virginia, 1992), interprets Nanny's fall somewhat differently: "Gaskell in her shorter fiction has already used literal falls in this metaphoric way. As soon as Lizzie Leigh is redeemed, her daughter, for instance, assuming her state, instantly tumbles down the stairs. . . . The fallen is the daemonic state, and being rejected in one guise, it must somehow be achieved in another"(125). I would argue that Nanny's death precipitates Lizzie's redemption.

    41. Gaskell, "Lizzie Leigh," 37, 38, 39, 16.

    42. Gaskell, "Lizzie Leigh," 25, 48.

    43. Homans, *Bearing the Word*, 231.

    44. Gaskell, "Lizzie Leigh," 49, 48.

    45. Elizabeth Gaskell, *Mary Barton*, ed. Stephen Gill (New York: Penguin, 1988), 43.

    46. Gaskell, *Mary Barton*, 111, 112, 324.

    47. Homans cites Gaskell's sonnet, "On Visiting the grave of my stillborn little girl," and J.L. Uhland's poem that serves as epigraph to the novel as evidences of Gaskell's remembrance of her stillborn daughter as well as that of her son William's death from scarlet fever as the origin of her writing: "Thus, behind the myth of the writer as mother grieving over her son and directed by her husband's wisdom, who writes novels and publishes them immediately, lies hidden another writer who grieves alone over a daughter and writes a poem and a story she is reticent to publish" ["Lizzie Leigh"] (*Bearing the Word*, 223–24). Susan Morgan, on the other hand, observes that "in the example of Gaskell's son, the psychological explanation is implicitly sexist, as if Gaskell's novels were substitute babies, her aesthetic commitment a sort of sidetracked mothering instinct. While she may have begun to write to distract her from her grief at her son's death, her novels were not her children. She had four daughters who satisfactorily filled that role" (*Sisters in Time: Imagining Gender in Nineteenth-Century British Fiction* [New York: Oxford University Press, 1989], *n.* 243).

    48. Gaskell, *Mary Barton*, 327.

    49. In *The Industrial Reformation of English Fiction: Social Discourse and Narrative Form 1832–1867* (Chicago: University of Chicago Press, 1985), Catherine Gallagher points to "the romances which Miss Simmonds' young ladies were in the habit of recommending to each other" (*Mary Barton*, 121) as well as Esther's influence in encouraging Mary's aspirations to be a lady. This critique of what Gallagher terms the "truly

pernicious" (68) effects of romances puts Gaskell right in the line of the Austen of, in particular, *Sense and Sensibility* and *Northanger Abbey*, as well as an unwitting inheritor of Wollstonecraft's legacy. Of course, Gaskell is expressing a criticism taken up a decade later by Eliot in "Silly Novels by Lady Novelists" (1857).

50. Gaskell, *Mary Barton*, 337.

51. Gaskell, *Mary Barton*, 85, 83, 82, 84, 85.

52. Gaskell, *Mary Barton*, 43, 58, 43.

53. Gaskell, *Mary Barton*, 67, 287.

54. Gaskell, *Mary Barton*, 297, 209.

55. Catherine Gallagher discusses the generic inconsistency of the first half of the book that results from what she analyzes as Gaskell's "ambivalence about causality." Gaskell "consequently seeks refuge from the contradictions of her tragedy in other narrative forms, primarily melodrama and domestic fiction. The resulting formal multiplicity is most apparent in the first half of the book. Only in the second half, after the tragic action is complete, does she temporarily achieve a kind of generic consistency by retreating into the domestic mentality of her heroine" (*Industrial Reformation of English Fiction*, 67).

56. Gaskell, *Mary Barton*, 180.

57. Gaskell, *Mary Barton*, 170.

58. Michael Wheeler, *The Art of Allusion in Victorian Fiction* (London: Macmillan, 1979), 50.

59. Gaskell, *Mary Barton*, 389, 438.

60. There are two other scenes in which a child has symbolic Christian significance in *Mary Barton*. In the first scene, John Barton is on his way to murder Harry Carson, and he soothes a child whose cry reminds him of his dead boy Tom. He soothes the child "with beautiful patience" and returns him to his mother, who blesses John Barton with "an eloquent Irish blessing" (251). In the second scene, Mary has gone to see Jane Wilson, Jem's mother, after Jem is arrested for Harry Carson's murder. She is "turned out of the house, which had been *his* home, where *he* was loved, and mourned for, into the busy, desolate, crowded street" (283). She feels outcast, but as she approaches her home, a hungry little Italian boy begs her for food, and calls for his "Mamma mia!" Mary gives him the last food in the house and is kissed by the child and "diverted from the thought of her own grief by the sight of his infantine gladness; and then bending down and kissing his smooth forehead, she left him . . ." (284).

61. Gaskell's brief sentences themselves recall the Bible and its solemn language:

Mr. Carson stood in the door-way. In one instant he comprehended the case.

He raised up the powerless frame; and the departing soul looked out of the eyes with gratitude. He held the dying man propped in his arms. John Barton folded his hands as if in prayer.

'Pray for us,' said Mary, sinking on her knees, and forgetting in that solemn hour all that had divided her father and Mr. Carson.

No other words could suggest themselves than some of those he had read only a few hours before.

'God be merciful to us sinners.—Forgive us our trespasses as we forgive them that trespass against us.'

And when the words were said, John Barton lay a corpse in Mr. Carson's arms.

So ended the tragedy of a poor man's life. (441)

62. Gaskell, *Mary Barton*, 131.

63. Patsy Stoneman, *Elizabeth Gaskell* (Bloomington: Indiana University Press, 1987), 69.

64. Jenn Morey, "Subtle Subversion: Gaskell's Use of Scripture in Her Social Purpose Novels" (Master's thesis, College of William and Mary, 1990). Morey also discusses the maternalized Christian imagery of this scene.

65. Catherine Gallagher analyzes the novel's ending in terms of theodicy: "The povidential resolution of John Barton's story partly mitigates his tragedy. Although moral freedom was an increasingly important idea in Unitarian theology in the 1840s, Gaskell was still writing within a teleological tradition. John Barton feels responsible for his crime, but in the end the very intensity of his remorse leads to both his own and his enemy's spiritual regeneration. There is not even a hint of possible damnation in the novel; evil is eventually self-effacing and productive of good, although sin is not explicitly ordained by God. The close of Barton's life, therefore, hardly appears to be tragic; his life veers from its tragic course in the final episode . . . " (*Industrial Reformation of English Fiction*, 67).

66. Gaskell, *Mary Barton*, 460, 465.

67. I use the term from Richard Poirier, *A World Elsewhere* (New York: Oxford University Press, 1966). Although Poirier is of course discussing an American vision of utopia embodied in the style of certain American writers, his term is evocative for Gaskell's final vision of *Mary Barton's* American New World.

68. Gaskell, *Mary Barton*, 76, 466, 342, 360.

69. Gaskell, *Mary Barton*, 68, 309.

70. Among the best resources for consideration of the reality and image of the fallen woman are Mayhew's contemporary account in the fourth volume of *London Labour and the London Poor* (New York: Dover Publications, 1968); Judith Walkowitz, "The Making of an Outcast Group: Prostitutes and Working Women in Nineteenth-Century Plymouth and Southampton," in *Suffer and Be Still: Women in the Victorian Age*, ed. Martha Vicinus (Bloomington: Indiana University Press, 1977), 72–93; Raymond Lister, *Victorian Narrative Paintings* (London: London Museum Press, 1966); Susan Casteras, "Down the Garden Path: Courtship Culture and Its Imagery in Victorian Painting" (Unpublished Dissertation. Yale, 1977); Helene Roberts, "Marriage, Redundancy or Sin: The Painter's View of Women in the First Twenty-Five Years of Victoria's Reign," in Vicinus, *Suffer and Be Still*; Elizabeth Helsinger, Robin Sheets, and William Veeder, *The Woman Question* (See n. 2). See especially Nina Auerbach's "The Rise of the Fallen Woman," chap. 3 in Auerbach's *Woman and the Demon: The Life of a Victorian Myth* (Cambridge: Harvard University Press, 1982).

71. Winifred Gérin, *Elizabeth Gaskell* (Oxford: Oxford University Press, 1980), 127–28.

72. John Pfordresher points out in his fine paper, "A Rhetoric for Urania Cottage," that in his interviews with prostitutes in magdalen houses Dickens makes clear his belief that fallen women had some moral defect; their prostitution was evidence of "a diseased state of mind" (unpublished 1990 MLA talk, page 3, from the session "Figuring Women's Bodies in Victorian Fiction").

73. Rosemarie Bodenheimer, *The Politics of Story in Victorian Social Fiction* (Ithaca, NY: Cornell University Press, 1988).

74. Coral Lansbury disagrees with my interpretation of Ruth's sacred childhood experience of her mother: "As the only child of a stupid old farmer and an ineffectual but amiable curate's daughter, Ruth was brought up to be lady without the means to enable her to maintain that station" (*Elizabeth Gaskell* [Boston: G.K. Hall, 1984], 26).

75. Elizabeth Gaskell, *Ruth* (Oxford: Oxford University Press, 1987), 36–37.

76. Gaskell, *Mary Barton*, 64.

77. Gaskell, *Ruth*, 37, 46, 37, 38.

78. Gaskell, *Ruth*, 35, 48, 38.

79. Gaskell, *Ruth,* 54, 31, 29.

80. Gaskell, *Ruth,* 15, 18.

81. Stoneman, *Elizabeth Gaskell,* 100.

82. Gaskell, *Ruth,* 5.

83. Gaskell, *Ruth,* 41, 39, 27, 22, 39.

84. Gaskell, *Ruth,* 33, 44, 40, 4, 5, 50–51.

85. Lansbury, *Elizabeth Gaskell.* See p. 23, where Lansbury compares Mary Barton's urban savviness and Ruth's country innocence.

86. Gaskell, *Mary Barton,* 183.

87. Gaskell, *Ruth,* 58.

88. See especially Bodenheimer, *The Politics of Story,* and Stoneman, *Elizabeth Gaskell.*

89. Gaskell, *Ruth,* 74–75.

90. This scene in which children enact the gendered cultural values is reminiscent of a scene in Anne Brontë's *Agnes Grey,* in which young Master Tom Bloomfield, seven years old, demands that he rule both his sisters and his governess; his sister Mary Ann, meanwhile, opposes all authority by remaining absolutely inert, a kind of parody of static Victorian womanhood in the face of overwhelming male dominance. See chapters 2 and 3.

91. Gaskell, *Ruth,* 71, 72–73, 92.

92. Gaskell, *Ruth,* 96, 100.

93. Gaskell, *Ruth,* 70, 462n, 70.

94. Gaskell, *Ruth,* 135, 141, 149.

95. Bonaparte, *The Gypsy-Bachelor of Manchester,* 123. See n. 40.

96. Lansbury, *Elizabeth Gaskell,* 24.

97. Bonaparte, *The Gypsy-Bachelor of Manchester,* 130.

98. Gaskell, *Ruth,* 448.

99. Gaskell, *Ruth,* 316. W.A. Craik, in *Elizabeth Gaskell and the English Provincial Novel* (London: Methuen, 1975), 86, discusses the "Pre-Raphaelite" effect of this scene.

100. See Meaghan Hanrahan, *'A Transitory Splendour': Portrayals of the Fallen Woman in the Mid-Century Victorian Novel* (Honors thesis, College of William and Mary, 1990), 32–33, for a good discussion of the erasure of Ruth's narrative.

101. Gaskell, *Ruth,* 448.

102. Bonaparte, *The Gypsy-Bachelor of Manchester*, 107.

103. Gaskell, *Ruth*, 185.

104. Gaskell, *Ruth*, 338, 57, 341, 457, 429.

105. Lansbury, *Elizabeth Gaskell*, 33.

106. Morey, "Subtle Subversion," 35.

107. Gaskell, *Ruth*, 458. Tears are a resonant Gaskell symbol. For a discussion of the significance of tears in another Gaskell text, see Deborah Denenholz Morse, "'Where there are no more tears': Elizabeth Gaskell's New Eden in *Sylvia's Lovers*." Unpublished article.

108. Gaskell, *Ruth*, 458.

God's House, Women's Place

Laura Fasick

It is one of the minor ironies of history that although spinsters in Victorian England were denied a place in social recognition and approval, they were nonetheless among the few women who could have a literal place of their own. Prior to 1870, the year in which Parliament passed the first married Women's Property Act, a married Englishwoman could only hold property—including houses—under the provisions of a special trust. This "device" worked only because trusts were "governed by equity rather than the common law," under which women's property passed to their husbands upon marriage.[1] As a result, spinsters were set apart partly by their unambiguous and unqualified ability to create their own households.

Yet Martha Vicinus, in her study of women's communities in Victorian and Edwardian England, has shown the psychological and social constraints that constricted women's ability to enjoy independent lives even when they were legally and financially able to establish them.[2] Central to the concern felt about "redundant" women was the belief, more or less openly stated, that single women had missed out on their one opportunity for a fulfilling life, and that what remained were necessarily "existences manquées," as the influential social critic and essayist W.R. Greg put it, when writing in 1862 on the "wretchedness and wrong" of an increase in spinsters. Greg explained that he did not count domestic servants among "redundant" women because they fulfilled "both essentials of woman's being: *they are*

75

supported by, and they minister to, men" (emphasis in original).[3]
According to this view, even an affluent spinster able to live in
her own home was out of place, while a menial laboring in
somebody else's residence was filling an appropriate place in a
harmonious home order.

By putting men at the center of "normal" women's lives,
Victorian domestic ideology situated single women in an aimless
psychological limbo. Thus W.G. Hamley's 1872 *Blackwood's* essay, "Old Maids," distinguishes between the *real* life of the wife
and mother, which leaves its imprint on the heart and mind and
features of a woman, and the spinster's essential detachment
from the highs and lows of experience. The spinster's cheerfulness is a shallow enjoyment that has no "memory of tears in it
. . . [no] resolute forgetting of worries and cares lurking just
around the corner." The old maid will seem younger than the
matron because "sympathy in other's trials" does not age a
person as "cares do in our own case." The independent woman
apparently has no "case" of her own: she will not or cannot feel
for herself alone as she might—indeed, must!—if she had family
responsibilities. Spinsterhood in this interpretation is not just
absence of marriage but absence of deep emotion, meaningful
activity, any center of gravity. "Single women often have no
obvious duties," Hamley explains. "They can only talk." No
wonder that while the wife has "an acknowledged position," the
"old maid knows herself in the world's eye a cipher."[4]

Both Greg and Hamley demonstrate a view of women as
relative creatures, "incomplete" when "independent."[5] This belief in female contingency has been one major target of later
feminist analysis and theory, leading to such developments as
the selection by some of lesbianism and/or of female separatism
as political choices. Yet physical love for women and physical
separation from men was not a psychological or practical possibility for many nineteenth-century women, especially women
committed to "respectability." How, then, could women establish a sense of independent self while remaining within the
bounds of social conventionality at a time when female dependence was an ideal?

Ironically, Victorian religion, although patriarchal itself
and embedded in a patriarchal society, could also become an

opening through which women could locate themselves outside of masculine territory. A church that allowed only male clergy and that worshiped "God the Father and the Son" might not appear promising as a source for female empowerment, but the uses women made of religious ideology could be liberatory indeed. Emphasis on a universal divine could justify women in rejecting the centrality of romantic love and of an individual man. It could also justify women in attention to the self—here defined as "soul"—and in a faith in spiritual equality that erased supposed masculine superiority. Admittedly, these liberatory tactics are never easy or clear-cut. The High Church novelist Charlotte Yonge began her treatise *Womankind* (1877) with the brisk declaration that Genesis proves and justifies women's inferiority to men. Yet Yonge's fiction, which she wrote specifically to promulgate her religious views, consistently presents women as beings responsible for themselves before God and not simply relying on heterosexual relationships to supply them with purpose and meaning. Indeed, Yonge's fiction, like that of Elizabeth Sewell and Dinah Mulock Craik, shows some intriguing resemblances to the arguments of far more radical theorists, such as Frances Power Cobbe. These resemblances are certainly not a straightforward case of influence: many of Craik's, Yonge's, and Sewell's novels were written before Cobbe's self-declared goals: radical changes in female education, employment, and freedom from social convention. Yet in their construction of characters and plots, these authors anticipate and illustrate many feminist ideas about the arrangements for female life.

In this essay, I will examine the spaces—literal and figurative—that single women establish for themselves in these authors' avowedly didactic novels. These works were among the popular fiction of their day, appealing to a large (and largely female) audience.[6] The books were respectable best-sellers not only because the plots and characters were confined to the domestic life of the middle class, but also because they openly preached a conservative belief in women's innate differences from (and intellectual inferiority to) men. All three authors wholeheartedly accepted the ideal of lady-like decorum and the importance of family cohesion. Yet by placing religious faith, not an individual man, at the center of a woman's life, these writers subtly ques-

tioned and overturned some of the most constricting Victorian
assumptions about female nature and roles. This revisionary
process is particularly apparent in the treatment of the spinster's
home as an alternative space to the patriarchal domains ruled by
husbands and fathers. It also emerges in the spinster's handling
of finances as one aspect of home management that has wider
implications for the self. Finally, an appreciation of female autonomy provides the basis for attitudes toward nineteenth-
century England's most controversial example of spinster life:
vowed religious celibacy. This appreciation shows especially
clearly when contrasted with the values whereby the comparable
male religious writers Charles Kingsley and William Sewell
handle the same issue.[7]

The Spinster's Relationships and Responsibilities

Although Victorian gender ideology assigned women to the private rather than the public sphere, it did not authorize women to
assert themselves openly even in the home. Nina Auerbach has
insisted that "the [Victorian] mother's power is seen as all-infus-
ing," with "father" no less than "children . . . a ritual praiser,
rather than sharer, of her reign." Yet her image of the God-like
materfamilias is emphatically based on the power of the maternal and thus, in Victorian terms, the wifely: it assumes the nuclear family unit. And within that unit the father, however
"absent," remains "omnipotent."[8] Indeed, in W.R. Greg's ideal
household, described above, the male absorbs all female members of the establishment—from wife to housemaids—into one
large amorphous harem of ministrants and dependents. In this
pattern, the paterfamilias, subsuming the limited powers of the
mother, could model for offspring the authority that sons later
would acquire for their own, and that daughters would defer to
in husbands as well as in fathers. Thus the family roles and
structure could reproduce themselves endlessly.

A single woman's house, however, could become an alternative space, one in which a woman could not only hold authority in her own right, but could also transmit the knowledge that
deference to a man should not be a woman's highest value. This

is the situation, for instance, in Charlotte Yonge's *Hopes and Fears: or, Scenes from the Life of a Spinster* (1860). Honor Charlecote, the spinster of the title, must undergo during the course of the novel an education not often imposed on Victorian heroines. She learns not to love any individual man too devotedly, but rather to remain clear-sighted and judicial even as she enjoys the warmth of human attachments. Honor offers the one young daughter of a neighboring couple refuge from an environment that might almost have been constructed as a parody of hierarchical gender relations. Mr. Fulmort is the undisputed head of the household, while his wife is so spiritless that one commentator suggests she "must probably be classified as mentally retarded, like at least one of her daughters."[9] Even the dutiful Phoebe cannot feel toward the aggressive Mr. Fulmort what Yonge suggests is a girl's typical attitude toward her father: that what he does "cannot be wrong." In comparison with the emotionally barren Fulmort household, where father knows best, or at least gets his way as though he does, Honor's home "was a region of Paradise to Phoebe Fulmort."[10]

Phoebe gains more than momentary peace and quiet through visiting the Holt (Honor's estate). She gains also the knowledge that a woman's concerns go beyond one personal relationship. Phoebe does eventually wed but not before she has demonstrated her willingness to forego marriage at a time when marriage would only be possible were she and her fiancé to accept the "immoral" profits of a gin manufacturery. Morality, not freedom, is Phoebe's keyword, but by granting preeminence to other values, she does show her freedom from women's supposed subjection to romantic love. The result is not endorsement of female independence for its own sake, but it nonetheless establishes female independence as a prerequisite even for honorable union.

Honor's mentorship of Phoebe and Phoebe's subsequent dilemma and choice thus link Yonge's fiction with the theories of avowed feminist writing. Frances Power Cobbe, whose enthusiastic support for women's suffrage was one of her many differences from Yonge, nonetheless was among those who argued that only women psychologically and practically willing to be spinsters should they be unable to attain a satisfactory marriage could be more than glorified prostitutes if they actually did marry.[11] Indeed, Cobbe argued at length in "Celibacy v. Marriage" that celibacy must be "common and desirable" in order for "the wife [to be] what wife should be": not a consumer whose husband must "grow more mercenary and more worldly to supply her wants," but a "brave" and "honorable" partner in "the noblest of his aspirations." Only when a woman feels "able to make for herself a free, useful, and happy life alone" can a man feel confident that marriage will not interfere with his ability "to pursue his calling disinterestedly."[12] Yonge never deals as openly as Cobbe with the need for educational and employment opportunities to give women financial options other than marriage. Her characters live in such upper-middle-class affluence as to make economic considerations superfluous. But Yonge does dispel the emotional bugbear of spinsterhood: she consistently treats an unmarried life as a plausible—and sometimes attractive—possibility, not a doom. Religion underlies this treatment; her ability to reject Victorian matrimonial fixation rests on her belief that in proportion as she is recognized as one of the "members of the one great Body" of the Church, "the single woman ceases to be manquée and enjoys honour and happiness." Church membership and duties give women a status that in pre-Christian times had belonged to them only "as appendages to some individual man."[13]

Yonge's emphasis on female autonomy is similar to that of Dinah Craik, whose *A Woman's Thoughts About Women* (1858) does "not concern married women." In that book Craik urges her readers toward that "dependence upon God" that in worldly terms is "self-dependence." Perhaps men will not be pleased, but "is a woman's divinity to be man—or God?"[14] To renounce man as a divinity is also to renounce the belief in romantic love as the crux of a woman's life. In two Craik novels, entry into a spinster's sphere becomes a way for lovelorn heroines to learn the range of life beyond fixation on a man. The eponymous heroine of *Olive* (1850) retires for the night in the abode of spinster Flora Rothesay. Her "last waking thought was still of Harold," the object of her apparently hopeless love, but already Flora's "pleasant stream of talk" has sunk "the one weary pain that ever pursued her . . . into momentary repose":

> Just between waking and sleeping Olive was roused by
> what seemed an almost spirit-like strain of music. Her
> door had been left ajar, and the sound she heard was
> the voices of the household, engaged in their evening
> devotion. . . .

> Poor lonely Olive lay and listened. Then rest, deep and
> placid, came over her, as over one who, escaped from a
> stormy wrack and tempest, falls asleep amid the murmer
> of "quiet waters," in a pleasant land.[15]

Flora's home is "another world" to Olive, who finds in it a
refuge from grief and frustration. It is "another world" in more
senses than that, however: it opposes the world that denies the
possibility of single female happiness. Flora herself, the mistress
of the house and of this "other" world of female comfort, is proof
that an old maid can live "not only to feel, but to impart
cheerfulness."[16]

Decie, the narrator of Craik's "Miss Tommy," comments,
looking back, that she is glad to have

> learned my lesson—the lesson first taught me by her dear
> old self [Miss Tommy] in her pretty house at Dover, dur-
> ing the peaceful three months when she 'took me in'—me,
> almost a 'stranger'—and returned me back to my parents
> healed in body and mind. At least I was so much better
> that I endured the ensuing three years without making
> myself unendurable to my family, as is the way with so
> many young people who have been 'crossed in love.'[17]

The house in which those important three months elapse—
three months with the power to shape the following three
years—is explicitly presented as "an old maid's house." That, it
turns out, is its strength.

> Even now—to me who had just gone through a great do-
> mestic convulsion, to say nothing of the small tempests in
> teapots that were always brewing in our numerous and
> tumultuous family—the exceeding repose of the maiden
> household I had dropped into, where nobody squabbled
> and nobody "fussed," was most soothing and pleasant.

> It was, of course, a silent house—no children running
> about or girls singing up and down the stairs; but when

one has had rather too much of domestic noise, silence is
agreeable for a time.[18]

Victorian domesticity, complete with an abundance of
children, here becomes a distraction from that inner exploration
and growth in self-knowledge that Craik implies is essential for
female maturity. Miss Tommy does not discourage her protégée
from marrying, but she does inculcate in her the realization that
marriage—that romantic love itself—cannot be the one concern
of a woman's life. Miss Tommy, who is "busy day after day, occupied from morning to night with duties domestic and duties
social," is the first model to young Decie of a woman who can be
busy and beloved outside the context of married life. Craik does
not abjure a few declines into pathos, but she emphasizes Miss
Tommy's customary "placid gayety."[19] The example Miss
Tommy sets is one of energy and vitality, not the "deep sadness
and resignation" that Sally Mitchell finds presented as "the inevitable consequences of woman's lot."[20] Miss Tommy's message
to Decie is to "rise superior" to her sorrows. The experience
teaches Decie that to "waste one's life, with all its duties, all its
blessings—and few lives are void of the latter, none of the former—to sacrifice it on the shrine of any one human being, is, as
some statesman said of a great political error, 'worse than a
crime—a blunder.'"[21]

The mixture of terminologies in Decie's observation
demonstrates the blurring of gender roles that occur as the role
of spinster becomes a valid alternative to that of wife.
"Blessings" and "shrine," even "duties," suggest the religious rationale by which Miss Tommy herself—and the other spinsters
in this essay—constructs her life. At the same time, the allusion
to political affairs and the acceptance of a pragmatic political
judgment indicates how the spinsters' version of religion—deliberately divorced from the emotionalism inherent in idolizing
another human being—allows the religion to co-exist with a
healthy and shrewd self-care.

That same mixture of terminologies appears in Aunt
Sarah, presiding genius in Elizabeth Sewell's *The Experience of
Life* (1853). She seamlessly combines "wisdom that cometh from
above" with "short, sharp maxims of worldly policy," thereby
establishing a pattern of "proper energy" and "confidence in

[one's] one powers" that her great-niece Sally Mortimer chooses to follow, never marrying. Sally remarks that "there is something in every household to which all other objects or pursuits must give away. In Aunt Sarah's it was religion."[22] Such is not the case in her own home, where her father insists on retaining all control over household affairs, even as he shows his incompetence over and over again. The result is constant tension between the idea of masculine acumen and the reality of mismanagement. Since none of the family dare to challenge male authority, they must endure the financial and practical hardships that ensue. Aunt Sarah's home, by comparison, is one in which the only inviolable authority belongs to God, and it is thus possible to assess all merely human—even when masculine—figures on their own merits.

Aunt Sarah's home is the stage on which Sally can witness the potential richness of a spinster's life. It is within this framework that Sally learns to appreciate that "there's a better chance of respect . . . in setting one-self to please God than to please man." Suspecting from youth that spinsterhood is her "destined . . . lot," Sally learns that this lot may be a "blessing" as much as any other. That blessing is specifically allied with independence of mind and action, rather than with bland acquiescence in the patterns of other people's lives. The effect on the young girl is to convince her of the dignity and happiness possible to spinsters: "that it is possible for single persons to be superior"—superior not only in their own merit, but superior to the shallow judgment of a world where "if one is not married, one shall not be so much respected."[23] Rather than the displaced person of W.R. Greg's imagining, the spinster here is someone who has made a place for herself. This was a deliberate strategy on Sewell's part. In her *Autobiography*, Sewell defines a "regular novel" as "a story in which love is the essential interest," too often "misleading to young people" because of the usual ending—'and so they were married, and lived happily ever after.'" Such novels make the climax the heroine's wedding. Marriage is obviously not exceptional in human life, but Sewell was keenly aware that many novels treated it as such, and she wrote many of her novels "to show that life could be happy, and its events of importance apart from marriage."[24]

Like Yonge's, Sewell's fictions here fit into the framework of far more explicitly feminist debates than occur in *The Experience of Life* itself. Greg feels free to place "the sentiment of love" (married heterosexual love) at the center of women's lives because he dismisses all other emotional outlets as unsatisfactory for them, specifically including religious feeling in the category of unnatural and ineffectual palliatives. A few highly exceptional women, he grudgingly admits, may be so "spiritual" that "human ties and feelings seem pale and poor by the side of the divine; and to such marriage . . . would assuredly be a mistake." But even of those "really thus called, the voice, alas, far oftener comes from a narrow intelligence or a defective organization than from the loftier aspirings of the soul."[25] In a few sentences—all he bestows on this subject—Greg simultaneously equates "marriage" with all "human ties and feelings," elevates strong religious feeling to an all-but-unobtainable and far from desirable height, and dismisses such feeling as a source of strength or satisfaction for all but a tiny fraction of (not very attractively described) women. By essentially removing religion from the realm of deeply felt and motivational human emotions, by allowing only heterosexual love the power to inspire active and contented lives, Greg constructs a schema of women's psychology that equates celibacy with emotional impoverishment and distortion.

Frances Power Cobbe, in her reply to Greg, touches upon this theme when she argues that women's "tenderness and devotion," a gift from God that enriches marriage, "is yet meant to be subordinated to the great purposes of the existence of all rational souls—the approximation to God through virtue." Cobbe states, "God is the only true center of life for all of us, not any creature he has made"—an unexceptional statement for a nineteenth-century Christian, save that Cobbe is making it in the context of her argument that "it is desirable that women should have other aims, pursuits, and interests in life beside matrimony." That a woman's "single life" could be "useful and happy"[26] was neither a piece of received wisdom nor, as Susan Gorsky and Kathleen Hickok point out, a literary convention of the time. It was far more common to show the spinster as pathetic or ridiculous or both,[27] and one special sign of the spinster's emotionally crippled state was that she sought in "religious affections a pale ideal substitute for the denied human ones"—a substitution "seldom wholly satisfactorily or wholly safe."[28] In insisting upon a religiously founded and *therefore* independent female life as indeed safe and satisfactory, Cobbe was able to employ the weight of Victorian patriarchy. This version of spinsterhood, by subordinating marital love to existential concerns, denied that the single woman was particularly prone to emotional danger or imbalance. Sewell's novel contains a similar version of spinsterhood in which the single woman's "pious resignation and service" actually facilitates her status as "a self-sufficient, active and respected member of society whose life has been rewarding in purely human terms."[29] In her portrayal of Aunt Sarah and of Sarah's protégée, Sally, Elizabeth Sewell could almost be offering a point-by-point illustration of the old maid's capacity for health, sanity, inner fulfillment, and rich human relations that deliberately do not include the marital.

A spinster's separate household entails separate finances and requires the spinster to manage her own money: a problematic matter at a time when women were assumed to be illogical rather than practical. In these novels, however, financial responsibility becomes a synecdoche for general self-responsibility and competence. Finances also become an arena in which women can reject the ideal of total feminine self-sacrifice. After all, the same moral code that dictated selflessness in the (feminine) domestic sphere insisted on probity and sobriety in the (masculine) economic sphere. This difference between public and private virtues was part of what Cobbe describes as a "morality . . . divided between [men and women]."[30] Entering the economic sphere made it possible for women justifiably to guide their conduct by values of moderation and balance, rather than ecstatic self-forgetfulness. The ethically compelling need for financial balance provides the model for other kinds of balance, such as that between fulfilling one's own needs and the needs of others. It also provides a way out of the division of attributes that constituted the basis of Victorian gender identity.

Miss Tommy's use of money, for instance, breaks down the gender divisions whereby masculine "self-respect" is defined as difference from, and material superiority to, the female. When Miss Tommy, "accustomed for years to manage her large fortune entirely herself," grows too physically frail to maintain the records of her "very wide . . . responsibilities and sphere of action," she employs the retired soldier Major Gordon as a steward. The Major, whose fierce pride and loathing of dependence has not kept him from idleness and inutility since he left the army, finds new satisfaction in renewed occupation. No longer longing for death to relieve him from the curse of "nothing to hope for, nothing to do" . . . "the deadened heart of him burst out into full flower."[31]

The Major's acceptance of both a salary from, and a relationship of almost conjugal tenderness and intimacy with, Miss Tommy, is a movement away from his earlier equation of a poor man's love for a rich woman with the man's loss of self-respect.[32] He no longer identifies male selfhood with superiority over the female. Yet his new position is in fact a direct challenge to Victorian standards of masculinity. Miss Tommy insists on making the Major a paid employee not only in order to alleviate his poverty, but because she wants to maintain the clarity of a business relationship in their business dealings. Their growing intimacy never interferes with her independence because she always maintains the distinction between the private model of masculine protectiveness toward feminine delicacy and the public model of employer authority. Since they are linked emotionally as well as financially, however, their relationship reverses the accepted roles of Victorian marriage. Miss Tommy is the provider of money and financial security, the ultimate authority on expenditure and investment, while the Major attends to daily details and financial "housekeeping." Craik softens the subversive implications of this reversal by casting most of Miss Tommy's financial concerns as charitable contributions and involvements. The innate dignity of "good works" makes the Major's employment as much a mission as a job. By switching material roles, however, Craik undermines the fixed categories that justified Victorian gender hierarchy.

The same hierarchy, of course, placed single women as receptacles of others' unwanted responsibilities. Yet a reinterpretation of the nature of duty could radically revise the expectations for a single woman's life. In *The Experience of Life,* Aunt Sarah, always eager to save her grand-niece from excess, warns Sally to care for others, but not as if her life had no definition aside from such devotion: "Never undertake a responsibility which does not belong to you."[33] After their father's death, Sally's older siblings give Sally sole responsibility for their mother's support, as well as for the two youngest Mortimer children. The supposedly practical reasoning behind this is that Sally, as a budding old maid, has none of the expenses that a career brings upon a man, or that a husband and children bring upon a matron. Sally's older siblings have judged the matter by standards based on the importance of conventional gender roles. The men must get ahead in the world (their career success, of course, is also a prerequisite for marriage, thereby linking their professional and personal satisfactions). The women, for whom marriage is a business, must either maintain their husband's status through their own conspicuous consumption or else cultivate an (expensive) appearance that will enable them to marry. Sally, in her elder brothers' and sisters' eyes, is the logical choice to care for their mother because she has none of these responsibilities: her schoolteaching does not require material display, and it already seems obvious that she will never marry. As a result, her siblings see her life as a void into which they can cast their unwanted burdens—for so they regard their mother.

Sally sees the selfishness of her siblings' excusing themselves from even monetary assistance to their mother by claiming the priority of their career or household expenses. Nonetheless she is prepared to assume the burden they wish to load on her. Aunt Sarah, however, puts a stop to Sally's willingness to martyr herself. If Sally actually does take entire responsibility for her mother's care, Aunt Sarah warns,

> I will tell you what will surely come to pass. . . . You will begin by allowing that it is your duty to support your mother, and they will all praise you, and thank you, and call you an angel; and by-and-by, you will go to them and ask for help, and maybe they'll give it; but they won't think they are giving to *her*, but to *you*; and so they will talk about debt and obligation, and you will know that there is no obligation, and say they are unjust; and they will be angry, because they have never learnt to see their

duty clearly, and then you'll quarrel. No, child,—take
your own share, and let them take theirs, and then see if
you can't make the world go smoothly between you.[34]

Aunt Sarah is the spokesperson for Sewell's view that "a
single woman, with her own particular set of duties, has as much
personal significance as a wife, and should not regard herself as
a useless parasite,"[35] duty-bound to accept whatever tasks others
assign her. To her, the single female life is equal in rights and responsibilities with those of men and of married women, and
equality of rights and responsibilities is therefore her keynote in
decreeing how the Mortimer children should divide their mother's care. "Some of you may make more money, and some less,
and so some may give more and some less," Aunt Sarah declares, "but the duty of giving is the same share for each, and if
you take all the shares, you do wrong to them and wrong to
yourself."[36] Aunt Sarah's argument thus denies the special virtue
of female self-sacrifice by asserting the necessity of equal virtue
for *all*.

Her argument operates from both an idealistically religious and a pragmatically business-like perspective. From an
idealistic perspective, depriving another of the opportunity to
fulfill an undesired duty is doing wrong to him or her. After all,
if the preservation of the soul from sin is the greatest good toward which one can assist others, then any refusal to countenance others' sinful selfishness is good not only for oneself, but
for others, too. They may choose not to benefit from the chance
for self-reform, but at least they have had the opportunity. The
need to offer such opportunities, of course, also makes it morally
as well as psychologically and practically preferable for women
to refuse the extreme self-abnegation offered as one feminine
ideal. However, from a perspective of business morality, this solution offers a marketplace emphasis on justice rather than charity, on good sense rather than on delicacy or self-devotion. As
Aunt Sarah tartly remarks, "We can all be martyrs as we fancy,
but we can't be sensible men and women."[37] In the interests of
sense, of justice, of equity, Sally not only can but should ignore
the feelings and preferences of her older siblings. She should, in
short, live by a model of hardheadedness and clear-sightedness
that violates standards of domestic tact even as it satisfies stan-

dards of business efficiency. By doing so, she incorporates public (masculine) virtues into her female life, creating a self that transcends stereotypical gender categories.

Celibate Sisterhoods

Female celibacy clearly had its enemies in Victorian England, but vowed celibacy aroused even stronger condemnation, particularly when the vowed women lived as a community.[38] Among nineteenth-century British Protestants, anti-Roman Catholicism ensured a general distrust of convent life, even as a minority of Tractarians fought for the establishment of Anglican sisterhoods.[39] Not only were such associations redolent of "Popery" for most English observers, they also were seen as opposing self-chosen duties to God-appointed ones. Family responsibilities must come first: to leave the home circle for convent life was an act at once of presumption and of laziness.[40]

At the same time that sisterhoods were condemned as a refuge for the idle and self-willed, they were also viewed as hotbeds of sexual frustration. Susan Casteras has traced the theme of "repressed sexuality" in early Victorian art. The "majority of nuns" in the paintings Casteras studies[41] would have preferred marriage. In this way, woman's romantic passion is seen as preceding the religious passion into which it may perforce be channeled. Even more pointedly, Charles Kingsley distinguishes the "English matron['s] . . . unsullied purity of thought" from the "prudish and prurient foulmindedness" that surrounds the Roman Catholic exaltation of virginity.[42] Focusing this sexual scrutiny upon nuns, of course, destroys the rationale for the celibate life itself, since it assumes that sexuality can never be sublimated—or at least non-destructively sublimated.

Kingsley focuses almost exclusively on chastity and passion in his treatment of female religious life. In *Yeast* (1849), Argemone's desire to join a High Church sisterhood is subtly denied even religious grounding by being linked to Argemone's admiration for the pagan Sappho. Argemone, who wishes for convent life partly out of a guilty need for enforced asceticism, believes herself joined with Sappho in disgust at the "unsatisfying, unloving" physical world. The narrator, however, steps in to lecture her, linking in his diatribe female attempts at self-sufficiency, the pretense of female friendship, and the inevitable collapse of both "self-sufficiency" and "friendship" into the reality of female passion, a passion degrading and destructive when it is denied.

> Sweet self-deceiver! had you no other reason for choosing as your heroine Sappho, the victim of the idolatry of intellect—trying in vain to fill her heart with the friendship of her own sex, and then sinking into mere passion for a handsome boy, and so down into self-contempt and suicide? [43]

The assumption here is that the thirst for masculine love dominates female life, with everything from intellect to friendship a mere distraction from this essential element. Kingsley links even the assumed uselessness of vowed life to the themes of misplaced sensuality and of women's inability for friendship with members of their own sex. "[A]shamed of her own laziness by the side of [her sister] Honoria's simple benevolence," Argemone "longed to outdo her by some signal act of self-sacrifice" such as joining a convent. Visions of "romantic asceticisms and mystic contemplation, which gave the true charm in her eyes to her wild project" dominate her idea of a nun's life, reducing to fanciful trimming the performance of some "menial services towards the poor," which nonetheless must remain "distasteful to her."[44] Argemone's strongest motivation in seeking celibacy, however, is her desire for autonomy. Realizing that Lancelot Smith loves her but not yet willing to admit her love for him, she is consumed with horror at the thought of having to "give up my will to any man! to become the subject, the slave of another human being! I, who have worshipped the belief in woman's independence . . . who have felt how glorious it is to live like the angels single and self-sustained!"[45]

For Kingsley, this "belief in woman's independence" is a fantasy that a man's passionate love can dispel—as it does when Argemone falls in love and willingly foregoes her earlier dreams. Clearly the most disturbing element in convent life for Kingsley is the denial of male authority—authority that he associates to an almost embarrassing extent with male sexuality. Only when

Argemone responds sexually to a man, or more specifically, to the "delicious feeling of being utterly in [a man's] power,"[46] is she in touch with real life.

William Sewell, brother to Elizabeth, takes an attitude toward sisterhoods almost as favorable as Kingsley's is negative. Yet he, like Kingsley, emphasizes the need for male authority: he differs only by locating that authority not in sexuality but in male guardianship over a female cloister. In Sewell's 1845 novel *Hawkstone*, religious organization is a masculine corporation in which women form one small and subservient part. Sewell's hero, Ernest Villiers, restores a ruined priory to serve as the setting for his Anglican fellowship. An admiring peasant describes its inhabitants thus to an inquisitive passer-by:

> There are twelve gentlemen . . . clergymen most of them. And there is a head—the warden they call him. . . . And they have often other gentlemen staying with them, mostly clergymen; but some of them Mr. Villiers's friends, lords, and others, who come here to read and be quiet, generally about Lent time. And there are a number of other young gentlemen who are going to be clergymen. And there is a school . . . [47]

In this combination of gentlemen's retreat, seminary, and boys' school resides the dignity of the church. The "lofty" hall of the Priory, setting of a communal meal among the scholars, in which they are ritually joined by "twelve poor people," is as "simple but solemn" as the grace with which it concludes. The evening service, which even the schoolboys attend in a "grave, and composed" manner, is inspiration for "holy, peaceful, grateful thoughts."[48]

By contrast, the Beguinage (sisterhood) is only the site for female subordination. Unlike the establishment of the brotherhood, an act of positive creation and religious dedication, the sisterhood came into being as Villiers' response to a bank crash that impoverished many of Hawkstone's single "gentlewomen." Humbled by their financial ruin, the women enter the Beguinage as a refuge, not as a place of honor. The "chastened" Mrs. Bevan, the formerly powerful Mabel, "now quiet, regular, self-disciplined, trained in habits of obedience and order," and the fallen woman Margaret, now "the servant and menial of those who had not sinned as she had,"[49] seem alike in their humiliation.

The Beguinage is also the setting for Villiers's beloved, the formerly Catholic Lady Eleanor, to undergo her last struggle with temptation before bowing to her male religious tutors and joining the Anglican communion. The warden accurately judges that even Mrs. Bevan, the most "judicious" of the sisters, will be incompetent to cope with Lady Eleanor's final doubts, "temptations which could only be counteracted by one more deeply experienced in the controversy." Before masculine wisdom and holiness, both the pure lady Eleanor, who "would have fallen on her knees before [the warden] . . . so deep was her reverence for him," and the reclaimed Margaret, "abashed, yet grateful for his notice" and answering with "reverence,"[50] are joined in humility.

The real point of all this seems to be that even in religious life, women cannot do without men. We find here a desexualized version of patriarchal authority equivalent to the daily supervision possible in marriage. These women earlier had misused their freedom and financial means; Mabel, in particular, had sought individual aggrandizement through service on meaningless committees and ineffectual personal charity. Life in the Beguinage deprives her of power to misuse by depriving her of power altogether. The element of her new religious life that Sewell most endorses is her submission to male guidance.

By contrast, when Frances Power Cobbe writes on sisterhoods in "Female Charity—Lay and Monastic," she condemns them for exactly the reasons that Sewell supports them and offers as an ideal for women exactly what Kingsley fears. It is absurd, Cobbe argues, for a "woman accustomed to all the liberty of an English lady in our time" to enter into "the trammels of every convent life." Women require "the invigorating influence of freedom of movement—of intercourse with the sound strong minds of men—or even [sic] of women mixing freely in the world." They require, in short, precisely that "woman's independence" that Kingsley sees as the threat of convent life and that William Sewell sees as the threat that convent life overcomes. The gravest danger that Cobbe perceives in the cloistered life is that "the intellect" as well as the "affections" "grow[s] starved and sick as it is denied." Denied "the fresh feelings of free work followed intelligently," nuns are too likely to sink into "mechanism," even "a sort of dotage" that renders them "not so much unhappy as idiotic." The alternative to this is for women to be "rational free agent[s],"[51] not necessarily wives and mothers and certainly not mere adjuncts to a man.

Elizabeth Sewell does not deal with sisterhoods directly, but Charlotte Yonge and Dinah Craik do, and in their qualified sympathy, we find reasoning similar to Cobbe's, but significantly different from that of Kingsley and William Sewell. For the two female writers, the limitations in convent life spring not from insufficient contact with men but from insufficient purpose and meaning. Indeed, Craik and Yonge both draw parallels between the vacuity that leads some women to a cloistered life and the vacuity that in other circumstances makes those same women dependent on men for a sense of self. They celebrate the possibilities of female comradeship even when they question whether the cloister truly facilitates such comradeship. Nor do they follow the pattern of many conservative opponents of convent life who condemned sisterhoods for substituting "self-sacrifice" possible at "home."[52] The implicit ideal for Craik and Yonge, as for Cobbe, is the "rational free agent."

Dinah Craik, in *Olive*, offers a reasonably friendly, yet condescending, picture of a Roman Catholic cloister: the nuns are harmless, irresponsible children, not moral exemplars. A convent eventually becomes the refuge of a woman whose only previous definition has been through the admiration of men. In Craik's novel, Christal, beautiful but shallow, lacks the strength and dignity that allows Olive to possess and enjoy independence. Instead, Christal craves male attention, and only when the revelation of her illegitimacy and of her own violent nature removes her from the marriage market does she find shelter among nuns. The weakness of convent life is not, then, identified with separation from men: rather, it is allied with the *same* weakness that would make romantic involvement with a man a woman's main goal in life. Individual self-sufficiency constitutes woman's true dignity.

Craik explicitly states this idea in her essay on Anglican sisterhoods, in which she pronounces this organized life, with

"work to do, authority to compel the doing it, and companionship to sweeten the same," helpful to women who "are not clever
enough, or brave enough, to carry out anything single-
handed."[53] Such women, however, are not to be compared to the

> single woman, who having inherited or earned sufficient
> money and position, has courage to assume the status and
> responsibilities of a married woman. She has, except the
> husband, all the advantages of the matronly position, and
> almost none of its drawbacks. So much lies in her power to
> do unhindered, especially the power of doing good. She
> can be a friend to the friendless and a mother to the or-
> phan; she can fill her house with happy guests, after the
> true Christian type—the guests that cannot repay her for
> her kindness. Being free to dispose of her time and labour,
> she can be a good neighbor, a good citizen—whether or
> not she ever attains the doubtful privilege of female suf-
> frage. Her worldly goods, her time, and her affections are
> exclusively her own to bestow wisely and well.[54]

There is, Craik declares, "no position more happy, more
useful (and therefore happy)."[55] Unlike Kingsley's version of
women's happiness, which centers upon sexual love, this vision
includes independence, free choice, and meaningful activity as
prerequisites of a fulfilled life.

Yonge, unlike Craik, tends to distinguish between Roman
Catholic and Anglican sisterhoods. Orders tainted with Roman
Catholicism are shown as generally inactive and useless. Vigorous Anglican sisterhoods, on the other hand, receive high praise
from her and from her characters.[56] Sisterhoods become com-
promised in Yonge's eyes only when they represent a selfish
withdrawal from life's possibilities for action. Thus in *Heartsease*
(1854) the timid Emma Brandon is led astray by her overenthusi-
astic friend Theresa into dreams of a contemplative life. Originally Emma had planned to restore the Priory on her property as
a place for charitable care-taking and religious services for all.
Under Theresa's influence, she begins to dream of the Priory as a
conventual home, divorced from useful life.

Like Craik, however, Yonge parallels irresponsible attraction to convent life with an equally irresponsible eagerness for
masculine attention. Emma's weakness for the blandishments of

a money-hunting suitor reveals not the necessity of masculine presence in female life, but the particular weakness of Emma's nature, and its susceptibility to amorous, as well as pseudo-pious, evasions of life's duties. Her wooer uses the language of piety as a form of amorous flattery, praising Emma's "purity and devotedness . . . [for] having been such powerful instruments in leading him to a better course." In reality, his debts would "swallow two-thirds" of the money that Emma still intends for the Priory's restoration. This masculine capacity for absorption is a contrast to the wholesome system of checks and balances by which Emma earlier had allowed her enthusiasm to be "chastened by her mother's sound sense." Under her mother's guidance, Emma had been willingly to plan, work and wait for the active charity of transforming the Priory into an "alms-house, with old people and children."[57] Mother and daughter had formed a partnership, united by respectful attention and by shared values.

Emma's renunciation of her convent scheme is associated with an access both of power and of strengthened ties with the women around her. She does lose contact with Theresa, it is true, when Theresa converts to Roman Catholicism. But, significantly, Emma also abjures her suitor, having learned of his secret machinations. Fittingly, it is a woman, Theodora Martinsdale, with whom Emma had never previously been comfortable, who first persuades her to return to a fold filled both with female contact and with duties—a secular sisterhood indeed. Her relations with her mother, her responsibilities to "all the poor people" whom formerly she tended and, in her stage of showy religiosity rather than religion, has neglected: these are compelling arguments for Emma to hear. But she further craves, and the usually reserved Theodora grants, the sisterhood of reciprocity: Theodora tells her the story of her own struggle toward peace.

This new equality, and Emma's renewed companionship with her old friend Violet and with her own mother, are both herald of, and response to, Emma's picking up of her "allotted work" in a circle of female inspired moral dignity. Reassured of her steadiness, Emma's mother now is "quite ready to promote her plans" for the orphanage and the details of orphans "doubled in numbers," soon to need "the restoration of the ruin" for the sake of more lodging, show matters "actually in train for the fulfillment of Emma's aspiration.[58] This is a contrast not only to Emma's convent dreams, but also to the self-indulgent and self-destructive marriage plans into which she had been tempted: plans that revealed the possibility of marital love being at least as threatening as a convent life to women's usefulness and dignity.

Conclusion

As Yonge's statements in *Womankind* and her strategies in her fiction indicate, religion could work two ways: justifying female subordination on the one hand, but on the other hand encouraging women in an attention to the self or soul that denies male centrality to female existence. It is this ambiguity that distinguishes the works by Yonge, Craik, and Sewell from more secular—and today, more canonical—treatments of spinsterhood such as Elizabeth Gaskell's *Cranford* (1864). It also sets these didactic novels apart from Anthony Trollope's breezily areligious clerical fictions, in which "common sense" dismisses spiritually as an adequate substitute for heterosexual love.

However pleasant (or not) one finds *Cranford*'s wistful comedy, the Cranfordians themselves are eccentrics whose freedom from the world's constrictions consists largely of total separation from the world outside their community. Nina Auerbach celebrates the alignment of "the Jenkyns sisters . . . with incompetence and unreality" because Cranford itself is "a sanctuary of unreality," an entire town that can be "defined . . . as insane." To Auerbach, this very derangement makes Cranford "a repository of sudden, quasi-magical power that destroys or appropriates the reality it excludes."[59] She obviously intends her argument as a feminist reclamation of *Cranford* from such earlier readings as Martin Dodsworth's view that Gaskell "underlines the essential unrealism" of female "desire to equal the male" and "deplores [the] anti-social nature" of female "assertions of independence."[60] She can only do so, however, by reversing Dodsworth's standards of approval and disapproval, not by challenging his descriptions: Miss Matty *is* "feminine, fluttery . . . self-hating";

the townswomen *are* "half-awed" by the "autocracy and mysterious skill the male seems to embody."[61] In their "singularities"
and "oddities" the Cranfordians fit one contemporary definition
of women best off as single because "unfitted for married life."[62]
Gaskell hints, however, that single life has itself produced their
common eccentricity: a clue that singleness for women is perhaps inevitably a distorting process. Their self-enclosure, moreover, if anything exacerbates their susceptibility to masculine
presence: throughout *Cranford*, the appearance of a man triggers
extreme reactions ranging from delight to horror. The Cranfordians display what Richard Steele (in *The Tatler* 126) defines as
the distinguishing feature of both the prude and the coquette:
they remain constantly conscious of "the distinction of sex,"[63]
and that consciousness itself is perhaps the highest "emblem of
masculine power."[64]

Anthony Trollope, meanwhile, plays with the idea of spinsterhood through such characters as Miss Mackenzie in the novel
of that name (1865) and Lily Dale in *The Small House at Allington*
(1864) and *The Last Chronicle of Barset* (1867). Yet he consistently
rejects the single life as a possibility for a single healthy woman.
Lily Dale condemns herself to lifelong celibacy after being rejected by an unscrupulous fiancé, but she does so out of the
feeling that she has been fatally damaged and therefore is unfit
for marriage. Miss Mackenzie is only able to think of marriage
after her invalid brother's death and her inheritance of his
money liberate her for a life of her own. A life of her own, however, turns out to mean nothing more than a choice among suit-
ors—a choice simplified by the fact that all but one are arrant
fortune-hunters. Trollope pokes fun at the foibles of confirmed
old maids (as opposed to the poised-for-marriage Miss
Mackenzie): women who relieve their sexual frustration in
exhibitionistic devotion to a charismatic preacher. For Trollope,
in fact, religious fervor in women is almost always linked with
some sexual maladjustment and connected with some masculine
authority figure. Thus even the zealous harridan Mrs. Proudie of
the Barsetshire novels must first unite with the slimily seductive
Mr. Slope in order to further crush her already cowed husband.
Mrs. Proudie's ultimate goal clearly is to assume the powers of
her husband's bishopric as completely as she has already

usurped his domestic authority. Mrs. Proudie represents no serious alternative to female subordination, however; if anything, she illustrates the outrages of which power-seeking women are capable. Trollope's resolutely secular concerns simply cannot allow religion as a possible source of psychologically healthy empowerment for women. Like Greg and other conservatives, he hedges any acknowledgment of piety as a factor in women's inner lives with "common-sense" qualifications and reservations. Thus Madeline Staveley's momentary flirtation with religious austerities in *Orley Farm* (1862) is the subject of Trollope's amused irony and (though perhaps not consciously on Madeline's part) an immediately successful strategy to win her parents' approval of a previously forbidden match. For Trollope, a female life that draws its main springs from piety is subject to skepticism that does not necessarily attend one organized around a man.

One might argue, however, that Craik, Yonge, and Elizabeth Sewell retain one major reservation of their own: despite their spinsters' virtues, the old maids usually offer their counsel and example to women who themselves marry. Of the books discussed here, only *The Experience of Life* is an exception to this pattern. Dinah Craik is particularly indebted to sexual conventions: Shirley Foster points out that "romantic relationships form the core of nearly all of her tales; most of her heroines accept the primacy of love."[65] Marriage is still the climax of most women's lives and a happy marriage is still the most popular reward for a good woman's virtue. The importance of these spinsters, then, is perhaps what they suggest about the possibilities of female strength. With religion replacing romantic love, and the idea of God replacing the actuality of a man, the spinster could displace men from their otherwise central position in the lives of Victorian women. As a result, although fully involved in human life and human relationships, she need not seek validation through male approval. Through their presentation of spinsters' stories, Yonge, Craik, and Elizabeth Sewell celebrate women's potential for autonomy and dignity. In their eagerness to foster female self-respect and to promote women's independent spaces, perhaps the creators of these spinster characters can be seen as unconscious allies of women whose feminist projects went far beyond their own.

NOTES

1. See Mary Lyndon Shanley, "One Must Ride Behind: Married Women's Rights and the Divorce Act of 1857," *Victorian Studies* 25 (1982): 361.

2. Martha Vicinus, *Independent Women: Work and Community for Single Women, 1850–1920* (London: Virago, 1985), 8. This work is an invaluable study of the most prominent organized means for single women to live and work together during the period. It does not concern itself, however, with the single woman on her own: the subject of this essay.

3. W.R. Greg, "Why Are Women Redundant?" *National Review* 14 (1862): 437, 436, 451.

4. W.G. Hamley, "Old Maids," *Blackwood's Edinburgh Magazine* 112 (1872): 100, 105, 107.

5. Greg, "Why Are Women Redundant?" 436.

6. Margaret Mare and Alicia C. Percival's biography of Yonge, *Victorian Bestseller: The World of Charlotte M. Yonge* (London: Harrap, 1948), provides an ample account about her contemporary popularity. Information about the careers of Dinah Craik and Elizabeth Sewell appears in Shirley Foster's *Victorian Women's Fiction: Marriage, Freedom and the Individual* (London: Croom Helm, 1985). Sally Mitchell offers a rewarding discussion of the reasons for Craik's popularity in "Sentiment, and Suffering: Women's Recreational Reading in the 1860's,"*Victorian Studies* 21 (1977): 29–45. Despite their success during their lifetimes, these authors have faded into obscurity during the twentieth century. The few recent studies of their work (in addition to those listed above) include Barbara Dennis's "The Two Voices of Charlotte Yonge," *Durham University Journal* 34 (1973): 181–88, and her "The Victorian Crisis: A Contemporary View," *Durham University Journal* 42 (1980): 27–36; David Brownell's "The Two Worlds of Charlotte Yonge," in *The Worlds of Victorian Fiction*, ed. Jerome Buckley (Harvard: Harvard University Press, 1975), 165–78; Sarah C. Ferichs's "Elizabeth Missing Sewell: Concealment and Revelation in a Victorian Everywoman," in *Approaches to Victorian Autobiography*, ed. George

Landow (Athens: Ohio University Press, 1979), 175–99; the anthology *A Chaplet for Charlotte Yonge*, ed. Georgina Battiscombe and Marghanita Laski (London: Cresset, 1965); Sally Mitchell's *Dinah Mulock Craik*, Twayne's English Authors' Series 364 (Boston: Twayne, 1983); Catherine Sandbach-Dahlstrom's *Be Good Sweet Maid: Charlotte Yonge's Domestic Fiction: A Study in Dogmatic Purpose and Fictional Form*, Stockholm Studies in English 59 (Stockholm: Almquist and Wiksell, 1984), and her "Perceiving the Single Woman: Elizabeth Sewell's *The Experience of Life*," in *Proceedings from the Second Nordic Conference for English Studies*, ed. Haan Ringbom and Matti Rissanen (Åbo Akademi, 1984), 497–504; Patrick Scott's "Genre and Perspective in the Study of Victorian Women Writers: The Case of Elizabeth Missing Sewell," *Victorian Newsletter* 66 (1984): 5–10; Valerie Saunders's "Absolutely an Act of Duty: Choice of Profession in Autobiographies of Victorian Women," *Prose Studies* 9, no. 3 (1986): 54–70; Elaine Showalter's "Dinah Mulock Craik and the Tactics of Sentiment: A Case Study in Victorian Female Authorship," *Feminist Studies* 2.2/3, (1975): 5–23; and Elliot Engel's "The Heir of the Oxford Movement: Charlotte Mary Yonge's *The Heir of Redclyffe*," *Études Anglaises* 33 (1980): 132–41. These writers also receive attention in Margaret Maison's *The Victorian Vision: Studies in the Religious Novel* (New York: Sheed and Ward, 1961); Raymond Chapman's *Faith and Revolt: Studies in the Literary Influence of the Oxford Movement* (London: Weidenfeld and Nicholson, 1970); Joseph Baker's *The Novel and the Oxford Movement* (New York; Russell and Russell, 1965); Robert Lee Woolf's *Gains and Losses: Novels of Faith and Doubt in Victorian England* (London: Garland, 1977). Claudia Nelson provides an excellent discussion of Craik's and Yonge's children's fiction in *Boys Will Be Girls: The Feminine Ethic in British Children's Fiction, 1857–1917* (New Brunswick: Rutgers University Press, 1991).

7. Although all of these authors were Anglican (Craik joined the Anglican Church after childhood in a Dissenting household), they spanned the spectrum of the Established Church. Charlotte Yonge and Elizabeth and William Sewell all wrote from a Tractarian High Church perspective, while Dinah Craik and Charles Kingsley were Broad Church latitudinarians. Similarities in religious orientation, however, prove no indicator of similarity in treatment of gender: the difference between William Sewell's and Elizabeth Sewell's novels are perhaps the most dramatic example of this.

8. Nina Auerbach, *Communities of Women: An Idea in Fiction* (Cambridge: Harvard University Press, 1978), 35.

9. Catherine Storr, "Parents," in *A Chaplet for Charlotte Yonge*, ed. Georgina Battiscombe and Margharita Laski (London: Cresset, 1965), 108.

10. Charlotte Yonge, *Hopes and Fears; or Scenes from the Life of a Spinster* (London: Parker, 1860), vol. 1, 216, 146. The richness and mutual benefit of Honor's friendship with Phoebe disproves Barbara Dennis's contention that "wherever human relationships are concerned [Honor] fails conspicuously." Dennis's comment appears in her "The Two Voices of Charlotte Yonge," *Durham University Journal* 34 (1973): 181–88.

11. Frances Power Cobbe, "What Shall We Do With Our Old Maids?" *Fraser's* 66 (1862): 595.

12. Frances Power Cobbe, "Celibacy v. Marriage," *Fraser's* 65 (1862): 232, 230, 235, 234.

13. Charlotte Yonge, *Womankind* (New York: Macmillan; London: Mozley and Smith, 1877), 6.

14. Dinah Craik, *A Woman's Thoughts About Women* (New York: Rudd and Carleton, 1858), 1, 42, 41.

15. Dinah Craik, *Olive* (London: Chapman and Hall, 1850), vol. 3, 98, 99–100.

16. Craik, *Olive*, 3: 100, 105.

17. Craik, "Miss Tommy: A Mediaeval Romance," in *Miss Tommy: A Mediaeval Romance and In a House Boat: A Journal* (New York: Harper, n.d.), 77–78.

18. Craik, "Miss Tommy," 14–15.

19. Craik, "Miss Tommy," 22, 23.

20. Mitchell, *Dinah Mulock Craik*, 93. See n. 6.

21. Craik, "Miss Tommy," 73, 78.

22. Elizabeth Sewell, *The Experience of Life; Margaret Percival: The Experience of Life*, in *A Garland Series: Victorian Fiction: Novels of Faith and Doubt* (New York: Garland, 1977), 23, 31, 199.

23. Sewell, *The Experience of Life*, 198, 200, 199.

24. Elizabeth Sewell, *The Autobiography of Elizabeth M. Sewell* (New York: Longmans, Green, and Co., 1907), 145–46.

25. Greg, "Why Are Women Redundant?" 439.

26. Cobbe, "What Shall We Do With Our Old Maids?" 598.

27. Kathleen Hickok, "The Spinster in Victoria's England: Changing Attitudes in Poetry by Women," *Journal of Popular Culture* 15

(1981): 119–20. For Susan Gorsky's comments, see her article, "Old Maids and New Women: Alternatives to Marriage in Englishwomen's Novels, 1847–1915," *Journal of Popular Culture* 7 (1973): 68–85.

28. Greg, "Why Are Women Redundant?" 437.

29. Catherine Sandbach-Dahlstrom, "Perceiving the Single Woman: Elizabeth Sewell's *The Experience of Life*," 502. See n. 6.

30. Cobbe, "Celibacy v. Marriage," 235.

31. Craik, "Miss Tommy," 174, 208, 209–10, 158, 211.

32. Craik, "Miss Tommy," 110.

33. Sewell, *The Experience of Life*, 312.

34. Sewell, *The Experience of Life*, 312–3.

35. Foster, *Victorian Women's Fiction*, 117. See n. 6.

36. Sewell, *The Experience of Life*, 312.

37. Sewell, *The Experience of Life*, 313.

38. For a full account of the considerable controversy attending the establishment of Anglican sisterhoods and the presence of Roman Catholic ones, see A.M. Allchin's *The Silent Rebellion: Anglican Religious Communities 1845–1900* (London: SCMP, 1958); Peter F. Anson's *The Call of the Cloister: Religious Communities and Kindred Bodies in the Anglican Communion* (London: SPCK, 1955); Brian Heeney's *The Women's Movement in the Church of England 1850–1930* (Oxford: Clarendon Press, 1988); Michael Hill's *The Religious Order: A Study of Virtuoso Religion and Its Legitimization in the Nineteenth-Century Church of England* (London: Heinemann, 1973).

39. Norman Vance, *The Sinews of the Spirit: The Ideal of Christian Manliness in Victorian Literature and Religious Thought* (Cambridge: Cambridge University Press, 1985), 36–41.

40. Vicinus, *Independent Women*, 63–64.

41. Susan Casteras, "Virgin Vows: The Early Victorian Artists' Portrayal of Nuns and Novices," in *Religion in the Lives of English Women, 1760–1930*, ed. Gail Malmgreen (Bloomington: Indiana University Press, 1986), 130.

42. Charles Kingsley, "The Poetry of Sacred and Legendary Art," *Fraser's* 39 (1849): 289, 287.

43. Charles Kingsley, *Yeast: A Problem, The Life and Works of Charles Kingsley in Nineteen Volumes* (London: Macmillan, 1902), 32–33.

44. Kingsley, *Yeast*, 132–33.

45. Kingsley, *Yeast*, 134.

46. Kingsley, *Yeast*, 144.

47. William Sewell, *Hawkstone*, in *A Garland Series: Victorian Fiction: Novels of Faith and Doubt* (New York: Garland, 1976), vol. 2, 325.

48. Sewell, *Hawkstone*, 2: 326, 327, 333·

49. Sewell, *Hawkstone*, 2: 327, 384, 385.

50. Sewell, *Hawkstone*, 2: 368–69, 385.

51. Frances Power Cobbe, "Female Charity—Lay and Monastic," *Fraser's* 66 (1862): 786, 787, 782, 788.

52. Vicinus, *Independent Women*, 64.

53. Dinah Craik, "On Sisterhoods,"in *About Money and Other Things: A Gift Book* (London: Macmillan, 1886), 160, 158.

54. Craik, "On Sisterhoods," 155.

55. Craik, "On Sisterhoods," 155.

56. Examples of laudable Anglican sisters occur frequently in Yonge's fiction. Sister Constance in *Pillars of the House* is a model of virtue and domestic helpfulness; nursing sisters are heroines during epidemics in *The Three Brides* and *The Trial;* endeavors to set up a sisterhood meet with full approval in *The Heir of Redclyffe*. Barbara Dennis gives other examples of favorably presented sisterhoods, and she also notes that in 1868 Yonge herself became an Exterior Sister ("Victorian Crisis": 32). See n. 6.

57. Charlotte Yonge, *Heartsease; or The Brother's Wife* (London: Parker, 1854), vol.1, 182, 100.

58. Yonge, *Heartsease,* vol 2, 281, 375.

59. Auerbach, *Communities of Women*, 81–82, 80.

60. Martin Dodsworth, "Women Without Men at Cranford," *Essays in Criticism* 13 (1963): 135, 134.

61. Auerbach, *Communities of Women*, 82–83, 84.

62. Hamley, "Old Maids," 102.

63. Richard Steele, "The Tatler: No. 126," in *The Tatler*, ed. George A. Aitken (London: Duckworth, 1899), vol. 3, 68.

64. Auerbach, *Communities of Women*, 84.

65. Foster, *Victorian Women's Fiction*, 50–51.

Women Artists at Home

Julia M. Gergits

> The rooms differ so completely; they are calm or thunderous; open on to the sea, or, on the contrary, give on to a prison yard; are hung with washing; or alive with opals and silks; are hard as horsehair or soft as feathers—one has only to go into any room in any street for the whole of that extremely complex force of femininity to fly in one's face. How should it be otherwise? For women have sat indoors all these millions of years, so that by this time the very walls are permeated with their creative force, which has, indeed, so overcharged the capacity of bricks and mortar that it must needs harness itself to pens and brushes and business and politics.[1]

Reflecting on the history of ancestral women writers, Virginia Woolf laments that almost none of the most brilliant women had the economic ability to secure privacy. Jane Austen, Woolf reminds us, wrote her novels while sitting amongst her friends and relatives in a busy parlor. Yet, despite the hardships, women have become artists, and novelists have, in turn, portrayed women artist characters undertaking the support of their own homes, not simply caring for men's homes, not ruling over the home as the proverbial angel of the house, but actually sustaining and controlling their own homes. In a sense, writers have envisaged that for some time: Charlotte and Anne Brontë, Dinah Mulock Craik, George Eliot, and Wilkie Collins present women artists wrestling for their own homes, for the right to independence and peace. Women artists who thus support themselves "unprotected" by a man violate two central Victorian tenets: that women cannot be artists and that respectable women cannot live without the guidance of fathers, brothers, or husbands. And the fictional battle for a "room of one's own" is just as difficult as the real one.[2]

It is not too strong to say that, in the nineteenth century, women were property, helpless to determine their own fate, considered too unintelligent to comprehend complex ideas, too gentle, repressed, and tender to survive in the "outer" world. As so clearly articulated by Sarah Stickney Ellis's *The Wives of England, Their Relative Duties, Domestic Influence, and Social Obligations* [3] (1844) and Coventry Patmore's "Angel in the House"[4] (1854–56), women's talents were domestic, private, and personal, unsuitable for the competitive world of commercial art. Women's intellect was thought to be derivative and imitative: if they painted, drew, or sang, they mirrored male achievements; they supposedly had no creative genius. Woolf explains, "Women have served all these centuries as looking-glasses possessing the magic and delicious power of reflecting the figure of man at twice its natural size. Without that power probably the earth would still be swamp and jungle."[5] In "Lilies: Of Queens' Gardens," John Ruskin voices the archetypal Victorian definition of women's abilities:

> . . . her intellect is not for invention or creation, but for sweet ordering, arrangement, and decision. She sees the qualities of things, their claims, and their places. Her great function is Praise: she enters no contest but infallibly judges the crown of contest. By her office, and place, she is protected from all danger and temptation. The man, in his rough work in the open world, must encounter all peril and trial. . . . But he guards the woman from all this; within his house as ruled by her, unless she herself has sought it, need enter no danger, no temptation, no cause of error or offense. This is the true nature of home—it is the place of Peace; the shelter, not only from all injury, but from all terror, doubt, and division.[6]

Ruskin connects women's supposed ability to create a home to the lack of creative genius; a "true" woman is not at all creative and certainly not a genius—she admires and judges. Since the ability to create a peaceful home is inimical to artistic genius, a woman who chooses to pursue a creative career is clearly unnatural—in violation of the God-given order of things. Women, according to Ruskin, define "home": it surrounds them naturally. If they are "good," home will be wholesome and restorative; if they are "bad," home will be endangered. Women are responsible for the nature of their homes; men are simply responsible for guarding them, ensuring the economic continuance of the "home." She does not own this home; her husband, father, or brother does. She resides "within his house"—although it is "ruled by her," she is only a caretaker.

In *Suffer and Be Still* (1972), Martha Vicinus writes that "before marriage a young girl was brought up to be perfectly innocent and sexually ignorant. . . . Once married, the perfect lady did not work; she had servants."[7] While lower-class women regularly slaved twelve hours a day as servants or factory workers, middle-and upper-class women were not supposed to work, not supposed to earn money, not supposed to support their own households. Their absence from the professional world lent credibility to class claims: few men aspiring to middle-class status would permit their wives or sisters to work. Women were to exercise their "womanly tenderness, meant by Heaven to comfort the stranger and cherish the desolate."[8] Men arranged financial security, determined where the family was to live, and secured their future; women ran the household and raised the children. Running the household was no mean feat, of course, as Rona Randall explains: "The average nineteenth-century household kept the average nineteenth-century housewife busy from morning till night, even with servants to help her. . . ."[9] Victorian women were the ornaments and ornamentors of their homes, both objects and actors, decorating their homes with endless needlework, hand-hooked rugs, painted fire screens, and lace work. While women were given considerable authority in the management of the household, this authority was delegated to them by men. True, women had a measure of freedom in deciding the arrangement of the home or its decor, but even that freedom depended upon the male's absence or willingness to let them pursue such trifles.

Of course, intelligent women fought this definitional box. Dinah Mulock Craik argues passionately against it in *A Woman's Thoughts About Women* (1861), saying that women simply had to have the right to self-support: ". . . the chief canker at the root of women's lives is want of something to do," and "in this much-suffering world, a woman who can take care of herself can always take care of other people."[10] In *Cassandra* (1928), Florence Nightingale insists that women have a call to hard and vital work, but "the stimulus, the training, the time, are all three wanting to us."[11] In a famous passage, Jane Eyre expresses the frustration of many Victorian women:

> Nobody knows how many rebellions besides political rebellions ferment in the masses of life which people earth. Women are supposed to be very calm generally: but women feel just as men feel; they need exercise for their faculties and a field for their efforts as much as their brothers do; they suffer from too rigid a restraint, too absolute a stagnation, precisely as men would suffer; and it is narrow-minded in their more privileged fellow-creatures to say that they ought to confine themselves to making puddings and knitting stockings, to playing on the piano and embroidering bags. It is thoughtless to condemn them, or laugh at them, if they seek to do more or learn more than custom has pronounced necessary for their sex.[12]

Realistically, it was simply impossible for all women to stay quietly in the house; many had to support themselves and their families. The frequent discussions of the "woman problem" and proposals for sending "excess" women abroad to find husbands reveal that even the most conservative Victorians recognized the difficulty of accommodating all women within the house.

Talented Victorian women were able to earn enough money to secure comfortable homes. Charlotte, Emily, and Anne Brontë, Elizabeth Gaskell, and George Eliot improved their families' lives considerably through their writing. In *Woman and the Demon* (1982), Nina Auerbach argues that independent women such as these formed a strong mythic center in Victorian fiction in defiance of the popular stereotype of the ideal woman:

> ... the three paradigms that animate the fictional imagina-
> tion [angel/demon, old maid, and fallen woman] are out-
> casts from domesticity, self-creating rather than selflessly
> nurturing, regal but never maternal. Solitaries by nature
> and essence, they transcend the culture that creates
> them.[13]

Women writers worked both within and without the patriarchal
system for support, and their success was tangible. The Brontës
purchased freedom from the servitude of teaching; Gaskell secured a good education for her children; Eliot guaranteed the financial security of George Henry Lewes's children and her own
family. These women were able to buy, decorate, and at least
partially control their homes. They were "angels in the house"
and breadwinners, with roles both in and out of the home, regardless of their attempts to pretend they were anonymous, inoffensive, and retiring.

Women's growing protest and assumption of professional
as well as domestic responsibilities stirred a hornet's nest of opposition, sometimes quite vicious. In *The Bourgeois Experience:
Victoria to Freud,* Peter Gay writes:

> Woman's increasingly open display of her power seemed
> the public counterpart of that private power that men
> evoked, more and more anxiously, in the second half of
> the nineteenth century: both furnished them with
> formidable arguments against woman's emancipation. For
> most males luxuriating in dominance, a woman deserting
> her assigned sphere not only became something of a freak,
> a man-woman; she also raised uncomfortable questions
> about man's own role, a role defined not in isolation, but
> in an uneasy contest with the other sex.[14]

Fictional women artists face much the same double bind as
real women. Women artist characters solve their conflict with
Victorian definitions of womanly capabilities through compromise and redefinition: they require the right to paint, sing, and
act; but they yield to the overpowering romantic code. Marriage
replaces art for nearly all women artists. In Charlotte Brontë's
Jane Eyre (1847), Anne Brontë's *Tenant of Wildfell Hall* (1848),
Dinah Craik's *Olive* (1850), Wilkie Collins's *No Name* (1862), and
George Eliot's *Daniel Deronda* (1876), a woman artist is forced by

misfortune to defy societal definitions of womanly capabilities, thereby at least temporarily unsexing herself to establish a secure home. Abandoned or driven from normal society, each painfully achieves a new identity that includes a new inner space, at least a faint image of "home." They furnish it with their own property to fulfill their needs. They do not simply decorate their family's home; they purchase, select, and sustain themselves in their own homes. Although independence supplies their homes, the home symbolizes female dependence, and the inherent contradiction causes serious conflict as the novels progress. In the end, the artistic woman, able to express and support herself, works hard to achieve independence and then decides to share her home with the man she loves, thus rejoining the patriarchal family.

Failure of the Partiarchy

Charlotte Brontë's Jane Eyre *(Jane Eyre)*, Anne Brontë's Helen Huntingdon *(The Tenant of Wildfell Hall)*, Dinah Craik's Olive Rothesay *(Olive)*, Wilkie Collins's Magdalen Vanstone *(No Name)*, and George Eliot's Mirah Lapidoth *(Daniel Deronda)* supply their own homes. Injustice or misfortune prevent their falling into typical women's roles: Jane is cast off by her relatives; Helen runs away from an adulterous, drunken husband; Olive is left to support her mother when her father dies; Magdalen loses her name and fortune when it is discovered that she and her sister are illegitimate; and Mirah runs away from a father about to sell her to a wealthy man. If it is women's birthright to be protected by men and maintained in the home, as Ruskin and Patmore insist, the patriarchy has disinherited these women. They are left with no recourse: they must supply their own homes or starve. The "fathers" fail to supply the necessary support, and the "daughters" are left to repair the loss. If there is blame, it is the fathers', not the daughters'.

Several of the women artists are betrayed or abandoned by their actual, not figurative, fathers. Olive's, Magdalen's, and Mirah's childhood homes are destroyed by their fathers, thus justifying independent reconstruction. Olive Rothesay's birth defect disgusts her father, although it is not terribly severe: "It was not a humpback, nor yet a twisted spine; it was an elevation of the shoulders, shortening the neck, and giving the appearance of a perpetual stoop." Her father recoils from her: "He shook [his wife] off angrily, looked once more at the child, and then turned away, putting his hand before his eyes, as if to shut out the sight." Far more important to Olive than her mother's equally strong abandonment, his rejection goes "deep into her child's soul." Later, in a drunken stupor, he shouts, "My daughter! how dare you call yourself so, you white-faced, mean-looking hunchback."[15] His death sets Olive free to care for her mother; they are left with little money and no extended family.

Magdalen's and Mirah's fathers sin more seriously against their daughters; these fathers violate basic social and religious laws. Although Magdalen's father is not as reprehensible as Mirah's, his sins are visited on his children's heads. Mr. Vanstone is apparently a typical country squire: "An easy, hearty, handsome, good-humoured gentleman, who walked on the sunny side of the way of life." Mr. and Mrs. Vanstone lead a bucolic life, but their sudden deaths reveal the truth: Magdalen and her sister Norah are illegitimate. The Vanstones' deaths leave the girls with no legal standing, as Mr. Pendril, the family lawyer explains: "Mr. Vanstone's daughters are Nobody's Children; and the law leaves them helpless."[16] The protective father, Mr. Vanstone, leaves his daughters with no means of support and no social or legal standing. Mirah's case is similar, although more dramatic. Her father kidnaps her, tells her that her mother and brother are dead, trains her for the stage, and, finally, tries to convince her to agree to a wealthy man's scandalous proposals, arguing that she "had a splendid offer and ought to accept it."[17] Vanstone's sin of adultery makes his daughters homeless bastards; Lapidoth's multiple sins of abandonment, kidnapping, and, finally, pimping nearly makes his daughter a whore. These daughters flee, turning away from their homes and seeking justice.

When daughters voluntarily leave their homes, it is usually to become wives, not wandering artists, yet in two of these novels, husbands or lovers fail to provide as they should, driving the women artists out of their own homes. Jane Eyre, orphaned and abandoned by Aunt Reed, is betrayed by her fiancé, Edward

Rochester. The wedding-day revelation that he already has a wife and his subsequent invitation to join him as his pretend-wife dictate her departure. Rochester tries to seduce her—"You shall yet be my wife: I am not married. . . . Never fear that I wish to lure you into error—to make you my mistress"—but she has already resolved to leave: "I must part with you for my whole life: I must begin a new existence amongst strange faces and strange scenes."[18] His sin casts her out into the night, just as surely as Helen Huntingdon is driven out by her "protector." Her husband, Arthur, is a drunken beast, determined to teach his son to be as much a "man" as he is, which means drinking, carousing, and adultery. She writes in her diary, ". . . it is not enough to say that I no longer love my husband—I HATE him!"[19] She runs away from her husband's house with only bare necessities to protect her son from his corrupting influence. Her flight is literally illegal; her husband "owns" her and her son. If he chooses, he can pursue her and force her to relinquish their son; Arthur's unfitness as a father is irrelevant in Victorian law.

Representatives of society—the fathers, lovers, and hus-bands—drive the women out into the world. The novels set up situations in which the artists must take care of themselves; it is impossible for Victorian readers to blame the women for being "unwomanly" when the men responsible for taking care of them have failed so miserably. The homes and careers that the women etch out for themselves are freed, at least temporarily, from blame.

Earning a Home through Art

With some help from adoptive fathers or brothers, the women establish new homes that are at best precariously preserved. Their resources are limited (limiting language always defines their abilities), but they are sufficient for modest homes, never on a scale of the paternal home. In various ways, these orphaned women rely on their intellect and artistic ability for salvation. It is important to understand the link between their abilities and their homes: these unnatural women, far too intelligent and in-dependent for "normal" Victorian women, must earn their peaceful homes. As products of their work and lives, their homes reflect the women's natures, talents, and state of mind. Ruskin argues that "wherever a true wife comes, this home is always round her";[20] "true" women carry "home" with them wherever they go—they cannot avoid recreating it, even when cast out on their own. Charlotte and Anne Brontë, Dinah Craik, Wilkie Collins, and George Eliot make it clear that their women artists are "true" women, despite their "manly" talents: Jane, Helen, and Olive create their own homes; Mirah discovers a woman-defined home in the Meyrick household; and Magdelan collects a "home" when she throws her lot in with her dishonest uncle and absent-minded aunt, determined to use them in her plot to regain her name.

Jane Eyre is not usually discussed as an artist, although her water-colors, pastels, and drawings are essential to the plot, and she most certainly is an author, as the first-person narrative demonstrates. To most critics, Jane is the little, fiercely independent governess relying upon her own resources after being thrown out of her aunt's family. Yet she is an artist, and a considerable one at that. Her watercolor paintings of imaginary scenes captivate Rochester; they speak of an inner life only vaguely suggested by her day-to-day demeanor. Rochester comments, ". . . you have secured the shadow of your thought; but no more, probably. You had not enough of the artist's skill and science to give it full being: yet the drawings are, for a schoolgirl, peculiar. As to the thoughts, they are elfish."[21] Jane relies on her art to provide recreation, to calm an overly excited imagination, to tame an unruly passion (her portrait of Blanche Ingram and self portrait), to remember loved ones (Rochester's portrait), and to ensure friends (portraits of cousins and of Rosamond Oliver). Art even betrays her identity and thus ensures her inheritance from her uncle: she daubs her name on a piece of sketch paper; St. John Rivers recognizes it. Thus, even if she earns her living by being a governess, she is an artist. Jane is a paradox: a quiet, tiny woman swallowed up by vast thoughts, dreams, and passions. She earns her livelihood through being a governess, but she lives in her art—at least until she falls in love with Rochester.

Jane's first real home is Rochester's mansion, Thornfield; from this home, she is cast out into the wilderness. She declares to Rochester, "I grieve to leave Thornfield: I love Thornfield—I love it, because I have lived in it a full and delightful life,—momentarily at least." Yet, when she discovers Rochester's sin, she tears herself from this comfortable home:

> Not one thought was to be given either to the past or the future. The first was a page so heavenly sweet—so deadly sad—that to read one line of it would dissolve my courage and break down my energy. That last was an awful blank: something like the world when the deluge was gone by.[22]

Her homes in exile, Moor House and the school mistress's cottage, grant her time to heal. The school mistress's house is truly a solitary home, one she decorates and tends alone, while unsuccessfully trying to become accustomed to her separation from Rochester. St. John Rivers secures the living for Jane: "Her salary will be thirty pounds a year; her house is already furnished, very simply, but sufficiently . . . " Jane's virginal home is a two-room cottage:

> My home, then,—when I at last find a home,—is a cottage: a little room with white-washed walls and a sanded floor; containing four painted chairs and a table, a clock, a cupboard, with two or three plates and dishes, and a set of tea-things in delft. Above, a chamber of the same dimensions as the kitchen, with a deal bedstead, and chest of drawers; small, yet too large to be filled with my scanty wardrobe. . . . [23]

In the wreck of her romantic hopes, Jane lands in a scrupulously clean, diminutive cottage, entirely defined and controlled by women. Her Moor House friends, the Rivers sisters, provide her with clothes and necessary toiletries. Rosamund Oliver, the wealthy, unmarried heiress, arranges the school and cottage, providing furnishings. By ironic contrast, she reminds Jane of her own orphaned condition; Rosamund is "a vision," a "perfect beauty"—"Nature had surely formed her in a partial mood; and, forgetting her usual stinted stepmother dole of gifts, had endowed this, her darling, with a granddame's bounty." Rosamund lives a pampered life, the darling of her father and the entire neighborhood; Jane certainly has not had an easy life, nor is she the darling of any doting father. Her students, all women and girls, are not entirely disappointing; even though they seem "wholly untaught, with faculties quite torpid," they improve quickly: "The rapidity of their progress, in some instances, was even surprising . . . "[24] The women combine to form a sanctuary for Jane, a place in which she can heal, maybe even forget, her wounds:

> To live amidst general regard, though it be but the regard of working-people, is like 'sitting in sunshine, calm and sweet:' serene inward feelings bud and bloom under the ray. At this period of my life my heart far oftener swelled with thankfulness than sank with dejection. . . .[25]

In this scrupulously clean house, protected by a fire against the winter cold, however, Jane is intensely lonely, rushing "into strange dreams at night: dreams many-coloured, agitated, full of the ideal, the stirring, the stormy . . . " The cottage represents a serious social fall for Jane; she has gone from living in a grand mansion, the well-trained governess of a wealthy child, tutoring her in French and English, painting and reading widely to living in a two-room cottage, the teacher of lower-class women, focusing on plain sewing, personal hygiene, and basic reading and writing. Thornfield offered huge, grandly decorated rooms—and love; her cottage offers tiny, sparsely furnished rooms—and "regard." Instead of a "many-coloured" existence, she has routine and a "scoured floor, polished grate, and well-rubbed chairs."[26]

This cottage is only a temporary home, despite Jane's reflections that it may be her final home. She begins to paint again, this time a portrait of Rosamund; subconsciously she paints her name on a scrap of paper. St. John's discovery of her name and identity reinstates her in the patriarchy: inheriting her uncle's money enables her to behave "independently"—but the money simply places her safely back into the patriarchal organization. She proclaims to St. John that she will share her inheritance and live with her cousins: "I never had a home, I never had brothers or sisters; I must and will have them now."[27] The discovery pulls her out of her maidenly retreat and pushes her to marriage with either St. John or Rochester. She does, of course, marry for "love," but she is no longer independent.

Like Jane Eyre, Helen Huntingdon (*The Tenant of Wildfell Hall*) marries for love, but her story is not "happy ever after"; the story of her first marriage, captured in the journal she gives to Gilbert Markham, is one of disillusionment and enforced hiding. When Helen first appears in the novel, she has assumed a false identity and veiled her relationship to her brother, Frederick Lawrence, to ensure that her husband will not find her. Unlike Jane, Helen earns her living from her paintings; she is truly an independent artist, using her wits to sustain herself and her son in exile. She is a work-a-day artist, a practical painter with an eye for what will suit her customers. She spends a great deal of time searching for appropriate scenes, dragging her art equipment up steep escarpments, across fields, and down hills. Her art fascinates Gilbert Markham, soon to fall in love with this supposed widow; he describes one of her works: "It was a view of Wildfell Hall, as seen at early morning from the field below, rising in dark relief against a sky of clear, silvery blue, with a few red streaks on the horizon, faithfully drawn and coloured, and very elegantly and artistically handled." He is surprised when she says she sells the works, but she retorts, "I cannot afford to paint for my own amusement."[28] Helen notes in her diary that she plans to earn her keep proudly and openly:

> I am working hard to repay my brother for all his expenses on my account. . . . I shall have so much more pleasure in my labour, my earnings, my frugal fare, and household economy, when I know that I am paying my way honestly, and that what little I possess is legitimately all my own; and that no one suffers for my folly—in a pecuniary way at least. . . .[29]

Ironically, she is incorrect in assuming that what she earns is "legitimately all" her own; legally, everything she earns is her husband's property. Caught up in the illusion of escape, she forgets just how tightly she is bound to Arthur Huntingdon.

Her sanctuary is a few rooms reclaimed from the ruins of Wildfell Hall, her family's ancestral home. Time, history, and weather have invaded Wildfell Hall. Wilderness, in "bilberry plants and heather," is reclaiming the grounds. Wildfell Hall is a "superannuated mansion of the Elizabethan era, built of dark grey stone"; Gilbert thinks it looks "cold and gloomy enough to inhabit, with its thick stone mullions and little latticed panes, its time-eaten airholes, and its too lonely, too unsheltered situation."[30] The old mansion is an appropriate symbol of Helen's life. Her marriage is only rubble and ruin; she has reclaimed a few clean, weatherproof rooms by dint of hard work and stubbornness. Weather and ruin are literally at her doorstep, even at her inner doors; she is "too lonely" and in an "unsheltered situation," susceptible to neighborhood gossip, in eminent danger of losing her son. However, she views Wildfell Hall more positively than Gilbert; her first view of the home reveals glimmers of hope within the destruction:

> We entered the desolate court, and in breathless anxiety surveyed the ruinous mass. Was it all blackness and desolation? No; one faint red glimmer cheered us from a window where the lattice was in good repair. . . . Besides the kitchen there were two bedrooms, a good-sized parlour, and another smaller one, which I destined for my studio, all well aired and seemingly in good repair, but only partly furnished with a few old articles, chiefly of ponderous black oak—the veritable ones that had been there before, and which had been kept as antiquarian relics in my brother's present residence. . . . [31]

She is happy here: ". . . each separate object seemed to echo back my own exhilarating sense of hope and freedom."[32] Wildfell Hall is a practical yet romantic space, resonating with personal history, an ancient mansion reclaimed from destruction. It restores her to her brother, Frederick, and allows her to weave a fiction of a new life freed from Arthur; in a sense, she rediscovers her childhood.

Her studio is the homiest room, exuding industry and creativity, encapsulating her past and present. Gilbert and his sister are shown into this room:

> To our surprise, we were ushered into a room where the first object that met the eye was a painter's easel, with a table beside it covered with rolls of canvas, bottles of oil and varnish, palette, brushes, paints, etc. Leaning against the wall were several sketches in various stages of pro-

gression, and a few finished paintings—mostly of land-
scapes and figures. [33]

To sit down, they are forced to clear chairs of their "artistical
lumber that usurped them." Helen's studio is the only room
regularly warmed with a fire; here, she spends many peaceful
hours. Her studio suggests light and industry, looking out onto
the open air (as it must to serve as a studio). Here, she works off
her debt to her brother and pretends that her husband no longer
exists. Her studio holds clues to her past: portraits of her son and
Arthur as a young man before she discovered his weaknesses.
Gilbert studies both portraits but does not yet know the truth.
He notes that Arthur's portrait was clearly an early work, with
"far more careful minuteness of detail," and observes that the
sitter "was prouder of his beauty than his intellect." Helen snaps
that touring her studio without permission "*is* an act of very
great impertinence,"[34] thus annoying Gilbert. He takes an un-
warranted liberty in this female sanctuary when he assumes the
right to look at and judge her works—and by implication, her
life. His unintentional unearthing of her past indicates the
fragility of her sanctuary; she cannot count on remaining
anonymous. This home will not last.

As Jane's governess's cottage was a downfall, Wildfell Hall
indicates a social fall, but Helen does not care: in fact, she rejoices
in her haven. This old mansion, her old ancestral home, is her
sanctuary from her husband's obscene influence. Wildfell Hall is
an island in the middle of desolation, a relatively safe place for a
shipwrecked woman and her son. Here, her husband cannot
trace her; he cannot take her son. She believes she can start again,
rebuilding her life, just as she has rejuvenated a few rooms in the
mansion. The well-meaning community soon ruins her peace by
spreading rumors about her supposedly shameful relationship
with Lawrence, and her husband's illness recalls her to her
"duty." Her return to Arthur not only enables her to marry
Gilbert without guilt when her first husband drinks himself to
death, but allows her to pay for the "sin" of demanding independence and freedom from persecution and for daring to create
a home of her own.

Dinah Craik's *Olive* also offers an independent woman
artist. Unlike Jane or Helen, however, Olive becomes a real artist,

a genius devoted to her art, at least as long as she maintains her virginal naiveté. Jane and Helen know sexual love before they seek independence; their homes are havens from the turbulence of romantic disappointment. Olive has been cut out of romance by her deformity; no man, the narrator tells us, would marry a hunchback. She seeks an independent home because she has no other option; she must make a home for her mother and herself.

After her father's death, she takes an apartment under Vanbrugh, a crotchety genius who does not believe women can paint:

> I am not such a fool as to say that genius is of either sex, but it is an acknowledged fact that no woman ever was a great painter, poet, or musician. Genius, the mighty one, does not exist in weak female nature, and even if it did, custom and education would certainly stunt its growth.[35]

His sister brings Olive into his notice. Olive proclaims, "Woman as I am, I will dare all things—endure all things. Let me be an artist!" The narrator explains that Olive's genius is "nearly" a man's; she does not paint "mere prettinesses" but reaches for the greatness of Michelangelo. Because of her deformity, she is free to focus her energy: "But sometimes chance or circumstance or wrong, sealing up her woman's nature, converts her into a self-dependent human soul. Instead of life's sweetnesses, she has before her life's greatnesses."[36] This artist seeks an instructor, Michael Vanbrugh, and a career that will fulfill her ambitions—as well as providing additional income. Her home will be enriched by her work.

After her father's death, she takes her mother to Woodford Cottage in a quiet part of London:

> It was the queerest of all queer abodes, was Woodford Cottage. The entrance-door and the stable-door stood side by side; and the cellar-staircase led out of the drawing-room. The direct way from the kitchen to the dining-room, was through a suite of sleeping apartments; and the staircase, apparently cut of the wall, had a beautiful little break-neck corner, which seemed made to prevent any one who once ascended from ever descending alive. Certainly, the contriver of Woodford Cottage must have

had some slight twist of the brain, which caused the
building to partake of the same unpleasant convolution.[37]

Like Olive, who is twisted from birth, this house seems quite
lopsided and uncomfortable, yet the narrator insists that
"altogether, the house was a grand old house—just suited for a
dreamer, a poet, or an artist." The maker of the house, like
Olive's maker, had a peculiar sense of humor. He produced an
illogical, circuitous house, with no privacy and inconvenient
corners, yet, although Olive and her mother are considerably
poorer than they were, they "feel cheerful—even happy" here in
solitude and peace. With her artistic instincts, Olive enlivens the
old cottage, making it vibrant with flowers and drawings. She
becomes indispensable to the Vanbrughs, her landlords: "Miss
Rothesay was needed everywhere; first in the painting-room, to
assist in arranging its various treasures, her taste and tact assist-
ing Mr. Vanbrugh's artistic skill."[38]

Later, her successful sale of paintings affords them modest
luxury; she tames the gardens: "Trim it is not, and never would
be—thanks to Olive. . . . But its wild luxuriance is that of flowers,
not weeds. . . " And their home is brighter: "Its once gloomy bar-
renness has been softened by many a graceful adjunct of comfort
and luxury. Half of it, by means of a crimson screen, is transformed into a painting-room."[39] Olive is so happy here that she
forgets her birth defect; she studies her craft under Vanbrugh; he
arranges for her first sale. She does not venture out from Woodford Cottage, selling her works from her flat, meeting patrons
and negotiating with agents here. Her work enables her to live in
comfort, in fact to repair the damage her father did: she repays
his debts. She replaces the patriarchal breadwinner and hearth-
provider quite well, adjusting to her position deftly. The narrator
insists on Olive's modesty and womanly goodness, but it is clear
that Olive creates a full life; she does not notice that she is missing romantic love.

This life is interrupted when Vanbrugh suddenly becomes
fashionable; affluence encourages him to go to Rome—which he
does. Thus, a surrogate father figure once again fails the two
women, and they leave for a country house. Olive describes part
of it for her blind mother:

It is a charming sleeping-room, with its white draperies, and its old oak furniture; and the quaint pier-glass, stuck round with peacocks' feathers, country fashion. And there, mamma, are some prints—a "Raising of Lazarus," though not quite so grand as my beloved "Sebastian del Piombo." And here are views from my own beautiful Scotland—a "Highland Lock," and "Edinburgh Castle"; and oh, mamma! there is grand old "Stirling," the place where I was born! Our good fairy might have known the important fact . . . [40]

Olive observes closely. Although this home is not of their own design, it is home, at least for a while. It has "country" details—the Rothesays are from the country. The cottage reminds Olive of her birthplace. This temporary home is a link between her past and future, although she does not realize it. Here "had dawned a new era in her life." Rejected by her Scottish father, left to support her mother after his death, devoted to "Art," Olive discovers romantic love here; she rejoins the patriarchy, abandons art, and accepts her lover's motherless daughter as her own. Only in London, in the odd cottage, does she maintain her determination to be an artist. As soon as she rejoins the country, i.e. "nature," she finds Harold Gwynne and his daughter—love, marriage, and motherhood. Instead of an independent artist, she becomes a "true woman"—"with her clinging sweetness, her upward gaze";[41] she nestles in his strong bosom and forgets art. The small independent space does not last.

George Eliot's and Wilkie Collins's artists are more problematic, even more confused and confusing than the Brontës' or Craik's. Eliot's Mirah in *Daniel Deronda* seems passive, lifeless, unable to make her own decisions, determined to "do good" and to obey Deronda or her brother. In Collins's *No Name*, Magdalen is set on revenge; she is aggressive, defiant, and "unwomanly." Mirah's and Magdalen's homes in patriarchal exile reflect their very different personalities and conflicts. Mirah is succored by the Meyrick women, who willingly take her in on Deronda's recommendation. The Meyrick women are truly independent: they support themselves while Hans, the only son, wanders around Europe trying to find his niche. Magdalen runs away from her upright sister and governess to set her plan of revenge in motion;

her exiled home is make-shift and absurd, a mockery of "home." Mirah is too passive, Magdalen too aggressive.

Mirah's singing voice is small, not strong enough for a grand career, although Eliot tells us she is a true artist; Mrs. Meyrick adds that she is a "pearl: the mud has only washed her." Mirah is altogether diminutive with "tiny rings" of hair, "delicate nostrils, and "little feet and hands"; even her voice is small and childish: "It was the sort of voice that gives the impression of being meant like a bird's wooing for an audience near and beloved." Klesmer, the great composer, judges her "a true musician" who "will do: if she doesn't attempt too much and her voice holds out, she can make an income." Her motivation for professional singing is solely to gain independence; she is not ambitious, unlike Gwendolyn Harleth or Deronda's mother, who left him to be brought up by a casual lover to pursue her career unimpeded. Mirah will always do her duty; as Mrs. Meyrick explains, "It is not her nature to run into planning and devising: only to submit."[42]

Deronda deposits Mirah in the Meyrick home, an entirely female domicile, in which all Meyrick women paint, write, or sew to support the household. Mirah is not responsible for the household, but the Meyrick women are. Brother Hans is clearly too irresponsible to help them sustain themselves. Eliot describes their impoverished household, with its little people and industrious lives:

> [The Meyricks] all clung to this particular house in a row because its interior was filled with objects always in the same places, which for the mother held memories of her marriage time, and for the young ones seemed as necessary and uncriticised a part of their world as the stars of the Great Bear seen from the back windows. . . . The chairs and tables were also old friends preferred to new. But in these two little parlours with no furniture that a broker would have cared to cheapen except the prints and piano, there was space and apparatus for a wide-glancing, nicely select life, open to the highest things in music, painting, and poetry.[43]

Although the Meyricks are tiny ("All four, if they had been wax-work, might have been packed easily in a fashionable lady's travelling trunk"),[44] they are hard-working artists, determined to remain independent. Their house matches their limited abilities and diminutive bodies, but they are good-hearted and generous. They keep their old prints and furniture, as wealthier families keep valuable heirlooms; they work hard together, collaborating in making a comfortable life. Like Sleeping Beauty finding the dwarves, Mirah finds a comfortable home with these little women artists.

In *Daniel Deronda*, female accomplishments seem terribly small: the Meyricks' home is poor and ill-furnished; their skills barely sufficient to sustain even a modest lifestyle. Herr Klesmer's visit reinforces this impression: "But when he entered, the rooms shrank into closets, the cottage piano, Mab thought, seemed a ridiculous toy, and the entire family existence as petty and private as an establishment of mice in the Tuileries." The life of these hard-working female artists is insignificant, unimportant, trivial. His is the world of "a multitudinous audience";[45] theirs is the world of toy pianos and dolls. They are playing; he is doing.

Their home is secure, but not a permanent place for Mirah, who leaves them when her brother, Mordecai, is discovered. Much like the Rivers sisters' rescue of Jane Eyre after her flight from Rochester, the Meyricks supply a female-defined and defended space while she recovers from her shock. As tiny as the Meyricks, she fits in comfortably and sees nothing absurd or limiting in the household's ambitions. Inspired by their example, Mirah asks Deronda to help her get employment so she can be as independent as the Meyricks, but she is a passive agent, using her art only as required for sustenance. Men control her fate: she follows her father until he violates her morality; she follows Daniel's dictates until Mordecai reclaims her; she follows Mordecai's guidance until his death; and, of course, she will be a dutiful wife to Daniel. Except for her brief stay with the Meyricks, her "home" is always defined by men.

No Name pivots on the loss of home and the impossibility of reclaiming it; the emphasis is on naming and ownership, on inequity and inequality. The artist, Magdalen Vanstone, seeks vengeance for the loss of her name and fortune; her uncle has effectively dispossessed her and her sister Norah. Magdalen determines to repair the loss by forcing him or his hapless son to give up their inheritance. Magdalen is a born actress, a dangerous talent in typical Victorian wisdom, since actresses verged on fallen women and were seldom accepted into "good" society. Her protector, Miss Garth, reflects, "Magdalen, in the capacity of a thoughtless girl, was comparatively easy to deal with. Magdalen, in the character of a born actress, threatened serious future difficulties." Her first attempts are a stunning success: "By a dexterous piece of mimicry, she had made a living reality of one of the most insipid characters in the English drama; and she had roused to enthusiasm an audience of two hundred exiles from the blessings of ventilation. . . . " After her parents' death, she uses this ability to earn money, to barge into her cousin's presence unrecognized, and to trick her cousin into marrying her. She ruthlessly manipulates her talents to gain an end that the narrator defines as unladylike, unnatural, and sheer madness. When her "husband" dies, however, she pays richly for her sins: "She had never felt the means taken to accomplish her end so unutterably degrading to herself, as she felt them on the day when the end was reached."[46] This artist is driven to misuse her talents, and her "home" reflects this aberration.

As noted, it is the loss of the paternal home that initiates Magdalen's criminal behavior. While she plans her revenge, she takes refuge with her criminal half-uncle and his idiot wife. Although they provide an effective cover-story, she provides the money required for the "home." Their poor rooms are hers. They live in the "front parlor" of a dilapidated house when she first encounters them; her uncle places her in "the spare-room, the landlady's spare-room, on the third floor front."[47] It is a sad room for Magdalen:

> The room was small, close, and very poorly furnished. In former days, Miss Garth would have hesitated to offer such a room to one of the servants, at Combe-Raven. But it was quiet; it gave her a few minutes alone; and it was endurable, even welcome, on that account. She locked herself in; and walked mechanically, with a woman's first impulse in a strange bedroom, to the rickety little table, and the dingy little looking-glass.[48]

She has embarked on a journey that will degrade her even further than this room suggests. It indicates merely the beginning of her downward slide into revenge: she assumes false characters to gain information, lies to her enemies, and tricks her most hated relative into marrying her. Her little dingy room suggests that she has fallen very far from the ladylike Miss Vanstone of Combe-Raven. The dingy mirror reflects her misery and compulsion: she has accepted degradation; her goal, theoretically, justifies her means. She knows her plot is evil, yet she cannot resolve to leave it. The artist with No Name can have no "home" until she has taken revenge or, perhaps, died; her resting places after the dissolution of her home are depressing temporary, poorly furnished rooms that are an affront to a lady—dirty, noisy, scantily furnished, impersonal. To avoid questioning, Magdalen and her relatives must stay at places that are far less than honorable. Magdalen had always been a pampered favorite of wealthy parents; her room was richly furnished, full of dainty objects and luxurious toiletries. She is reduced to borrowing necessary personal items from her weak-minded aunt and securing the protection of her scoundrel uncle.

Her independence is involuntary; her revenge is compulsory—she cannot stop seeking the destruction of her uncle or cousin. This terribly unladylike goal makes her "homes" completely unhomelike; for a time, she behaves as a siren or witch, tempting and manipulating men—her uncle and Noel Vanstone—to gain her ends. Ruskin's argument that the true woman carries "home" everywhere she goes is pertinent; Magdalen cannot find "home" because she has violated her womanly nature. Until she has paid for her crimes, she can find no peace. Interestingly, Collins does not punish Magdalen very severely for her determination to get revenge. She does sink into depression; her sister and friend Miss Garth do abandon her temporarily when Magdalen tricks her cousin into marriage; and she does become seriously ill after her successful plot. Yet she also recovers and gains the love of an upright man, and her sister restores their name and inheritance. Her independent "homes" may have been dishonorable and damaging to the reputation of a lady, but she rebounds after her illness, supposedly contrite and prepared to rejoin the respectable male-dominated world.

Conclusion

The conflict between the women artists' lifestyles and society is sharp, and Charlotte and Anne Brontë, Dinah Mulock Craik, George Eliot, and Wilkie Collins strive to justify their artists' un-ladylike strength. These women, even hunch-backed Olive and mild Mirah, are powerful artists, striking other characters with their talents and strength. To nervous Victorians, this indepen-dence and creative power need careful explanation and defense; womanly power is normally inexcusable, so the authors create abnormal situations in which women are free to exercise their strength. Because men have failed these women, they must com-pensate by doing everything: conduct a career and create a home. The authors assure the readers that the women's homes and careers are unthreatening: the solitary women artists gener-ally do not succeed as well materially as they might within the patriarchy as married women or pampered daughters. The artists' homes are smaller, more barren (literally and figura-tively), less secure, and readily abandoned as soon as "good" men volunteer to marry them. Most of the descriptive details are limiting or indicate impoverishment ("small," "tiny," "ill-fur-nished," "deal chairs," "toy piano," "dingy mirror"); none of these women becomes wealthy on her own. Only male-domi-nated homes offer wealth and plenty. Women artists, however, juggle the supposedly separate spheres competently. Although they seem embedded in poverty or captured in smallness, they generally describe their independent lives as happy and fulfill-ing. For a while, at least, they do not miss the "protection" of men; Jane, Helen, Olive, Mirah, and Magdalen become absorbed in their work, generally ignoring the blandishments of various men to quit working for marriage. They refuse marriage or en-tombment in various "safe" refuges in order to pursue their goals until there is nothing left to prove: the author need not pro-long the artists' solitary lives once they have proven that they can survive on their own; although marriages end each woman's career, they no longer need to demonstrate their genius. They are clearly brilliant women willingly abandoning their careers for the men they love; all the credit goes to the women, little to the men. Modern readers may take exception to the stereotypical endings, but it is important not to underestimate the importance of the heroines' careers and independent homes; marriage does not eradicate the earlier non-traditional lives and careers.

Jane, Helen, Olive, Mirah, and Magdalen are different from run-of-the-mill Victorian heroines. Yes, other heroines lose their homes, and others contend with evil fathers. Victorian literature is full of cruel fathers; fleets of irresponsible parents occupy Victorian literature (Dickens's novels, for example, are replete with them). Yet, unlike the usual heroine, the woman artist is not a passive pawn; she is an intelligent, active character, determined to make a comfortable home for herself when men have failed. She does not die or quietly accept whatever men wish to foist off on her; she chooses among options intelligently and acts according to her conscience. When she is hurt, she shakes loose from passivity and determines a course of action, which includes finding or making surrogate homes, freed at least temporarily from patriarchy.

NOTES

1. Virginia Woolf, *A Room of One's Own* (New York: Harcourt, Brace and Jovanovich, 1929), 91.

2. The list of distinguished feminist critics who have commented on the trials of talented, intelligent heroines is quite long. For further reading, however, the following are extremely useful: Lynne Agress, *The Feminine Irony: Women on Women in Early-Nineteenth Century English Literature* (Rutherford, NJ: Fairleigh Dickinson University Press, 1978); Sandra M. Gilbert and Susan Gubar, *The Madwoman in the Attic: The Woman Writer and the Nineteenth-Century Imagination* (New Haven: Yale University Press, 1979); Jean E. Kennard, *Victims of Convention* (Hamden, CT: Shoestring Press, 1978); Ellen Moers, *Literary Women* (New York: Doubleday, 1976); Judith Lowder Newton, *Women, Power, and Subversion: Social Strategies in British Fiction, 1778–1860* (New York: Methuen, 1981); Susan Siefert, *The Dilemma of the Talented Heroine: A Study in Nineteenth-Century Fiction* (St. Albans, VT: Edens, 1979); Patricia Meyer Spacks, *The Female Imagination* (New York: Knopf, 1975); Elaine

Showalter, *A Literature of Their Own* (Princeton: Princeton University Press, 1977).

3. Sarah Stickney Ellis, *The Wives of England, Their Relative Duties, Domestic Influence, and Social Obligations* (New York: n.p., 1844).

4. Coventry Patmore, *The Angel in the House,* in *Poems,* ed. Basil Channeys (London: Bell, 1921).

5. Woolf, *Room of One's Own,* 35.

6. John Ruskin, "Lilies: Of Queens' Gardens," in *Essays English and American* (New York: Collier, 1910), 145.

7. Martha Vicinus, ed., *Suffer and Be Still: Women in the Victorian Age* (Bloomington: Indiana University Press, 1972), ix.

8. John Ruskin, "On Domestic Art," in *The Lamp of Beauty: Writing on Art by John Ruskin,* ed. Joan Evans (Ithaca, NY: Cornell University Press, 1959), 115.

9. Rona Randall, *The Model Wife, Nineteenth-Century Style* (London: Herbert, 1989), 48.

10. Dinah Mulock Craik, *A Woman's Thoughts About Women* (Philadelphia: T. B. Peterson and Brothers, 1861), 11, 34.

11. Florence Nightingale, "Excerpts from *Cassandra,*" in *The Norton Anthology of English Literature,* vol. 2 (New York: Norton, 1971), 1649.

12. Charlotte Brontë, *Jane Eyre,* ed. Richard J. Dunn (New York: Norton, 1971), 96.

13. Nina Auerbach, *Woman and the Demon: The Life of a Victorian Myth* (Cambridge: Harvard University Press, 1984), 61–62.

14. Peter Gay, *The Bourgeois Experience: Victoria to Freud,* vol. 1 (New York: Oxford University Press, 1984), 169.

15. Dinah Mulock Craik, *Olive,* 3 vols. (New York: Garland, 1975), 1: 57, 58, 210.

16. Wilkie Collins, *No Name,* ed. Virginia Blain (New York: Oxford University Press, 1986), 2, 98.

17. George Eliot, *Daniel Deronda,* ed. Barbara Hardy (New York: Penguin, 1967), 259.

18. Brontë, *Jane Eyre,* 267.

19. Anne Brontë, *The Tenant of Wildfell Hall,* ed. G. D. Hargreaves (New York: Penguin, 1979), 318.

20. Ruskin, "Lilies," 146.

21. Brontë, *Jane Eyre,* 111.

22. Brontë, *Jane Eyre*, 222, 282.

23. Brontë, *Jane Eyre*, 312, 315.

24. Brontë, *Jane Eyre*, 319, 322.

25. Brontë, *Jane Eyre*, 322.

26. Brontë, *Jane Eyre*, 323, 326.

27. Brontë, *Jane Eyre*, 341.

28. Brontë, *Wildfell Hall*, 68, 69.

29. Brontë, *Wildfell Hall*, 397–98.

30. Brontë, *Wildfell Hall*, 45.

31. Brontë, *Wildfell Hall*, 396.

32. Brontë, *Wildfell Hall*, 397.

33. Brontë, *Wildfell Hall*, 68.

34. Brontë, *Wildfell Hall*, 68, 70, 71.

35. Craik, *Olive*, 2:45.

36. Craik, *Olive*, 2: 52, 55.

37. Craik, *Olive*, 2: 3.

38. Craik, *Olive*, 2: 4, 5, 82–83.

39. Craik, *Olive*, 2: 298.

40. Craik, *Olive*, 2: 164–65.

41. Craik, *Olive*, 2: 168, 375.

42. Eliot, *Daniel Deronda*, 264, 422–23, 543, 265.

43. Eliot, *Daniel Deronda*, 237.

44. Eliot, *Daniel Deronda*, 238.

45. Eliot, *Daniel Deronda*, 539.

46. Collins, *No Name*, 38, 42, 444.

47. Collins, *No Name*, 147.

48. Collins, *No Name*, 151.

Female Acquisition in
The Spoils of Poynton

Sandra Kumamoto Stanley

Henry James's *donnée* for *The Spoils of Poynton* (1897) originated from "a small and ugly matter": the legal case between, on the one side, a young Scottish man who, at the death of his father, had inherited his parents' "rich old house" and, on the other side, his mother who had taken valuable treasures from the house. In his *Notebooks*, James writes: "It presents a very fine case of the situation in which, in England, there has *always* seemed to me to be a story—the situation of the mother *deposed*, by the ugly English custom, turned out of the big house on the son's marriage and relegated. One can imagine the rebellion, in this case (the case I should build on the above hint) of a particular sort of proud woman—a woman who had *loved* her home, her husband's home and hers (with a knowledge and adoration of artistic beauty, the tastes, the habits of a collector)."[1] Indeed, the case James cited actually reflected the attitude of more than one rebellious, proud woman toward an "ugly English custom"; in the late 1800s many people agitated to allow married women the right to own and handle their property, and their fight resulted in the passing of the Married Women's Property Acts (1870–1908). But when James wrote his actual novel, his conception for his *Spoils* underwent a significant change. Although James, in his fiction, had the opportunity to pit his rebellious woman, Mrs. Gereth, against the patriarchal forces of the legal system that propagated such an "ugly English custom," or even the masculine force represented in her son, Owen Gereth, James chose to pit Mrs. Gereth against another woman: her son's fiancée, the Philistine Mona Brigstock. In one stroke, James transformed this potential tale of male power into a tale of female acquisition. Moreover, James is quite critical of these two acquisitive women, for his novel highlights the danger of the desire for possession, which as Fred See notes, always involves the act of entrapment, of "one will [attempting] to circumscribe and use another."[2] Thus, paradoxically, at a time in which married women were seeking independence—specifically, the right to handle their own property—James writes a novel in which a woman's desire for possession signifies a corrupting desire for the control and despoilment of the independent will. James's change indicates a corresponding conflict adumbrating the social and economic tensions of Victorian England; although James realizes the injustice done to Mrs. Gereth, he ultimately defends the underlying traditions of ownership which have betrayed this woman who loved "the rich old house."

For a number of women in the Victorian era, female acquisition signified economic liberation. Political activists in England were attempting to reshape the master narratives of the politics, law, and economics of their own culture, to redefine a woman's place in relationship to society, and especially, in relationship to property. Thirty years before the publication of *Spoils*, John Stuart Mill, in his classic work *The Subjection of Women*, argued that women historically had been rendered morally and economically dependent upon men, and that the present law concerning women discriminated against, if not enslaved, them. Mill's argument was also articulated by a number of activists such as Elizabeth Clarke Wolstenholme, Josephine Grey Butler, and Emilia Jessie Boucherett. Married women, especially, were vulnerable to the law which reflected the common assumption that the husband held dominion over the wife. As Sir William Blackstone stated, "In law husband and wife are one person, and the husband is that person." Because such a legal assumption concerning married women relegated them to a weak and subordinate position, many feminists agreed that the first platform of the woman's charter should be the reform of the married woman's property law. Such a charge reflected the changing social, economic and philosophic tenets of the time. One of the central principles of nineteenth-century liberalism espoused the value of individual freedom and natural human rights, which, according to John Locke, included life, liberty, *and* property. Moreover, feminists perceived a clear connection between the institution of private property and the institutionalized inferiority of women. The existing institutions sought to protect not a woman's but a man's right to private property. How was a woman protected? Conventional society would answer: she was protected by the patriarchal ideal, the paternalistic traditional family unit. But that paternalistic ideal, if it ever existed, was under siege. In the first place, the economic realities of the industrialized nineteenth century saw the crumbling of small family-based enterprises and the rise of commercial industries. In the second place, feminists, as well as others, were asking why should the patriarchal ideal, which was based on an authoritarian and hierarchical model, be the ideal? Society itself was evolving toward an individualistic and democratic model. Influenced by social Darwinism, many feminists believed society was evolving from an atavistic male-dominated society to a civilized equality-based society—from status to contract. The call for the reform of the English common-law which deprived wives of the right to own and control property culminated in the success of the 1882 Married Women's Property Act.[3]

Others, however, feared that female acquisition could also signify economic subjugation, for as the middle class became increasingly wealthy, more and more women, delegating chores to the servant class, played the status-conscious role of the idle wife of leisure and functioned, as one early British critic noted, not as contributors to, but parasites on, the family unit.[4] A number of American feminists agreed with their British sisters. In 1898, just a year after James published his novel, Charlotte Perkins Gilman, in *The Economic Relations between Men and Women,* would warn that in seeking the status of the idle bourgeois wife, women would ultimately trap themselves within their own ostensible social privileges. She writes: "For the woman there is . . . no relation maintained between what she does produce and what she consumes. She is forbidden to make, but encouraged to take. Her industry is not the natural output of creative energy, not the work she does because she has the inner power and strength to do it; nor is her industry even the measure of her gain. She has, of course, the natural desire to consume; and to that is set no bar save the capacity or the will of her husband."[5] Gilman recognizes the oppressive forces of religiously and socially sanctioned institutions (including marriage) which would forbid a woman to make and encourage her to take. In one lecture, Gilman, portraying domestic servitude, compares the economically subjugated mother to a "she-hornbill, who while in her nest, is all walled in by mud, with only her big beak protruding; and into this the he-hornbill puts the food to sustain her."[6] Here, the woman's very nest—her house—and her passivity become her means of entrapment. Gilman, however, also warns that women are responsible for their subjugation, for a "woman as non-productive consumer" is not far from a "woman as parasite"—a completely economically dependent woman. Gilman posits her "woman as consumer" theory, however, in order to urge women to assert their political and economic will—as a means of liberation, not entrapment. The female desire for acquisition and consumption is only a danger if it lulls her into economic subjugation, preventing her from becoming a maker, instead of a taker, a producer, instead of a consumer. For her part, Charlotte Gilman urged women that the true standard of women's progress would not be the vote, but rather "economic equality and freedom."

Given the nineteenth-century discussion on "the woman question," I find James's fictional exploration of women and property revealing. In *Spoils*, female acquisition is a metaphor neither for economic freedom, on the one hand, nor for economic subjugation, on the other hand; instead, it signifies narcissistic desire, the desire to remake the world in one's own image. By attempting to challenge her son's right to ownership, the "wronged" woman, Mrs. Gereth, becomes the perpetrator of wrongs, the acquisitive woman who will sacrifice motherhood for ownership. Although James's reason for writing his novel was initiated by his sense of injustice done to the mother, in the end, Mrs. Gereth, in insisting upon her right to have her "things," becomes a symbol of a failed mother, the mother who values her "things" rather than her son. In a time of changes which threaten traditional patriarchal values, James, despite his initial sympathies, ultimately defends the status quo, reinforcing, rather than challenging, traditional values concerning ownership and property. In fact, throughout much of the work, Owen's right to the property will constitute one of the prevailing social virtues of the novel.

Of course, James has long been critical of characters—both male and female—who are driven by their acquisitive desire; such characters all too often treat individuals as commodities and treat commodities as signifiers for both social and, even, transcendental power. As Donald Mull has observed, this "objectification of persons and personification of objects "is linked to what James has described as the 'business imagination': the self is defined by the things it possesses. In James's boyhood, his father denigrated the business imagination, and, instead, exalted what one might call the 'converting imagination,' in which the self, through the imaginative apprehension of things, transforms experience into social virtue." As Mull further notes, Henry James, Sr., in his article "Socialism and Civilization," had harsh words for the concept of ownership: "We degrade by owning and just in the degree of our owning. . . . We degrade and disesteem every person we own absolutely, every person bound to us by any other tenure than his own spontaneous affection."[7]

Certainly, much of James, Jr.'s attitudes toward acquisition is tinged by James, Sr.'s attitude. But we should make a specific clarification: in *Spoils,* James is not questioning the concept of ownership but foregrounding the struggle for ownership. Within this struggle, each character clarifies his or her relationship to "the things," which James states in his "Preface to *The Spoils of Poynton"* constitute "the real centre," the "citadel of the interest" of the work.[8] The two acquisitive females in *The Spoils of Poynton* are seeking to define their familial relationships by the ownership of things. When Mrs. Gereth discovers that her son intends to marry Mona Brigstock, a sensible girl without aesthetic taste, she absconds to Ricks with Poynton's spoils. Rather than allow the Philistine Mona to own her precious artifacts, Mrs. Gereth challenges her son's ownership. Mona, whose family owns the Victorian house Waterbath, will not marry Owen until he recovers the spoils for Poynton.

In *Spoils*, inasmuch as the two acquisitive characters are female, James's redemptive character is his heroine Fleda Vetch, the one character who refuses to seize possession of the spoils. Mrs. Gereth wishes Fleda to marry her son because she sees that Fleda, a woman of taste, has the ability to appreciate Poynton's beauty. Fleda, however, is also a woman who embodies Victorian morals; she not only defends traditional values but she also becomes a central transmitter of these cultural values. Refusing to own either Owen or the things, she seeks, instead, to protect Owen's legal rights to ownership, which is a social value Fleda ultimately accepts as fixed and given.

While Poynton represents the grand old Victorian house, a repository of cultural ideals, Waterbath represents failed bourgeois tastes. In James's novel, the Victorian house and its artifacts serve as a rich nexus of meaning. Critics have long noted how James's houses often embody the aesthetic and moral tensions within his novels (his own "houses of fiction"). Even recent criticism concerning *Spoils* reflect this standard view. For instance, Philippa Tristram, aligning the central houses of the novel—Waterbath and Poynton—with actual houses that James lived in (De Vere Mansions and Lamb House, repectively), has noted that the spoils become the "ground over which middle-class taste and middle-class vulgarity fight it out." While Mrs. Gereth is endowed with an aesthetic sensibility, her son is endowed with a moral sensitivity; while Mona has neither good taste or moral judgment, Fleda has both.[9] Richard Lyons, noting that James seemed especially preoccupied with inheritances and houses in the 1890s, has observed that James long regarded the old English house as a symbol of a cultural ideal, an ideal which Poynton embodies. But in the late 1800s, James, disillusioned by an increasingly commercialized English society, felt that few people were worthy of such a European cultural inheritance.[10] Once Poynton's artifacts become a battleground for ownership, James foregrounds the moral conflict of an acquisitive culture. The fight between Mona and Mrs. Gereth represents the fight between two houses, a fight of aesthetic tastes; the fight also raises moral questions concerning issues of the right of ownership.

In focusing upon female—rather than male—powers of appropriation, James explores ways in which women enact power in the domestic sphere to acquire objects of social status and to acquire men who would allow them to collect these objects. The spoils of Poynton represent both the treasure of the house as well as the trophy of a possible marriage: Owen Gereth, himself. Both Mrs. Gereth and Mona Brigstock stand ready to take control of the spoils. For Mrs. Gereth, "things" represent sacred artifacts; as she states to her son, "The best things here, as you know, are the things your father and I collected, things all that we worked for and waited for and suffered for. . . . They were our religion, they were our life, they were *us.*"[11] Mrs. Gereth's sense of herself has been absorbed into the material world; even the transcendent ideal—religion—disappears into the landscape of objects. Inasmuch as Mrs. Gereth's desire is governed by the things which "were of course the sum of the world," they represent the sum of her subjective and objective world. When she loses her spoils, she is alienated from her supreme Other.

For Mona Brigstock, the "things" function not as worshipped ends, but as pragmatic means of asserting her will; in fact, James describes Mona as *"all will."* The possession of the spoils are part of the marriage contract: material proof of fulfilled social obligations. Owen must recover Poynton's furniture and art works before Mona will marry him; Mona, hardly a damsel in distress, has ordered her knight, accompanied by solicitors if need be, to go in search of the contracted holy grail. Like Jean Giraudoux's Bertha, Mona risks, however, losing her fiancé by the very demands of her test.

Caught between these two women's desires, Owen has difficulty in either articulating or enacting his own desires. *The Spoils of Poynton* hardly seems to be a model for Levi-Strauss's theory of kinship which posits that women function as objects of exchange; they are circulated among men. In the symbolic order of society, they do not desire or produce meaning for themselves. Instead, Owen seems to be buffeted by female desires; the women have no difficulty in producing meaning for themselves. Mona and Mrs. Gereth are women who insist upon their own hegemony. As such, we may say that Owen appears to be an Adam in the midst of Eves, a Jason in the midst of Medeas. Thus, Owen is not cast in the role of the oppressor, rather he is the negotiator, attempting to reestablish some form of order which is threatened by the women's power struggle.

Despite the fact that James does not chose to foreground male power, we must remember that the female struggle was essentially initiated by an absent male—the dead husband/father who left Poynton to his son—and as such Mr. Gereth inevitably inscribes himself on the entire subsequent narrative. Although male power may "speak softly," it nonetheless, "carries a big stick." Female power is ultimately contained, circumscribed within larger phallocentric structures. Owen only has difficulty articulating his desires in the domestic and private sphere, the traditional domain of the woman; in the end, despite the women's ostensible appropriation of power, Owen still maintains his legal right over the house, the institutionally sanctioned right of possession, a dictum of the master social narrative.

In any case, Owen will not have to fight for his legal rights, for James's heroine Fleda Vetch, who is cast in the middle of the struggle by Mrs. Gereth, will "redeem" the inert Owen and his property. Mrs. Gereth, hoping that Owen will marry Fleda rather than the implacable Mona, has elected Fleda as the appropriate caretaker/priestess of the sacred Things. Owen, who in time does fall in love with Fleda, relies upon Fleda as an arbiter of social value, someone who will advise him to do the right thing. In contrast to the other two acquisitive women, Fleda—"a young lady without fortune" or home—struggles against her desire for appropriation, against her temptation to "consume" both Owen and the treasures of Poynton. James uses Fleda, whom he calls his "free spirit," as his emblem of the independent will—the one who refuses to dominate another. In his "Preface," James states that "from beginning to end . . . appreciation, even to that of the very whole, lives in Fleda." She is the only one who "both sees and feels, while the others but feel without seeing."[12] As such, Fleda possesses James's "converting" rather than "business" imagination; imaginatively apprehending the things, she refuses to be defined by them, and instead, attempts to maintain a virtuous position in the struggle. She does not want to be accused of exploiting the situation for her own personal gain; she does not want to be cast as "one of those bad women in a play" who steals

Owen and Poynton away from his fiancée Mona: "Her problem was to help him to live as a gentleman and carry through what he had undertaken: her problem was to reinstate him in his rights." Yet, in defining her problem as the reinstatement of Owen's rights, Fleda—this "free spirit"—is not challenging but defending the maintenance of a conventional social order. She obliterates her own desires and displaces those desires onto altruistic abstractions: "Now, won over as she was to heroism, she could see her use only as some high and delicate deed."[13] Although Mrs. Gereth identifies her transcendental ideal with her "things," Fleda perceives the "things" as her temptation, her "bitter tree of knowledge"; thus, her refusal to fall—in this case, determined by her inaction and silence—will constitute her heroism. As such, Fleda fights to remain an unfallen Eve, one who refuses to give Adam the apple, to tempt him away from his obligations to his fiancée Mona. In her refusal to possess either the spoils or Owen, Fleda may be exercising her independent will, but she does so by subsuming her will to what she believes is her moral agenda, by displacement and repression.

Ironically enough, even though Fleda tries not, to use Gilman's word, "take," she is the only character described as parasitical: "People *were* saying that she fastened like a leech on other people—people who had houses where something was to be picked up."[14] James recognizes the tricky problem: not to have property sets one free, but it also makes one dependent upon others. He notes this irony in his "Preface": "The free spirit, always much tormented, and by no means always triumphant, is heroic, ironic, pathetic, or whatever, and, as exemplified in the record of Fleda Vetch, for instance, 'successful,' only through having remained free."[15] Refusing to possess the "husband and home," Fleda is instead dispossessed.

Paradoxically, her independence signifies that she is caught in the interstices of social and economic structures; Fleda's geographical dispossession (she is not mistress of any home) emphasizes her marginal position in society. Several times, conscious of the fact that she has no proper home, she fears that others—especially Owen—might perceive her position as false. At one point, she wonders if "her tendency had begun to define itself as parasitical." At another point, realizing that Fleda would support his position rather than his mother's, an uncomfortable Owen asks, "'You don't—a—live anywhere in particular, do you?' . . . She [Fleda] could see that he felt himself to have alluded more grossly than he meant to the circumstances of her having, if one were plain about it, no home of her own."[16] In essence, Owen recognizes Fleda's economic and social plight; he recognizes what she might sacrifice if she challenges his mother. As Martha Vicinus has noted about women in nineteenth-century England, "The genteel poor woman had a choice of three underpaid and overcrowded occupations— governess, companion or seamstress."[17] Although Fleda's position is undefined—she is not a paid servant—she does serve as Mrs. Gereth's companion. Having "no home of her own," Fleda occupies an incongruous social and economic position. Neither wife nor mother, she lives not in the center, but on the edge, of the nuclear family (she finds no real place either with her married sister Maggie or at her father's modest lodgings). It is no wonder that Fleda feels most at home at Ricks, the house that once belonged to Mrs. Gereth's maiden aunt, a home existing, as such, on the margins of Poynton. Her own refusal to circumscribe Owen's will prevents her from appropriating and marrying Owen, an act which would allow her to claim a clearly defined place within conventional society. Although Fleda occupies a marginal social position, it is worth noting that she does not identify with such liminal characters as the trickster or picaro—like Moll Flanders. While such characters often assume defiant, although creative roles—challenging old values and modes of social control—Fleda affirms the normative social order. She does not seek for a means to restructure her life apart from society. Internalizing Victorian conventions, Fleda plays the ideal spinster who denies her desires and participates in what Anna Freud would call "altruistic surrender."[18]

We see a complex tension enacted in the dynamics of Fleda's own internal struggle for self-possession, as well as the external struggle for the possessions. In the end, both struggles are shaped by James's underlying assumptions concerning power and control—assumptions which are not always so clearly defined. Quoting from Michel Foucault's *La Volante de Savoir*, Leo Bersani highlights the problematic issue of power, especially for those who are tempted to locate power in a clearly definable construct: "Power *[le pouvoir]* 'is not an institution, it is not a certain power *[la puissance]* with which certain people would be endowed: it is the name given to a complex strategic situation in a given society.'" Bersani goes on to note that James, for instance, does not focus upon the power of those who govern, but, like Foucault, he is "interested in the types of discourse produced by the exercise in power." Thus, Jamesian dialogues, with all their "Foucaldian flavor," become a continual means of negotiating and redressing the balance of power between two "points," or human subjects. Bersani notes that in James's rules of discourse, for instance, there is a correlation between those exercising power and knowing: those who are most powerful are those who understand, who apprehend, who "see."[19] In *Spoils*, one can argue, Fleda is the character who sees, who, in this sense, is the most powerful character in the novel. She, in fact, can advise Owen what to do; he repeatedly asks her to guide his action. He stands helplessly before her—a Galatea asking her to be a Pygmalion. Thus, the question of the male gender as locus of power per se may seem moot. In fact, Peggy McCormack has argued that James's novels are not so much about gender as they are about economics, for both men and women are subject to the dominating forces of economics; both are victimized in the power-broking marriage market society.[20]

Although I understand the sticky polemics concerning power and gender, a simple question still remains for me: what is it that Fleda "sees?" Very early in the narrative she establishes her "truth:" "Ah, the truth—there was a limit to the impunity with which one could juggle with it! Wasn't what she had most to remember the fact that Owen had a right to his property and that he had also her vow to stand by him in the effort to recover it?"[21] Fleda chooses to let the master narratives of her society be the dominant narrative, the narrative she will identify as her truth. Containing her desires, she allows social decorum to prevail; she does not want the socially unsanctioned role of seductress: "one of those bad women in a play." Although critics have argued that Fleda's limitations are more psychological than social, I would argue that Fleda finally is trapped within the social and psychological strictures of James's own narrative rules. How might Fleda become that "bad woman in a play"? Fleda becomes that "bad woman" if she over-steps her self-imposed psycho-social boundaries. Although the hero in Greek tragedy oversteps his human bounds, challenging the domain of the gods, James's heroine only desires not to cross the conventions of the drawing room drama. According to the rules that govern James's discourse, Fleda, as this "independent agent," must choose to limit herself.

Within the anxiety of the changes of his time, James chooses as his heroine one who does not extoll change, but tradition. In fact, James's shaping of Fleda's role reflects his own idealized role for the mid-Victorian schoolmistress. In an essay written in the early twentieth century, James praises the nineteenth-century governess who served as "the closed vessel of authority, closed against sloppy leakage." Such a woman was "an exquisite, an almost unconscious instrument of influence to a special end . . . embodying, for her young companions, a precious ripe tradition."[22] In this essay, although James acknowledges that these women have authority, he trusts they will use that authority to transmit the dominant cultural values of the time. In this sense, these women are also free, inasmuch as they remain "closed," inasmuch as they do not seize the authority that James claims they have, thus remaining female subordinates. As such, James values these women who, like Fleda, occupy the roles of cultural transmitters and protectors of tradition—these "closed vessels."

As a "closed vessel,"[23] Fleda, repressing her sexual and social desires, contains rather than disrupts her society's system of signification; as James states of this young Englishwoman earlier in the novel: "This young lady's repressed emotion began to require still more repression."[24] As part of the social body, she regulates her desires; thus, in the end, Fleda, without social legitimization (i.e. marriage), cannot possess the spoils or Owen. And, in the end, she does not really possess herself, for, finally for Fleda, "self-possession" signifies self-denial and repression rather than possession of the self. Although Fleda may be a seer, James controls what it is that she sees. Moreover, Fleda, acting as a "teacher" to Owen, enculturates him with "the truth" of what she sees.

For his passive heroine, James does not finally pose the alternative which Gilman suggests: Fleda refusing to take, could aspire to make, to achieve social and economic independence. Gilman and other feminists were calling for the emergence of the New Woman, a literary phrase actually popularized by James. James typically depicts this New Woman—such as Daisy Miller and Isabel Archer—as a young unmarried American woman who challenges social conventions; of course, she suffers the consequences of her autonomous actions. For feminists, however, this New Woman would not only reject social conventions, she would also claim a voice and career in her society.

Fleda is not a "New Woman" in either sense. Although James celebrates Fleda's ability to imaginatively apprehend "the things," he does not allow her to materialize that imagination. We learn that she does a little painting, but at best she is a "failed painter." In a rather painful moment, when the reader confronts Fleda's social condition, we see Fleda looking at some paintings in the window—some "shy experiments . . . placed there for sale and full of warning to a young lady without fortune and without talent." Feeling like a "servant girl taking her 'afternoon,'" Fleda contemplates a time "when she would resemble such a person more closely." Even Poynton, which she worships, does not invite an "active art," only a passive "Buddhistic contemplation."[25]

In the end, an exasperated Mrs. Gereth writes to Fleda that "for action you're no good at all." In the last scenes of the novel, when Fleda does in fact allow herself to act, to possess an item from Poynton, she does so only at Owen's invitation. Owen suggests that she take the Maltese cross, because he wants her to have "something of mine—something of real value . . . 'the gem of the collection.'" Interestingly enough, Owen has easily appropriated his mother's things; with the legal right of ownership, he feels no discomfiture in describing the Maltese cross as "something of mine." For Owen, the things seem to represent a series of possible meanings: a site of commercial, spiritual and sexual desire (he wants Fleda to take the most precious and beautiful of objects as a remembrance), a site of possession and loss (he has gained Poynton's spoils, but has lost Fleda). Fleda's response is interesting, for she has difficulty interpreting his message which "had mysteries for her that she couldn't meet."

Once she decides to act upon Owen's invitation, she is "capable of feeling it as an hour of triumph, the triumph of everything in her recent life that had not held up its head. . . . She would be able to say to herself that, for once at least, her possession was as complete as that of either of the others whom it had filled only with bitterness."[26] Both Owen and Fleda are mistaken about their assumption concerning possession; like Malta, an island emblematic for its own appropriation and reappropriation, Owen and Fleda are both characters who have been appropriated and re-appropriated—Owen by Mona and Fleda by Mrs. Gereth. In the end, as we shall see, both Fleda and Poynton's things become exhausted metaphors.

At the moment she decides to possess, Fleda feels a secret rapture "burned in her successful stillness."[27] When she arrives at Poynton, however, she discovers that the house literally is burning. Critics have interpreted this final scene in various ways. On the one hand, Arnold Goldsmith draws a connection between the Maltese cross and Fleda's "intense suffering"; the cross becomes a "symbol of her renunciation and self-denial and sublimation of her love." The house burns because it is only right that Fleda, like Lambert Strethers, be "right" without getting anything out of it for herself.[28] On the other hand, Nina Baym argues that when Fleda decides to accept the Maltese cross, she reveals her egotistical core: "To the extent she believes herself worthy, she becomes unworthy." Essentially, James burns Poynton to punish Fleda, demonstrating that she has "done nothing to merit reward."[29] Although Goldsmith and Baym focus upon the burning as a replication of Fleda's ethical conflict, Richard Lyons highlights the importance of Poynton's things as a representation of a cultural ideal that no one is worthy to inherit. Fleda, as the most worthy possessor, can reclaim the things in her imagination.[30]

I, however, cannot help but be reminded of Hélène Cixous's statement that when "'The Repressed' of their culture and their society come back, it is an explosive return, which is *absolutely* shattering, staggering, overturning, with a force never let loose before."[31] Once Fleda allows herself to desire and to act upon that desire, the "closed vessel" bursts asunder; the secret rapture which burns in her has been transposed to the house.

Once Poynton's artifacts signified the site of conflict; once Fleda, refusing to act or to possess, signified the independent will, the defender of recipricol freedom. Both Fleda and Poynton's social signification has been depleted, has burned away. From the station, Fleda watches Poynton—with its things, its exhausted metaphors of power—burn. Fleda, too, this "free spirit," is an exhausted metaphor.

In the end, she will return to Mrs. Gereth, that deposed "queenmother," that emblem of imperial power. Fleda promises to return to Mrs. Gereth with "an acceptance as responsible as the vow of a nun." When Mrs. Gereth writes her that she regards Fleda as a bit of furniture, Fleda is glad "if only by its acknowledgement that her friend had something left: it still implied recognition of the principle of property."[32] In her metaphors, ironic or not, Fleda is accepting the social values of a nun-like self-renunciation and a recognition of private property (she is now part of that property). Refusing to possess, Fleda is dispossessed, then finally repossessed by another.

In *Spoils of Poynton,* James, in focusing upon female acquisition, deflects a number of the political and social implications of the question of women and property. In the social, political and economic sphere of the late 1800s, Charlotte Gilman and the women who fought for the Married Women's Property Acts were asking women to redefine themselves in terms of their relationship to their property and possessions. On the one hand, property—if, as Gilman warns, women only seek it through men—could be a form of subjugation; on the other hand, the right to property—as implemented in the Married Women's Property Acts—could be a means of empowerment. James sets his two acquisitive women, Mona Brigstock and Adela Gereth, against each other: Mona is the ultimate "taker," acquiring Poynton through Owen; Mrs. Gereth, unable to subvert the social system of her time, loses the signs of her wealth and work. Although James warns against the desire to possess and to control, he does not offer his women an alternative model. In the end, he leaves his heroine Fleda Vetch dependent. She may have achieved a modicum of moral freedom, but finally she is economically and even metaphorically impoverished. Fleda is the "independent spirit" who is also a

"parasite"; she is the woman of rich imagination who is economically impoverished. Ironically, as James's emblem of the independent will, Fleda actually makes the choices women have historically made: self-sacrifice, renunciation, and self-denial. Set
against the conflicts of the Victorian era, *Spoils* is ultimately a
novel which reinforces the master socio-political narratives of
nineteenth-century England.

Although James, as well as a number of Victorian men and
women, could be appalled at individual acts of injustice done to
specific women, ultimately he perceived the erosion of patriarchal values as a threatening erosion of traditional values. Thus,
in his tale, the victim, who dares to desire and act, becomes the
acquisitive villainness. The woman who holds on to the moral
claims of an older tradition is the heroine. Although, in James's
novel, patriarchal voices seem silenced by the complaining
voices of the acquisitive women, the patriarchal voices which are
aligned with Fleda's vision of "truth" are the most powerful
voices of the culture. Victorian feminists, however, would refuse
to enculturate such a vision of "truth" to a future generation.
Burning old cultural ideals in their own conflagration, feminists
would seek new metaphors for a new age. For them, female acquisition would be defined not as an act of selfishness, but as an
act of empowerment: an effort not to despoil, but to preserve, the
independent will. Women who desire and demand their possessions can symbolize, rather than denigrate, a future cultural
ideal, providing a worthy inheritance for a new generation.

NOTES

1. Henry James, *The Complete Notebooks of Henry James*, ed. Leon
Edel and Lyall H. Powers (New York: Oxford University Press, 1987),
79.

2. Fred G. See, "Henry James and the Art of Possession," in
American Realism, ed. Eric J. Sundquist (Baltimore: Johns Hopkins
University Press, 1982), 120.

3. For an in-depth examination of the evolution of these laws, see Lee Holcombe, *Wives and Property: Reform of the Married Women's Property Law in Nineteenth-Century England* (Toronto: University of Toronto Press, 1983).

4. Lee Holcombe, *Victorian Ladies at Work: Middle-Class Working Women in England and Wales 1850–1914* (Hamden, Connecticut: Archon Books, 1973), 4.

5. Charlotte Perkins Gilman, *Women and Economics: A Study of the Economic Relation between Men and Women as a Factor in Social Evolution* (Boston: Small, Maynard, 1898), 118.

6. Charlotte Perkins Gilman, *New York Times,* 26 February 1914.

7. Donald L. Mull, *Henry James's "Sublime Economy": Money as Symbolic Center in the Fiction* (Middletown, Connecticut: Wesleyan University Press, 1973), 7–9.

8. Henry James, "Preface to *The Spoils of Poynton,*" in *The Art of the Novel,* ed. R. P. Blackmur (New York: Scribner's, 1962), 126.

9. Philippa Tristram, *Living Space in Fact and Fiction* (London and New York: Routledge, 1989), 160. Tristram also argues that the dower house Ricks, with its modest functional possessions, promises to restore "moral content" to good taste in a way that the purely aesthetic Poynton fails to do so.

10. Richard S. Lyons, "The Social Vision of *The Spoils of Poynton,*" *American Literature* 61, no. 1 (Mar. 1989): 59–77. Lyons also argues that James's disillusionment with English society leads him—as indicated in *Spoils*—to shift from social themes to dramas of consciousness.

11. Henry James, *The Spoils of Poynton* (New York: Penguin, 1978), 24.

12. James, "Preface," 129.

13. James, *Spoils of Poynton,* 69, 77.

14. James, *Spoils of Poynton,* 45.

15. James, "Preface," 129–30.

16. James, *Spoils of Poynton,* 31, 71.

17. Martha Vicinus, *Independent Women: Work and Community for Single Women 1850–1920* (Chicago: University of Chicago Press, 1985), 3.

18. Carroll Smith-Rosenberg, *Disorderly Conduct: Visions of Gender in Victorian America* (New York: Oxford University Press, 1985). See Smith-Rosenberg's intriguing argument concerning liminal characters.

19. Leo Bersani, "The Subject of Power," *Diacritics,* 7, no.3 (Sept. 1977): 2–21.

20. Peggy McCormack, "The Semiotics of Economic Language in James's Fiction," *American Literature* 58, no. 4 (Dec. 1986): 540–56. Of course, the issue of gender itself further problematizes the issue of power. Heavily influenced by the deconstructive and psychoanalytic thinking of Jacques Lacan, Jacques Derrida and Gilles Deleuze, French feminists, in their exploration of *l'écriture feminine,* have challenged the idea of simple male and female dichotomies, the boundaries set up by "Western Thinking." In fact, Gilles Deleuze identifies James, who is able to "trace lines of flight" into multiplicity, as a writer who is *le devenir femme* (women-becoming).

21. James, *Spoils of Poynton,* 114.

22. Alfred Habegger, *Henry James and the "Woman Business"* (Cambridge: Cambridge University Press, 1989), 235.

23. Noting the prescriptive nature of late nineteenth-century sexuality, historian Charles E. Rosenberg has observed that "the omnipresent images of control and physiological penury" highlight the mercantilist nature of sexuality: "The body is visualized in this metaphor as a closed energy system, one which could be either weakened through the discharge of energy or strengthened through its prudent husbanding." *No Other Gods: On Science and American Social Thought* (Baltimore: Johns Hopkins University Press, 1976), 87.

24. James, *Spoils of Poynton,* 44.

25. James, *Spoils of Poynton,* 106.

26. James, *Spoils of Poynton,* 188.

27. James, *Spoils of Poynton,* 188.

28. Arnold Goldsmith, "The Maltese Cross as Sign in *The Spoils of Poynton,*" *Renascence* 16, no. 1 (Fall 1963): 73–77.

29. Nina Baym, "Fleda Vetch and the Plot of *The Spoils of Poynton,*" *PMLA* 84 (1969): 102–111.

30. Lyons, "Social Vision," 76–77.

31. Hélène Cixous and Catherine Clément, *The Newly Born Woman* (Minneapolis: University of Minnesota Press, 1986), ix.

32. James, *Spoils of Poynton,* 175, 177.

Playing House
Frances Hodgson Burnett's Victorian Fairy Tale

Eileen Connell

In *Sara Crewe, Or What Happened at Miss Minchin's?* (1888), Frances Hodgson Burnett re-imagines the Cinderella story for children and adults who were still enchanted with her first romantic, rags-to-riches tale, *Little Lord Fauntleroy* (1886). English and American audiences so enjoyed *Sara Crewe* and its theatrical adaptations that Burnett expanded it, and this longer version, *A Little Princess* (1905), remains popular today.[1] Burnett modeled *Sara Crewe* on the fairy tales about princesses that were first widely read in the nineteenth century.[2] In such tales, a wicked queen or stepmother figure punishes her rival and tries to prevent her from assuming her royal station. Despite an enforced slumber that lasts one hundred years or a childhood spent sweeping cinders, the adolescent girl preserves her princess's soul and, in the end, she escapes to a castle with maid service. The torture or the trial the heroine endures often involves housekeeping. Cinderella sweeps her step family's fireplaces; Sleeping Beauty pricks her finger on a spindle and falls asleep; the miller's daughter in "Rumpelstiltskin" must spin straw into gold or lose her life; and Snow White survives her stepmother's wrath by keeping house for seven dwarfs.

These tales of the horrors of housework would seem to disenchant the middle-class home life that Victorian culture made the locus of personal happiness and fulfillment.[3] Consid-

ered in isolation from the rest of the narrative, the representation
of Cinderella sweeping fireplaces while the rest of the family
frolics exposes what other sentimental representations of domestic life obscure: The British home may need a virtuous woman's care and supervision, but it also requires the physical labor
of several servants who are excluded from the middle-class domestic comfort they manufacture. The subversive origins of such
fairy tales as "Cinderella" are lost, however, in modern translations that engage in the most direct form of mystification.[4] While
the tales mentioned above represent real social problems and describe some of their concrete ramifications, each invokes magic
to make them disappear. Everything that gets in the way of the
happy ending is attributed to mysterious causes, and everything
that brings it about, to felicitous magic. In the case of the princess
in rags, housekeeping becomes imaginative play that transforms
the unpleasant realities of the work intended to punish her into
magical keys to an enchanted, leisured life. For example, Cinderella's rats and garden vegetables turn into the elegant coach
that takes her away from her garret; and the miller's daughter
not only manages to spin straw into gold but captures a king in
the process. The vision of "happily ever after" domestic bliss the
fairy tale offers so enchants readers that they forget that while
powerful household magic saves the princess from the less than
romantic aspects of housekeeping, somewhere in the margins of
the story there is a maid who must keep the castle clean. Fairy
tales also banish to untold regions the far away, exploited lands
that supply the castle's wealth.

Because Burnett represents classes and races that are usually omitted from the fairy tale domestic narrative, one can more
readily discern the exotic "dark-faced . . . man-servant" and the
"ugly" maid hard at work in the corners of the idyllic British
home.[5] Located within an ancient tradition of fairy tales about
the horrors and delights of housekeeping, *Sara Crewe* contributes
to our understanding of the "domestic woman" recent studies of
the domestic novel have helped to make a rising star of feminist
literary scholarship. More clearly than such novels as *Pamela* or
Jane Eyre, *Sara Crewe* shows that the production and maintenance
of English domestic life depends upon the hierarchies of class
and race domestic discourse ostensibly critiques. Like

"Cinderella," Burnett's representation of a princess who is forced to be a maid both reveals and conceals the physical, dirty work swept under the rug in most fictions about household romances.[6] Burnett includes more details about Sara's domestic life in *A Little Princess*, explaining: "Between the lines of every story there is another story.... When I wrote *Sara Crewe* I guessed that a great deal more had happened at Miss Minchin's than I had time to find out just then."[7] Stories told "between the lines" of *Sara Crewe* and elaborated more fully in *A Little Princess* show that the housework would-be princesses perform can be torture that produces only an "ugly" house with a "severe varnished look." But for a privileged few, love and imaginative labor make housekeeping an effortless game of turning tissue-paper into "golden platters."[8] In a backwards game of hide and seek, the story uncovers the social and racial oppression within the domestic sphere and then hides it with a little magic, some other-worldly glamour, and a home-made love potion. In *A Little Princess* the objects of this game are Ram Dass the Indian servant and Becky the un-princess-like scullery maid.

"If Sara had been a boy and lived a century ago . . . ."

Ram Dass and Becky are two of the "things and people who had been left out," or merely sketched into, *Sara Crewe*.[9] *A Little Princess* also includes other stories and characters only alluded to in *Sara Crewe*, but in each version of the story the main events of the plot are the same. As the story begins, Sara, who strives always to behave "like a princess," arrives in "strange" London from India, where she has lived all her seven years with her devoted young father, a wealthy officer in the British regiment. Because her mother died after her birth, she is his "little Missus." Sara's fondest wish is to return to India and "keep the house for her father": "to ride with him, and sit at the head of the table when he had dinner parties; to talk to him and read his books— that would be what she would like most in the world, and if one must go away to . . . England to attain it, she must make up her mind to go."[10] Captain Crewe buys his seven-year-old a doll and a lavish wardrobe and regretfully leaves her at Miss Minchin's

Select Seminary for Young Ladies, where a greedy Miss Minchin pampers her wealthiest and most select young lady. When Sara is eleven, Captain Crewe dies after losing his entire fortune, and she becomes Miss Minchin's "little drudge and an outcast."[11] Days spent running errands for the cook, mending, and learning "to dust a room well and to set things in order" teach Sara a much different form of "keeping house" than the one she imagined when she first arrived at the school.[12] Through it all, she remains "a princess in rags and tatters" who escapes her household drudgery by constructing detailed fantasies of a domestic comfort that appears magically. Her virtue and imaginative effort are rewarded when her neighbor and his Indian servant furnish her comfortless attic. This neighbor, Mr. Carrisford, turns out to be the friend who supposedly lost Captain Crewe's fortune, and Sara, now wealthier than ever, moves next door to keep house for him and to live happily ever after.

Sara Crewe repeats the theme of Burnett's runaway bestseller *Little Lord Fauntleroy* (1886), which by 1888 had launched in England and America a Fauntleroy fad that outlasted the generation of boys who were cajoled into wearing velvet and lace Fauntleroy suits.[13] Both books overtly preach that boy "frogs" and girl "Cinderellas" can become princes and princesses because nobility and virtue are interior qualities rather than matters of title, fortune, or rank. Like most children's literature of the period, however, Burnett's two stories differ in significant ways because each reproduces the dominant late Victorian narratives of gender identity. In *Sara Crewe*, Burnett teaches female children the rewards of discovering, after enduring domestic hardships, whether they are really "nice" or "horrid" girls. The reward for surviving the torture of household toil is the realization of the heroine's domestic daydreams and the fulfillment of her childhood desire to "keep the house for her father."[14] Sara becomes a "little Missus" of a substitute father and of a house that requires only her virtuous presence to be a home. *Little Lord Fauntleroy*'s triumphant Cedric, on the other hand, has many adventures before he becomes, despite his unmanly velvet breeches, the future "master of everything" in his earldom.[15] Cedric has stereotypically feminine characteristics as well as clothes and Sara is far more intelligent and well read than most story book girls, but both stories clearly reinforce the familiar message that it is "natural" for men to take action to reach their goals and for women to take a more indirect route through the realm of emotion and imagination. In *Sara Crewe*, for instance, Sara imagines how her attic could be made comfortable and beautiful, and Mr. Carrisford and his Indian servant make it so.[16]

Burnett's tale about a "little princess" who is rescued from one form of housekeeping and transported to a higher one does more, though, than remind us that traditional gender roles are drummed into children's heads from the moment they can follow a story. As *A Little Princess*'s representation of Becky suggests, nineteenth-century culture's association of femininity with a powerful interiority encodes class as well as gender difference. Born and bred scullery maids were excluded from the ideology of Victorian "true womanhood" that reified feminine morality and self-restraint and turned the physical work of housekeeping into a spiritual endeavor.[17] As several recent critics of nineteenth-century fiction have argued, these two related domestic ideologies both enforced women's subordination to men and extended the power and influence of middle-class women in the home and in the public sphere. The way in which Sara passively endures her indentured servitude calls attention to the limitations of a "feminine" inner power, but the lower-class female characters who inhabit the margins of Burnett's story have not even the ability to imagine and to dream their way out of the kitchen.

If the Shoe Fits . . .

Like "Cinderella," Burnett's story depicts an adolescent heroine who closely resembles the domestic woman Nancy Armstrong argues emerged about the time of Richardson's *Pamela, or Virtue Rewarded* (1740). Although Burnett's Sara Crewe is eleven when her trials begin and is tortured by a greedy woman rather than a lustful man, she can be usefully compared to Richardson's slightly older adolescent domestic woman. Armstrong reads *Pamela* to describe how in the modern period an ideology that elevated a sexually pure and morally superior middle-class woman above her aristocratic counterpart helped to construct the modern, privatized self, as well as to bolster the ideology of separate spheres and to authorize middle-class hegemony.[18] She shows how Richardson's Pamela epitomizes the woman who is valued for her moral virtue, which is evidence of an interior subjectivity, rather than for her sexual attributes, appearance, or economic status."[19] In *Pamela* as in many eighteenth- and nine-teenth-century novels, the romantic love plot often works to manage and to displace "the more politically volatile issue of class."[20] In other words, such novels as *Pamela* appear to argue for the equality of all individuals and to maintain that virtue en-dows even a servant girl with an upwardly mobile status, but the political content of this argument is counteracted by romance plots in which gender difference emerges as a magical solution to the economic, class, and other differences represented.

In *Sara Crewe*, on the other hand, the minimal romantic love interest of the story concerns a girl and her father, and the father figure who replaces him. Both "fathers" are of the same economic class as Sara herself. Thus, when Sara finally achieves domestic bliss, the social inequities the story represents are not formally resolved as they are in *Pamela* or in "Cinderella." Bur-nett instead attempts to make the fellowship and affection that characterizes Sara's relations with Becky and the male Indian servant Ram Dass perform the magic that marriage does in other domestic narratives. Compared to a romantic love potion that can displace one form of difference with another though, pla-tonic love is a weak form of magic that barely conceals the sto-ry's more potent celebration of hierarchy.

Throughout most of *A Little Princess* Sara and Becky per-form the same sort of domestic chores and inhabit adjoining attic "cells," but Sara possesses imaginative powers that Becky does not. These powers are paradoxical, given the social disenfran-chisement of women and the domestic incarceration of Sara her-self. But to the reader, Sara's vivid imagination is a sign that al-though she no longer has an extravagant, womanly wardrobe and must spend her days cleaning, she retains the essence, if not the status, of the princess she was when she "gobbled" books, told exotic stories to herself and to others, and provided for the other girls in the school an example of "perfect" manners and morality. Like Richardson's Pamela, Sara never deviates from her commitment to virtue, she daydreams constantly, and only the most extreme kind of physical stress causes her to lose self-control. Becky is as consistently kind and generous as Sara, but she lacks the other "royal" attributes that make Sara a princess whether she wears rags or silk gowns.

In both "Cinderella" and *Sara Crewe*, a princess must have access to both an interior nobility and a royal wardrobe. A perfectly sized "glass slipper" that signifies wealth and external beauty may not be all it takes to transform a girl into a princess, but it does contribute to and symbolize her unique powers. As I have suggested, recent interpretations of the domestic novel maintain that the Cinderella-like heroine signifies the end of the reign of the aristocratic woman and the ascendancy of the middle-class housekeeper who, unlike her predecessor, does not wear flamboyant, costly clothing to display her husband's income but rather imparts her inner virtues to the household.[21] This argument suggests that in a capitalist culture any virtuous woman can attain the democratic "authority" of the domestic woman, whether or not she has the money necessary to buy clothing that signifies a privileged class position. Fairy tales reveal, however, that this is wishful thinking. While Sara's internal virtues constitute an essential worth that does not alter when she becomes a shabby maid, in the beginning of the story, her possessions add another dimension to her value. Just as her "odd" expression signals her internal singularity, her "extraordinary wardrobe" of dresses of "silk and velvet and India cashmere" causes people to speculate about her father's status: "That odd little girl with the big, solemn eyes must be at least some foreign princess—perhaps the daughter of an Indian rajah."[22] Dressed-up, she serves the same purpose as does the female aristocrat the domestic woman supposedly replaces: she displays the wealth of the man who heads the household and "authorize[s] a political system that made sumptuary display the ultimate aim of production."[23] In 1888, the political system Sara's "much too grand" wardrobe authorizes is British Imperialism. Burnett represents the "business" of the British occupation of India as something mysteriously removed from life in London. The diamond mines are, as Sara puts it in *A Little Princess*, like something from

"'Arabian Nights,'" and she imagines that "strange, dark men" dig for the diamonds."[24] Dressed in her exotic, "ridiculous" clothing, she embodies the most important "product" of the British Indian venture, the enigma of India itself.[25]

This adolescent domestic woman also epitomizes characteristics of the undecorated, vigilant, and unseen housekeeper Armstrong says authorizes "the power of the middle classes."[26] Although as a student and as a maid, Sara has little authority over the household, her ability to regulate her desire and to observe others gives her a moral authority that helps her to control her own fate. In one of the most memorable scenes in the story, a ravenous Sara gives a starving street child five of the six buns she bought with a six pence she found in the mud. Sara can also control her anger. When Miss Minchin subjects her to verbal or physical abuse, she retaliates in the same way Richardson's Pamela does; she withholds the interiority the abuser strives to violate: "When people are insulting you, there is nothing so good for them as not to say a word—just look at them and *think*. Miss Minchin turns pale with rage when I do it."[27] In her unobtrusive rags, Sara does what she can to empower herself. Once her finery is gone, "nobody took any notice of her except when they ordered her about," or they notice "her odd little habit of fixing her eyes upon them and staring them out of countenance."[28] Just as Cinderella's tiny feet symbolize the moral worth that makes her suitable for the prince, the haunting eyes staring out of Sara's thin face distinguish her from Becky and signal an indestructible interior value. The inner spirit no punishment can crush reveals itself in an expression that makes even Miss Minchin wonder, "What is the child made of?"[29]

"If you keep house for us, cook, make the beds, wash, sew, and knit, if you'll keep everything neat and orderly, you can stay with us, and we will provide you with everything you need."[30]

Because Sara is made of the qualities that constitute idealized Victorian womanhood, she never becomes like Becky and the other "machines who carried coal scuttles and made fires."[31]

When Sara loses both her money and her father, Miss Minchin offers her a housekeeping contract that is far less good-hearted than the one that the seven dwarfs offer the orphaned Snow White. Moments after Sara learns of her father's death, Miss Minchin tells her: "If you work hard and prepare to make yourself useful in a few years, I shall let you stay here."[32] Since Sara is "a sharp child," Miss Minchin plans to use her as a housemaid only until she is old enough to save the school the cost of a real teacher's salary. Although Burnett implies that Sara's reversal of fortune bridges the distance between Becky and Sara, this addendum to the housekeeping contract alone indicates that Sara is not, as Miss Minchin cruelly puts it, "like Becky" now. The maid's work the "princess in rags" performs does not alter her essential identity as an "exceptional girl," but Becky has no identity apart from her work. A "machine," "not a little girl," Becky does not possess the "feminine" attributes Victorian culture most prizes because that culture defines her as a lower-class worker rather than as a woman. Without these attributes, she has little chance of even imaginatively escaping her life of blacking boots and grates, scrubbing floors, and cleaning windows. Burnett gives Sara everything a character in a fairy tale needs to survive her banishment to the kitchen and to become a princess again, but Becky is not the type of character who can be taken for a fairy tale princess: ". . . [Becky] was in a deep sleep as if she had been, like the Sleeping Beauty, slumbering for a hundred years. But she did not look—poor Becky!—like a Sleeping Beauty at all. She looked only like an ugly, stunted, worn-out little scullery drudge. Sara seemed as much unlike her as if she were a creature from another world."[33]

When Sara first meets Becky, she is still the wealthiest child in the school, but she insists that she and Becky "are just the same" and begins to give her the lessons in genteel femininity that would make them more alike. After Sara loses her princess's wealth, her ability to tell stories, to remain self-controlled before Miss Minchin, and to be kind continues to provide Becky with an example of princess-like behavior. These lessons do not transform Becky's prosaic thoughts into imaginative ones or cure her tendency to respond to Miss Minchin's abuse with wild tears, but they do teach her the "feminine" preference for spiritual rather than material comfort, an important precept of the Victorian ideology of womanhood. Although Becky is always hungry, she soon learns to enjoy the stories Sara tells her more than the food she offers: "The mere seeing of Miss Sara (in her sitting room) would have been enough without meat-pies." Even when Sara becomes a maid too and has nothing but stories to offer, Becky needs only to listen to them and to serve "Miss Sara" to endure her miserable life. Unlike the beggar Sara encounters, a "little ravening savage" on the lowest rung of the social ladder, Becky has mental capabilities that distinguish her from "a poor wild animal." But while the beggar may not know enough to thank Sara, her "wolfish" behavior does get her food. Becky's cultivation of a spiritual nature merely teaches her to be an ascetic and obedient servant who resigns herself not to "mind *how* heavy the coal-boxes was—or *what* the cook done."[34] Sara, on the other hand, frequently likens her own stoicism to that of a soldier in battle or of a prisoner of the French Revolution. She invents a reason for her suffering, inwardly rebels against the injustice of that reason, and convinces herself that she will be rewarded and empowered if she serves her temporary sentence bravely.

Burnett's "ugly" Sleeping Beauty cannot impart such meaning to her suffering, nor can she become "like" "Princess Sara," who insists that "it's just an accident" that Becky is not the princess. Indeed, the rest of the narrative undermines the tentative suggestion that the qualities the culture attributes to upper- and middle-class women can be attained and exploited by all women. In fact, the dynamic of the two girls' friendship indicates that these qualities may help to construct and to maintain class divisions between women rather than work to dissolve them. Sara's condescending desire to "scatter largess to the populace" motivates her to befriend and to educate Becky who, in turn, expresses her gratitude by worshipping and "wait[ing] on" Sara. Becky gives Sara a homemade pincushion that inspires Sara to exclaim, "I love you Becky!" but neither love nor loss of wealth alters the hierarchical positions of "Miss Sara" and Becky. They remain creatures from different worlds, because even when they inhabit the same world in the attic, Sara's mental skills raise her to an immaculate palace far above Becky and her coal scuttle.

While Sara can learn to "dust a room well and set things in order,"[35] Becky cannot learn to pretend.

As Sara carries out her chores, she plays house. She imagines, for instance, that the attic, "almost like a nest in a tree," is "really a beautiful little room," and she tries to "guess something about . . . people" by imagining how furniture reveals personalities. In *A Little Princess*, the scene in which Sara plays her most elaborate game of house illustrates the ways in which the story as a whole shores up class differences as it reproduces the class-specific identity of the Victorian woman who presides over and sanctifies the household. Just before the climatic transformation of the attic, Sara's friend Ermengarde, the only school girl who has not re-defined the erstwhile school "princess" as an inconsequential "under servant," offers to sneak up to the attic with some food. Becoming her own fairy godmother, Sara decides to turn her dismal room into a grand banquet hall. Becky and Ermengarde join in her game. Although Sara is "pretending" that they are the princess and the "maids of honor" of a fairy land castle, each of the three girls imitates the role of one of the members of an English middle-class household. Like the male provider, Ermengarde goes off to get the food for the meal. Meanwhile, Sara "devote[s] herself to "the wifely" effort of accomplishing an end so much to be desired," the transformation of the attic into a play house, and Becky carries out "Miss Sara's" polite orders. Sara pretends that odds and ends from her attic room are golden plates, garlands, and embroidered napkins for the "royal feast." She instructs Becky to "pretend" along with her as well as to fetch a soap dish, but Becky's attempt to pretend only underlines, and naturalizes, the difference between the two girls. "Pretending" comes easily to Sara, but for Becky "it takes a lot o' stren'th" to even "almost" "see it like [Sara] does." Obediently, Becky undertakes the challenge, "twisting her face in strange, convulsive contortions, her hands hanging stiffly clenched at her sides." After this effort, Becky returns with relief to her usual task of following more concrete instructions and allows Sara to do the pretending for both of them. In this way, Becky plays along, but while she can "view the splendors" Sara describes, she does not have the ability to create them herself. Although she sits at the same table with Sara and Ermengarde as a "maid of honour," she is transformed again into an "impudent creature" when Miss Minchin comes in and breaks the spell Sara has cast.[36]

Ram Dass the Magician

Sara's attempt to create a fairy tale household provokes Miss Minchin to make Sara's life at the boarding house more miserable than ever, but the reward for her efforts outweighs the punishment. In both *Sara Crewe*, which does not include the scene in which Sara and her friends play house, and *A Little Princess*, the "magical" transformation of Sara's attic into a miniature domestic paradise follows the heroine's most memorable displays of her unique morality and exceptional imaginative power.[37] In *Sara Crewe*, Sara's reward of "magical surroundings" and abundant food follows her gift of buns to a beggar child who cannot, as she herself can, imagine that one bun is more than a whole meal. The game of house that in *A Little Princess* precedes the arrival of "the magic" indicates that Sara is rewarded not just for being virtuous in a general sense, but for mimicking the task of the ideal Victorian housewife. As I have suggested, the nineteenth-century image of domestic life as a realm separate from an alienating market place depended upon the displacement of the physical household labor lower-class women were paid to perform with the imaginative household labor women of the upper classes did supposedly free of charge. The idealization of domesticity and the magic of the fairy tale plot depend upon this displacement. Although Miss Minchin interrupts Sara's imaginative labor to punish her with additional housekeeping chores, *A Little Princess* ends with a celebration of enchanted domestic life. Sara falls asleep without dreading these chores because she dreams again of an attic that does not require labor or commodities to be homey: "Suppose there was a bright fire in the grate. . . . Suppose there was a comfortable chair before it. . . ."[38]

When Sara awakens to find that a "magician" has decorated her attic to correspond to her vision, she exclaims that "it is bewitched!" The narrator tells us that "the little, cold, miserable room seemed changed into Fairyland."[39] This "Fairyland" is merely an attic room furnished with the simple comforts of middle-class Victorian domestic life: a brass kettle on the hob, a blazing fire, books, a rug, a chair, and a table spread with a meal. Burnett's rendering of a comfortable room also transports readers to a "Fairyland" they imagine, with Sara, was created by "something glittering and strange—not at all like a real person, but bearing resemblance to a sort of Eastern magician, with long robes and a wand."[40] Just as readers of *Peter Pan* (1904) enjoy Peter and Wendy's flight from a mundane English nursery to Never Never Land, the moment when an aura of exoticism enters Sara's attic has always captivated fans of Sara Crewe. Although Sara remains in "dull" London, India makes her private part of the city "like something fairy come true."[41]

India's contribution to nineteenth-century domestic life helps to explain the "rapturous awe" in the narrative that accompanies the appearance of terrestrial chairs, decorations, and food. Ram Dass, who at his English master's request secretly brings the "magic" to Sara's dreary attic, does bear a "resemblance to a sort of Eastern magician." Although he does not have long robes and a wand, he does have a turban, a monkey, and a "picturesque, white-swathed form."[42] Like many Western representations of Eastern men, this one is feminized.[43] Burnett aligns Ram Dass with female, disenfranchised identities: "There was a head and part of a body emerging from the skylight, but it was not the head or body of a little girl or a housemaid; it was the . . . dark-faced, gleaming-eyed, white-turbaned head of a native Indian man-servant."[44] This "Lascar" who embodies the India of Sara's past gives the story much of its magic and romance. Even before "the magic," the arrival of the Anglo-Indian gentleman, his servant, and his "rich," "Oriental" furniture enliven Miss Minchin's "big, dull brick house."[45] Like other discourses of this period, the story represents India as the locus of the exotic. In doing so, Burnett obscures the reality that the imperialist exploitation of India contributed significantly to the economic expansion in nineteenth-century Great Britain that both produced and upheld the ideology of separate spheres informing British domestic life. In *Sara Crewe* this unpleasant reality is contained in several ways, but the most interesting is the reversal of the positions of the imperialist invader and of the native implied when the Lascar enters Sara's home in order to bring her the comforts of civilization.

As many scholars have pointed out, in the mid-nineteenth century, Great Britain successfully disguised the economic and political motivations of its exploitation of India by mobilizing the rhetoric of domestic ideology.[46] In political, social, and literary discourses of the period England is habitually constructed as a mother figure who benevolently undertakes the task of providing uncivilized, child-like Indians with moral guidance and material domestic comfort. The British "parent" also justifies its control over India by representing the East as the locus of the mysterious, the wayward, and the irresponsible. Toward the end of the century, as resistance at home and abroad to the British venture in India increased, the domestic narrative became a less effective means of masking the racism and avarice behind imperialism. Burnett's revision of these dated narratives symbolically resolves the tension surrounding Great Britain's exploitative relation to India.

Instead of representing an Indian who gratefully receives the fruits of English civilization, Burnett constructs an Indian who gives Sara the services and commodities representing his subjugation to a country that robs his own country of its resources. The first morning after Ram Dass visits the attic Sara receives simple, typically English elements of household comfort, but on the second morning she awakens to the superfluous "odd and luxurious things" that make the room "like a fairy story come true." These decorations are Indian exports: "odd materials of rich colors," "brilliant fans," "large cushions," "a curious wadded silk robe." Just as India finances the British economy that makes the idealization of domestic life and its female superintendent possible, Ram Dass and the Indian commodities he provides turn a mundane domestic setting into a magical "fairy story." Sara's notion that she "might wish for anything—diamonds or bags of gold—and they would appear" reveals what the audience already knows: the source behind the magic is the return of the Indian diamond mines her father had lost. Mr. Carrisford, Ram Dass's master and Sara's neighbor, is in fact the friend who mistakenly was said to have "robbed" Sara's father. To distract himself from his obsessive search for the daughter of

Captain Crewe, heiress of the diamond mines, Mr. Carrisford undertakes Ram Dass's plan to make the "visions" of the "maid" next door "real things."[47]

This far-fetched scenario would be less entertaining if the narrative exposed and censured the political realities behind the diamond mines that supply Sara and Mr. Carrisford with their wealth. In *A Little Princess*, however, any suspicion that Ram Dass is unhappy in his servitude, or that he is coerced into performing his "magic" for Sara, disappears when he explains to Mr. Carrisford's English secretary why he suggested the "plan" to his master: "It is true that the first thought was mine, Sahib. . . . I am fond of this child; we are both lonely. . . . Being sad one night, I lay close to the open skylight and listened. The vision she related told what this miserable room might be if it had comforts in it." When Becky and Sara play house, Becky follows Sara's instructions, and in this game, Ram Dass follows his master's. The home he makes with treasures from his country belongs to Sara and to Mr. Carrisford, and his imaginative housekeeping does not magically transform his own class position. As Sara's claim that she and Becky are "just the same" is refuted, so is Ram Dass's more qualified suggestion that he and Sara are alike. When Sara meets Ram Dass, they are both domestic servants, yet when she returns his monkey he thanks her with "grateful obeisance," "as if he were speaking to the little daughter of a rajah." The English secretary's interpretation of the scheme to help Sara also emphasizes Ram Dass's radical difference from the little housemaid he watches with such empathy and affection: "It will be like a story from 'Arabian Nights' . . . Only an Oriental could have planned [the transformation of Sara's attic]. It does not belong to London fogs."[48]

The rhetorical construction of Ram Dass and his "magic" as utterly different from, yet benevolently sympathetic to, his English master and mistress lifts the "London fogs," beautifies Miss Minchin's "respectable and well furnished" but "ugly" house, and allows Mr. Carrisford to claim this alien magic as his household property. After Sara ascends to her position as a "little Missus" of Mr. Carrisford's household and ceases to be "little drudge," Ram Dass becomes "her devoted slave," and Mr. Carrisford becomes her "magician."[49] This division of household labor resembles the one between Sara, who keeps Mr. Carrisford "amused and interested," and Becky, one of the many servants who cares for the house in which Mr. Carrisford and his "princess" live."[50]

And They All Lived Happily Ever After. . . .

As all fairy tales do, *A Little Princess* ends with the comforting implication that "they all lived happily ever after." In tales that create a magic circle around a royal couple, this sudden gesture of inclusion, "all," casts out any problems the story has not already resolved. Stepping outside the enchanted circle, however, one wonders: Will Becky live happily ever after as Sara's "delighted attendant"? Is Ram Dass's life as Sara's "devoted slave" as fulfilling as Sara's life as a "princess" who "can give buns and bread to the populace"?[51] Can these household servants ever become household spirits who hover over a castle that maintains itself without agency? Like many domestic novels and fairy tales, Burnett's romantic story transports its readers to a land where such questions do not seem to matter. Poverty and injustice evaporate once the protagonist reaches her goal. The magic along the way, disenchanted, is merely the comfort of home, and one of the magic's most insidious messages is that even the most clever and bookish adolescent girl should above all things desire to keep the house for the man who loves her. Yet for over one hundred years the story has enchanted readers and has encouraged them to desire the particular form of gratification and power Burnett conjures up for Sara. Like other fairy tales, *A Little Princess*'s magic appears to be available to all who wish for it hard enough, but it visits only the princess, and not the lower-class "ugly Sleeping Beauty" in the "adjoining cell."[52]

The book ends with an event designed to put the class issues it raises behind closed doors. In the last chapter of both versions, Sara returns to the bakery where she once saw the beggar girl in order to give the baker money to feed other hungry children. Anne, the beggar, no longer sits outside in the gutter but stands "clean and neatly clothed" behind the counter of the bakery that is now her home. Unlike Miss Minchin, the owner of the bakery bases her domestic arrangement with the destitute girl on affection: "I told [Anne] to come here when she was hungry, and when she'd come I'd give her odd jobs to do, an' . . . she was willing, an' somehow I got to like her; an' the end of it was I've given her a place an' a home, an' she helps me."[53] Ironically, Sara's punishment resembles Anne's reward. Like Becky, Anne attains a happy ending that involves little change in fortune or in class position, but merely a more pleasant life of domestic servitude. And like Becky, Anne will do some of the physical work required to realize Sara's imaginative schemes. Since Sara wishes to "give bread and buns to the populace," she asks the no longer "savage" Anne to distribute the food for which she once begged.[54] This final unglamorous transformation of a "wolfish" beggar to a cherished bakery worker is hardly the stuff of a "fairy story come true," but it does help to keep the spell *Sara Crewe* casts over readers from breaking. In the story, class differences are not symbolically managed in a marriage union, but rather naturalized and contained in friendly, well-managed households. Becky, Ram Dass, and Anne cannot play house along with Sara because they are too busy keeping house for her, but in this fairy tale, they do not seem to mind.

Everyone should be able to experience the fun of playing house, but current middle-class domestic ideologies show that many versions of the game are as exclusive as they were a century ago. The lasting appeal of a story based upon one of the most enduring and popular stories of all should encourage us not to recognize in it an "essential truth" about social organization, but to consider more carefully the various, historically specific messages of each variation of the Cinderella plot. *A Little Princess* remains a well-loved, charming story because even grown-up twentieth-century readers try in their own lives to transform domestic drudgery into domestic joy. Playing house can be a harmless and pleasurable pursuit as long as, like Goldilocks, we invade and examine the home when the family is away and the dirty dishes are on the table.

NOTES

1. Frances Hodgson Burnett, *Sara Crewe, Or What Happened at Miss Minchin's?* (New York: Scribner's, 1888) and *A Little Princess* (New York: Scribner's, 1905). In this essay, I refer to both published versions of the story to support my argument. On the differences between the two versions of Burnett's story, as well as a brief discussion of the story's many stage productions, see Marion E. Brown, "Three Versions of *A Little Princess:* How the Story Developed," *Children's Literature in Education* 19, 4 (1988): 199–210.

2. The publication in 1823 of an English translation of the brothers Grimm tales popularized fairy tales in England and in America. *German Popular Stories* included "Snow-Drop" (Snow White) and "Hansel and Gretel." English translations of Frenchman Charles Perrault's versions of "Cinderella" and "Sleeping Beauty" also became available in the nineteenth century. See Iona and Peter Opie, *The Classic Fairy Tales* (London: Oxford University Press, 1974),1–26; and Maria Tartar, *Off With Their Heads!: Fairy Tales and the Culture of Childhood* (Princeton: Princeton University Press, 1992). Tartar notes that the "myth of folk tales as sacred, 'natural' texts was deftly propagated by Charles Dickens" who "praised the tales as powerful instruments of socialization" (17). For a discussion of Burnett's literary relation to fairy tale and popular children's literature traditions, see Phyllis Bixler, "The Oral-Formulaic Training of a Popular Fiction Writer: Frances Hodgson Burnett," *Journal of Popular Culture* 15, 4 (1982): 42–52; and Phyllis Bixler Koppes, "Tradition and the Individual Talent of Frances Hodgson Burnett: A Generic Analysis of *Little Lord Fauntleroy, A Little Princess,* and *The Secret Garden,*" *Children's Literature* 7 (1979):191–207.

3. As nineteenth-century domestic novels so clearly show, Victorian England's industrial, capitalist economy came to depend upon an ideology of separate spheres, the gender-based division of private and public spaces which held that a "true" woman, as the weaker and intellectually inferior but morally superior sex, should remain enshrined in a home she could make a refuge for a man weary of the world of public affairs. There have been several studies in the past two decades of the ways in which nineteenth-century domestic novels and domestic ideology represent and help to construct the female subjectivity that was a crucial part of the organization of nineteenth-century consumer culture. These critical and historical works provide an important background and context for my argument. Some argue that many nineteenth-century domestic and sentimental novels written by women were a literary

reaction against and subversion of an ideology of separate spheres. Others suggest that the majority of these novels offered romantic, conservative responses to domestic ideology, in part because the women who wrote them wanted their work to be marketable. See, for instance, Monica Correa Fryckstedt, "Defining the Domestic Genre: English Women Novelists of the 1850's," *Tulsa Studies in Women's Literature* 6, 1 (1987): 9–23; Helen Papishvilly, *All the Happy Endings* (New York: Harper's, 1966); Nancy Armstrong, *Desire and Domestic Fiction: A Political History of the Novel* (New York: Oxford University Press, 1987); Mary Poovey, *Uneven Developments: The Ideological Work of Gender in Mid-Victorian England* (Chicago: University of Chicago Press, 1988).

4. For an extended analysis of this aspect of the fairy tale genre, as well as a suggestion about how "fairy tales can still be told . . . so that they challenge and resist, rather than simply reproduce, the constraints of a culture," see Tartar, *Off with Their Heads!* 229–38.

5. Burnett, *A Little Princess*, 51, 141.

6. In her analysis of eighteenth- and nineteenth-century British texts, Armstrong proposes that "the power of the middle classes had everything to do with the power of middle class love" *(Desire and Domestic Fiction,* 4). She argues as well that novels that enclose class conflict within a domestic sphere "demonstrate that despite the vast inequities of the age virtually anyone could find gratification within this private framework" (38). Because Armstrong limits her discussion, for the most part, to representations of relatively powerful, middle-class domestic women, her study neglects the laboring classes who were excluded from this particular "gratification."

7. Burnett, *A Little Princess*, v.

8. Burnett, *A Little Princess*, 7, 202.

9. Burnett, *A Little Princess*, vii.

10. Burnett, *A Little Princess*, 6. The suggestion of father-daughter incest pervades fairy tales. In one of the oldest versions of Cinderella, for example, a widower is bound by a spell not to marry until he finds a woman who is as beautiful as his dead wife and can also wear her ring. The only woman who fits this description is his own daughter. She runs away when he tries to force her to marry him (Opie, *Classic Fairy Tales*, 13). For a feminist interpretation of such tales, see Tartar, *Off with Their Heads!* 120–40.

11. Burnett, *Sara Crewe*, 17.

12. Burnett, *Sara Crewe*, 19; *A Little Princess*, 100.

13. According to Ann Thwaite, *Waiting for the Party: The Life of Frances Hodgson Burnett, 1849–1924* (London: Secker and Warburg, 1974), *Little Lord Fauntleroy* has sold well over a million copies in English and has been translated into a dozen languages (94). For years after the book's publication, representations of the sweet, virtuous, fantastically dressed Cedric proliferated in America and in England. Plays adapted from the novel were produced successfully as late as 1911, and in 1924 Mary Pickford starred as both Cedric and his mother in a film version (231, 118). *Little Lord Fauntleroy* inspired Victorian mothers to dress unwilling boys in velvet and lace "Fauntleroy suits" which remained faddish until the early years of the twentieth century.

14. Burnett, *A Little Princess*, 35, 6.

15. Frances Hodgson Burnett, *Little Lord Fauntleroy* (New York: Scribner's, 1914), 281.

16. An advertisement in the back of the original edition of *Sara Crewe* synopsizes these fundamental Victorian gender roles. In a single advertisement, Scribner's offers a "handybook" for girls subtitled "how to amuse yourself and others," and a "handybook" for boys subtitled "what to do and how to do it." A reviewer quoted in the advertisement writes of the girl's book: "It is an invaluable aid in making a home attractive, comfortable, artistic, and refined. The book preaches the gospel of cheerfulness, industry, economy, and comfort." Another reviewer makes the boy's book sound much more exciting: "It tells boys how to make all kinds of things—boats, traps, toys, puzzles, aquariums, fishing tackle . . . how to rear wild birds, to train dogs, and do the thousand and one things that boys take delight in." For further instructions about these two distinct types of fun, consult Lina and Adelia B. Beard, *The American Girl's Handybook; Or, How to Amuse Yourself and Others* (New York: Scribner's, 1888); and Daniel C. Beard, *The American Boy's Handybook; Or, What to Do and How to Do It* (New York: Scribner's, 1888).

17. In addition to Armstrong's study of the ideology of domestic womanhood, see, for example, Martha Vicinus, ed., *A Widening Sphere: Changing Roles for Victorian Women* (Bloomington: Indiana University Press, 1977); and Carol Smith-Rosenberg, "In Search of Woman's Nature, 1850–1920," *Feminist Studies* 3,1/2 (1975): 141–54. See also Barbara Welter's study of the Englishwoman's American counterpart, "The Cult of True Womanhood: 1800–1860," in *Dimity Convictions: The American Woman in the Nineteenth Century*, ed. Barbara Welter (Athens: Ohio University Press, 1976).

18. The story of "Cinderella," which is at least one thousand years old, indicates that the construction of the domestic woman began long

before the age of eighteenth- and nineteenth-century English domestic novels (Opie, *Classic Fairy Tales*, 12).

19. Armstrong, *Desire and Domestic Fiction*, 108–34.

20. Armstong, *Desire and Domestic Fiction*, 18.

21. For example, see Armstrong, *Desire and Domestic Fiction*, 86.

22. Burnett, *Sara Crewe*, 10–11; *A Little Princess*, 10.

23. Armstrong, *Desire and Domestic Fiction*, 73.

24. Burnett, *A Little Princess*, 58.

25. For an extended analysis of the English relation to the Orient, see Edward Said, *Orientalism* (New York: Pantheon Books, 1978). Said argues that "Europe . . . articulates the Orient": "This articulation is the prerogative, not of a puppet-master, but of a genuine creator, whose life-giving power represents, animates, constitutes the otherwise silent and dangerous space beyond familiar boundaries" (17).

26. Armstrong, *Desire and Domestic Fiction*, 4. In Armstrong's archeology, as discourse rather than physical force becomes the primary practice through which subjects are constituted, the cultural meaning the publicly displayed female body carries is displaced by the signifying power of a feminine interiority (*Desire and Domestic Fiction*, 73–82). What modern capitalism needs is "not a woman who attracts the gaze as she did in an earlier culture, but one who fulfills her role by disappearing into the woodwork to watch over the household." Situated in the woodwork, this nearly invisible housekeeper wields power by supervising the household. Like the surveyors Foucault describes in *Discipline and Punish* (New York: Pantheon Books, 1977), the domestic woman subjects herself as well as her surroundings to disciplinary practices: "The domestic woman executes her role in the household by regulating her own desire . . . . self-regulation became a form of labor that was superior to labor. Self-regulation alone gave a woman authority over the field of domestic objects and personnel where her supervision constituted a form of value in its own right and was therefore capable of enhancing the value of other people and things" (81).

27. Burnett, *Sara Crewe*, 21.

28. Burnett, *Sara Crewe*, 19–20.

29. Burnett, *A Little Princess*, 217.

30. Jacob and Wilhelm Grimm, "Snow White and the Seven Dwarves," in *The Complete Fairy Tales of the Brother's Grimm*, trans., Jack Zipes (Toronto: Bantam, 1987), 199.

31. Burnett, *A Little Princess*, 74.

32. Burnett, *Sara Crewe*, 17.

33. Burnett, *A Little Princess*, 51.

34. Burnett, *A Little Princess*, 67, 170, 57.

35. Burnett, *A Little Princess*, 57, 88, 100.

36. Burnett, *A Little Princess*, "a beautiful little room": 112–16; "something about . . . people": 135; "wifely effort," "royal feast": 199; "see it like [Sara] does": 200; "clenched at her sides": 200; "impudent creature": 204.

37. When *Sara Crewe* was produced for the stage as *A Little Princess*, New York and London audiences were treated to an expanded representation of the scenes in which the attic is transformed (Brown, "Three Versions of *A Little Princess*," 206).

38. Burnett, *A Little Princess*, 207.

39. Burnett, *Sara Crewe*, 53; *A Little Princess*, 221.

40. Burnett, *Sara Crewe*, 55.

41. Burnett, *A Little Princess*, 221.

42. Burnett, *Sara Crewe*, 55; *A Little Princess*, 141.

43. See, for example, Said's *Orientalism*. Said argues that the "'threatening otherness' [of India and other Eastern countries] is often gendered 'feminine' and sexually available, so that it can be penetrated, catalogued, and therefore contained by the 'superior' rationality of the Western mind" (56).

44. Burnett, *A Little Princess*, 141.

45. Burnett, *Sara Crewe*, 6.

46. For example, in "A Housewifely Woman: The Social Construction of Florence Nightingale," Poovey discusses how England's late nineteenth-century imperial campaigns "appropriated the terms of the domestic ideology that underwrote the separation of spheres, male identity, and female nature, and by which Nightingale masked her own territorial ambitions" (*Uneven Developments*, 194–95).

47. Burnett, *A Little Princess*, "fairy story come true": 221, 222; "odd materials . . . silk robe": *Sara Crewe*, 1, 56–57; *A Little Princess*, 209, 221; " . . . they would appear": *A Little Princess*, 221; "real things": A *Little Princess*, 179.

48. Burnett, *A Little Princess*, 179, 144, 180.

49. Burnett, *A Little Princess*, 153; *Sara Crewe*, 74.

50. Burnett, *A Little Princess*, 260, 262.

51. Burnett, *A Little Princess*, 263, 262.

52. Burnett, *A Little Princess*, 51, 109.

53. Burnett, *Sara Crewe*, 82; *A Little Princess*, 265.

54. Burnett, *Sara Crewe*, 82; *A Little Princess*, 265, 264.

PART TWO

A Woman's Work Is Never Done: Women's Work and Domestic Space

The Chatelaine
Women of the Victorian Landed Classes and the Country House

Jessica Gerard

Many historians have dismissed the wives of the Victorian aristocracy and gentry as functionless parasites: "idle drones" who were "condemned to rot in idleness" and "forced by lack of activity into often totally wasted lives."[1] Though running the Victorian house was normally the woman's province, in the nation's greatest houses wives supposedly abdicated their domestic responsibilities to troops of well-trained servants. The assumption that ladies of the landed elite did no housekeeping reflects ignorance both of the distinctive role of the chatelaine, and of the wide range of experience within the landed classes. In all ranks, the mistress of the household was responsible for the smooth running of the household; she was in charge of the female staff; and as hostess, she had to make the arrangements for her guests. While duchesses never contemplated doing housework, the wives of the lesser gentry turned their hand to a surprising range of domestic chores.

It is true that the Victorian theory of gender, separate spheres, which designated the home as the wife's arena, and the world outside it as the male breadwinner's sphere, could not fully apply to the country house. In this leisure class men did not leave the home daily to work long hours at earning a living. Men frequently remained at home to supervise estate administration, to act as host to numerous guests, and to enjoy field sports. They therefore had the time and the opportunity to intervene in household management. The revival of paternalism early in the century, moreover, stressed the landowner's obligation to rule over his household. Thus a few pious and domineering men continued to retain a traditional authority over household management.

Unlike the housewife in lower ranks, the landowner's wife could not regard the family's home as her own space, a territory over which she had complete personal control. The mansion was the family seat, the home of past and future generations of the dynasty. The current owner was merely a life tenant, obligated to pass the house on intact, preserving all the valuable furnishings and works of art accumulated over decades or centuries. A landowner's bride entered the household in which her husband had grown up, with its own long-established routines and customs. She stepped into the shoes of her predecessor, as it were; when Margaret Child-Villiers, eighth countess of Jersey, arrived at Middleton, she found her mother-in-law's needlework and letters in the boudoir drawers, her china on her dressing table, and blotters on the writing table.[2]

The Victorians' insistence on clearly defined functions for each room limited ladies' access to many rooms. Male territory included the study, the gunroom, the library and the billiards room, and the dining room after dinner. The ladies' territory comprised the drawing room, the morning room, the boudoir, and their dressing rooms. Upon arriving at Blagdon, Lady Ridley found she had a suite of three rooms upstairs: bedroom, dressing room and sitting room, all "newly done up" for her.[3] Sir James Kay-Shuttleworth also recognized this female territory when he refurbished the boudoir at Gawthorpe for his son's bride.[4] In a large mansion, the servants held sway over the regions behind the green baize door; the maze of kitchens, laundries, servants' hall, butler's pantry, housekeeper's room, storerooms, and so on. Their employers were not free to wander into the servants' domain at will; the master and mistress arranged their incursions ahead of time, or scheduled a regular daily visit to consult with the cook or housekeeper. Mistresses of small manor houses, on the other hand, claimed the entire house as their territory, inspecting any room at will. Mary Ann Dixon of Holton freely went into the kitchen, laundry, dairy and attics to direct and help her servants.[5]

Running the country house might also be considered too demanding and difficult a task for these supposedly weak and ineffectual ladies. As a class, the aristocracy and gentry owned the largest and most complex type of domestic household in nineteenth-century Britain. The country house served not just as a family home, but as a power house, headquarters of the family's economic enterprises, stage for status-enhancing public display and rituals of social performance, and venue for community events. The sheer size of the mansion and its gardens, the high levels of consumption, with elaborate clothing, meals and furnishings, and the high standards of service and constant entertaining made the country house very labor-intensive. Housekeeping was further complicated by the Victorian enthusiasm for specialization and subdivision, which assigned each group of inhabitants separate quarters and meals, according to age, sex and occupation, and allocated a room to each function. At dinnertime, for instance, different menus would be ordered for the dining room, the schoolroom, the nursery and the servants' hall. Country houses contained many servants, hired not just to do the enormous amount of housework, cooking, laundry, gardening, stablework and gamekeeping required to keep up a first-class establishment, but to confirm publicly the family's social superiority with their submissive deference and obedience. The average country house had around ten indoor servants, and about six outdoor men, but great houses kept many more.[6] In larger houses, these servants were thoroughly trained, highly skilled and insistent on strict job demarcation and rules of precedence below stairs. A new mistress lacking in knowledge, confidence and experience could find it difficult to establish authority over her staff. "English servants are *fiends*," complained George Curzon's American bride to her mother, "They seem to plot among themselves. . . . I should like to hang a few and burn the rest at the stake."[7]

Another feature of the Victorian country house which limited a bride's initiative was the inflexiblity of its routines. In order to coordinate the activities of such a large and complex household, and to meet industrial society's ideals of order and efficiency, a rigid daily timetable was imposed. Everyone had to get up, eat meals, go to bed, and even use certain rooms at a certain time each day. Individual families had also developed their own, sometimes bizarre, domestic customs. Upper-class Englishwomen were brought up within this system, and never questioned it, but American heiresses who married English aristocrats were initially bewildered and frustrated, for they had been raised in "organized chaos," with family members and guests coming and going at will, and "all the servants were at the beck and call of each and every clamoring family member."[8]

The Victorian landed classes, nevertheless, did not consider the country-house establishment beyond the capacities of their womenfolk. Running the country house was the responsibility of the women of the nineteenth-century landed classes, not the men. As far as the household was concerned, the majority of landed husbands confined themselves to hiring and managing the male servants, and to the male preserves of the stables and gamekeeping. The ninth duke of Marlborough was typical in assigning his young American bride the management of the household at Blenheim Palace and its finances, and reserving estate adminstration for himself.[9] "For work," Lord Rosslyn advised his newly-married stepdaughter, "have you not your poor . . . your servants and domestic affairs? . . ."[10] And at Hawarden, recalled his son, William Gladstone "in household affairs, so long as I can remember . . . took no part beyond keeping exact knowledge of general cost; my mother managed everything."[11]

The ladies' housekeeping role had expanded over the centuries, as the landowner's household became smaller and less mobile and more female, and the country house became more of a family home. By the seventeenth century, the chatelaine personally supervised the wide-ranging activities of a largely self-sufficient household. She had to ensure that servants performed their tasks and that all the necessary supplies were stocked. She often assisted in the dairy herself, and was skilled in the still-room, making preserves, cordials and medicines to administer to family, servants and the poor. Early in the nineteenth century, when many country houses were still remarkably self-sufficient, mistresses supervised cheese and butter-making, bread-baking, preserving and distilling, and the curing of hams and bacon. From the eighteenth century, however, fashionable great ladies, if not gentry wives, often hired a housekeeper to perform all these functions.

By the early nineteenth century the ideology of separate spheres further idealized and elevated the female role of household management and introduced the home-making role. Prescriptive literature reinforced the pervasive social norm that housekeeping was the special province of women. Females were held to have more suitable personality traits than men to deal with the endless small crises and myriad chores of keeping house: unselfishness, sensitivity, patience, attention to detail, and skill in personal relationships. Men were not expected to be bothered with the details of domestic problems. "A gentleman is not always at home and even if he was," noted a former head housemaid, "one cannot run to him with every worry."[12] In all classes, girls were taught that they would become wives and mothers who would run the household and care for husband and children. Keeping servants relieved a wife of the actual work, but not of responsibility for the results, or, indeed for the servants themselves. "A large house misses a lady, as we cannot get on so well without her," explained the same housemaid. In one establishment lacking a mistress, the servants endured badly-cooked dinners and ruined clothes. "We never saw a lady that would let that go on."[13] Housewives were urged to adopt industrial principles of efficiency, rationalization and order to household management, implementing strict schedules, carefully-kept accounts, and inventories.[14] The wife was now responsible for the home's decor and atmosphere, for creating an attractive and morally inspiring haven where a contented, virtuous family life could flourish. A housekeeper could never diffuse an atmosphere of home for the family, or set a lady's example to servants. Nor could a housekeeper grace the house as its chief ornament or act as hostess.

The landed classes had their own motives for adhering to Victorian norms of gender. Traditions of loyalty to lineage and kin, the sense of belonging to a dynasty, and the duty to uphold family honor and promote family interests still shaped the landed classes' behavior and attitudes. Early in the century, the

upper classes were widely criticized for their self-indulgence, ir-
responsiblity, frivolity and extravagance. Fearing the loss of their
ascendancy, the early Victorian landed classes reformed themselves, adopting middle-class piety, morality and seriousness. To
justify their wealth and power, the landed classes emphasized
that privilege carried with it the obligation to serve family, class,
the poor and the nation. Thus, a strong sense of duty became a
crucial part of the upper-class code of conduct. Marriages were
typically a working partnership dedicated to the preservation
and improvement of the family's property and reputation.
Ladies' eagerness to assume personally their domestic duties as
mistress of the house and servants and hostess was thus partly
image-building to appease the middle classes. The lady of the
house ultimately determined its reputation among the upper
classes and their servants too.

Most male landowners, therefore, felt obliged to find a
lady to act as mistress of the country house. An unmarried
owner turned to his mother, his sister or even a cousin, and wid-
owers commandeered a daughter. Before the third Baron
Northwick's marriage, his sister Georgiana supervised his
household. After his wife died, Richard Congreve asked his sister-in-law to run Burton Manor, and on her death, his three
unmarried daughters took over.[15]

Few upper-class girls were trained in household management. Lady Middleton taught her daughters by requiring each to
take turns as her assistant. "No trouble was too great which ensured the smooth working of the big machine," they learned. "A
calm unruffled demeanour was essential for the Mistress of the
House, and . . . above all things under no circumstance, however
trying, must you lose your temper." The "early habits formed of
method and attention to details" enabled them to manage competently their own country houses in turn.[16] A few girls had to
assume their deceased mother's duties, as did Meriel, Lucy and
Lavinia Lyttleton successively at Hagley.[17] Most girls, however,
had to learn from observation, watching their mothers at work.
The uniformity of domestic routines throughout the landed
classes must have been a great advantage to them. Lady Ran-
dolph Churchill believed the practical knowledge of housekeeping that girls somehow obtained was "one of the triumphs of

English education," arming the married woman "with the sinews of war."[18] Many heirs married and set up smaller households long before inheriting the estates, which gave their wives an opportunity to gain experience and confidence. When young couples resided with the heir's parents, the mother-in-law acted as instructor.

Brides of landowners had to learn their new duties rapidly. Lady Ridley did so with gusto. The day after her arrival, she inspected every room with the housekeeper, and on the following day she examined the gardens and kennels. Initially she felt rather overwhelmed, but by the third day she felt "nearly settled" and ready to alter the tea-making. Soon she was paying bills, planning the flower garden, prescribing and making medicines for a sick maid and reforming the butter-making. "I have the housebooks all my own way now," she wrote to her mother. "Matt does not even look at them."[19] Five days after her wedding, Lady Knightley wrote in her journal, "To-day I have entered on my housewifely duties and been all over the house with the housekeeper, Mrs. Eaton, and an upholsterer from Daventry, arranging, contriving, and glorying in my new domain."[20]

Some novices turned to their parents or books on housekeeping for advice. "Housekeeping looks alarming when I see the bills," Viscountess Amberley confided to her sister. "Would you ask Mamma what the book is she gave Rosalind on Domestic Economy and order it for me."[21] While visiting Hagley, Catherine Gladstone studied a book of instructions on household accounts written by her sister Mary's mother-in-law, Sarah, Lady Lyttleton. "You will yet, I think and hope, find me a good manager and a good accountant," Catherine Gladstone wrote to her husband.[22]

Normally, the mistress was responsible for the household accounts, for inspecting the housekeeper's books, paying the bills and ordering supplies as requested, approving or suggesting menus, and dealing with unresolved domestic crises. When the family migrated from one property to another, to London for the Season, or to Scotland for shooting, the mistress supervised the move, selecting servants and making sure that all the vast amounts of plate, china, clothing, nursery equipment and other luggage were safely packed and transported. Every time the

Kay-Shuttleworths stayed in London, they took all the indoor and stable servants, and everything from the house except large furniture, packed carefully into crates, chests and trunks, on a special train. Just before leaving, Lady Kay-Shuttleworth always inspected the empty house with the estate agent, giving instructions on which rooms should be redecorated, and which carpets and curtains were to be cleaned by the caretakers in their absence.[23] Some aristocratic families were utterly peripatetic, moving every month or two to yet another of their properties. Over and over again, the mistresss had to settle her travelling establishment into a different house in a new locality. She still had to keep in touch with staff remaining at all the other family properties, with letters and telegrams flowing back and forth between herself and department heads, perhaps arranging for supplies of fresh food to be sent from country estates and even for the laundry to be sent back and forth. The family, furthermore, often split into several smaller units: children left behind with their nurses and governess in the country, or sent to the seaside; or a husband and his men friends at the hunting lodge in Scotland.

Some landowners' wives, preoccupied with a frenetic social life, with philanthropy or other pursuits, delegated housekeeping to head servants. This was more common among fashionable and wealthy aristocrats, who could easily afford competent house stewards, housekeepers and butlers. Many great ladies did no more than confer with these head servants about the day's arrangements. The Countess of Macclesfield, for instance, headed a very efficient chain of command at Shirburn. After breakfast, she summoned the butler to the breakfast room, to give him his orders for the day: "how many visitors (if any) and which rooms they would occupy, the number that would be at meals, also orders for the carriages." He was followed by the housekeeper, then the cook. These department heads then gave the appropriate orders to their subordinates. "Everything went like clockwork," recalled the butler, "no confusion, no jealousies, no treading on each other's toes; no occasion for saying I don't know this or that; for each department got their orders and acted up to them."[24]

Less wealthy or fashionable mistresses were more involved in day-to-day housekeeping. Laura Cornwallis kept close tabs on the household at Linton Park, inspecting the linen, demanding lists of the china, glass and pewter, and the meat bill, giving out the tea and coffee herself, regularly going over the cook's accounts, and paying the servants' wages herself.[25] At late-nineteenth-century Petworth, Lady Leconfield and, in her absence, her daughter Maggie, attended to many day-to-day details of kitchen matters and finances, working in cooperation with the housekeeper.[26] Not all landowner's wives could afford a housekeeper; in a sample of 100 country houses from the 1871 census, nearly half of the baronet and gentry households lacked a housekeeper or cook-housekeeper, and one in ten contained only two or three female house servants.[27] Lower incomes necessitated closer supervision and accounting, and more household chores, even in the gardens and home farm. As late as the 1890s, according to Lady Violet Greville, "the ordinary *chatelaine*" superintended "her dairy, her poultry-yard and her garden."[28] Lady Shiffner not only paid household bills, hired and paid the female servants, and performed everyday housekeeping tasks like preparing an inventory of the linen and china, but sold home farm produce.[29]

Impoverishment forced even aristocratic ladies to take a greater interest in the household accounts: the fourth Baron Lyttleton's financial difficulties greatly worried his wife Mary. Her letters to her sister, Catherine Gladstone, were full of ideas for small economies. Her sister sent back "long letters of practical advice, questioning, for instance, the necessity of keeping a second laundry-maid, or urging enquiry into the amount of beer consumed in the servants' hall."[30] For the Gladstones were equally eager to economize after they took over the bankrupt Hawarden estate. Disorderly by nature, Catherine Gladstone forced herself "to keep careful accounts, to watch small expenditure, and to train herself in order and method."[31]

The mistress was most involved in housekeeping in the smallest households. Like other mistresses, Mary Ann Dixon did the household accounts and shopping lists, gave out stores, and arranged and supervised her servants' and daily helpers' work. But she also checked over the plate, bedding and linen, wrote inventories, labelled and put away wine and spirits, tidied her dressing room, helped shake carpets and gathered flowers. In the kitchen, futhermore, she processed the home-killed pig, cooked desserts for dinner parties, made pastries for the school feast, preserved fruit, and even cooked breakfast occasionally. Checking her own and her children's clothing, she cut out garments and household linen for seamstresses to sew.[32]

Home-making as opposed to simply housekeeping was a recent development, resulting from a more intimate and domesticated family life, the separation of home and work and a rising standard of living. The Victorian wife was supposed to create a cosy, comfortable, virtuous and aesthetically pleasing refuge from the harsh, immoral outside world, which would attract family members back to the home. Charlotte M. Yonge considered homemaking a wife's "paramount earthly duty." Even rich women, she insisted, should "keep a cheery family apartment for common life and ease."[33] Frances Power Cobbe was typical in regarding homemaking as women's "peculiar and inalienable right," a task reserved for them alone. "It is a woman, and only a woman . . . who can turn a house into a home." The primary goal of homemaking, she believed, was to create a "moral atmosphere," and thus contribute to "the virtue and happiness of mankind." She thus saw homemaking as an area of female independence and usefulness.[34]

Landowners' womenfolk residing in the ancestral mansion had less scope for home-making and home-decorating than middle-class wives, as much of the expensive decor and furnishings had been specially designed for each room, or accumulated over generations. Vast, formal staterooms, with their portraits and heirloom furniture, and atmosphere of chilly grandeur, were designed to impress visitors, not to promote domestic bliss. A new wife had little jurisdiction over the public rooms, except for her own drawing room. Men were sometimes reluctant to change the home of their childhood; at Hinton, Mr. Dutton strenuously opposed any structural alteration, despite his wife's "heroic efforts" to improve what she called "this barracks of a house," a Georgian manor house enlarged to become singularly poorly-designed and inconvenient.[35] At Calke Abbey, the only change Lady Harpur Crewe was able to bring about was the redecoration of the drawing room in 1856, which included placing loose-covers over late Georgian furniture.[36]

Victorian taste and the desire for comfort and coziness could lead chatelaines to introduce fashionable furniture and ornaments, and to modify existing interiors, particularly in their own territory of the drawing room and boudoir. "I have been busy this morning," wrote Cecilia, Lady Ridley, in 1841, "arranging flowers & making comfortable *corners* & trying to teach Bevan how to put books & chairs with an informal air."[37] On moving to Hinton Manor in the late 1850s, Mary Dutton crammed the drawing room with chairs, small tables, and whatnot stands piled with ornaments.[38] Upstairs, a bride could alter her own private rooms as she wished, and create a comfortable retreat for herself. When she first saw her suite, Lady Ridley resolved to place most of her own "pretty things" in her sitting room.[39]

Wives and daughters contributed to the heritage of country-house art and furnishings with their own embroidery and fine sewing, paintings, drawings, sketches and sculpture, or their collections of valuable objets d'art. Embroidery was a conventional pastime for gentlewomen. Lady Featherstonhaugh was typical in covering chairs, firescreens and footstools for Uppark.[40] Sketching and painting in watercolor were also ladylike pursuits, and the more agreeable results were often framed and hung. In some cases, genuine talent ensured that these works of art would become part of the family's heirlooms. Other ladies enjoyed purchasing beautiful objects for their homes. Lady Dorothy Nevill, for instance, collected old English glass, china and antique furniture.[41]

Late in the century, the aesthetic movement inspired some ladies to implement fashionable changes in decor. Madeline Wyndham befriended many famous artists and craftsmen. She and her contemporaries "fearlessly decorated their houses themselves," collecting fabrics on their travels which they cut up and sewed as covers for their sofas and chairs.[42] In 1880, Lady Bell and her daughters stitched the "splendid frieze of embroidery" designed by Edward Burne-Jones and William Morris for the Morris dining room at Rounton Grange.[43] Lady Wentworth was an advocate of the arts and crafts movement, a great admirer of

Morris and of the architect Voysey, whom she commissioned to replace the arcade on the front of Ockham. She had some eighteenth-century panelling torn out, removed antique furniture and redecorated with "plain unornamented tables, sideboards and rugs from the Home Arts Society."[44]

When a family rebuilt or bought a country house, the mistress had more scope. Before looking for a wife, Sir Rainald Knightley remodelled and updated his venerable family seat with new rooms on the south front. His bride found workmen still busy decorating them and hoped they would soon be gone, "and then we can arrange the furniture and chintzes etc."[45] Likewise, Bestwood was only just finished when the tenth Duke of St. Albans married Sybil Grey, so she was able to furnish the new mansion.[46] When her husband inherited Harewood House, Lady Harewood "dictated her own programme of alterations" with "forceful authority and unabated energy," employing Sir Charles Barry to remodel it extensively to accommodate a large family and Victorian ideals of domestic organization.[47] The higher a wife's rank, and the greater her family's riches, the more scope she enjoyed; Harriet Leveson-Gower, second Duchess of Sutherland, took notes on the houses and gardens she visited abroad, incorporating the features she admired most into her own houses. She was responsible for the alterations at Dunrobin and Lilleshall, and for the rebuilding of Trentham, while Cliveden was largely her own creation.[48] Also powerful, of course, were the widows and sisters who inherited landed estates. Anne Scarisbrook remodelled and redecorated her brother's Scarisbrick Hall, and the widowed Lady Buxton supervised the completion of alterations to Shadwell Hall, begun two years before her husband's death.[49]

Many country-house women exerted their talents and energies in the gardens. By the early-Victorian period, gardening had become an immensely popular pastime at all levels of society, with large numbers of exotic plants, shrubs and trees introduced. Some aristocrats were enthusiastic collectors of trees and plants. Lady Dorothy Neville, collected and grew a vast range of rare specimens at Dangerstein. Her collection was so extensive that Charles Darwin used it for his studies, and Kew Gardens exchanged plants with her.[50] On the landed estate, fashions in landscaping changed, giving ladies new opportunities to intervene. In the eighteenth century, mansions had stood in an idealised natural landscape of pasture, woodland and water. The early Victorians revived formal flower beds in parterres near the house, added shrubberies of exotic plants, and perhaps a rockery and a fernery. Botany was an approved subject of study for girls, and gardening was considered a genteel form of exercise for ladies. The gardens, moreover, were seen as an outdoor extension of women's aesthetic and moral influence on the home:

> In the country . . . the whole superintendence of the shrubbery, flower garden, and conservatory, should be appropriated by the ladies: the appearance of the ornamental garden is no equivocal exponent of the moral power of the female part of the family: it is very rare that either husband or brother will deny the exclusive control of this department.[51]

Though an expert head gardener was kept, with undergardeners to do all the labor involved, a lady could make the decisions as to what would be planted, and where. On small estates, the mistress could be very active. Mary Ann Dixon not only closely supervised the gardener and his helpers but did the annual pruning herself, altered the flower beds and chose planting sites for shrubs, helped with sowing and planting, gathered fruit, cut off deadheads and worked in her greenhouse.[52] When the young Belgraves were given a house on the Motcombe estate, Viscountess Belgrave delighted in making a garden. Her letters to her mother were full of enthusiasm for gardening. "I cannot tell you," she wrote, "the interest the garden gives my weak mind— to have the things sown and planted and then see them *evidently* come up and grow."[53] Lady Ridley studied garden books, determined to emulate a neighbor who managed the gardens of Brinkburn Priory herself "and expresses astonishment that anyone can live without gardening." Soon, Lady Ridley's plans to alter the flower beds were the despair of her head gardener. "He has no taste," she complained, "and does not enter into our views, and he suggests things which we do not agree to."[54] Many ladies engaged in amateur landscape-gardening. Margaret Hobhouse, for instance, designed the terraces, fountain, tennis court, rockeries, summer house and lily pond at Hadspen, and collected decorative lead figures and marble carvings.[55]

Two other important roles expanded housekeeping duties. Landowners' wives were expected to serve their families as hostesses and as philanthropists. These roles forced even wealthy mistresses to pay attention to the details of housekeeping. Chatelaines organized the transportation, accommodation, feeding and amusing of guests. A housekeeper could not be expected to know the intricacies of precedence, personalities and attachments which dictated the allocation of rooms and seats at the dinner table. In the smart set, particular skill was required to place adulterous lovers in adjacent bedrooms. Theresa Vane-Tempest-Stewart, sixth Marchioness of Londonderry, for instance, allocated bedrooms for her house-parties at Wynyard to suit lovers.[56] The lady of the house was responsible for the thoughtful details which made guests feel welcome.

> Everyone knows by comparison the difference between a house where a woman of education and refinement gives some of the thought and personal care to the comfort of her guests and one where all is left to the servants. We can all recall in certain houses the sheets scented with lavender, the enticing quill pens and the dainty bunch of flowers, the cosy fire on a cold day, that all whispered welcome to us as we entered our bedroom, and compare them favourably with the scrubby and torn blotting-book, the black and incapable pens, and sullen grate, that have been our gate in other places. In one house we have felt instinctively that the hostess has looked upon no details as too small or beneath her dignity; that no guest can come too late or go away too early.[57]

The role of hostess expanded over the period. In early and mid-Victorian England, social life was domesticated, intimate and private, within a close-knit circle of relatives and families of the same rank. When the landed classes were at home in the country, they entertained local elite families, family members descended en masse for weeks on end, and house parties were less frequent and longer than at the end of the century. During Lady Jeune's childhood in the 1860s, a dinner-party was a great event. She recalled how "the whole household was pressed into service;

how the family plate was taken out days before and cleaned, the chintz covers removed in the state rooms, clean curtains put up; and, when the eventful day arrived, how the mistress of the house was occupied from early morning superintending the details!" When shooting parties were arranged, "the small details relating to the bedrooms, such as seeing the fires lighted, the beds aired, and all the necessary accessories of a party, fell on the hostess, and only when her guests departed did she throw off the sense of anxiety which hospitality entailed."[58]

By the 1890s, with a rising standard of luxury and training, head servants had learned to handle all such details. "Now-a-days," Lady Jeune claimed, "no mistress need think of such small things. Her well-trained housekeeper attends to all those matters; and unless she likes to see for herself, it is unnecessary for her to trouble her head on the subject."[59] Autobiographies, however, reveal that many fashionable hostesses of the period still personally superintended the arrangements for guests. Indeed, it became an increasingly demanding task when the weekend party became so popular late in the century. Many a morning, Lady Elcho started preparing for her guests before she arose, littering the bed with sheets of paper "scribbled all over with tangled plans for the day." Even as she sorted out the trips to be made by carriage and dog-cart to the railroad station, the allocation of bedrooms and the seating arrangements at dinner, "a large fraction of her mind would be simultaneously engaged in planning ahead exactly how her next week's party should be occupied during every hour of their stay."[60] For the conscientious hostess, planning for numerous guests was burdensome. Having to ensure that the "vast machinery of service" operated smoothly and unobtrusively severely taxed her memory and energies, according to Lady Violet Greville.

> She must, in order to do justice to every one, be the first to rise and the last to go to bed. She must spare no effort and despise no trouble. She is for ever busy in her boudoir and her sanctum, interviewing servants, discussing arrangements, luncheons, dinners, and the distribution of bedrooms with her housekeeper, her butler and her steward, writing telegrams, answering letters. Her head must be a perfect encyclopaedia, with its varied and always ready knowledge. Then she must never forget, never be ruffled,

never be "caught napping". . . . It is she who suggests drives or rides, or plans expeditions, and ingeniously invents games and pastimes, and merry modes of passing the hours on wet days or long evenings. . . . If she does not do these things, and thinks only of amusing herself, she is no ideal hostess, and her parties are promptly stigmatized as dull.[61]

Consuelo Spencer-Churchill, ninth Duchess of Marlborough, came to resent the strain weekend parties entailed:

For my round of the thirty guest rooms, accompanied by the housekeeper, was apt to reveal some overlooked contingency too late to be repaired; a talk with the chef more often disclosed an underling's minor delinquency; orders to the butler invariably revealed a spiteful desire to undermine the chef . . . that, if realized . . . would jeopardize the culinary success of my party. Menus had to be approved and rooms allotted to the various guests. I had, moreover, spent hours placing my guests for the three ceremonial meals . . . for the rules of precedence were then strictly adhered to, not only in seating arrangements but also for the procession in to dinner. . . . There was . . . a considerable amount of purely mechanical work to be done—dealing with correspondence, answering invitations, writing the dinner cards and other instructions . . . which took up a great deal of my time.[62]

The role of Lady Bountiful also expanded women's housekeeping duties. As part of their rural philanthropy, country-house women dispensed charity to needy villagers. Visiting the sick, elderly and destitute in their own cottages, or interviewing them at the mansion, the ladies handed out food, medicine, clothing, or bedding as needed. Sometimes this was surplus food or cast-off clothing, the waste of an extravagant household. When the American Consuelo Vanderbilt became Duchess of Marlborough, she was disconcerted to find it was her job to cram the leftovers from lunch into large tins to distribute to the poor.[63] Lady Wantage sold dripping (the fat left after roasting joints) to the villagers for 4d a pound.[64] At Earlham, Laura Ripley stored leftovers from meals in a special cupboard, filling baskets for the poor. She also took small sums from the housekeeping money for beggars at the door.[65] Some ladies had supplies specially bought or made. Mrs Wroughton stocked her "Poor Person's Cupboard" at Woolley with flannel and calico, while Lady Fielding, kept hers filled with groceries and clothes, and her apron pockets filled with pennies ready to distribute.[66] Every year, Mary Ann Dixon provided gowns and shawls for the village women, frocks for the Sunday school girls, and, like other ladies, circulated four "baby's bags" containing layettes for newborns. Women also organized the traditional annual Christmas dole of beef and plum pudding, bedding, coals or clothing. Mary Ann Dixon presented villagers with shirts, petticoats and sheets (all cut out by her own hand), and coal.[67] At Blenheim, Consuelo Spencer-Churchill and her sisters-in-law spent their mornings before Christmas making up bundles of gifts for the duchess to deliver to the local poor.[68] When food ran short in harsh winters, ladies ordered their cooks to prepare soup to distribute to hungry villagers. In the 1840s, when farmers on her Sussex estate could not afford to raise their laborers' wages, Mrs. Day supplied soup twice a week for the five winter months, spending £25 on flour, rice, oatmeal and meat, and taking fresh vegetables from her own gardens.[69] School feasts, Sunday School treats, Christmas parties, tenants' balls, meetings of the militia or friendly societies, and community celebrations of family or national events were held at the Big House, all involving catering for large numbers, and a personal appearance as the hostess. Mary Ann Dixon bought or made the cakes and pastries for the Holton school feast herself.[70] Rosalind Howard, Countess of Carlisle, was famed for her estate Christmas parties. She purchased vast amounts of good-quality toys so that each child had a choice, personally supervised and participated in decorating a huge tree, and managed the three parties of schoolchildren, presenting the gifts herself.[71] The lady of the manor was also expected to host balls, bazaars, fancy fairs and garden parties to raise funds for charity.

Another important aspect of housekeeping was the management of servants. The role of mistress of servants was not instructing and supervising servants at work, but personnel management: hiring and firing the female staff, and issuing and enforcing rules governing their behavior both during and after work. Benevolent mistresses also took a personal interest in individual maids' welfare.

Every mistress of a country house devoted much time and energy to searching for new maidservants, firing unsatisfactory ones, and helping those leaving without fault find new posts. While the master was supposed to be responsible for the male staff, wives often took over; Lucy Arkwright interviewed and hired footmen, butlers and outdoor men.[72] Obviously, only the master or mistress could hire an upper servant like the housekeeper, lady's maid or cook, but many employers also concerned themselves with the lower staff as well, even though theoretically hiring and firing lower servants was delegated to department heads. Employers believed they gained greater control over the membership and quality of their household and reduced the risks of incompetence, immorality and crime. Servant-hunting was also an absorbing pastime for upper-class ladies, a constant topic of conversation and correspondence. Anne Sturges Bourne declared, "getting places & people to fit is one of the chief employments of life."[73] Often, however, the hunt was time-consuming, frustrating and fruitless. "One lives in hopes of getting quite the right thing (only to be disappointed probably!)" wrote Lucy Arkwright.[74]

Some mistresses exhibited distinctive preferences. Henrietta, Lady Hereford, shunned literate servants. Fanny Heneage, a Roman Catholic, wanted co-religionists, but the second Duchess of Sutherland, abhorred Roman Catholics, tolerating one in the Trentham laundry only because of her long service. Philanthropic mistresses attempted to help the underprivileged; Lady Carlisle, "took numerous boys and girls from the workhouse or outrelief cases."[75]

Ladies obtained the names of likely servants by asking their friends, relatives or servants for recommendations, concocting a shortlist from newspaper advertisements or applying to a registry office. They then interviewed candidates themselves or wrote for further particulars. An interview provided an opportunity to evaluate personality and appearance, and to enquire about a servant's intentions to marry, health, religion, and family background. Local servants' backgrounds could easily be investigated; Mrs. Coatesworth inspected prospective maids' own homes, rejecting one applicant because the door ledges were dusty.[76]

Once a servant was selected, the mistress demanded his or her "character," the letter of reference from the previous employer. While some upper servants vouched for underlings they had trained, and mistresses of the largest establishments sometimes relied on a report from a department head about a maid they had never encountered, most characters were written by the previous employer herself. Some letters simply followed the standard formula, affirming the essential requirements of honesty, sobriety, steadiness and respectability, and specifying why the servant left. Many surviving characters, however, reveal knowledge of the individual servant, describing relevant attributes, commenting on personality, and even evaluating a servant's problems and potential. Lady Braybrooke admitted that Emily Wise was not strong enough for the "*very* hard" work at Audley End in the winter, and Julia Ducie decided her lower housemaid was too inexperienced to take sole charge of a large house. When Lucy Shackleton gave notice, saying she wanted to better herself, Lady Donaldson suspected that "a disagreement with her cook was the real cause." Lady Falmouth noted that her dairymaid's weak wrist made baking difficult for her, and believed that Julia was "led away by others" in going out without permission. Alice Royce, wrote Lady Warwick, was very helpful when family members fell ill, being "willing to take on work that did not belong actually to her place."[77]

When they wrote for a character, some ladies expressed particular concerns. Lady Walsingham wanted to know if prospective footmen drank, swore or smoked, were amorous, dirty or smelly. Some recipients grew impatient with the virtues demanded; Lady Ruthven answered one letter: "If John Smith could answer to half your demands, I should have married him long ago."[78]

An anxious lady could take one further step to ascertain that she was obtaining a good servant. A character might be fraudulent, forged or falsified, and some people supplied undeservedly favorable references. So some mistresses also called on the previous employer to verify a written character, obtain fur-

ther information and judge the nature of the household, normally when both families were in London.

Involvement with the staff did not end with hiring. Early
in the century, Evangelicalism and the cult of True Womanhood
created a "maternalism" which paralleled the revival of
paternalism. The mistress was urged to show a motherly concern
for her servants' welfare, and to influence her servants by her
own character and example. In 1825, Samuel and Sarah Adams,
both experienced upper servants, insisted that the mistress
should always be aware that "the welfare and good character of
her household depends on her own active superintendence."[79]
Another author, Mrs. Dow, held that "no rank exempts a woman
from the duty of caring well for her household . . . she has a duty
before God to fulfil to her servants . . . in the place of rule."[80]
Even as late as 1883 Mrs. Eliot James urged that mistresses had a
duty to look after maidservants' "conduct, their comfort, their
general well-being, spiritual and bodily."[81]

The role of mistress included promoting desired work attitudes, controlling undesirable behavior and solving personal
problems and other crises. Her treatment of the staff, and the resultant atmosphere of the household, affected the servants' performance, behavior and turnover rate. Lady Violet Greville, admitted that "even in the largest establishment the mistress's eye
is absolutely invaluable. A cook soon loses heart in his work if he
is neither praised nor blamed, and the nattiest of family coach-
men . . . requires occasional commendation."[82] Some great ladies
were very autocratic; Lady Londesborough forbade her footmen
"to look at each other in her presence, or to speak excepting in
their professional capacity."[83] They were not even allowed to
look at the butler. She herself refused to speak to any servant except her butler and housekeeper. The seventh Duchess of Marlborough "ruled Blenheim and nearly all those in it with a firm
hand. At the rustle of her silk dress the household trembled."[84]
Likewise, Maria Brudenell-Bruce, Marchioness of Ailesbury,
"ruled her household with a rod of iron."[85]

Newly-hired servants seldom glimpsing the mistress felt
her influence through the rules governing the household. Employers had always sought efficient, deferential, obedient, law-
abiding and honest servants. By the early Victorian period, the

religious revival had prompted a preoccupation with religious observances and sexual morality; class-consciousness had instituted elaborate rituals of deference and codes of dress; and the family's desire for privacy demanded servants as anonymous and invisible as possible. Many Victorian mistresses were convinced they had the right and obligation to interfere in their servants' private lives. Pious ladies felt responsible for their servants' spiritual welfare. "It is my duty as the mistress of my family to attend to the spiritual welfare of my servants," resolved Lady Darnley, as she commenced to read scripture to her maids.[86]

Nineteenth-century mistresses were eager to impose a dress code on their maids. In earlier centuries maids had worn what they pleased. Eighteenth-century mistresses had even supplied their own cast-offs. Now lower maidservants were obliged to wear cotton print dresses with aprons and caps (housemaids changed into black dresses in the afternoon). Mistresses prohibited any alterations in accordance with current fashions, be they crinolines or bustles, and any ornamentation with lace, ribbons, artificial flowers and jewelry. Some mistresses forbade fashionable hairstyles; ringlets and, later in the century, fringes. Elizabeth Coke assured her fiancé she was determined to "put down with an iron hand all curl-papers and fal-lal."[87] For their afternoons off, however, maids bought or made outfits in the latest styles. Horrified mistresses believed maids were attempting to rise above their proper station in life; Lady Spencer-Stanhope made her female staff wear homespun; silk, she believed, was reserved for their betters.[88] Fashionable dress might also attract the opposite sex. Mistresses therefore insisted on dark, plain dresses and unfashionable black bonnets for church.

Many mistresses felt obliged to protect the virtue of the young women in their care. They had other motives for discouraging romance: among the staff it created jealousies; outside attachments introduced illicit guests, even thieves into the house; and both unwed pregnancy and marriage required a maidservant to leave service, necessitating a tiresome search for her replacement. Most mistresses immediately fired without a reference any maids caught in a sexual relationship, usually revealed by advancing pregnancy. Lady Carlisle utilized a more humane option, insisting that a groom and a laundrymaid legitimize their expected child with a hasty marriage.[89] To avoid such situations, mistresses laid down rules segregating the sexes both during and after work, restricted outings and often forbade courtship entirely. Like many other employers, Mary Ann Dixon issued the degrading command, "No Followers."[90]

After establishing rules, mistresses enforced them, as judges and arbiters. Typically, they dealt with servants' minor faults with a scolding, fired them for more serious ones, and dealt with the most serious crimes, like systematic theft, by calling in the law. When a fired but repentant housemaid pleaded with Anne Frewen to allow her to stay, her mistress "blew her up roundly" and granted her a reprieve. Lady Falmouth, however, fired Julia Simmons for disobeying the housekeeper and going out when she was supposed to remain in the house.[91]

Intervention as mediator and peacemaker in staff quarrels was "a recurrent and preoccupying worry."[92] Lady Cynthia Asquith later acknowledged that servants, "being human . . . always tended to quarrel with one another, so that domestic politics were often inflamed."[93] Thus, Lucy Arkwright dealt with a "domestic riot": "Housemaid confronting Mrs B. in my presence and so on. I have made Jane eat her words about the beer on Sat[urda]y, & given her a piece of my mind."[94] Anne Leveson-Gower, third Duchess of Sutherland, was called upon to settle a dispute over precedence at prayers.[95]

A final aspect of managing the staff was acting as a role model, setting a good example, and maintaining their respect. The mistress's dependents, one writer argued, were "unconsciously regulating their conduct by hers, and imbibing from her precepts and opinions favourable or otherwise to their morals."[96] Mrs. Beeton asserted that if servants "perceive that the mistress's conduct is regulated by high and correct principles they will not fail to respect her."[97] A strict code of conduct regulated and limited the family's lives, forcing everyone to adhere to the household's routines, attend prayers and church, and suffer excruciating boredom on Sundays, when Victorian ladies dared not knit, sew or play cards for fear of shocking the servants.[98] "Sundays were interminably long for a hostess," recalled Consuelo Balsan.[99]

The wide range of activities entailed in supervising house-keeping and servants, acting as hostess and Lady Bountiful, and perhaps engaging in landscape gardening and home decorating, kept the lady of the house busy. As the fictious but representa-tive "Lady Fanny Clermont" complained, "household duties are ever with you. Something in a large household has always to be ordered, and counter-ordered. Telegrams arrive at all hours. Fresh guests come, or friends that were expected write to say they are detained at the last moment. Nothing is too small, nothing is too trivial, for a woman's ears." She envied her hus-band, who could insist on uninterrupted solitude in his study when he wanted to write a speech. "I as a woman have no recognised leisure."[100] Even as a child, Lady Cynthia Asquith re-solved not to marry the owner of a large country house, regard-ing a chatelaine's life as "slavery of a kind." The role "involved too much organisation, too much thinking-ahead to be compati-ble with any rhythmic life of one's own."[101] Contemplating mar-riage to a landowner, twenty-year-old Emily Jowitt feared she was unfit. "It is an awfully responsible position for me."[102]

Late-nineteenth-century mistresses found their task in-creasingly challenging. "As the managers of households much more is demanded of them," claimed Catherine Milnes Gaskell in 1887.[103] Families moved from place to place more often and hosted a greater range of social occasions, more lavish and ex-pensive than ever, while ladies were now expected to demon-strate artistic talents with flower arrangements and interior dec-orating. Upper-class women became more active outside the home, serving in organized philanthropy and local government, promoting and participating in the arts, or writing articles and books. Less serious-minded ladies became preoccupied with a frenetic and opulent social life, and with a growing range of sports. The most wealthy and fashionable wives in High Society delegated many of their domestic responsibilities to the house-keeper or house steward. "Housekeeping is voted common now," declared Lady Greville in 1892. "Brides despise the details of the store closet and the larder."[104] Lady Jeune agreed: "No woman in modern society knows how to set about the ABC of her grandmother's work. She could not dust a room, or tell her cook how to make the most elementary dishes. Among the upper classes . . . everything devolves upon the servants. There is a good cook and a good butler, and the mistress never need give anything a thought."[105] In some ways, housekeeping was growing easier. A growing range of manufactured goods and commercial services eliminated the necessity for home brewing, baking, preserving, dairying and even laundries. Efficient employment agencies catering especially for the upper classes supplied regular and temporary servants on command, and catering companies could undertake the entire arrangements for a social event.

Why, when they could hire skilled and capable servants, did not more upper-class women evade the burdens of managing the household? Even those women temperamentally unsuited to the task struggled on. Though Catherine Gladstone lacked "organizational skills and a disciplined mind," and housekeeping at Harwarden was "rather chaotic," she "cheerfully muddled through," with the assistance of her daughters and loyal staff.[106] Mrs. Jebb of The Lythe "was not domesticated although she tried hard to be."[107] She "worried over expenses, accounts and servants. Her diaries are full of resolves to better look after her household."[108] In her study of politicians' wives 1860–1914, Pat Jalland found that the only woman who openly expressed distaste for household management was Alice Balfour, who most efficiently ran Whittinghame for her brother Arthur.[109] Significantly, she was a spinster, denied "a wife's compensation of status and affection."[110]

Most upper-class wives took their domestic roles for granted, thoroughly indoctrinated in the doctrines of separate spheres from every side as they grew up. Like all girls, they were conditioned from early childhood to subordinate their interests to those of others. In the nursery, nurses favored boys, and taught little girls to defer to and nurture their brothers. Girls played with dolls, dollhouses, miniature kitchens and so on, and read fiction idealizing women's domestic roles. Upper-class girls were educated at home, by middle-class governesses, who further inculcated accepted gender roles. Older girls became amiable, dutiful and submissive companions to their parents. They grew accustomed to the fragmentation of their time into disparate activities, and to putting aside their own pursuits to carry out family duties. "Women are never supposed to have any occupation of sufficient importance *not* to be interrupted," complained Florence Nightingale.[111]

Confined to the country house and its environs, landowners' daughters grew up regarding the home as the proper sphere for their activities. They saw themselves only in relation to the family, relatives and friends, the servants and the local poor. Girls envisaged their future roles with such groups, in subservience to their husbands, and in authority over their inferiors.[112] Proud of their birth into the elite, acutely conscious of their own social superiority, and served by deferential servants, these girls also acquired the self-confidence and assurance necessary to take on the demanding and complex task of running a country house.

Most important, however, was the strong sense of duty inculcated as part of the upper-class code of behavior. Females could advance the interests of the family by running a country house efficiently, and becoming a successful hostess. They helped preserve the reputation and authority of both their family and their class by engaging in philanthropy. For most wives, therefore, doing one's duty was a primary motivation for assuming the responsibility of running the household. It would be irresponsible and selfish to delegate the task to a housekeeper.

One more important reason why landed women chose to undertake housekeeping duties was that the role of mistress was a source of self-worth and self-esteem, a means of gaining status and respect within the family and household. The larger the establishment, the greater the power and the responsibility: chatelaines of country houses had under their control huge buildings, valuable furnishings, substantial funds, tons of supplies, and numerous employees. Some women relished their role, proud of their ability to run the household efficiently. Margaret Hobhouse "enjoyed being in the position of giving orders and superintending the smooth working of a large household."[113] Housekeeping was real work, which made a woman feel useful and active. Placed in charge of the stillroom, pantry and linen room, young Florence Nightingale reported she was "very fond of housekeeping. In this too highly educated, too-little-active age, it is at least a practical application of our theories."[114] The role of mistress of servants gave a woman considerable power over the lives of others: deciding who was to be hired, determining the rules governing the servants' daily lives, disciplining and firing servants, and writing or withholding references. When Lady Boughey caught Hannah Cullwick and another young maid larking about as they cleaned kettles, she gave them both notice to leave. Hannah was very sorry to leave her friends at Aqualate. "I was vex'd to leave & I ax'd Lady Boughy if she would please forgive me & let me stop. But she said 'NO,' very loudly, & I'd to look out for another place."[115] The role of hostess was a demanding and significant role too, which forced these women to become involved in the details of housekeeping and to seek the cooperation of servants. The mistress knew the family's reputation for hospitality, and part of her popularity as a hostess depended on guests' satisfaction with her arrangements.

The women who "married a country house," as the phrase went, were not frail and idle, but self-assured, energetic and willing to do their duty. The position of chatelaine gave them opportunities to exercise power over staff, to gain a reputation as a good hostess, to be benevolent towards the poor, and to make their own contribution to the family's heritage, be it by creating works of art, redesigning the gardens, redecorating rooms, or even remodelling the house. Their roles as housekeeper and mistress helped justify their privileged social position, and validated them as True Women. Far from being idle parasites, they performed real work demanding significant skills, time and effort, work which enhanced their own sense of worth, their value to the family, and their reputation among their contemporaries.

NOTES

1. Ronald Pearsall, *The Worm in the Bud: The World of Victorian Sexuality* (New York: Penguin, 1983), 64; O.R. McGregor, *Divorce in England: A Centenary Study* (London: Heinemann, 1957), 73, 74; Lawrence Stone, *The Family, Sex and Marriage 1500–1800* (London:

Weidenfeld and Nicholson, 1977), 396; Jonathan Gathorne-Hardy, *The Public School Phenomenon* (London: Hodder and Stoughton, 1977), 233.

2. Margaret Child-Villiers, Dowager Countess of Jersey, *Fifty-One Years of Victorian Life* (London: John Murray, 1922), 66.

3. Ursula Ridley, ed., *Cecilia: The Life and Letters of Cecilia Ridley, 1819–1845* (London: Rupert Hart Davis, 1958), 69–70.

4. Michael P. Conroy, *Backcloth to Gawthorpe* (Nelson, Hendon Publishing Co., 1971), 31.

5. Dixon MSS, diaries of Mary Ann Dixon, e.g. July 6, Dec. 10, 1870; May 22, 1872; July 18, 1875; Dixon 10/12/5–6, Lincolnshire Archives Office.

6. Jessica Gerard, *Country House Life: Family and Servants, 1815–1914*, forthcoming.

7. Gail Maccoll and Carol McD. Wallance, *To Marry an English Lord: The Victorian and Edwardian Experience* (London: Sidgwick and Jackson, 1989), 199.

8. Maccoll and Wallance, *To Marry an English Lord*, 193–94.

9. Consuelo Balsan, *The Glitter and the Gold* (London: Heinemann, 1953), 81.

10. Anita Leslie, *The Marlborough House Set* (New York: Dell, 1977), 147.

11. Georgina Battiscombe, *Mrs. Gladstone: The Portrait of a Marriage* (London: Constable, 1965), 71.

12. Anon. (Signed "M.S., An Old Servant"), *Domestic Service* (Boston: Houghton Mifflin, 1917), 35–36.

13. Anon., *Domestic Service*, 35–36.

14. Theresa McBride, *The Domestic Revolution: The Modernisation of Household Service in England and France 1820–1920* (London: Croom Helm, 1976), 27–30.

15. Northwick MSS, agreements with servants, 1859–68; 705:66 BA4221/23, Worcestershire Record Office; P.H.W. Booth, *Burton Manor: The Biography of a House* (Cheshire, England: Burton Manor, 1978), 34.

16. Edith Mary Gell, *Under Three Reigns 1860–1920* (London: Kegan Paul, Trench, Trubner and Co, 1927), 43–44.

17. Betty Askwith, *The Lyttletons: A Family Chronicle of the Nineteenth Century* (London: Chatto and Windus, 1975), 144, 160–61, 165.

18. Maccoll and Wallace, *To Marry an English Lord*, 197.

19. Ridley, *Cecilia*, 69–71, 73, 81, 83, 84, 86.

20. Julia Cartwright, ed., *The Journals of Lady Knightley of Fawsley* (London: John Murray, 1915), 173.

21. Nancy Mitford, *The Stanleys of Alderley: Their Letters Between the Years 1815–1865* (London: Chapman and Hall, 1973), 348.

22. Battiscombe, *Mrs. Gladstone*, 40–41.

23. Conroy, *Backcloth to Gawthorpe*, 42–43.

24. Ethel Thomson, *Clifton Lodge* (London: Hutchinson, 1955), 166–67.

25. Cornwallis MS, notes by Laura Cornwallis for the cook-housekeeper, n.d., U24 F25, Kent Archives Office.

26. Patricia Blackwell, " The Landed Elite in Decline: A Case Study of Five Sussex Country Houses" (Master's thesis, University of Sussex, 1978), 40–41.

27. See Gerard, *Family and Servants*, forthcoming.

28. Violet Greville, *The Gentlewoman in Society* (London: Henry and Co., 1892), 176.

29. Blackwell, "Landed Elite," 39–40.

30. Askwith, *Lyttletons*, 93–94.

31. Battiscombe, *Mrs. Gladstone*, 80.

32. Dixon MSS, Mary Ann Dixon's diaries, 1838–62, 1864–79; Dixon 10/12/1–9.

33. Charlotte M. Yonge, *Womankind* (London: Mozley and Smith, 1876), 162, 266.

34. Jenni Calder, *The Victorian Home* (London: Batsford, 1977), 103–105.

35. Ralph Dutton, *Hinton Ampner, A Hampshire Manor* (London: Country Book Club, 1969), 67, 79.

36. Howard Colvin, *Calke Abbey Derbyshire: A Hidden House Revealed* (London: The National Trust/George Philip, 1985), 70.

37. Ridley MS, Cecilia Ridley to Lady Parke, Oct. 1844; ZRI/30/27/5, Northumberland Record Office.

38. Dutton, *Hinton Ampner*, 63.

39. Ridley, *Cecilia*, 70.

40. Margaret Meade-Fetherstonhaugh and Oliver Warner, *Uppark and Its People* (London: George Allen Unwin, 1964), 96.

41. Ralph Nevill, *Reminiscences of Lady Dorothy Nevill* (London: Edward Arnold, 1907), 222–24, 236–41.

42. Edith Olivier, *Four Victorian Ladies of Wiltshire* (London: Faber and Faber, 1945), 90–91.

43. Mark Girouard, *The Victorian Country House* (New Haven: Yale University Press, 1979), 418.

44. Susan Tweedsmuir, *The Lilac and the Rose* (London: Gerald Duckworth and Co., 1952), 29.

45. Cartwright, *Journals of Lady Knightley*, 173.

46. Donald Anderson and Peter Beauclerk Dewar, *The House of Nell Gwyn: The Fortunes of the Beauclerk Family 1670–1974* (London: William Kimber, 1974), 156.

47. Mary Mauchline, *Harewood House* (Newton Abbott: David and Charles, 1974), 125–47.

48. George Sutherland, 5th Duke of Sutherland, *Looking Back* (London: Odhams Press, 1957), 35–36.

49. Girouard, *Victorian Country House*, 117–119, 194, 197.

50. Joan Morgan and Alison Richards, *A Paradise out of a Common Field: The Pleasures and Plenty of the Victorian Garden* (New York: Harper and Row, 1990), 229.

51. Anon. (signed "G.S."), *The Governess*, Houlston's Industrial Library no. 18 (London: Houlston and Stoneman, 186–?), 233–56.

52. Dixon MSS, Mary Ann Dixon's diaries 1838–77; Dixon 10/12/1–7.

53. Gervas Huxley, *Lady Elizabeth and the Grosvenors: Life in a Whig Family, 1822–1839* (London: Oxford University Press, 1965), 53.

54. Ridley, *Cecilia*, 116.

55. Stephen Hobhouse, *Margaret Hobhouse and Her Family* (privately printed, Rochester: Stanhope Press, 1934), 160–61.

56. H. Montgomery Hyde, *The Londonderrys: A Family Portrait* (London: Hamish Hamilton, 1979), 68.

57. Catherine Milnes Gaskell, "Women of To-Day," *The Nineteenth Century* Vol. 24 (Nov. 1889): 778–79.

58. Susan St. Helier, Lady Jeune, *Lesser Questions* (London: Remington and Co., 1895), 108–109.

59. St. Helier, *Lesser Questions*, 109.

60. Cynthia Asquith, *Remember and Be Glad* (London: James Barrie, 1952), 5–6.

61. Greville, *Gentlewoman in Society*, 173.

62. Balsan, *Glitter and the Gold,* 81.

63. Balsan, *Glitter and the Gold,* 87.

64. Pamela Horn, *Labouring Life in the Victorian Countryside* (Dublin: Gill and Macmillan, 1976), 16.

65. Percy Lubbock, *Earlham* (London: Jonathan Cape, 1926), 24–25, 47.

66. Winefride Elwes, *The Fielding Album* (London: Geoffrey Bles, 1950), 88–89.

67. Dixon MSS, Mary Ann Dixon's diaries, 1838–1880; Dixon 10/12/1–10; "Christmas Books" 1834–59, 1861–81; Dixon 10/12/20–21.

68. Balsan, *Glitter and the Gold,* 119.

69. Alice Catharine Day, *Glimpses of Rural Life in Sussex during the Last Hundred Years* (Idbury: The Countryman Press, 1927), 47.

70. Dixon MSS, diaries of Mary Ann Dixon. e.g. 8 August, 9 August, 1864, Dixon 10/12/3; 13 August, 17 August 1867, 24 July, 30 July 1868, Dixon 10/12/4; 22 June, 9 August, 10 August 1869, Dixon 10/12/5.

71. Dorothy Henley, *Rosalind Howard, Countess of Carlisle* (London: The Hogarth Press, 1959), 51–52.

72. Arkwright MSS, Lucy Arkwright to John Hungerford Arkwright 1869–1900, A63/IV/176, Herefordshire Record Office.

73. Pamela Horn, *The Rise and Fall of the Victorian Servant* (Dublin: Gill and Macmillan, 1975), 38.

74. Arkwright MS, Lucy Arkwright to John Hungerford Arkwright, May 24, 1896, A63/IV/176.

75. The Countess of Wemyss, *A Family Record* (privately printed, London, 1932), 29; L.E.O. Charlton, *The Recollections of a Northumbrian Lady* (London: Jonathan Cape, 1949), 91; Sutherland MS, Harriet, Duchess of Sutherland, to Mrs. Ingram, n.d. D543/R/10/2; Henley, *Rosalind Howard,* 88.

76. Mary Chamberlain, *Fenwomen: A Portrait of Women in an English Village* (London: Virago Press, 1975), 100.

77. Packe MSS, letters of reference sent to Lady Alice Packe, 1875–1883, DE 1346/437, Leicestershire Record Office.

78. Eric Horne, *More Winks* (London: T. Werner Laurie, 1932), 79; Augustus Hare, *The Story of My Life* 6 vols. (London: George Allen, 1896–1900), 4: 269.

79. Samuel and Sarah Adams, *The Complete Servant* (London: Knight and Lacey, 1825), 13.

80. Mrs. Dow, *Hints to Mistresses* (London: Bosworth and Harrison, 1856), 12–13, 17.

81. Mrs. Eliot James, *Our Servants: Their Duties to Us and Ours to Them* (London: Ward, Lock and Co., 1883), 26.

82. Greville, *Gentlewoman in Society*, 82–83.

83. Edith Sitwell, *Taken Care Of* (London: Hutchinson and Co., 1965), 64.

84. Pamela Horn, *Ladies of the Manor: Wives and Daughters in Country-House Society 1830–1918* (Wolfeboro Falls: Alan Sutton, 1992), 147.

85. Violet Greville, *Vignettes of Memory* (London: Hutchinson and Co., 1927), 249.

86. Elizabeth Cust and Evelyn Georgiana Pelham, eds., *Edward, Fifth Earl of Darnley and Emma Parnell His Wife* (Leeds, Richard Jackson, 1913), 229–30.

87. A.M.W. Stirling, *Life's Little Day* (London: Thornton Butterworth, 1924), 20.

88. Stirling, *Life's Little Day*, 20–21.

89. Henley, *Rosalind Howard*, 89.

90. Dixon MS, rules for servants, Dixon 22/5/36.

91. Prestwold MS, Lady Falmouth to Lady Alice Packe, Aug. 1, 1875; DE 1346/437.

92. Noel Streatfield, ed., *The Day Before Yesterday: Firsthand Stories of Fifty Years Ago* (London: Collins, 1956), 119.

93. Asquith, *Remember and Be Glad*, 4.

94. Arkwright MS, Lucy Arkwright to John Hungerford Arkwright, 6 Nov. 1894, A63/IV/176.

95. Sutherland MS, Anne, Duchess of Sutherland, to Mrs. Ingram, n.d. D593/R/10/2.

96. Mrs. Henderson, *The Young Wife's Own Book: Her Domestic Duties and Social Habits* (Glasgow: W.R. M'Phun, 1857), 7.

97. Isabella Beeton, *How to Manage House and Servants* (London: Ward, Lock and Tyler, 1871), 9.

98. Clodagh Anson, Lady, *Book: Discreet Memoirs* (London: G. Bateman Blackshaw, 1931), 360.

99. Balsan, *Glitter and the Gold,* 84.

100. Gaskell, "Women of To-Day," 782.

101. Asquith, *Remember and Be Glad,* 6–7.

102. David Verey, ed., *The Diary of a Victorian Squire: Extracts from the Diaries and Letters of Dearman and Emily Birchall* (Gloucester: Alan Sutton, 1983), 47, 49.

103. Gaskell, "Women of To-Day," 778.

104. Greville, *Gentlewoman in Society,* 173.

105. St. Helier, *Lesser Questions,* 107.

106. Pat Jalland, *Women, Marriage and Politics 1860–1914* (Oxford: Clarendon Press, 1986), 192.

107. Stella Margetson, *Victorian High Society* (New York: Holmes and Meier, 1980), 133.

108. Francesca Wilson, *Rebel Daughter of a Country House: The Life of Eglantyne Jebb, Founder of the Save the Children Fund* (London: George Allen and Unwin, 1967), 25–26.

109. Jalland, *Women, Marriage and Politics,* 192–93.

110. Jalland, *Women, Marriage and Politics,* 193.

111. Florence Nightingale, "Cassandra," in Ray Strachey, *"The Cause": A Short History of the Women's Movement in Great Britain* (Port Washington NY: Kennikat Press, 1969), 401.

112. See Leonore Davidoff, *The Best Circles: Society Etiquette and the Season* (London: Century Hutchinson, 1986), 51, 93; Carol Dyhouse, *Girls Growing Up in Late Victorian and Edwardian England* (London: Routledge and Kegan Paul, 1981), 43–45.

113. Hobhouse, *Margaret Hobhouse,* 67.

114. Cecil Woodham-Smith, *Florence Nightingale* (London: Reprint Society, 1952), 50.

115. Liz Stanley, ed., *The Diaries of Hannah Cullwick, Victorian Maidservant* (New Brunswick: Rutgers University Press, 1984), 38.

Decorating Domestic Space
Middle-Class Women
and Victorian Interiors

Thad Logan

> "Women have always been visible as objects within culture, but only recently have they been acknowledged as subjects of cultural production in their own right."[1]

In 1950, Scribner's published an unusually intelligent coffee-table book called *Decorative Art of Victoria's Era* by Frances Lichten. In two hundred fifty oversized pages, Lichten explored the fantastic variety of ornamental objects popular in the late nineteenth century. "Women," she observed, "lived out their lives in tangled thickets of them."[2] It was to these tangled thickets of ornament that middle-class British and American women were indeed confined by an increasingly hegemonic doctrine of separate spheres. The ideological construction of home as a woman's place coincided with the development of a distinct style of design—the detailed, curlicued, cluttered, sentimental, fringed and flowery style we call Victorian.[3]

Until somewhat recently, Victorian decoration was usually dismissed as being both aesthetically bad and morally unsound. A modernist aesthetic in art and literature soundly rejected Victorian excess in favor of the minimal. Similarly, Thorstein Veblen's *Theory of the Leisure Class* (1899) reproached Victorians for their excessive consumption of goods.[4] Yet as Theodor Adorno pointed out in *Prisms* (1967), Veblen bases his critique on a fantasy of some purely functional relation between people and the products of culture, whereas in reality all culture involves elements of display.[5] In "Beyond Veblen: Re-thinking Consumer Culture in America," Jackson Lears, following Adorno, argues that in Veblen's work "nothing was allowed its true, multivalent significance. Veblen realized that all consumption enacted cultural meaning, but he was willing to assign it only one meaning: status striving."[6] Since women played an important role in creating the cluttered interiors that became so fashionable during Victoria's reign, a reductive understanding of Victorian decoration contributes to a limited view of middle-class women. If, that is, the practice of decorating was primarily directed at gaining social status, then the women who presided over this practice must be seen either as venal themselves or as mere agents for their husbands. But decoration is in fact a complex activity which serves many cultural and psychic purposes. In this essay I will explore several aspects of decorative practice, and consider how domestic decoration was represented in the literature of the period. Initially, it will be necessary to situate Victorian decoration within its historical context: specifically, we need to consider decoration with reference both to the development of a consumer economy and to the ideology of separate spheres.

Compulsory domesticity was the context of life for middle-class Victorian women.[7] Only in the last two or three decades of the twentieth century has the domestic been deconstructed, both practically and theoretically. The link between women and home, which anti-feminist discourse insists is natural, has of course a history. Cynthia L. White's study of periodical literature, *Women's Magazines 1693–1968* (1970), demonstrates how attitudes about women had modified considerably during the first quarter of the nineteenth century: early in the 1800s, women's magazines were "frank, vigorous, and mentally stimulating," but by mid-century their focus had narrowed to "fiction, fancy-work, and gossip."[8] By about 1860, women had become primarily responsible for selecting and purchasing articles to furnish the home, and magazines became important sources of advice on this topic.

Advice on particulars of housekeeping and decoration, such as that found in Isabella Beeton's *Book of Household Manage-*

ment (1861), echoes and elaborates on the exhortations of "Victorian sages" concerning the social role of women. Perhaps the locus classicus of this latter discourse is John Ruskin's *Sesame and Lilies* (1865) in which the home is idealized as "the Place of Peace . . . the shelter from all terror, doubt, and division." A woman's duty toward the home is "to secure its order, comfort, and loveliness": "her intellect is not for invention or creation, but for sweet ordering, arrangement, and decision."[9] On a less exalted but perfectly harmonious note, an American book on etiquette and home, *Decorum* (1881), advises that "a sensible woman will always seek to ornament her home and to render it attractive."[10] Thus Thomas Carlyle writes approvingly of his wife Jane's work in completing their move to 5 Cheyne Row: after three or four days of confusion, "all was swept and garnished, fairly habitable; and continued incessantly to get itself polished, civilized, and beautified."[11] Carlyle's use of the passive voice here might suggest how such feminine practices came to be seen as so natural and so familiar that the *agency* of individual women tended almost to disappear from masculine view.

The middle-class woman was taught to consider the tasteful decoration of her home as an important part of her duty, a duty whose broader outlines included both the physical and spiritual well-being of her family. Decoration, in this context, became linked to morality. In *The American Woman's Home*, Catherine Beecher and Harriet Beecher Stowe argue that "the decoration of houses . . . contributes much to the education of the entire household in refinement, intellectual development, and moral sensibility."[12] As the home became (ostensibly) set apart from the vicissitudes of public life and the harsh economy of the marketplace, women presided over an interior space that was frequently linked to the "goodness" in contemporary discourse. The huge popularity of Coventry Patmore's poem, "The Angel in the House," testifies to a powerful conflation of the morally upright, the feminine, and the domestic for middle-class Victorians.

By the mid-nineteenth century, technological development within an industrial capitalist economy made the production and consumption of material goods possible on a scale never before realized in history. Mark Girouard, in his introduction to Susan Lasdun's *Victorians at Home* (1981), notes that in this era "more

and more people were collecting more and more objects, partly
because there was more money all around, [and] partly because
large numbers of mass-produced, decorative objects were available at comparatively little expense."[13] Women, insofar as they
were primarily responsible for domestic decoration, were thus
responsible for managing at a local level the plenitude of things
coming into being in the wake of industrialization and the rise of
a consumer economy.

    As we turn to consider decoration as a practice functioning
within the parameters I have sketched, it may be best to begin by
examining relations between domestic interiors and social status.
Like the Catholic Mass, Victorian social rituals required material
objects for their successful performance. In *The Victorian Girl and
the Feminine Ideal* (1982), Deborah Gorham (following J.A. Banks)
has characterized this set of objects as "the paraphernalia of gentility"—there was "a generally agreed upon set of possessions . . .
that formed the material base upon which the pattern for a successful middle-class way of life rested."[14] In the absence of this
paraphernalia, social rituals such as making and receiving calls
were perceived as parody or deception rather than the real thing.
Hence there was, as Patricia Branca has observed in *Silent Sisterhood* (1975) real anxiety among the lower ranks of the middle
class about acquiring and maintaining such possessions. If a family's prosperity increased, corresponding changes in domestic
decor were expected to occur; thus most books on housekeeping
carefully distinguish among different levels of income when offering advice about decoration. Since women were responsible
for the social life of the family, "Women, not men, managed the
outward forms that both manifested and determined social status. Through the creation of an appropriate domestic environment . . . women at all levels of the middle class were responsible
for assuming that the private sphere acted as an effective indicator of status in the public sphere."[15]

    While it is surely important to acknowledge that decorat-
ing worked within the elaborate Victorian system of social rank
and ritual, it is also important to ask what interests or needs
other than indicating status might be served by lavish domestic
decoration. Despite my argument with Veblen, his critique of
"conspicuous consumption" is potentially useful and interesting

because it foreshadows more sophisticated Marxist (and non-Marxist) thinking about the communicative work of objects. In *The World of Goods* (1989), for instance, Mary Douglas and Baron Isherwood attempt to reframe our understanding of commodities by considering all goods as operative parts of an extensive system of communication. For Douglas and Isherwood, "the essential function of consumption is its capacity to make sense."[16] Objects, including decorative objects displayed in the home, do say something about those who possess and display them; among the messages emitted by a lavishly decorated parlor was, surely, something like "this is the home of a successful man," yet there is no reason to believe that decoration was limited to signifying relative wealth. Many other aspects of a family's life were also on display in the parlor.

The characteristic Victorian accumulation of objects nearly always, for instance, included a proliferation of things crafted by the ladies of the household. These objects testified to their talent and industry, and when exchanged with friends and family could become signs of that "female world of love and ritual" discussed by Carroll Smith-Rosenberg.[17] Here is Elizabeth Gaskell's account, in *Cranford* (1853) of Miss Matty Jenkyns accomplishments:

> What she piqued herself upon, as arts in which she excelled, was making candle-lighters or 'spills' (as she preferred calling them), of colored paper, cut so as to resemble feathers, and knitting garters in a variety of dainty stitches.... A present of these ... a bunch of gay 'spills,' or a set of cards on which sewing silk was wound in a mystical manner, were the well-known tokens of Miss Matty's favor.[18]

Besides crafts, mementos, and souvenirs, the middle-class parlor was liable to contain many decorative objects with a straightforward narrative content, whose communicative value lay in their assertion of socially approved patterns of thought and behavior. Presumably, the presence of paintings, prints, sculptures, or Berlin work (what we would now call needlepoint) which told stories of filial devotion or religious faith would not only benefit the family but would also speak to outsiders of their sound opinions, thus helping to establish its respectability—an attribute linked to, but not subsumed by, financial status.

My point is simply that Victorian decoration carries a far more complex social meaning than has usually been acknowledged. Another dimension of that meaning which is sometimes not adequately discussed or understood involves aesthetic experience. The importance of such experience is well evidenced by an episode recounted in Zuzanna Schonfield's *The Precariously Privileged* (1987). In 1889, the upper middle-class Marshall family decorated a house in Chelsea prior to moving in. Ada and Jeanette Marshall, unmarried women in their twenties, "wallowed in pattern books and swatches," choosing colors and fabric for curtains, floor coverings, slipcovers, paint, and wallpaper. On moving day, they "unpacked the wine, the china, and the glass; they arranged trophies of ornaments on the overmantels and supervised the hanging of pictures." On their first "at home" day, visitors "exclaimed in delight over the beauties of the house and the skill of its amateur interior decorators"—"our taste was pronounced perfect," Jeanette confided to her diary.[19] If, following Jean Baudrillard's theories of cultural semiotics,[20] we consider the Marshall's home as a set of signifiers, it is clear that one signified is indeed something like "prosperity." Yet it is also evident that the meaning of this space is linked to aesthetic values. Victorian women almost certainly did find aesthetic pleasure for themselves and generate such pleasure for others in the decoration of their homes.

In her essay "In Search of Our Mother's Gardens" (1974), Alice Walker looked at the lives of poor southern black women in the early years of our century and asked, as did Virginia Woolf and Tillie Olsen in other contexts, what happens to the creativity of women who are brutally oppressed.[21] Her answer is that women did, against all odds, find in the materials and practices available to them a way to create beauty. While the degree and kind of oppression operative in the lives of middle-class Victorian white women is certainly different from that visited upon the black women whose work Walker celebrates, we can nonetheless recognize that in both cases aesthetic impulses found expression in forms unrecognized as "art" and undervalued by those in positions of cultural authority. We need at least to consider that the bric-a-brac, whatnots, and knickknacks that Victorian women chose, made, and cherished were as meaningful to them as the garden of Walker's mother, and that their cluttered parlors were at least in some cases generated in response to a desire for aesthetic pleasure.

It is possible to see, for instance, a kind of unquenchable aesthetic drive in a poignant passage cited by Frances Lichten about an American servant's decorative habits:

> Hannah had queer ways. She was given to interior adornments, and the fruits of her needlework were thick in the house. These were not fine, but considering the material from which she wrought them, they were worthy of praise. She pinned black broadcloth cats to the wall, brought out in silhouette upon red flannel . . . she hung novel comb-cases under all the bedroom looking glasses. These were of varied shapes and materials, some of broadcloth, some of straw, and less pretentious ones of covered cardboard, all much stitched with colored silks. The patchwork around the house was endless. Hannah hoarded scraps of silk and cambric, and pieced them into pin-balls, chair-cushions, and coverlets. She glued painted pictures to the inside of wide-mouthed glass jars, which she filled with flour and planted with asparagus, thus simulating quaint vases. She embossed blown egg-shells with the pith of bulrushes, coiled around bits of bright silk, and hung them upon pine boughs in the fireplaces of the front rooms.[22]

At least two significant objections can be raised, however, to the idea that Victorian decorative practices constituted some kind of creative work for women. Lichten herself pointed out, as long ago as 1950, that the sheer number of useless decorative objects produced by women might better be viewed as a manifestation of anxiety, boredom, and depression rather than a satisfying and healthy engagement with art. In what now seems a rare burst of feminist insight for a woman writing in that era for a major publishing house, she theorizes the causal link between oppression and the production of ornament:

> Most of the time-killing works to which the era was so zealously given resulted from . . . the social and emotional predicaments in which the Victorian woman floundered.

> For those who craved a really sound education, there were
> at first few opportunities. Men did not intend to make it
> easy for women to compete with them in the cultural,
> artistic or economic fields. Woman was constantly urged
> to be content and happy in the lovely home she had
> created with funds which her successful husband had
> supplied.[23]

In this context, to advance an argument that Victorian domestic
interiors might be viewed as art may seem at best irrelevant, and
at worst reactionary. Jenni Calder, for instance, in *The Victorian
Home* (1977) argues forcefully that there was no possibility for
creative self-expression in the domestic life of the middle-class
woman. To see the purchase, arrangement, or fabrication of decorative objects as a meaningful act of creativity is simply to reproduce the ideology of domesticity.[24]

There is, moreover, a serious question among writers on
design about the extent to which personality plays any significant role in Victorian interior decoration. While Osbert Lancaster
sees "the intrusion of an aggressively personal note into decoration" as a distinguishing mark of Victorian style, Denys Hinton
argues that "the rigidity of social structure left little scope for
originality of ideas in decorating or furnishing."[25] Poststruc-
turalism has, furthermore, taught us always to question any
simple notions of creativity and self-expression. Thus, in her
theoretically elaborate meditations on the collection, the souvenir, and the miniature, Susan Stewart considers that "the
function of belongings within the economy of the bourgeois
subject" is to construct—rather than express—what we know as
"personality."[26]

Despite these cogent objections to a reevaluation of domestic ornament as offering some scope for feminine creativity, I
think it is too early to foreclose on this possibility. While we need
to know more about women as historical subjects in the nineteenth century, we can be sure that they did exercise some control over the purchase, selection, and arrangement of objects in
their homes. Since all social practices are rule-governed, to point
out that a rigid code of correctness presided over interior decoration does not vitiate the potential for individual performance
within this system. To deny that individual choice played some

part in decorative activity, or that aesthetic value might accrue to its results, seems to me only to reproduce the all-too-familiar misogynistic devaluation of women's lives and works.

If we conceive, somewhat speculatively, of the decorating subject as analogous to the writer of literary texts, then the problematic issue of self-expression in middle-class domestic interiors becomes clearer. Certainly, Victorian women, like epic poets, operate within a set of historically contingent conventions; it would not have been possible for an individual woman to exercise transcendent freedom in decorating her parlor. Yet writers and decorators do make choices from the grammar and lexicon available to them to construct texts or rooms, and we may assume that what we call personality is involved in that construction. (It is interesting to note that the term "style" is important in the discourses of both literary criticism and interior decoration.) My point is that it is possible to use concepts like self-expression in thinking about the practice of decoration while acknowledging that selves are always embedded in the social world and that choices are always made within history.

Contemporary ethnographic studies of decoration, in fact, stress precisely the intersection of the individual and the social at the site of the domestic interior. In a special issue of *Environment and Behavior* devoted to home interiors (March, 1987), Roderick Lawrence argues that "the home is simultaneously a haven for withdrawal from society and a credential for esteem and the respect of others."[27] "The home," according to Maria Guiliani's article in the same journal, "catches the expression of the dialectic rapport between the individual and society in its physical and behavioral specificity."[28] The point, as I take it, is that the home is both public and private: its decoration articulates meaning both in the register of the personal (family photographs, souvenirs, handcrafts) and in the larger social system which envelops and enables private experience. Similarly, in *The Meaning of Things* (1981) Mihaly Csikszentmihalyi and Eugene Rochberg-Halton conclude that decorative objects both mediate between the self and others, and "constitute an ecology of signs that reflects [and] shapes the owner's self." They go on to suggest that "the organization of the household can be seen as a pattern of attention and intention made concrete in the artifacts and ambience they create."[29]

Is it possible, then, to read Victorian homes, insofar as we have access to them or to their representations, as symbolic of psychic experiences, needs, and drives? What patterns of attention and intention are revealed by the lavishly decorated interiors of this era, so often ridiculed by moderns. A brief outline of some possible psychological approaches to the characteristically cluttered Victorian style of domestic decoration can suggest some explanations for the emergence and popularity of this style.

Behavioral psychology suggests one interesting way to think about "excessive" Victorian design. In "Decorating Personal Places: A Descriptive Analysis," William Hansen and Irwin Altman explore the similarity between decorating and marking behaviors: many animals mark their territory "by scent, secretions, excretion, or other means," and humans exhibit comparable behavior when they decorate their homes.[30] The Victorian interior, then, would be identified by Hansen and Altman as a strongly marked space, full of material objects which combine in intricate patterns to intensify visual and tactile experience. In *For a Critique of the Political Economy of the Sign* (1981), Baudrillard discusses "redundance" in the decor of the bourgeois home in a way that further makes sense of Victorian marking behaviors: "The obsession of the small cottage owner and small capitalist is not merely to possess, but to underline what he possesses two or three times."[31] Baudrillard refers here to decorative objects like the doily, yet it is easy to see how redundancy operates throughout the Victorian interior—consider, for instance, the typical window, outlined in layers of elaborately-draped fabric. The practice of marking in the world of bourgeois Victorians is clearly related to concepts of territory, possession, and ownership, and thus would seem to be useful in substantiating a Veblenesque sense of ornament. Yet it is important here to remember that Victorian women did not stand in the same position vis-à-vis property as did middle-class men. Both Veblen and Baudrillard tend to assume a relation between the self, the possession, and the world that is descriptive of male, but not female, experience. If we try to reconstruct that female experience, then marking behaviors take on a somewhat different tone. Rather than the confident, aggressive statement "This is mine!" decoration can be instead an attempt to assert authority and control on the part of subjects whose autonomy was constantly being undermined by legal, medical, and religious discourse.[32] Thus excessive decoration, from a feminist perspective, is not only a question of surplus but of lack: women filled their parlors with objects not only because they had plenty of time, money, and consumer goods, but also because they lacked social power.

This projected logic of too much and not enough suggests a second kind of psychological analysis. Denys Hinton points the way to a Freudian reading of the parlor in the following observation: "We associate the name Victorian with a moral attitude and a distinctive mode of decoration: the one disciplined and puritanical, the other, paradoxically, licentious and undiscriminating."[33] From a classical Freudian perspective, the paradox is an obvious one: the erotics of decoration operate according to the general principles of psycho-sexual economy, in which primary drives are sublimated and find socially acceptable forms of expression. Thus the "tangled thickets" of Victorian ornament can represent a displacement of libidinal energy onto material things, and the Victorian parlor, in its sensual richness, can be read as a return of the repressed.

From a slightly different angle, it could be argued that the feminization of the home, in the sense of the coercive ideological link between women and the domestic sphere, produces a kind of hyper-femininity in decoration. In his essay on material culture cited earlier, Jackson Lears discusses "the resurfacing of instinctual energy that was submerged, though never absent, in the Victorian imagination," and makes some interesting though problematic assertions about decoration and the erotic:

> The Victorian interior embodied the iconography of female experience; it domesticated and moralized natural fecundity and sexual energy with floral wallpaper, globular lamps, cavorting cupids in the bedroom, and Ceres in the dining room. The vogue of potted plants epitomized the pattern of a domesticated nature straining at the seams of its civilized constraints.[34]

The sheer proliferation of forms, colors, and textures in the Victorian parlor must have constituted an intensely stimulating sensory environment. To what extent this environment was overtly or latently sexualized by the Victorians, however, is a difficult question. While Lear's conflation of female experience with "natural fecundity and sexual energy" is perhaps specious, his point about the iconographic feminization of the parlor seems to me a good one, although it needs careful development within the context of feminist studies in representation.

The "constraints of civilized life" that many Victorian women felt had perhaps less to do with sexual experience than with limits placed on the exercise of their ambitions and the play of their egos. Confined to the domestic sphere, Victorian women may well have attempted to make the best of a bad job by transforming their homes into small versions of the world, into microcosms full of objects and icons, something like the tombs of the Pharaohs. Recent work on museums and collections does, in fact, suggest links between the desire to accumulate objects and the formation of the bourgeois self. Writing for a collection of anthropological essays on museums and material culture, James Clifford observes that

> some sort of "gathering" around the self and the group—
> the assemblage of a material "world," the marking off of a
> subjective domain which is not "other"—probably is universal. . . . In the West, however, collecting has long been a
> strategy for the deployment of a possessive self.[35]

Clifford goes on to cite Susan Stewart's analysis of how the collection of objects works to create the illusion of a controlled world and a coherent identity. Stewart and Clifford, along with Baudrillard, whose work strongly influences theirs, seem to take an essentially Marxist view of the selfhood thus generated as guilty and illusory. But if we remember that nineteenth-century bourgeois women were not, in fact, fully empowered by a capitalist economy, then their strategies of collecting decorative objects as a means of forming identity and making a place in the world can be viewed less harshly.

Gaston Bachelard's *The Poetics of Space* (1964) considers home from a phenomenological perspective that is, despite differences in philosophical and political orientation, quite similar to the work of Stewart at certain points. Bachelard, too, develops a dialectic view of the relation between identity and the middle-class home. He imagines a fantasy of perfect congruence between outer and inner, self and world. "Before being cast out . . . we are laid in the cradle of the house" where "being reigns in a sort of earthly paradise of matter, dissolved in the comforts of an adequate matter."[36] It is not difficult to see Victorian interiors as womb-like bowers of materiality, a materiality that is literally domesticated and thus made safe and beneficent, capable of offering an antidote to existential anxiety. Mark Girouard is worth quoting again, at some length, as he explores this aspect of Victorian decoration.

> Most Victorians were incurable nest-makers; but their equivalents of twine, straw, and leaves were Japanese fans, vases, photographs, bronze statues, and clocks, which they wove together into a richly indistinguishable fuzz. Burne-Jones, on the other hand created a forest, lined with the leaves and foliage of Morris wallpaper and embroideries, and filled with mysterious light percolating through hangings and stained-glass windows. Other interiors combined elements of both nest and forest, the forest being almost literally provided by the potted palms and other greenery which spilled over from the conservatory into all the living rooms of the more prosperous Victorian homes. Both nests and forests suggest an element of escapism, just as the accumulation of objects suggests a desire for security. They probably do so with reason. It is so easy to think of the Victorian as a smug and self-confident age, but one has only to make a very superficial dip into Victorian letters and literature to see how far this was from being the case: doubt, despair, fear of revolution, dislike of the way the world was changing round them, mystification and worry at what science was up to, are all too apparent.[37]

In his wonderful study of detail in Victorian art and literature, Peter Conrad similarly considers the period's decorative intensity as linked to pleasure in a fantasied escape from the marketplace:

> The exuberance of the Victorian interior derives from the split between the prosaic and ugly environment of work

and the haven of comfort and relaxation of the home, devoted to dream and pleasure.[38]

While the perspective here is obviously masculine—for women,
the home was certainly not simply a site of dream and pleasure—Conrad's theorizing of ornament was an important
achievement in 1973. As Naomi Shor was to do some years later,
in an analysis focused on gender,[39] Conrad explored the concep-
tual and practical link between ornament and detail, and observed that Victorian novels, like Victorian interiors, are "stuffed
as full as possible."[40] The popularity of the three-decker novel,
then, coincides with the kind of decorative practice we have been
considering; the realistic novel, with its plenitude of "un-necessary detail,"[41] seems indeed to be the literary counterpart of the
Victorian parlor.

One of the oddest things about reading Victorian novels
with an eye out for descriptions of these parlors is how seldom
one finds them. We might expect these rooms, these nests of ornament, to have provided a field day for realists. Yet announced,
extended descriptions of these rooms are relatively uncommon
throughout the century. In her book *Living Space in Fact and
Fiction* (1989), Phillipa Tristram argues that while Jane Austen,
following eighteenth-century standards of decorum, gave us
little in the way of interior description, later novelists were much
more apt to fully set their characters in a material context.[42]
While this is accurate, I am not convinced that Tristram adequately acknowledges what I conceive to be the discrepancy
between the sheer number of decorative objects the writers she
discusses lived among and the scarcity of descriptions of such
objects in their texts. Michael Irwin, in *Picturing: Description and
Illusion in the Nineteenth Century Novel* (1979), addresses what
seems to me a lack, and offers one explanation for it:

> How often is the student of nineteenth-century fiction in-
> duced to visualise an almost completely alien world? How
> often is he made to recall that the city streets he is reading
> about are thronged with horse-drawn vehicles? that the
> drawing-rooms are over-furnished and over-decorated in
> the heavy Victorian manner? . . . Sights that would have
> been commonplace to the author and his contemporary
> readers were taken for granted. Everyone knew what a

> busy street or a middle-class drawing room looked like. Why should the novelist waste words in describing them?[43]

Why, on the other hand, should the novelist "waste" words at all? Irwin's observation seems to me on target, but his explanation does not. Perhaps the novelists suffered (or enjoyed) as we all do the invisibility of any contemporary style which is really pervasive and successfully hegemonic. We cannot, that is, literally *cannot* see the distinctive visual features of life in the 1990s as we can easily see those of the the sixties, the seventies, and, increasingly, the eighties. Some kind of distance (difference?) is a condition of the sort of visibility I am referring to. Yet, obviously, descriptions of domestic interiors do sometimes appear in the nineteenth-century novel. What conditions make their appearance possible?

An answer must shift our focus from any individual's perceptual experience to the rhetorical conventions which always to some degree control the production of narrative. The description of landscape, for instance, which may appear to be natural, or spontaneous, or simply a representation of what is "really there," is in fact governed by rhetorical practices which can be traced to Classical literature (and Academic painting) and are well-established by the Victorian era.[44] Description of the bourgeois domestic interior, however, is a practice being constructed by and within the nineteenth-century novel. The appearance of detailed description of the "normal" middle-class parlor, as I will argue for the remainder of this essay, is presided over by two categories, "coziness" and "excess." It is the coming into play of these intellectual or emotional categories that seems to preside over the appearance of the interior.

I want to begin by considering Thackeray and Henry James under the rubric of excess, looking first at a passage from *Pendennis* (1848–50). The description here is of Lady Clavering's drawing room. While it might be objected that the quality and expense of the individual items suggest an aristocratic rather than a bourgeois style, Lady Clavering and her sensibilities are presented as aggressively middle class, "nouveau riche."

> But what could equal the chaste splendor of the drawing room?—the carpets were so magnificently fluffy that your

foot made no more noise on them than your shadow: on
their white ground bloomed roses and tulips as big as
warming pans: about the room were high chairs and low
chairs, bandy-legged chairs, chairs so attenuated that it
was a wonder any but a sylph could sit upon them, mar-
queterie tables covered with marvellous gimcracks, china
ornaments of all ages and countries, bronzes, gilt daggers,
Books of Beauty, yataghans, Turkish papooshes and boxes
of Parisian bonbons. Wherever you sat down there were
Dresden shepherds and shepherdesses convenient at your
elbow; there were, moreover, light blue poodles and ducks
and cocks and hens in porcelain; there were nymphs by
Boucher and shepherdesses by Greuze, very chaste indeed; there were muslin curtains and brocade curtains, gilt
cages with parroquets and love birds, two squalling cockatoos, each out-squalling and out-chattering the other; a
clock singing tunes on a console-table, and another boom-
ing out the hours like Great Tom, on the mantel-piece—
there was, in a word, everything that comfort could desire,
and the most elegant taste devise.[45]

Lady Clavering's drawing room is presented, notably, in contrast
to Sir Frances' library, which was "filled with busts and books all
of a size, and wonderfully easy chairs, and solemn bronzes in the
severe classic style."[46] Obviously it is the library that for Thackeray represents genuine comfort and elegance. The key term,
however, in this description is "chastity."

By repeating the term several times, Thackeray asks us to
apprehend the scene in terms of sexuality, and when we do so,
we must read "chaste" as ironic, as evoking its opposite term,
promiscuous. First, the sheer proliferation of sensory experience,
the sounds, colors, textures, and surfaces, surround and threaten
to overwhelm the hapless observer. Thackeray here casts his narrative in the second person in order, I think, to emphasize the
sensually aggressive relation of the room to a visitor, especially a
male visitor. The objects themselves, seen as coherent "wholes"
as well as fragments of a total scene, suggest promiscuous sexuality: consider the shepherds and shepherdesses, the cocks and
hens, the nymphs and love birds and finally the frenzied pair of
cockatoos. Thackeray represents excessive decoration as a
version of unrestrained sexuality—a sexuality that is gendered

"feminine" by virtue of its specific association with Lady Clavering and its separation from the masculine realm of the library.

The link between vulgarity, wealth, and female sexuality is
to be repeated and elaborated in the novels of Henry James. We
might note, for instance, in *The Wings of the Dove* (1902), Merton
Densher's reaction to the drawing room of Kate Croy's Aunt
Maud, whom Merton has already described to himself as
"colossally vulgar."

> He hadn't known . . . that he should "mind" so much how
> an independent lady might decorate her house. It was the
> language of the house itself that spoke to him, writing out
> for him with surpassing breadth and freedom the associa-
> tions and conceptions, the ideals and possibilities of the
> mistress. Never, he felt sure, had he seen so many things
> so unanimously ugly—operatively ominously so cruel. . . .
> He felt it less easy to laugh at the heavy horrors than to
> quail before them. . . . He had never dreamed of anything
> so fringed and scalloped, so buttoned and corded, drawn
> everywhere so tight and curled everywhere so thick. He
> had never dreamed of so much gilt and glass, so much
> satin and plush, so much rosewood and marble and mala-
> chite. But it was above all the solid forms, the wasted
> finish, the misguided cost, the general attestation of
> morality and money, a good conscience and a big balance.
> These things finally represented for him a portentous
> negation of his own world of thought—of which, for that
> matter, in presence of them he became as for the first time
> hopelessly aware. They revealed it to him by their
> merciless difference.[47]

The relationship that obtains between Aunt Maud and her parlor
is more metonymic than that between Lady Clavering and hers:
here, the interior represents (stands for, symbolizes) for Densher
both the woman and her world. The revulsion he feels, I would
suggest, is linked to a fear and horror of mature women, women
who in 1902 surely would also have appeared as "fringed and
scalloped, buttoned and corded, drawn everywhere so tight and
curled everywhere so thick." If the language used here seems to
evoke the elaborately clothed, fleshy body of a Victorian matron,
then the last lines of the passage can be read a a re-statement of
the fear of being swallowed up, "negated" by the maternal body.

Densher explicitly invokes here the myth of patriarchal culture summed up by Judith Kegan Gardner: "cultures like ours ... define 'mind' as male and immaterial and mother as mindless mat(t)er."[48]

If Aunt Maud and her parlor are inimical to the male spirit, what are we to make of another famous description of wretched excess in James, the Brigstocks' home in *The Spoils of Poynton* (1897). It is, after all, Mrs. Gereth, a woman and a mother, whose sensibilities are horrified by "Waterbath." One answer is that it is vulgarity that is being pilloried here, vulgarity in the sense of wealth (rather than femininity) undisciplined by taste.

James's narrator notes in the lines leading up to his description of Waterbath that "the principle of taste" has been "extravagantly omitted" from the Brigstocks' "composition." If chastity and its unnamed opposite, promiscuity, preside over the description of Lady Clavering's drawing room, here James's language suggests an excessive pre-Oedipal energy. The Brigstocks are described as having an "abnormal" nature, and it first appears as though the description is to be primarily informed by the theme of strangeness. In the decoration of Bathgate, "some other principle [than that of "taste"] remarkably *active*, but *uncanny* and *obscure* had operated instead" (emphasis mine). Yet as the description progresses, the idea of strangeness is overtaken by the idea of "remarkable activity," and the passage ends with a barely displaced fantasy (attributed to Fleda Vetch) of excremental smearing. Here is James's description of the Brigstocks at work on their house:

> They had smothered it with trumpery ornament and scrapbook art, with strange excrescences and bunchy draperies, with gimcracks that might have been keepsakes for maid-servants and nondescript conveniences that might have been prizes for the blind. They had gone wildly astray over carpets and curtains; they had an infallible instinct for gross deviation and were so cruelly doom-ridden that it rendered them almost tragic ... the house was perversely full of souvenirs of places even more ugly than itself and of things it would have been a pious duty to forget. The worst horror was the acres of varnish, something advertised and smelly, with which everything

was smeared: it was Fleda Vetch's conviction that the application of it, by their own hands and hilariously shoving each other, was the amusement of the Brigstocks on rainy days.[49]

Social snobbery here merges with—and probably can be traced back to—a revulsion from the childish and primitive; for Mrs. Gereth there is a confusion of the Brigstocks, and babies, and excrement which is surely not unrelated to Mona Brigstock's relationship with Owen Gereth. When Mrs. Gereth imagines the marriage and Mona's coming to Poynton, "she saw in advance with dilated eyes the abominations they would inevitably mix up with them." "Them" refers ostensibly to the precious "things" of Poynton, but it is not farfetched to read here a concern for the possibility of Mona Brigstock's sexuality spoiling the purity of the Gereths just as the "little brackets and pink vases" of Waterbath would spoil Mrs. Gereth's "treasure."

Phillipa Tristram, in her discussion of the novel, perceptively notes that Poynton and its beauties are never described with the kind of detail James lavished on Waterbath. "They remain deliberately impressionistic, no more than a suffusion of colour, light, and texture."[50] For James, detailed description is equal to representing the ugly, but not the beautiful. To describe in detail, in Dutch-painterly fashion, is a lapse of taste for James. His characterization of the Victorian novel as a "loose, baggy monster," is (or can be read as) a re-statement in the realm of aesthetic theory of his aversion to the blowsy, sentimental, overly-ornamented British drawing room. I think a case could also be made that the loose, baggy monster is a decidedly feminine horror: a nightmarish version of the middle-class, middle-aged woman. James announces the advent of modernity in more ways than one. His distaste for the vulgar, feminized interior will be increasingly shared, especially by proponents of "modern" design, who will slay the dragon of Victorian excess with the sharp edge of minimalism.

Although the idea of the domestic and the category of the detail are extremely important for Dickens and George Eliot, a different set of principles—moral rather than aesthetic—seems to govern the appearance of domestic detail in their novels. Interestingly, however, neither gives us much "straight" description of a middle-class parlor. In Dickens, details of domestic interiors are associated with the eccentric, the grotesque, the odd, and the idiosyncratic. In Eliot's novels, detailed description of interiors is usually linked to nostalgia for the "old-fashioned." Both Dickens and Eliot value detailed description as a narrative technique which corresponds closely to the ethical norms established in their novels. Their valuation and presentation of the objects of domestic life, of bric-a-brac and ornament, is in both cases more closely linked to their sense of the good than to their vision of the beautiful.

What is particularly interesting from my perspective about Dickens is that he doubles (I might say obsessively) his own imaginative act as a novelist by describing characters who (compulsively?) create settings for themselves. They, like Dickens, are masters of the odd but exact detail, and they furnish their domestic spaces on some pure principle of metonymy. The objects they gather and collect around themselves constitute a repeated, polyphonic self-expression. These characters generate—at least when they are most blessed by circumstances—environments in which "Being reigns in an earthly paradise of matter."[51] We might think immediately of Mr. Peggotty, of Mr. Pumblechook and his shop, of Mrs. Gamp's apartment, even, though more grimly, of Miss Havisham.

In Dickens's novels, decoration and ornament tend to lose any strong association with the feminine. Here, ornament and detail are signifiers of the creative, romantic "self," which Dickens values so highly.[52] As signifiers of identity, domestic objects are too important to be left to women in general or a spouse in particular, to gather and arrange. Boffin's Bower, in *Our Mutual Friend*, (1864–65), illustrates my point:

> It was the queerest of rooms . . . There were two wooden settles by the fire, one on either side of it, with a corresponding table before each. . . . On the hob, a kettle steamed; on the hearth, a cat reposed. Facing the fire between the settles, a sofa, a footstool, and a little table, formed a centrepiece devoted to Mrs Boffin. They were garish in taste and colour, but were expensive articles of drawing-room furniture that had a very odd look beside the settles and the flaring gaslight pendent from the ceiling. There was a flowery carpet on the floor; but, instead

of reaching to the fireside, its flowing vegetation stopped short at Mrs Boffin's footstool, and gave place to a region of sand and sawdust. Mr Wegg also noticed, with admiring eyes, that, while the flowery land displayed such hollow ornamentation as stuffed birds and waxen fruits under glass-shades, there were in the territory where vegetation ceased, compensatory shelves on which the best part of a large pie and likewise a cold joint were plainly discernible among other solids.[53]

The divided room appears because Mr. Boffin asserts his right to select and arrange objects in the drawing room to please himself (his part of the space is fitted "like a luxurious amateur tap room"), yet does not appropriate the whole room. As he puts it to Wegg, "Mrs Boffin, she keeps up her part of the room in her way; I keep up my part of the room in mine."[54]

Dickens, it seems to me, envisions a social world of a beneficent mutuality here, composed of interiors that fully, openly, and transparently express the personality of their inhabitants. Several writers on Victorian style have discussed the parlor as a kind of personal or familial museum,[55] and it is this aspect of decoration that Dickens exploits and exaggerates in his fiction. When Dickens's characters do *not* operate out of a principle of creative self-expression in relation to their surroundings, then ornament begins to appear under the aegis of the "excessive" and/or the "bad." The Podsnap plate is a good example of this sort of thing in Dickens:

Hideous solidity was the characteristic of the Podsnap plate. Everything was made to look as heavy as it could, and to take up as much room as possible. Everything said boastfully, "Here you have as much of me in my ugliness as if I were only lead; but I am so many ounces of precious metal worth so much an ounce;—wouldn't you like to melt me down?" A corpulent straddling epergne, blotched all over as if it had broken out in an eruption rather than been ornamented, delivered this address from an unsightly silver platform in the centre of the table. Four silver wine-coolers, each furnished with four staring heads, each head obtrusively carrying a big silver ring in each of its ears, conveyed the sentiment up and down the table and handed it on to the pot-bellied silver salt-cellars.

> All the big silver spoons and forks widened the mouths of
> the company expressly for the purpose of thrusting the
> sentiment down their throats with every morsel they ate.[56]

In "Society," the world of the Podsnaps, of Lady Dedlock and
Edith Carker, people and objects tend to lose the beneficent,
cozy, metonymic relation I have discussed. Ornament ceases to
function as a fluid, multivalent signifier of the living "self," and
becomes a signifier whose signified is always and only "wealth"
and/or "status."

George Eliot's handling of the details of domestic interiors
is, like that of Dickens, governed by her profound commitment
to a certain moral position, but in Eliot's case a commitment to
expressing woman's condition also influences her work. It is
easy to see the famous jewel scene at the beginning of *Middlemarch* (1874) as a parable of the novelist's uneasy relation to
decoration. Dorothea begins by asserting to her sister Celia "we
should never wear them" (their mother's jewels—which are
referred to four times in this scene as ornaments), yet ends by
claiming for herself an emerald ring and bracelet "more beautiful
than any of them."[57] Dorothea justifies her act by spiritualizing
her pleasure in the beauty of the gems: one of the things Eliot
does in the scene is to enact for us the conflict within Miss
Brooke between religious asceticism and sensuality. I am arguing
that Eliot was similarly conflicted, that she both mistrusted
sensory detail and was drawn to it. We know that Eliot much
admired Dutch landscape painting, and one way she resolves the
tension I have described is to lavish her narrative attention only
on the rustic interiors of a recent (for Eliot) agrarian past. We see
the Poyser's kitchen in *Adam Bede* (1859), for instance,[58] and Mrs.
Tulliver's "chany" with gold sprigs in *The Mill on the Floss*
(1860),[59] but not, significantly, Gwendolyn Harleth's drawing
room in *Daniel Deronda* (1876). It is "safe" for Eliot to write about
these rustic interiors, I think, because their sensory details are
underwritten both by the concept of utility and by the rhetorical
category of pastoral. Thus they cannot lure her readers to an
admiration for rank and wealth, nor to a lust for the superficial
pleasures of the eye.

Eliot's realism is not, in any case, a matter of the representation of material objects. Her description of Tertius Lydgate's

medical research in chapter sixteen of *Middlemarch* can be read as an aesthetic manifesto, a statement of her project as a novelist. The "testing vision of details and relations" that "reveals subtle actions . . . through long pathways of necessary sequence" corresponds beautifully to her own narrative technique. What Eliot can tell us about Victorian domestic interiors is not so much what they look like, but how they come into being and how they are sustained or lost. Thus, we are never given much of a description of the Lydgate's home, but we follow it from its beginnings, through its threatened dissolution, to its final establishment (away from Middlemarch) as a luxurious upper-middle class residence—"all flowers and gilding."[60]

Eliot can give us insight into the "production" of Victorian interiors because she understands the material conditions of social life. Objects are made by hand (Miss Dodson's linen), inherited (Dorothea's jewels), or purchased (Rosamond Vincy's plate). To purchase objects, to maintain a bourgeois home, takes money: money is (if not inherited) acquired in exchange for labor. In the course of *Middlemarch*, we see Lydgate struggle to earn the money that will provide Rosamond with the kind of home she expects, and we see him finally sacrifice his talent and happiness in order to provide her with such a home.

Part of Rosamond's power over Lydgate lies in her utter refusal to acknowledge social and material reality: "She cared about what were considered refinements and not about the money that was to pay for them." When her husband attempts to explain that they must put their house on the market and put their furniture in hock to reduce expenses, she casts the situation in terms of free will and uses the language of choice; this, she complains, is what Lydgate "likes" to do.[61] Rosamond herself, with her "infantine blondness" and her "forget-me-not" blue eyes and her accomplishments, is a perfect symbol of decadent ornament as far as Eliot is concerned. Like the "trashy china" Edith Wharton warns us against in *The Decoration of Houses* (1907),[62] she destroys the "effect" of a "good piece" like Lydgate.

By developing a discussion of ornament in Thackeray, James, Dickens, and Eliot within the context of Victorian decorative practice, I have tried to open up new ways of thinking about domestic detail in the novel, to foreground "background" and reconsider the significance of what Kenneth Burke called "scene"[63] in relation to rhetoric, gender, and material culture. It has also been my purpose in this essay to reopen the doors of "real" drawing rooms, to look again at these interiors from a position on the other side of modernism.

We occupy now, of course, as scholars, a strange position with regard to these elaborate rooms constructed by the Victorians. We are in a sense voyeurs (voyeuses), peeking into what were hallowed sanctuaries of private life. We are the uninvited guests, the "world" whose gaze most Victorians were so anxious to shut out. If these rooms are in some way works of art, they were never intended to be open to the public. The art of the parlor is an intimate art: its emotional resonance must have depended, to a large extent, on the observer's familiarity with the memorabilia displayed while the visual, kinesthetic effect surely depended on an observer's being enclosed in the decorated space. We can, it is true, visit such rooms, as well as look at photographs or drawings of them, but unless the rooms belong to family or friends, rather than historical societies, we must miss out on some of their pleasure and "meaning," which—as I have been at pains to argue—cannot be wholly understood as a statement about wealth or status.

Neither, though, can the rooms be read as though they were *not* implicated in a capitalist economy. It is surely no accident that a major resurgence of Victorian style for the home accompanied the Reagan/Thatcher years. The 1980s saw the publication of an extremely successful new "shelter" magazine for women, *Victoria,* which celebrates in florid prose and gorgeous pictures the (often purely fantasied) world of the upper-middle-class Victorian woman. *Victoria* is, of course, a merchandiser's dream come true. And it's possible that in reading (or, more aptly, viewing) this magazine, with its curious mixture of the old and new, the sentimental and the materialistic, the beautiful and the absurd, that we are actually coming fairly close to some authentically Victorian taste in domestic decoration.

NOTES

1. Rosemary Betterton, *Looking On* (New York: Pandora's Press, 1987), 203.

2. Frances Lichten, *Decorative Art of Victoria's Era* (New York: Scribner's, 1950), 170.

3. The reader will observe that I play somewhat fast and loose with the term "Victorian" throughout this essay, using it to refer both to British and American interiors from the mid-nineteenth century up to the first world war. This is fairly common practice in the discourse of interior decoration. The distinction which is often made between Victorian and Edwardian interiors is not relevant to my purpose here, since the styles are so similar in the features I wish to discuss.

4. Thorstein Veblen, *Theory of the Leisure Class* (New York: Macmillan, 1899).

5. Theodor Adorno, "Veblen's Attack on Culture," in *Prisms*, trans. Samuel and Shierry Weber (Cambridge: MIT Press, 1967), 73–94.

6. Jackson Lears, "Beyond Veblen: Re-thinking Consumer Culture in America," in *Consuming Visions: Accumulation and Display of Goods in America, 1880–1920*, ed. Simon J. Bronner (New York: Norton, 1989), 75.

7. For discussions of middle-class domestic life, see Leonore Davidoff and Catherine Hall, *Family Fortunes* (London: Hutchinson, 1987), and Bonnie S. Anderson and Judith P. Zinsser, *A History of Their Own: Women in History from Prehistory to the Present*, vol. 2 (New York: Harper and Row, 1988.)

8. Cynthia L. White, *Women's Magazines: 1693–1968* (London: Michael Joseph, 1970), 38, 55.

9. John Ruskin, *Sesame and Lilies* (New York: H.M. Caldwell, 1865), 151, 172, 150.

10. S.L. Louis, *Decorum: A Practical Treatise on Etiquette and Dress of the Best American Society* (New York: Union Publishing House, 1881), 202.

11. Thomas Carlyle, *I Too Am Here: Selections from the Letters of Jane Welsh Carlyle*, ed. Alan and Mary McQueen Simpson (Cambridge: Cambridge University Press, 1977), 111.

12. Cited by Karen Halttunen in "From Parlor to Living Room: Domestic Space, Interior Decoration, and the Cult of Personality," in *Consuming Visions*, ed. Simon J. Bronner (New York: Norton, 1989), 161.

13. Mark Girouard, "Introduction" to Susan Lasdun, *Victorians at Home* (New York: Viking, 1981), 19.

14. Deborah Gorham, *The Victorian Girl and the Feminine Ideal* (Bloomington: Indiana University Press, 1982), 9.

15. Patricia Branca, *Silent Sisterhood: Middle-Class Women in the Victorian Home* (London: Croom Helm, 1975), 8.

16. Mary Douglas and Baron Isherwood, *The World of Goods* (New York: Basic Books, 1979), 62.

17. Carroll Smith-Rosenberg, *Disorderly Conduct: Visions of Gender in Victorian America* (New York: Knopf, 1985), 53–76.

18. Elizabeth Gaskell, *Cranford* (London: Macmillan, 1903), 245–46.

19. Zuzanna Schonfield, *The Precariously Privileged: A Professional Family in Victorian London* (New York: Oxford University Press, 1987), 176, 179, 180.

20. See especially Jean Baudrillard, *For a Critique of the Political Economy of the Sign,* trans. Charles Levin (St. Louis, MO: Telos Press, 1981).

21. Alice Walker, *In Search of Our Mothers' Gardens: Womanist Prose* (San Diego: Harcourt, Brace, Jovanovich, 1983); Virginia Woolf, *A Room of One's Own* (New York: Harcourt, Brace and World, 1957); Tillie Olsen, *Silences* (New York: Delacorte, 1978).

22. Lichten, *Decorative Art,* 172.

23. Lichten, *Decorative Art,* 170.

24. Jenni Calder, *The Victorian Home* (London: Batsford, 1977), 105.

25. Osbert Lancaster, *Home, Sweet Homes* (London: John Murray, 1939; 1948), 36; Denys Hinton, "High Victorian 1840–80," in *Great Interiors,* ed. Ian Grant (New York: Dutton, 1967), 179.

26. Susan Stewart, *On Longing: Narratives of the Miniature, the Gigantic, the Souvenir, the Collection* (Baltimore: Johns Hopkins University Press, 1984), xi.

27. Roderick Lawrence, "What Makes a House a Home?" *Environment and Behavior* 19:2 (March 1987): 163.

28. Maria Vittoria Guiliani, "Naming the Rooms: Implications of a Change in the Home Model," *Environment and Behavior* 19:2 (March 1987): 181.

29. Mihaly Csikszentmihalyi and Eugene Rochberg-Halton, *The Meaning of Things: Domestic Symbols and the Self* (New York: Cambridge University Press, 1981), 17, 184.

30. William Hansen and Irwin Altman, "Decorating Personal Places: A Descriptive Analysis," *Environment and Behavior* 8:4 (December 1976): 492.

31. Baudrillard, *For a Critique*, 42.

32. For a recent discussion see Mary Poovey, *Uneven Developments: The Ideological Work of Gender in Mid-Victorian England* (Chicago: University of Chicago Press, 1987).

33. Hinton, "High Victorian," 172.

34. Lears, "Beyond Veblen," 87.

35. James Clifford, "Objects and Selves: An Afterword," in *Objects and Others: Essays on Museums and Material Culture*, ed. George W. Stocking, Jr., History of Anthropology, vol. 3 (Madison: University of Wisconsin Press, 1985), 238.

36. Gaston Bachelard, *The Poetics of Space*, trans. Maria Jolas (New York: Orion, 1964), 7.

37. Girouard, "Introduction" to *Victorians at Home*, 10.

38. Peter Conrad, *The Victorian Treasure House* (London: Collins, 1973), 71.

39. Naomi Shor, *Reading in Detail: Aesthetics and the Feminine* (New York: Methuen, 1987).

40. Conrad, *Victorian Treasure House*, 9.

41. For a discussion of "un-necessary" detail as a mark of verisimilitude, see Tzvetan Todorov, *The Poetics of Prose*, trans. Richard Howard (Ithaca, NY: Cornell University Press, 1977), 137.

42. Phillipa Tristram, *Living Space in Fact and Fiction* (London: Routledge, 1989).

43. Michael Irwin, *Picturing: Description and Illusion in the Nineteenth Century Novel* (London: George Allen and Unwin, 1979), 113.

44. See, for instance, E. H. Gombrich's groundbreaking work in *Art and Illusion* (Princeton: Princeton University Press, 1961).

45. William Makepeace Thackeray, *The History of Pendennis* (New York: Scribner's, 1917), 429–30.

46. Thackeray, *Pendennis*, 429.

47. Henry James, *The Wings of the Dove* (New York: New American Library, 1964), 62–63.

48. Judith Kegan Gardner, "Mind Mother: Psychoanalysis and Feminism," *Making a Difference*, ed. Gayle Greene and Coppélia Kahn, (London: Routledge, 1985), 114.

49. Henry James, *The Spoils of Poynton* (New York: Scribner's, 1936), 6, 7.

50. Tristram, *Living Space*, 160.

51. Bachelard, *Poetics of Space*, 7.

52. Frances Armstrong discusses this principle of self-expression in *Dickens and the Concept of Home* (Ann Arbor, Mich.: UMI Research Press, 1990), 24–37. See also Conrad, *Victorian Treasure House*, 73.

53. Charles Dickens, *Our Mutual Friend* (New York: Penguin, 1971), 99–100.

54. Dickens, *Our Mutual Friend*, 100.

55. See Tristram, *Living Space*, 260; Hinton, "High Victorian,"180; Lancaster, *Home, Sweet Homes*, 36; and Lichten, *Decorative Art*, 42.

56. Dickens, *Our Mutual Friend*, 177.

57. George Eliot, *Middlemarch* (New York: Norton, 1977), 5–7.

58. George Eliot, *Adam Bede*, ed. Gordon S. Haight (New York: Rinehart, 1948), 72.

59. George Eliot, *The Mill on The Floss*, ed. Gordon S. Haight (Oxford: Clarendon Press, 1980), 177–78.

60. Eliot, *Middlemarch*, 113, 575.

61. Eliot, *Middlemarch*, 81, 450.

62. Edith Wharton and Ogden Codman, Jr., *The Decoration of Houses* (New York: Scribner's, 1907), 190.

63. Kenneth Burke, *A Grammar of Motives* (New York: Prentice Hall, 1945). For Burke's development of his "pentad" of terms for literary study, see 127–70.

"Ladies—Loaf Givers"
Food, Women, and Society in the Novels of Charlotte Brontë and George Eliot

Francis L. Fennell
Monica A. Fennell

> [Cooking] means the knowledge of Medea, and of Circe, and
> of Calypso, and of Helen, and of Rebekah, and of the Queen
> of Sheba. It means the knowledge of all herbs, and fruits,
> and balms, and spices; and of all that is healing and sweet
> in the fields and groves, and savoury in meats. . . . [It] means
> much tasting, and no wasting; it means English thorough-
> ness, and French art, and Arabian hospitality; and it
> means, in fine, that you are to be perfectly, and always,
> "ladies"—"loaf givers."[1]

In this advice to his young female pupils John Ruskin,
with that combination of blind arrogance and penetrating insight which so often characterizes him, adumbrates the thesis
which we will argue in this paper: that Victorian society prescribed for women a variety of roles associated with food
(ladies as loaf-givers), and that women were able to convert
these roles into a means of empowerment through the forms of
privileged knowledge (Medea, Circe, Calypso) and control
(Helen, Rebekah, Queen of Sheba) which the roles provided.
An examination of the preparation and serving of food in the
major novels of the two most prominent women novelists of the
period reveals much about the social structure and the position

of women in nineteenth-century Britain. We shall demonstrate also the ambivalence which so often characterizes this association of cooking and serving food with women, an ambivalence which carries over into Brontë's and especially Eliot's social philosophy. And we shall go on to show that these prescribed roles gave women the power to assert control over their own lives and the lives of others—a power which often could be a source of liberation, but which at other times could constitute the means for expressing the dark secret of how women direct their anger inward by denying themselves the nourishment they need.

Preparing and serving food often seems the simplest, the humblest of women's work, despite the time and energy and creativity which many have given to it. Perhaps for this reason critics have found it easy to ignore the many ways in which Charlotte Brontë and George Eliot have depicted women engaging in these activities, and they have therefore missed the subtextual commentary which emerges when these subjects are considered.[2] This essay will try to attune the reader to the muted discourse which the novels reveal. At the same time it will be possible to observe significant differences between Brontë and Eliot, differences which go some way toward defining the characteristic strengths of each.

Witch or Priestess?

That both Brontë and Eliot should know about and use food and food preparation in their novels will not surprise those familiar with their personal histories. Charlotte Brontë's years at Haworth were marked by many happy hours in her beloved Tabby's kitchen, as Emily's diaries clearly show,[3] and when a reviewer of *Jane Eyre* objected that "Currer Bell" could not be a woman because "no woman *trusses game* and garnishes dessert-dishes with the same hands," an indignant Brontë dismissed "that rather coarse observation" as proof that its author simply did not understand the subject as well as she did.[4] Similarly, we know of the young Marianne Evans that her household duties at Griff included overseeing the dairy, supervising the kitchen, and making pies, damson cheese, and currant jelly.[5]

Both novelists offer a rich variety of scenes associated with cooking and eating. The reader encounters simple breakfasts of porridge and milk, elaborate breakfasts of ham, potatoes, and pie, Belgian-style breakfasts of stewed pears and tartines. The midday meal can range from sandwiches taken in deserted schoolrooms to elegant luncheons *sur l'herbe*. Social occasions often focus on a special dinner, from Louis Moore's market-dinner and Arthur Donnithorne's coming-of-age dinner to Gwendolyn Harleth's archery dinner and Mrs. Bretton's Christmas dinner. The more intimate family meal can be as familiar as the milk and bread which Shirley Keeldar and Caroline Helstone share and as elaborate as the Jewish ritual dinner which Daniel Deronda observes in Ezra Cohen's house and as abundant as the Sunday feasts which attract young Martin Yorke. The reader can also find careful and knowledgeable descriptions of the food itself, of Victorian theories of diet, and of disputes about the best way to prepare certain items: the proper way of making *café au lait*, for example, or whether to use sugar or treacle in the preservation of black cherries, or how much thickening to put in porridge.

But more important than the food and the meals themselves is what they reveal. Both novelists use the serving of food as a device for illuminating the structure of the societies they portray. For example, Mr. Yorke in *Shirley* (1849) very quickly separates unexpected guests into gentry, who are ushered into the parlor for one kind of food, and men of the lower classes, destined for the kitchen and another kind. Meanwhile Mrs. Yorke calculates the social favor she will bestow on Hortense Moore by agreeing to come and "take tea," while the curate Mr. Donne stands revealed as no gentleman by his lack of proper table manners. With Middlemarchers like Mrs. Bulstrode who have risen above their class, society gains its revenge by criticizing "her complacency . . . in light dishes for a supper-party,"[6] a showiness and temerity incompatible with her position as the wife of a newly-disgraced man. As for the Dodson sisters in St. Ogg's, they believe that for the honor of the family's social position "it was of equal necessity to have

the proper pall-bearers and well-cured hams at one's funeral."[7]
Mr. Tulliver remembers that as a boy he had equated the
prosperity of their new malt house with a celebratory plum
pudding and had assumed his mother would make the pudding
every day so their diet could reflect their new, more elevated
social position. And Esther Lyon, while she has come to like
the cooking odors which permeate the small living quarters she
shares with her father, cannot help but reflect on the fact that
rich people like the Transomes never have to have that
experience and do not understand what it means.

Not surprisingly, both novelists depict a society which
assigns the preparing and serving of food almost exclusively to
women. Caroline Helstone rages at this limitation and sees it
as imposed by patriarchy:

> What do [fathers] expect [daughters] to do at home? If you
> ask,—they would answer, sew and cook. They expect them
> to do this, and this only, contentedly, regularly, uncom-
> plainingly all their lives long, as if they had no germs of
> faculties for anything else: a doctrine as reasonable to
> hold, as it would be that the fathers have no faculties but
> for eating what their daughters cook . . . [8]

Every novel offers illustrations of this duty devolving upon
women. Sometimes the responsibility for cooking and serving
may fall to someone hired for this purpose: the novels abound in
the Hannahs and Lyddys and Mrs. Galeses and Mrs. Fairfaxes
who served in every Victorian middle- and upper-class household (and whose hospitality, as Mrs. Gale pointedly observes
regarding the curates, was so often abused). But even if most of
the preparation fell to someone else, ultimate responsibility for
overseeing the cooking and serving still belonged to the wives,
mothers, and daughters of the family. If domestic help was not
available they were the ones who served instead. In short,
cooking and serving sometimes might be linked with *class* in
terms of physical labor, but were always linked with *gender* in
terms of responsibility.

For Brontë no woman escapes this role. Jane Eyre, for example, can protest that women "need exercise for their faculties, and a field for their efforts as much as their brothers do;
. . . and it is narrow-minded in their more privileged fellow-

creatures to say they ought to confine themselves to making puddings . . ." But Jane makes puddings anyway. And at the end of the novel she renews her relationship with Rochester by appearing at his Ferndean retreat in the guise of a woman servant carrying his tray, saying "I must mind not to rise on your hearth with only a glass of water, then: I must bring an egg at the least, to say nothing of fried ham."[9] Similarly, Shirley may affect her "Captain" Keeldar role as the emancipated woman who dares do and say what any man would dare do and say, but she still supervises luncheon parties and nurses Louis Moore with grapes and toast. Even Lucy Snowe in *Villette* (1853) who explicitly denies that she fits the normal Victorian stereotypes for women, finds it natural that Monsieur Paul should require her and the girls to spread butter on fifty rolls while a farm woman makes *café au lait* for their country outing.

Eliot more frequently portrays women who have little to do with food or its preparation. Maggie Tulliver, Dorothea Brooke, and Gwendolyn Harleth, for example, rarely fix or serve meals. But all of them at one time or another preside at tea, that most essential (it sometimes seems) of an upper-middle-class woman's duties.[10] And for every Maggie, Dorothea, or Gwendolyn in her novels there are dozens of female characters like Lisbeth Bede, who rises early to fix Adam's breakfast and will not believe her day's work is over until she can put out his late supper, and Mrs. Tulliver, who fusses to get Tom's supper and worries if his new school will allow him a second helping of pudding. Even the formidable Mrs. Glegg serves food to her insipid husband and adheres to the Dodson proprieties in "making the cowslip wine, curing the hams, and keeping the bottled gooseberries."[11] Such psychological and social opposites as Rosamond Lydgate and Mrs. Garth share a common lot:

> "Have you dined, Tertius? I expected you much earlier," said Rosamond...
>
> "I have dined. I should like some tea, please," said Lydgate, curtly, still scowling . . .
>
> [Mrs. Garth] said, "There you are, Caleb. Have you had your dinner?"
>
> "Oh yes, a good dinner . . ."[12]

And in *Felix Holt* (1866) when Esther Lyon, stung by Felix's rebukes of her laziness, wants to prove her accuser wrong, she does so by serving tea to her father and then later preparing his porridge.

On a more ominous note, both Brontë and Eliot show how women's very identities can sometimes be absorbed by their relationship to the food they prepare. Stephen Guest, for example, can declare that Mrs. Tulliver "should be represented by her brandy-cherries and cream-cakes" and that they are "agreeable proxies" for her actual presence;[13] Mrs. Tulliver's acquiescence in this identification of who she is with what she bakes is shown by the way she sees her pies as extensions of herself. Similarly, Lisbeth Bede, in imagining her future death, assumes the principal effect on Adam will be that she can no longer get his breakfast in the morning, while Mrs. Poyser is astonished anyone in her family would want to see her before "foddering-time." In *Middlemarch* (1872) the only characterization given of Miss Noble is the image of her snitching sweets from the table. Mrs. Bretton of *Villette* has her identity confirmed for Lucy Snowe when she sets out "an English tea whereof . . . I knew the very seed-cake of peculiar form."[14] Jane Eyre knows Grace Poole, keeper of the demented Bertha, only by her routine of bringing food trays.

Grace Poole suggests another aspect of women as food-preparers. One of the few visual images of Grace in the novel shows her bending over a saucepan on the fire, stirring a "boiling mess" like a witch out of *Macbeth*."[15] George Eliot offers a similar scene in *The Mill on the Floss* (1860) when Maggie meets an old gypsy woman "poking a skewer into the round kettle that sent forth an odorous steam." Like the witch of "Hansel and Gretel," the old woman entices the innocent Maggie to eat: "'We've got nothing nice for a lady to eat,' said the old woman, in her coaxing tone. 'And she's so hungry, sweet little lady.'"[16] Nina Auerbach has reminded us of the frequency and the power of this image of woman-as-demon. Victorian literature, she observes, often evokes the image of women's nature as "broadly demonic rather than fallibly human" because it suggests the deeper belief that "woman is not frailer than man is, but stronger and more powerful."[17]

If cooking sometimes partakes of the demonic, more often in these novels it assumes a quasi-religious, almost sacramental value. Consider, for example, Christmas morning at the Tullivers, with food as the symbol both of renewed hope and of Saturnalian abundance:

> The midnight chant had helped as usual to lift the morning above the level of common days; and then there was the smell of hot toast and ale from the kitchen, at the breakfast hour. . . . The plum-pudding was of the same handsome roundness as ever, and came in with the symbolic blue flames around it, as if it had been heroically snatched from the nether fires into which it had been thrown by dyspeptic Puritans . . .[18]

Similarly, Jane Eyre makes cooking a beautiful religion, an "ambition" worthy of a woman's devotion—and worthy too of description in language more commonly associated with religious liturgy:

> [T]he two days preceding that on which your sisters are expected will be *devoted* by Hannah and me to such a beating of eggs, sorting of currants, grating of spices, compounding of Christmas cakes, chopping up of materials for mince pies, and *solemnizing* of other culinary *rites*, as words can convey but an inadequate notion of to the *uninitiated* like you (italics ours).[19]

Cooking in sum is a priestly ministry. It has its sacred rites known only to those privy to its secrets. Its priesthood is open to, is in fact reserved almost exclusively for, the sex which has been so pointedly excluded from other priesthoods and positions of power. As Lisbeth Bede mutters, no man could ever master the art of making even a good porridge or oatcake—much less understand its importance in creating an environment within which human beings can thrive.

Cooking as Self-Empowerment

If cooking is sometimes religious and sometimes demonic, what unites these two conceptions is the idea of cooking as a means of empowerment. Through their roles as preparers and servers of food the women in these novels, denied other kinds of influence by a patriarchal society, still gain some measure of control over those with whom they live. More importantly, they also use food to gain control over their own lives, either positively by taking responsibility for their own nourishment, or negatively by using this power to will their own destruction.

One form of control is economic. Patricia Branca has estimated that in mid-century food represented 54 percent of the budget of a typical Victorian middle-class family.[20] Supervision of that portion of the budget fell almost exclusively to women and gave them an economic power of no mean significance. Potentially the exercise of that power could offer independence from the control of fathers or husbands, and these novels do show some women who exhibit financial self-sufficiency through their "women's work" associated with food. Mrs. Poyser in *Adam Bede*, for example, manages her kitchen and her dairy with knowledge and authority. She pronounces *ex cathedra* on such topics as the amount of milk yielded by shorthorn cows and the ethics of the egg market, and it is clear that the family's substantial income is owing to the way she superintends her work and her workers. Through subordinates Shirley Keeldar exhibits a similar kind of mastery. Economic independence through food-related activities can also manifest itself in less obvious ways, as when women hold bake sales to raise money for projects of their own devising.

But in these novels the most frequently exercised power is social rather than economic: the use of food preparation to stimulate affection and fellowship. Affection in this context means giving food as a sign of love, while fellowship means sharing food as a sign of mutuality.

Brontë more often portrays women using food as affection. In *Villette* little Polly delights in serving her father:

> "Put papa's chair here, and mine near it, between papa and Mrs. Bretton; *I* must hand his tea. . . ."

> And again, as she intercepted his cup in passing, and would stir the sugar and put in the cream herself, "I always did it for you at home, papa; nobody could do it as well, not even your own self. . . ."

> [H]er father, blind like other parents, seemed . . . wonder-
> fully soothed by her offices.[21]

Hortense Moore in *Shirley* expresses her love for her brother by fixing his breakfast plate and then relishing the appetite with which he eats. Meanwhile Miss Ainsley shows her favoritism among the curates by giving little Mr. Sweeting "slices of sponge-cake, and glasses of cowslip or primrose wine"[22] while Shirley nurses *her* secret love with grapes and toast. Jane Eyre, having felt welcomed at Thornfield because Mrs. Fairfax brought her negus and a sandwich, in turn woos little Adèle with chicken and tarts. Related to these gestures of affection is the use of food as consolation: Mrs. Bretton ministers to the lonely Lucy Snowe with tea and toast, for example, and both Helen Burns and Miss Temple bring Jane Eyre special seed-cakes to alleviate her misery at Lowood school.

For Eliot also food can be a means whereby her female characters express their affection. Lisbeth Bede, for example, puts out Adam's supper "in the loving expectation of looking at him while he ate it"[23] and later makes him his favorite ket-tle-cake, while Mrs. Poyser expresses her appreciation of him by serving the kind of potatoes he likes. Mrs. Tulliver sneaks the hungry Tom an extra portion of supper despite the compara-tively barren cupboard which has resulted from the disastrous lawsuit.

But Eliot more frequently than Brontë will depict sym-bolic moments of the kind described a generation earlier by Jean Brillat-Savarin in his *Physiology of Taste* (1825). "[A] table," says Brillat-Savarin, "establishes a kind of tie between two parties to a bargain."[24] This tie constitutes a fellowship of equals created and maintained by the sharing of food. *The Mill on the Floss* affords numerous examples of such bonds. By the simple gesture of packing Tom and Maggie a food basket for their journey, Mrs. Stelling, the narrator tells us, performs one of those "bare offices of humanity which raises [people] into a bond of loving fellowship."[25] During their childhood Tom brings Maggie a piece of plum-cake:

> Maggie's sobs began to subside, and she put out her mouth
> for the cake and bit a piece; and then Tom bit a piece, just
> for company, and they ate together and rubbed each other's

cheeks and brows and noses together, while they ate, with
a humiliating resemblance to two friendly ponies.[26]

But the next time there is a dessert to share Tom unjustly criticizes Maggie for taking the better half of a jam puff. This deliberate disruption of their fellowship prefigures his later betrayal of Maggie's love, a betrayal which would not be mended
until the final flood when brother and sister are at last "one
with each other in primitive mortal needs."[27] Just as food can
celebrate fellowship, it can also mark its absence. One needs
only to remember the scene from *Daniel Deronda* (1876) of
Gwendolyn and Grandcourt dining alone on their yacht, their
stony silence at that meal symbolizing their severed relationship and the unbearable tension between them.

More overt forms of control emerge when we examine the
feminine subtexts of these novels. Of particular interest is the
way female characters use their role as "loaf-giver" to subvert
the power structures of a patriarchal society which has prescribed this role for them.

On the simplest level both Eliot and Brontë show women
withholding food to control the behavior of men. Aunt Glegg,
for example, "can't bear" her husband's disagreement with her
views on money matters, so she resigns her duty: "Mr. Glegg,
you'll please to order what you like for dinner. I shall have
gruel." When this stratagem fails to move him, she withholds
his tea, then responds to his demand for the milk jug by
"pouring out the milk with unusual profuseness, as much as to
say, if he wanted milk he should have it with a vengeance." [28]
Mr. Glegg capitulates almost immediately. Dorothea Brooke,
wounded by her husband's suspicions, cancels dinner so that
Casaubon "might wonder and be hurt at her message."[29] Mrs.
Yorke in *Shirley* punishes young Martin for missing tea by giving him dry bread instead of muffins. For a similar offense of
tardiness Mrs. Bretton of *Villette* threatens to deprive John
Graham of his tea. By contrast we almost never see women
withholding food from each other (Mrs. Reed in *Jane Eyre* is an
exception) or men withholding food from women, although men
do occasionally use food for disguised aggression, as when John
Graham Bretton uses ale to tempt and thus gently taunt Polly.

The giving of food can sometimes be just as controlling a device as the withholding of it. As a child Polly gives the same attention to John Graham at tea-time as she had bestowed on her father, using treats as a way of enkindling his love and thus prefiguring their later attachment:

> "What will you have besides tea—what to eat?"
>
> "Anything good. Bring me something particularly nice; that's a kind little woman. . . ."
>
> She selected a portion of whatever was best on the table. . . . Graham was shortly after heard lauding her to the skies; promising that, when he had a house of his own, she should be his housekeeper, and perhaps—if she showed culinary genius—his cook . . . [30]

Mrs. Caldwallader *of Middlemarch* believes "It is the same thing, the dinner or the man,"[31] and exercises the identical kind of firm control over both. Less calculating but no less effective is Lucy Deane, who, we are told, "was fond of feeding dependent creatures, and knew the private tastes of all the animals about the house"—this just moments before we learn that the most manageable of her "animals about the house," Stephen Guest, had decided "this slim maiden of eighteen was quite the sort of wife a man would not be likely to repent of marrying."[32]

On a deeper level, attitudes toward food and food preparation offer an index by which the reader can judge the male characters in the novels. This judgment of men constitutes an increasingly important dimension of women's empowerment, as we shall see in a moment.

For Brontë the test regarding a male character is simple: can a man at least on occasion relinquish his society-given "rights" and prepare food, especially for a woman? If so, according to Brontë's implicit social philosophy he has an innate goodness and humility which will compensate for his sins, whatever they may be. Thus Robert Moore in *Shirley* first appears in the novel as a man dismissing his maid so he can make his own supper. Moore's basic simplicity and integrity have been established in the reader's mind and will not be dislodged, whatever stubbornness and folly Moore may exhibit later on.

Similarly Mr. Helstone, Caroline's uncle and guardian, appears cold and withdrawn almost to the point of being psychologically abusive. Yet when Caroline falls ill he insists that he can make tea "better than any housewife can"[33] and then patiently nurses her back to health. This "housewifely" side to his nature liberates his tenderness and allows him to show both his love for her and that he "understands nursing." Young Henry Sympson makes tea when Shirley demurs, an office which seems to suit this favored "poor lame darling" whose description partakes much more of the feminine than the masculine.

In *Jane Eyre* the heroine arrives, cold, wet, and hungry, at the doorstep of St. John Rivers. Her first image of him is associated with food: "'[She is] famished, I think. Hannah, is that milk? Give it me, and a piece of bread. . . . Not too much at first—restrain her . . . she has had enough.' And he withdrew the cup of milk and the plate of bread."[34] This observation reveals at once both his generosity and his severity, the very qualities which first attract and then repulse Jane. As for Rochester, his initial unsuitability as a lover is illustrated by his decadent taste for *bon bons*[35] and by the trenchant observation of little Adèle, who when Rochester jests that he will take "mademoiselle [Jane] to the moon," comments drily, "She will have nothing to eat: you will starve her. . . . If I were mademoiselle, I would never consent to go with you."[36] Rochester's ultimate redemption is signalled by his effort to bring food and wine to a despairing Jane. Although she refuses this first offering and leaves Thornfield, his solicitude regarding food makes the reader aware of his tenderness and his recognition of the enormity of the pain he has inflicted on her.

Finally, in *Villette*, Lucy Snowe falls in love with M. Paul in part because he seems so liberated from gender roles. He divines Lucy's taste: "How he guessed that I should like a *petit pâté à la crème* I cannot tell; but he went out and procured me one."[37] Later on he divides a portion of fruit intended by Lucy for his plate and insists that she eat a generous share. And at the end, the depth of their newfound intimacy finds an appropriate symbol in a kind of engagement dinner: Lucy sets out new china and delights in serving M. Paul, while he responds by arranging for the food to be brought in from a nearby restaurant.

This element of Brontë's social philosophy applies to everyone, not just men. Anyone, for example, who ignores conventional class roles regarding cooking or serving food also gains her praise: Caroline Helstone earns her maid's gratitude by helping make coffee in the kitchen, and the Rivers' servant Hannah celebrates her new fellowship with Jane by sticking out her floury hand as the two of them make gooseberry pie. But gender roles seem even harder to break out of than class roles, and part of the muted discourse in Brontë's novels concerns the suitability as marriage partners of those men who are willing to do so.

Eliot develops the same theme, but adds to it her characteristic irony. *Middlemarch* affords the most interesting example, illustrating as it does Eliot's convictions about the relationship of men and women to their community. Tertius Lydgate, for example, has a commendable lack of social pretension regarding meals: "He would have behaved perfectly at a table where the sauce was served in a jug with the handle off, and he would have remembered nothing about a grand dinner except that a man was there who talked well."[38] The narrator clearly endorses Lydgate's egalitarianism. But this imperviousness to distinctions which are important to almost everyone else in Middlemarch society prefigures the misunderstandings and cross purposes which will dog Lydgate's every step in the hospital affair and result in his financial and social disgrace.

In the case of Fred Vincy, readers can gauge the maturation of his character by observing his changing attitudes toward food. At first he exhibits a "gentlemanly" selfishness about a late breakfast:

> "Have you got nothing else for my breakfast, Prichard?" said Fred, to the servant who brought in coffee and buttered toast; while he walked round the table surveying the ham, potted beef, and other cold remnants, with an air of silent rejection, and polite forbearance from signs of disgust.
>
> "Should you like eggs, sir?"
>
> "Eggs, no! Bring me a grilled bone."[39]

Later, thinking of the possibility he might not inherit old Featherstone's money, Fred cannot imagine the "thoroughly unpleasant position" of eating cold mutton. But after undergoing suffering and humiliation and then learning the redemptive value of work, he comes to admire and imitate Caleb Garth, the same Caleb who can say "Oh yes, [I had] a good dinner— cold mutton and I don't know what."[40]

Among the other male characters in the novel Will Ladislaw exhibits the greatest willingness to flaunt conventional gender roles: he provides gingerbread feasts for children, for example. But this trait Middlemarchers call an "oddity" in Will, part of the evidence for his "dangerously mixed blood and general laxity."[41] He will pay severely for these social sins, despite the fact that the narrator clearly approves of his unconventionality.[42]

Eliot, while implicitly endorsing the same destruction of sexual stereotyping as Brontë does, underscores the pain which such disruptions can bring to those who cause them. She makes us aware of the cost attendant upon any movement toward liberation. Yet at the same time her social philosophy, while emphasizing the role of the community as a living organism resistant to abrupt change, still affirms the truth that the liberation of one person, however painful the process, cannot help but loosen bonds for others. Her novels illustrate the truth of Marx's dictum that "every emancipation is a restoration of the human world and of human relationships."

For both writers the connection between judging males and female empowerment is subtle but decisive. Our analysis supports Nancy Armstrong's argument that Victorian novels both endorsed and helped to create a "feminized household" and thus exercised enormous political power, a power all the more effective for being concealed. Reading such novels did not merely offer examples of desirable social change, she contends. Rather it caused them to happen: in her words, such reading *"initiate[d]* the historical transformations."[43] If one accepts Armstrong's thesis, then Brontë's and Eliot's tests for judging male characters assume special importance. To ratify the destruction of a gender stereotype and to broaden the definition of maleness, as we have shown these novelists do, is both to recommend a choice and to help women make it. If in the 1990s current social models for both men and women contain fewer gender restrictions, so that cooking can be seen as no more a woman's work than a man's, the persuasiveness of these models—indeed even their very existence—may be attributed in part to the image of Robert Moore making his own supper or of Will Ladislaw distributing his gingerbread.

Cooking as Self-Wounding

If giving or withholding food serves as a means of control for women whereby they can gain some measure of governance over the sex and the social structure which oppress them, the darkest undercurrent in these novels has still to be explored: the way this controlling power can be turned inward—in other words, the way women can literally starve themselves. Both Brontë and Eliot depict women victimized by self-hatred, by feelings of unworthiness, and by an anger towards others which they have turned back upon themselves. Both novelists clearly know, long before such terms as anorexia nervosa and bulimia would gain popular currency, that food could be the principal means for this self-destructive reaction to patriarchy—knew that the angel in the house was often ethereal because she was malnourished, and she was malnourished as an enduring sign of the starvation of her opportunities.

Brontë's novels show this self-starvation as taking two forms: either a passive refusal by women to control their own nourishment, or else an active determination to renounce food. Passive refusal occurs, for example, when Miss Temple, the mistress at Jane's school, will not openly oppose Mr. Brocklehurst's policy of semi-starving the orphan girls. Instead she suffers with her pupils, only occasionally smuggling them bread and cheese to supplement particularly wretched meals. In *Villette*, Lucy will suffer for nine days without solid food while everyone at Mme. Beck's school is away on vacation before she dares go to Père Silas, who ministers to the "deadly famine" in her soul while taking her to Dr. John for physical fortification. Caroline Helstone's severe illness is brought on most directly by the exertion of walking back from Hollow's Cottage, but she had already weakened herself by eating little and allowing herself to decline from the "rounder and rosier" young woman she had been two years before, and Sandra Gilbert and Susan Gubar have demonstrated the pervasiveness of the hunger motif throughout the depiction of her in the novel.[44]

The willed renunciation of food is more dangerous yet. Feminist psychoanalysts have noted how "throughout history, women's feeding others has been coupled with the necessity of self-denial."[45] For a woman to hunger for food is the same as for her to hunger for a future; to renounce food is to renounce a future. "That is why eating seems forbidden and food dangerous," observes Kim Chernin. "When we eat, we know."[46]

Brontë's novels offer several characters who illustrate this trait. Jane Eyre as a child thinks that if she starves herself the Reeds will realize how she needs to be fed, emotionally as well as physically. Injustice compels her to summon this "precocious though transitory power; and Resolve, equally wrought up, instigated some strange expedient to achieve escape from insupportable oppression—as . . . never eating or drinking more, and letting myself die."[47] Later on, when she discovers the "insupportable oppression" both of her and of Bertha represented by Rochester's proposal to her while he yet harbors the "madwoman in the attic," she responds by refusing every bit of food offered to her. Then she steals away in the middle of the night and wanders through fields and hedgerows for three days until, quite literally, she almost starves to death.

Similarly, in *Villette* little Polly, like Jane, practices self-denial, and refuses to touch the marmalade with what the narrator ironically terms "nice perceptions and delicate instincts." She also renounces sweets and justifies it by claiming her sex does not deserve them: "One little piece—only for him [John Graham]—as he goes to school: girls—such as me and Miss Snowe—don't need treats, but *he* would like it." Later Lucy Snowe takes a position as companion to Miss Marchmont where she deliberately accustoms herself to eat the tiny meals served the invalid. She explains, "I had wanted to compromise with

Fate: to escape occasional great agonies by submitting to a whole life of privation and small pains."[48]

Not all women in Brontë's novels starve themselves, and the same woman who denies herself in one scene can, as a sign of her growing emancipation and empowerment, reassert control over her own nourishment at a later point in the novel. Jane Eyre realizes that she gets more intellectual nourishment at Lowood than she had received from the abusive Reeds at Gateshead, so despite her hunger she can control her desire to imagine the rich Gateshead supper of hot roast potatoes, white bread, and new milk. As an adult she refuses to let the arrogant guests at Rochester's dinner party annoy her; instead she leaves them in order to create a feast for her little women's circle of Adèle, Sophie, and herself. Later she confronts Rochester with an angry determination to secure her own food:

> Do you think I . . . can bear to have my morsel of bread snatched from my lips[?]

> . . . Do you think, because I am poor, obscure, plain, and little, I am soulless and heartless? You think wrong—I have as much soul as you, and full as much heart.[49]

And when she banishes herself from Thornfield and is taken in by the Rivers, she covets a cake of bread because "the wish to have some strength and vigor returned to me as soon as I was amongst my fellow-beings."[50]

Lucy Snowe also takes crucial steps to better her lot through controlling her own nourishment. She finds the courage to tell M. Paul that she will not starve in a garret while rehearsing for his play, and she avowedly craves both the physical nourishment of butter and biscuits and the spiritual nourishment of friendship which Mrs. Bretton provides. The very act of moving first to London and then to the continent shows her willingness to take charge of her life, and she celebrates her victories by explicitly equating her physical and spiritual hungers:

> [M]y spirit shook its always-fettered wings half loose; I had a sudden feeling as if I, who had never yet truly lived, were at last about to taste life. . . . [It] was years since I had

felt such a healthy hunger. . . . I dined on two dishes—a
plain joint, and vegetables.[51]

Both appetites earn their satisfaction.

Eliot too recognizes the dark secret of female self-depri-
vation. Sometimes she only hints at the secret, as when the
saucy Rosamond Lydgate threatens not to eat in order to have
her own way: "You [her father] would not like me to go into a
consumption, as Arabella Hawley did."[52] At other times the
self-denying strain becomes much more direct. Dinah Morris, we
are told, eats only the odds and ends of food left over from other
people's plates. Mrs. Poyser claims Dinah eats only "a bit o'
sparrow's victual"[53] and worries that when she returns to
Snowfield, where no family can look after her, she might
starve herself. Young Maggie Tulliver, thinking life useless if
Tom does not love her, resolves: "Well, then, she would stay up
there [in the attic] and starve herself . . . and then they would
all be frightened, and Tom would be sorry."[54] While the threat
itself is merely comic, the form that the threat takes is revealing. Later on, when the two children are served Aunt Pullet's
tea-cakes, Maggie feels she must deny herself and refuse them
while Tom, troubled by no such instinct, gobbles them up. Then
as a young adult Maggie falls under the spell of Thomas à
Kempis and his doctrine of renunciation, imposing on herself as
many privations as she can, including food—although fortu-
nately, we are told, her innate physical strength prevents her
from suffering long-term effects.

Unlike Brontë, Eliot can portray men denying themselves
food. Bulstrode regiments his diet, drinking water and eating
thin sandwiches; Will Ladislaw "experiments in ecstasy" by
fasting until he faints; Felix Holt prides himself on his
willpower: "As for me, I can live on bran porridge. I have the
stomach of a rhinoceros. . . . I'll never marry, though I should
have to live on raw turnips to subdue my flesh."[55] The difference is that her male characters use food deprivation as a
means of increasing their power over others or over their circumstances. (Bulstrode's dieting, we are told, gives him "a
vampire's feast in the sense of mastery."[56]) The women by contrast express a redirecting inwards of an anger which would be

focused on the injustice of their lot were it not for the powerful social strictures which inhibit that anger.

Eliot, like Brontë, recognizes that the power to control one's nourishment means the power to control one's life. Dinah Morris, for example, seems to intuit that her sparrow's appetite reflects the restriction of other appetites. Some of these restrictions she has imposed upon herself (e.g., celibacy), some she has not (e.g., her society's distrust of women preachers). In the novel's epilogue, when she has married Adam, borne children, and made peace with both her social and religious communities, in short when she has made the adjustments which Eliot's social philosophy requires, we find that her face is "fuller" and her figure has taken on a more "matronly" form.

As we noted earlier, the preparation and serving of food seems among the simplest, most humble of women's work. But the very plenitude of references to and images associated with food in these novels suggests that we recognize its importance as a way of understanding the characteristic themes of both Brontë and Eliot. For Brontë the most driving concern is psychological: the deep inner torment experienced by unhappy young women who find their present desolate and their future hopelessly restricted. The most natural response to that constriction is anger, and Brontë's novels contain a great deal of direct and sublimated anger. The most fitting image is Rose Yorke's shuttered china closet:

> I will *not* deposit [my talent] in a broken-spouted teapot, and shut it up in a china-closet among tea-things. . . . [L]east of all, mother—(she got up from the floor)—least of all will I hide it in a tureen of cold potatoes, to be ranged with bread, butter, pasty, and ham on the shelves of the larder. [57]

For Eliot by contrast the most driving concern is social: the sense of alienation experienced by intelligent young women who find themselves torn between what they themselves desire and what those whom they love expect of them. Here the most natural response is sadness, the natural consequence of anger turned inward. The most fitting image is young Maggie Tulliver's repeated attacks of hunger:

[T]his hunger of the heart [is] as peremptory as that other
hunger by which Nature forces us to submit to the yoke,
and change the face of the world. . . . [Tragedy] lies in the
conflicts of young souls, hungry for joy, . . . thirsty for all
knowledge. . . . [E]very rational satisfaction of [their] nature that [they] deny now, will assault [them] like a savage
appetite. [58]

Sadly, Maggie's appetite for life can be quieted only by death.

Those images of shuttered closets and spiritual hungers
prove to be extraordinarily powerful both in what they describe and what they demand. For individual women in these
novels, their work as "loaf-givers" becomes subsumed in the
role prescribed for them by their society, and images of closets
and hungers speak eloquently of how confining and how mal-
nourishing that role was proving to be. The only proper adjective to describe the plight of a Rose Yorke or a Maggie Tulliver
is tragic.

But these novels also move beyond the level of the individual and the anger or sadness her "dark secret" might inspire. They operate as well on the level of society and the constructs by which it organizes and thus understands itself, which
is to say they operate on the level of ideology. For Brontë and
Eliot, to be a loaf-giver, in other words to undertake work
which seems so unimportant, so easily ignored (as indeed it has
been), is nevertheless to enact a role of genuine political significance, a significance which extends far beyond the fictional
lives depicted in these novels. Both novelists contest the dominant ideology of their day. That ideology posited a binary opposition between the sexes with men and women inhabiting
separate spheres because of ineradicable differences, as Mary
Poovey and others have shown.[59] Brontë and Eliot suggest that
such opposition is a social construct, and thus a political construct. They accept that cooking and serving food have been
women's work historically, and for the present continue to be
women's work. At the same time they explicitly deny that such
an appropriation of labor is either just or inevitable. To borrow
a relevant political distinction, they observe that cooking has
been and is women's work *de facto*. But they repudiate the
premise that it is women's work *de jure*, if we understand "law"

here to mean any kind of natural law argument. Loaf-giving emerges in these novels as an undervalued service—undervalued because of its association with women, undervalued because the ideals of affection and fellowship which it embodies and promotes run counter to the aggressive materialism of the dominant ideology. Neither Brontë nor Eliot sees the feminine ideal of a woman preparing a meal or serving at the urn as insidious in and of itself. Rather they call for a broad infusion of this ideal into society as a whole so it becomes part of the norm for men as well as women.

Both Charlotte Brontë and George Eliot, we have argued, destabilize the ideology of their time by demonstrating its consequences and exposing its illogic. Moreover, since ideologies are always in process, to destabilize is also to help create. If contemporary ideology departs from Victorian models, credit given to writers like Brontë and Eliot may not be misplaced. To return to Ruskin, cookery now means the knowledge of Merlin as well as of Medea. A skill worthy of English thoroughness and French art and Arabian hospitality, it stands open—"perfectly, and always"—to "gentlemen" as well as "ladies," in other words to whoever wishes to serve. And as both the work and the role are redefined, the door can begin to open and the hunger can start to be satisfied.

NOTES

1. John Ruskin, "The Ethics of the Dust," *Works*, vol. 18, ed. E. T. Cook and Alexander Wedderburn (London: Allen, 1905), 298.

2. The significance of hunger in *Shirley* has of course been given prominence by Sandra Gilbert and Susan Gubar in *The Madwoman in the Attic: The Woman Writer and the Nineteenth-Century Literary Imagination* (New Haven: Yale University Press, 1979), 372–398. In addition, Ann A. Carter wrote an unpublished Ph.D. dissertation on "Food, Feasting, and Fasting in the Nineteenth Century British Novel" (University of Wisconsin, 1979), but her anthropological and theological approach differs considerably from ours. As for how the topic of food

preparation by women has been ignored, one need only look at Barbara Kanner's otherwise excellent three-volume bibliography on *Women in English Social History, 1800–1914* (New York: Garland, 1987, 1988, 1990), where headings are provided for 107 different subjects, including "domestic service" and "artists and craftswomen"—but not including the part of women's work which has been the most constant and which has required the greatest effort.

3. Winifred Gérin, *Charlotte Brontë: The Evolution of Genius* (Oxford: Clarendon Press, 1967), 22.

4. Appendix to Charlotte Brontë, *Shirley*, ed. Herbert Rosengarten and Margaret Smith (Oxford: Clarendon Press, 1979) 798, 804. Subsequent references to Brontë's novels will be page numbers from the appropriate volume of the *Clarendon Edition of the Novels of the Brontës* under the general editorship of Ian Jack.

5. Gordon S. Haight, *George Eliot: A Biography* (Oxford University Press, 1968), 28.

6. George Eliot, *Middlemarch*, ed. David Carroll (Oxford: Clarendon Press, 1986), 731. Subsequent references to Eliot's novels will be to page numbers from the appropriate volume of the *Clarendon Edition of the Novels of George Eliot* under the general editorship of the late Gordon S. Haight, except for *Adam Bede*, not yet available in the Clarendon and therefore requiring the text of the Standard Edition as made accessible by F.R. Leavis (New York: New American Library, 1961).

7. Eliot, *Middlemarch*, 239.

8. Brontë, *Shirley*, 442.

9. Brontë, *Jane Eyre*, 133, 561.

10. Serving tea seems to be the one duty which all women had to assume, regardless of class or other circumstance. Even for upper-class women the role of "presiding" at tea was inescapable, and training for it could be a source of considerable anxiety for a young girl—witness Caroline Helstone's "speechless panic, the cups shaking in the little hand, the overflowing teapot filled too full from the urn" when she first undertakes this ritual in public (*Shirley*, 318). Victorian instruction manuals like Isabella Beeton's *Book of Household Management* (1861) contain information on the preparation and serving of what she called "a necessary of life." The image of the woman beside her tea-table is an important part of Victorian iconography.

11. Eliot, *Mill on the Floss*, 38.

12. Eliot, *Middlemarch*, 577, 814.

13. Eliot, *Middlemarch*, 321.

14. Brontë, *Villette*, 247.

15. Brontë, *Jane Eyre*, 370.

16. Eliot, *Mill on the Floss*, 94, 97.

17. Nina Auerbach, *Woman and the Demon: The Life of a Victorian Myth* (Cambridge: Harvard University Press, 1982), 108.

18. Eliot, *Mill on the Floss*, 135.

19. Brontë, *Jane Eyre*, 498–99.

20. Patricia Branca, *Silent Sisterhood: Middle-Class Women in the Victorian Home* (Pittsburgh: Carnegie-Mellon University Press, 1975), 48.

21. Brontë, *Villette*, 19.

22. Brontë, *Shirley*, 303.

23. Eliot, *Adam Bede*, 51.

24. Jean Authelme Brillat-Savarin, *The Physiology of Taste*, trans. Arthur Mechen (New York: Doubleday, 1926), 37.

25. Eliot, *Mill on the Floss*, 167.

26. Eliot, *Mill on the Floss*, 34.

27. Eliot, *Mill on the Floss*, 456.

28. Eliot, *Mill on the Floss*, 109–110.

29. Eliot, *Middlemarch*, 417.

30. Brontë, *Villette*, 29–30.

31. Eliot, *Middlemarch*, 166.

32. Eliot, *Mill on the Floss*, 325.

33. Brontë, *Shirley*, 482.

34. Brontë, *Jane Eyre*, 430.

35. A taste for *bon bons* seems to have been a frequent mark of male decadence: Arthur Donnithorne's self-centered disregard for what a girl like Hetty might suffer is signalled to the reader by his conclusion that "if he should happen to spoil a woman's existence for her, [he] will make it up to her with expensive *bon-bons*, packed up and directed by his own hand" (128).

36. Brontë, *Jane Eyre*, 336.

37. Brontë, *Villette*, 190.

38. Eliot, *Middlemarch*, 340.

39. Eliot, *Middlemarch*, 98.

40. Eliot, *Middlemarch*, 227, 814.

41. Eliot, *Middlemarch*, 455.

42. Bartle Massey of *Adam Bede* provides a perhaps even more interesting example of unconventionality. An avowed misogynist, he paradoxically embodies those feminine traits he so vigorously denounces. Bartle prides himself on his cooking, and it is Bartle who nurses Adam with bread and wine during the crisis of Hetty's imprisonment and trial.

43. Nancy Armstrong, *Desire and Domestic Fiction: A Political History of the Novel* (New York: Oxford University Press, 1987), 87.

44. Gilbert and Gubar, 372f.

45. P.E. Garfinkel and D.M. Garner, "Accepting the Symptom: A Feminist Psychoanalytic Treatment of Anorexia Nervosa," in *A Handbook of Psychotherapy for Anorexia Nervosa and Bulimia*, ed. David M. Garner and Paul E. Garfinkel (New York: Guilford Press, 1985), 86–87.

46. Kim Chernin, *Reinventing Eve: Modern Woman in Search of Herself* (New York: Random House, 1987), 180.

47. Brontë, *Jane Eyre*, 13.

48. Brontë, *Villette*, 32, 50.

49. Brontë, *Jane Eyre*, 317.

50. Brontë, *Jane Eyre*, 401.

51. Brontë, *Villette*, 64, 66.

52. Eliot, *Middlemarch*, 345.

53. Eliot, *Adam Bede*, 448.

54. Eliot, *Mill on the Floss*, 32.

55. Eliot, *Felix Holt*, 56, 66.

56. Eliot, *Middlemarch*, 153.

57. Brontë, *Shirley*, 452.

58. Eliot, *Mill on the Floss*, 34, 172, 205, 289.

59. Mary Poovey, *Uneven Developments: The Ideological Work of Gender in Mid-Victorian England* (Chicago: University of Chicago Press, 1988), 8.

Housework, Mill Work, Women's Work
The Functions of Cloth in Charlotte Brontë's Shirley

Maura Ives

Charlotte Brontë's *Shirley* (1849) documents the effects of the separation of public and private domains on the lives of middle-class women.[1] The novel does this by showing how women's occupation of private spaces removes them from economic and social power, which Brontë situates in male-controlled or occupied "public" spaces such as the mill and the church. Brontë's middle-class female characters always find themselves either kept out of or suppressed within men's spaces, and consequently have little choice but to remain within the home, carrying out activities that serve explicitly to define women and the private spaces they inhabit as domestic, decorative, and dependent.

For Brontë, the greatest distinction between men's public and women's private spaces has to do with the concept of work: which activities are designated as "work," how those activities are rewarded or valued, and the consequences of participating or refusing to participate in them. A separation between male "work" and female "home" appears near the beginning of *Shirley*, when Brontë describes the contrast between Robert Moore's mill and his house. Though the two are only a "short distance" away from each other, the house has an "appearance and feeling of seclusion." Brontë further distances Robert's home from the workplace by identifying it as a pleasant, nurturing haven, complete with "sheltered nooks" for early spring flowers.

But there is something wrong with this picture: "Such was Mr. Moore's home: a snug nest for content and contemplation, but one within which the wings of action and ambition could not long lie folded." The "snug nest" is supposed to be cozy; instead, it is tight, cramped, and static, offering no room for Robert's "action" and "ambition." Robert feels "no particular attraction" for his cottage, or for the limitation that it represents.[2]

Like Robert, several of Brontë's female characters respond to domestic space with feelings of confinement and frustration. Some women, like Hortense Moore and Hesther Yorke, respond by proclaiming their mastery of the "duties of woman" and by eagerly instructing younger women in various housekeeping tasks, especially needlework. Through these means women in Shirley produce valuable goods and services; professional seamstresses and embroiderers earned their livings (though not very good ones) from the same activities that Caroline and other women perform for free.[3] But Brontë shows that the activities of the home are nonetheless viewed by men and women in terms of consumption rather than production. Situating this attitude within the cloth-based economy of West Riding, Brontë represents cloth production as a process located outside the home and controlled by men, while cloth consumption occurs within the home as part of women's housekeeping duties; the economic value of women's work as producers of goods made from cloth is ignored by men and women. Caroline, who devotes substantial energy to sewing clothing, is dissatisfied because she is "making no money—earning nothing."[4] This is just one instance in which Shirley shows how the economic devaluation of women's work maintains the ideological separation of home and workplace and increases the sense of economic powerlessness that was felt by middle-class women like Caroline.

Brontë's text delineates the economic and social significance of cloth consumption as one of the "duties" of Victorian housekeeping, and consequently of Victorian women. The first part of this essay explores the Victorian ideology of "women's work" as it appears in Brontë's invocation of two traditional models of domesticity and propriety, Lucretia and Solomon's "virtuous woman." Brontë's use of Lucretia and the "virtuous woman" underscores the historical irony of middle-class women's exclusion from paid work, and it also provides insight into Brontë's own exclusion of female mill workers from her text. In part two, I discuss Brontë's text as a commentary upon middle-class women's efforts to organize and redefine domestic space as a site of productive, meaningful activity. The last section examines the role of clothing as a sign of women's economic subordination that, since it also represents the product of women's work (paid and unpaid), might be manufactured and worn in ways that allow women to renegotiate the boundaries of gender and class.

Lucretia and the "Virtuous Woman"

To understand the significance of women's household activities, especially sewing, one needs to keep in mind the larger economic structure of Brontë's fictional community. The staple product of Briarfield, as every reader knows, is cloth. With the exception of wealthy landowners such as Sam Wynne and Sir Phillip Nunnelly, almost every male character in *Shirley* actively participates in the cloth trade. Even the clergy, who do not depend on the local economy for their income, are "men of the cloth" in more than name, as Reverend Helstone's eager participation in the battle between Robert Moore and his mill workers demonstrates. Many of the novel's other male characters are cloth producers (Christopher Sykes owns a "wool-warehouse," and both Robert Moore and Hiram Yorke own mills) or mill workers, such as Joe Scott and William Farren.

Brontë's female characters also depend upon cloth. Shirley derives a portion of her income from the mill Robert Moore runs for her, and the economic well-being of most of the other women in the novel depends upon that of husbands or other male relatives employed in the mills. Even Caroline Helstone, the rector's niece, finds that her future rests upon Robert Moore's success or failure: if the mill prospers, she will marry him and share his wealth; if not, she will become an impoverished "old maid." There is, however, a crucial difference between the economic lives of Brontë's male and female characters: nearly all of the men take an active role in cloth production, while none of the women do.

Through this division, *Shirley* reflects middle-class women's shift from paid work in cloth production to unpaid domestic work, with marriage as the primary means by which women could improve their economic status. Cloth production is a form of economic activity in which women had formerly taken an important role. In *A History of Their Own: Women in Europe from Prehistory to the Present* (1988), Bonnie Anderson and Judith Zinsser describe all aspects of cloth production, from "collecting the raw wool and flax to finishing the shirt or coverlet," as a primary responsibility of peasant women "beyond written memory."[5] Women made cloth to meet the needs of their families and also sold it for profit. Later on, the wives of members of craft guilds often participated in their husbands' work: "A weaver would need the efforts of his whole family, since his wife and daughters spun the thread for his loom. Wives took responsibility for selling the goods."[6]

The fact that women were usually barred from membership in guilds underscores the economic losses that they suffered in the textile industry. Anderson and Zinsser show how, from the thirteenth through the seventeenth centuries, European women were gradually relegated to the production of the least lucrative kinds of cloth and to spinning.[7] As textile production (along with other forms of manufacture) moved from the home to the factory, the idea of the home as women's "proper sphere" made it increasingly difficult for middle-class women to participate in cloth production at any level without compromising their social status. In *Family Fortunes: Men and Women of the English Middle Class, 1780-1850* (1987), Leonore Davidoff and Catherine Hall explain that by the beginning of the nineteenth century,

> the consolidation of textile production in the market, the first sector to be so organized, had already had a strong impact on women's by-employments such as spinning which had been carried on in even quite prosperous families. The loss of opportunities to earn increased the dominance of marriage as the only survival route for middle-class women as illustrated by the metamorphosis

of the term 'spinster', from one who spins to an unmarried woman.[8]

Shirley explores Caroline's fear of becoming a spinster, in both senses of the term. She tells Robert that she would "be apprenticed to . . . the cloth-trade" *if she were a boy;* what she cannot, and of course does not need to say is that she hopes to avoid becoming an impoverished old maid by marrying him. The only paid work that Caroline seriously considers is that of a governess, which would allow her to remain within the domestic setting, and even this threatens the social status of her uncle who "will not have it said that my niece is a governess."[9]

A middle-class woman in the nineteenth century could participate in production by inheriting a mill and a productive estate, as Shirley does. But as Brontë makes clear, Shirley does not run the mill and maintains only a limited involvement in her own business affairs. The novel's only female entrepreneurs, Mrs. Gale and Mrs. Farren, do little to offset the overall picture of economic powerlessness. The novel's opening scene, in which Mrs. Gale endures the abuse of the curates, underscores working women's loss of status. Mrs. Farren, who contributes to her family's income through "a bit of a shop,"[10] escapes censure only because of special circumstances: she is working-class to begin with, she works only because her husband has lost his job at the mill, and she works in a shop that has the explicit sanction of Cyril Hall, who provided the necessary capital.

In the latter half of the novel, Caroline recognizes that in the past the home and the workplace were not necessarily separate. To make this point, she introduces Lucretia and Solomon's "virtuous woman" as examples of women who profited from cloth that they manufactured within the home. Caroline finds it strange that these particular women were "often quoted as patterns of what 'the sex' (as they say) ought to be:" why should Victorian women, who "have no earthly employment, but household work and sewing,"[11] be expected to "pattern" themselves after a linen manufacturer or a spinner? The only nineteenth century women who still worked in textiles were seamstresses and factory hands, whose lives knew little of the prosperity or the praise shared by Lucretia and the "virtuous woman." The point is that the culture that chose the "virtuous woman" and especially Lucretia as exemplars did not see them as successful entrepreneurs, but as women who knew and respected the limitations of the female sphere.

Caroline's preference of "virtuous woman" over Lucretia ("on the whole, I like her a good deal better") indicates that the two function differently in Brontë's text. The "virtuous woman" is, for Caroline, a "worthy model" who suggests that women might someday reclaim their former freedom. Unlike Lucretia, the "virtuous woman" participates in both the public and the private spheres, in both "men's" and "women's" work. Whereas Lucretia works only in the home and is limited to spinning, the "virtuous woman" "was a manufacturer—she made fine linen and sold it: she was an agriculturalist—she bought estates and planted vineyards."[12] The "virtuous woman" also combines feminine traits such as "kindness" with masculine attributes such as "strength," "wisdom," and the ability to beat the likes of Mr. Armitage and Mr. Sykes in a bargain. Caroline thus reclaims the "virtuous woman" by redefining "virtue" as androgyny.[13]

Caroline also attempts to reclaim Lucretia by referring only to the beginning of her story, in which Lucretia's husband, Tarquinius Collatinus, sought to prove her superiority to other women by showing up unannounced at his home, where he and his friends found Lucretia "spinning at midnight in the midst of her maidens."[14] Interestingly, Caroline's reference disconnects this part of Lucretia's story from its traditional ending, in which one of Collatinus's companions, Sextus Tarquinius, returns to Collatinus's home and rapes Lucretia, who then summons her kinsmen, tells them of the rape, and kills herself. In omitting this part of the narrative, Caroline deliberately attempts to shift attention away from the usual depiction of Lucretia as a symbol of sexual virtue to emphasize instead her productivity within the home. Caroline's ultimate rejection of Lucretia shows the impossibility of reclaiming her story, which continued to represent an ideologically charged linkage of textile work, domesticity and chastity within Victorian culture.

The history of this linkage was a long one. Brontë's rejection of Lucretia marks her refusal to participate in the tradition of defining female nature and sexuality according to classical heroines that reflect, as Ian Donaldson explains in *The Rapes of*

Lucretia: A Myth and Its Transformations (1982), a "mythology invented, sustained and extended largely by men." Donaldson claims that "the number of women who have chosen to treat this subject in literature and the visual arts is exceedingly small,"[15] and as if to substantiate this point, Artemisia Gentileschi's painting *Tarquin and Lucretia* (c. 1645-50) and Madeleine de Scudery's *Clélie* (1654-1660) are the only works by women that he discusses in detail. Arthur Young's earlier study, *Echoes of Two Cultures* (1964) mentions only Christiane de Pisan's treatment of Lucretia in *Cyte of Ladyes* and *Lavision*.[16]

Though Lucretia seems to appear rarely in women's writing, in *The Subversive Stitch*, Roszika Parker identifies Lucretia as a frequent subject of Renaissance women's needlework, along with other heroically chaste women who "transcended in virtue all women and all humans." Parker specifically mentions a set of sixteenth-century wall hangings that included "Lucretia . . . accompanied by Chastity and Liberality." But even these early depictions showed women artists to have had mixed responses to Lucretia, for Parker observes that such women became "a favorite theme not only of those who demanded respect for women but also of those who advocated limiting women's sphere of action."[17] As Ian Donaldson explains in *The Rapes of Lucretia*, Lucretia's "respect" derived from her acceptance of the limitations her culture placed upon women; as a woman, she could not seek revenge for the rape, and had she lived, she would have brought dishonor upon her male relatives.[18]

Thus Lucretia remained a "pattern" precisely because she stood for the circumscription of female behavior within the domestic space. By linking spinning, sewing and other forms of domestic work to female virtue, the story of Lucretia did more than just imply that other forms of work were inappropriately "male." Lucretia stood for the way in which women's work, paid or unpaid, inside or outside the home, came to be seen not as an economically but a sexually significant activity that demonstrated female "virtue." And insofar as the rape of Lucretia represented a violation of the private space of the body as well as of the home (both of which were male "property"), her suicide also reinforced the connection between domesticity, privacy and chastity that was reflected in the Victorian concept of separate spheres.

Brontë allows Caroline to subtly question this connection between domestic space and activities and female sexual propriety. One of the lessons to be learned from Lucretia's story is that the woman who obeys the dictates of her culture by remaining within the domestic sphere will pay for her choice. What is ironic about Lucretia's story is that her domesticity essentially cost her her chastity. Drawing upon contemporary examples, Caroline makes the same point, demonstrating that although a woman's presence in the home was supposed to encourage virtue, the opposite was true: women's improper behavior—"they scheme, they plot, they dress to ensnare husbands"[19]—resulted from women being shut up in the house with nothing to do except household work and sewing, from women having no legitimate activities in which they could participate outside the home, and from women's need to marry in order to survive economically.

Although Brontë criticizes the legacy of Lucretia, the connection between domesticity, consumption and propriety nevertheless circumscribes not only the lives of her characters but also the scope of her own text. It is Brontë, after all, who keeps Shirley and Caroline securely within the home, and Brontë who seems to perpetuate the stigmatization of women who worked outside the home by making them all but invisible in her own text. One might explain Brontë's neglect of working women by considering it in the context of her neglect of the working class as a whole; the workers themselves play a surprisingly small role in a book that builds its plot upon the resentment and potential violence of workers who found themselves victims of a slowdown in production and of "certain inventions in machinery" which "threw thousands out of work."[20] Even so, Brontë does manage to include a few representative male workers (Moses Barraclough and William Farren), a choice that makes the absence of female mill workers even more striking.

I think that it is wrong to read this absence as a dismissal. Instead, it demonstrates Brontë's sense of the risks, revealed through the fears and experiences of her middle-class characters, of an open alliance with women who lived outside of the domestic sphere. The contrast between Caroline's nostalgic reference to a past in which women were honored for their roles as cloth manufacturers, and the contemporary exploitation of Victorian factory women was stark.[21] The very fact that Brontë attempts to keep the economically degraded world of the mill women out of *Shirley* suggests that she is not as oblivious to them as she might seem to be. It is much more likely that Brontë was acutely aware of, even threatened by the popular disapproval that mill women—and all "public" women, including women writers—incurred when they were thought to have abandoned the domestic sphere. Brontë's nervous awareness of the mill girls appears both in her failure to directly introduce them into the text, and especially in the instances in which she indirectly invokes them, ultimately making the shadowy mill girls into fearsome reminders of the consequences of crossing into spaces and behaviors that Victorian culture designated as "male."

Contemporary mill girls contrasted sharply with Brontë's main female characters. Though mill workers earned low wages, factory work paid better than other forms of work,[22] and the simple fact that they earned a wage, rather than depending upon a male wage earner, made them independent in ways that middle-class women could not be. The earning power of mill girls gave them access to personal and social freedoms of a kind that middle class women, confined to the home and to a network of family members and female friends, could not attain. As John Rule points out in *The Labouring Classes in Early Industrial England, 1750-1850* (1986), the money that mill girls earned supposedly encouraged them to escape the control of their families either by abandoning submissive or deferential behavior, or by leaving home altogether.[23] Critics of mill girls held that this independence—in essence, the separation of the mill girls from the domestic sphere—led to wilfulness, frivolity, and sexual impropriety. These traits were supposedly evidenced by the showy clothing of the mill girls, who, like prostitutes, were accused of earning money primarily to satisfy their personal vanity.[24]

In constructing the story of the mill girls, Victorian commentators in essence constructed a companion narrative that endorsed the story of Lucretia, with its emphasis upon the propriety of private/domestic/female spaces, by making working women into unfeminine, promiscuous monsters. The bad reputation of Victorian factory women stemmed from the fact that they worked outside of the home, participating in activities that were no longer considered "feminine." By the end of the eighteenth century, it had already become particularly dangerous for women to dissociate themselves from "woman's work," that is, unpaid work in the home, especially sewing. Cecilia Macheski[25] and Laurie Lieb[26] have pointed out that, as Macheski puts it, "the word 'work' when applied to women in the eighteenth century generally means needlework,"[27] a usage that persists in Brontë's novel. Lieb's analysis of eighteenth and early nineteenth-century fiction shows "how pervasive needlework is, how normative, how automatic."[28] Women who did not sew were abnormal, unfeminine; women who abandoned consumption for production were even more so.

This explains why the young women who worked in the mills were criticized not only for their independence and supposedly unchaste behavior but also condemned for their failure to carry out the household tasks that had come to signify one's identity as a woman. In *Victorian Working Women* (1976), Wanda Neff describes this attitude and its appearance in literary works:

> Critics of the factory age were shocked by the whole system of domestic economy. They attacked the improvidence of mill women who hired the family washing, even that of their caps, a grave moral lapse in the eyes of worried factory inspectors who supplied much of such information. The women did not know how to sew or to mend. Out of thirteen wives in one mill, only one could make her husband a shirt. The average girl in the mill, like Anne Dixon in *Libbie Marsh's Three Eras*, knew nothing of housework. Wordsworth in *The Excursion* (1814) had earlier pointed out the neglect of the homes when the daughters left them for the factory. Mrs. Gaskell portrayed Mrs. Wilson in *Mary Barton* as marrying with no knowledge of housework.[29]

John Rule, among others, has argued that "contemporary criticism of working women was based less on any real investigation of intolerable conditions than on the image of the nature of the work contrasting with the idealized vision of a proper woman's sphere."[30] On the issue of housekeeping, he points out that most female mill workers were unmarried, and that working wives lived under conditions that rendered "good housekeeping" virtually impossible.[31]

The widespread condemnation of working women informs Brontë's characterization of Caroline, whose social and economic vulnerability is expressed both by her similarity to the young women who work in Robert Moore's mill and by her need to distance herself from them. Caroline shares the mill girls' ignorance of domestic work, a connection that is made early in the novel: shortly after we learn that Caroline is "profoundly ignorant" of stocking-mending, Robert Moore makes the common observation that mill girls were poorly suited to become domestic servants: "they were most of them, he was informed, completely ignorant of household work." Less obviously, Caroline's precarious social and economic status places her in a position that parallels that of the mill girls. Both Caroline and the mill girls depend upon Robert for economic security, and both are commodities that Robert takes up or leaves alone according to his own economic needs. Caroline herself recognizes that unmarried women are "cheap" goods on the "matrimonial market";[32] underpaid female workers were also "cheap." The oppression of Caroline and the Yorke girls by sewing-masters such as Hortense and Mrs. Yorke also suggests a link between single middle-class women and female mill workers. Most important, however, is Robert's vision of Caroline among his workers:

> I was standing at the top of one of my long rooms, girls were working at the other end, and . . . I seemed to see a figure resembling yours. It was some effect of doubtful light or shade, or of dazzling sunbeam. I walked up to this group; what I sought had glided away: I found myself between two buxom lasses in pinafores.[33]

Brontë assigns this passage to Robert to emphasize his unwillingness to "see" Caroline among the working-class women in his mill, but also to show that he nevertheless does envision her there. Robert's double vision actually confirms a single way of viewing women: he sees them in economic terms, either as sources of income (both the mill girls and Shirley fit into this category) or as expensive commodities.

Brontë's representation of Caroline suggests a reading of *Shirley* which recognizes that all women, regardless of class distinctions, shared a common experience of economic exploitation. One effect of this exploitation was to separate working and middle class women by stigmatizing the former and isolating the latter. Caroline's lack of recognition of the closeness of her experience to that of working women mirrors Brontë's own reluctance to openly introduce working women into her text. In the same contemplation in which the figures of Lucretia and the "virtuous woman" illustrate women's lost economic opportunities, Caroline leaves out the present-day working women who carry on the legacy of cloth production, even as she complains that "old maids" are not supposed to "ask for a place and an occupation in the world." Caroline's distaste for domestic tasks and her desire to participate in paid work prompt her to fantasize about working in the mill, but as a clerk, not a "hand." Such a wish perhaps registers a faint protest against the forces that prevented women from working in the counting-house as well as the carding-room. It seems more likely, however, that Caroline is playing it safe, since both she and Robert know that she does not dare invade his territory. Thus Caroline responds to Robert's vision of her among the mill girls by assuring him that she knows her limits: "I shall not follow you into your mill, Robert, unless you call me there."[34]

For Caroline, the mill girls are a reminder of the dangerousness of her wishes, and of the grim consequences of stepping beyond the limits imposed upon her by Victorian definitions of femininity. For Shirley, the mill girls are also a powerful reminder of the consequences of abandoning the domestic sphere. At first glance, it seems as if Shirley's wealth and social status allow her to get away with things Caroline and the mill girls cannot. She wears fancy clothing and suffers no criticism, she rarely sews, and she experiments with masculine behaviors without compromising her femininity. But Shirley can only do these things as long as her independence does not seriously challenge the status quo. Brontë minimizes the independence that Shirley's wealth and social status supposedly give her: though she playfully designates herself as an "esquire," in reality Shirley exercises little control over her own wealth and allows Robert to think of the mill as *his* property. Once Shirley transgresses the standards of her class and her sex by assuming the masculine prerogative of choosing her own spouse, her Uncle Sympson concludes that she is "not proper"and refers to her with a "coarse epithet" and other "words" unpleasant enough to nearly make her faint.[35] Uncle Sympson's unprintable words place Shirley on a level with the unspeakable, equally improper mill girls, making the point that no amount of money and social status will allow a woman to assert real independence without censure. For both Shirley and Caroline, the missing mill girls in Brontë's novel demonstrate the frightening consequences of departing from the domestic sphere and its attendant duties.

Redefining the "Duties of Woman"

In *Shirley*, working women serve as bitter, frightening reminders of women's past glory and present limitations. Like the "woman-titan" Shirley imagines and the ruined nunnery to which Shirley, Caroline and Mrs. Pryor retreat, Lucretia and the "virtuous woman" recall a lost world of female power, solidarity and dignity. Brontë's female characters cannot recapture the lost world of productivity by engaging in paid work because they lack skills and opportunities and because of social pressures: "hard labour and learned professions, they say, make women masculine, coarse, unwomanly."[36] Instead, they engage in consumption rather than production, and try to make the former take the place of the latter. As Davidoff and Hall observe in *Family Fortunes*, "By mid-century, whenever family finances would permit, the energy, organizational skill and sense of commitment which middle-class women had put into economic activity were deflected into domestic affairs."[37] Instead of making and selling cloth, middle and upper-class women in *Shirley* spend their days sewing various goods for private use.

Sewing clearly has an economic significance in *Shirley*. Wealthy, more independent women are less likely than poor or dependent women to spend their time sewing. If they do sew, they do fancywork, such as embroidery, rather than plainwork (the sewing of garments or necessary household goods). Thus Shirley embroiders violets on silk canvas while Caroline makes clothing for herself and for the parish. For the eighteenth century, Lieb suggests that "the distinction between useful, practical plainwork and frivolous, decorative fancywork becomes in the novels a reliable signal of moral worth, since women are characterized by the type of needlework they do: poor, good women do practical plainwork, often for someone else; wealthy or selfish women waste their time on fancywork. You are what you sew."[38] For the nineteenth century, Roszika Parker found that "unless embroidery was performed as a moral duty, in the spirit of selfless industry, it was regarded as sinful laziness—redolent of aristocratic decadence."[39] This attitude appears in Hortense Moore, who thinks of her needlework, especially stocking-mending, as "one of the first duties of women": "She would give a day to the mending of two holes in a stocking any time, and think her 'mission' nobly fulfilled when she had accomplished it."[40]

For Brontë, however, there seems to be little moral significance in what or how much one sews. Brontë does not show industrious sewing to be the mark of a good woman, but of a poor one. The financially independent Shirley is the only woman in the book who is "lax of her needle."[41] But Shirley's disinclination for sewing is not a symptom of moral laxity; rather, it comes from the fact that she has a variety of possessions and pastimes available to her. Shirley's wealth allows her to vary the means by which she combats her boredom, whereas Caroline, who has few books and no estate, turns to her sewing. If anything, Brontë condemns household sewing as a waste of women's energy and abilities. Rose Yorke uses the Biblical parable of the talents to argue against sewing and other household tasks as women's primary "duty":

> the Lord who gave each of us our talents will come home some day, and will demand from all an account. The tea-pot, the old stocking-foot, the linen rag, the willow-pattern tureen will yield up their barren deposit in many a house:

suffer your daughters, at least, to put their money to the exchangers. . . . [42]

This Biblical reference allows Brontë to reverse the usual moral value attached to domestic work while also bringing its economic aspect to the fore: the "barren deposit" of the woman who wastes her talents in the household is both spiritual *and* financial.

The direct link of sewing to economic status helps Brontë to unsettle subtly the notion of sewing and other domestic work as woman's "natural" occupation: women occupy themselves with household tasks not by choice, but because they have (or can afford) nothing else to do. Although Shirley's embroidery and Rose Yorke's sampler both illustrate this point, Brontë's sharpest focus is on practical sewing, and on the fact that angelic sewers like Caroline are in reality frustrated, discontented seamstresses forced to channel their energy into the domestic production of cloth goods rather than cloth. This kind of sewing, taken up most noticeably by women who are cut off not only from the industrialized workplace but from the acceptably domestic female careers of wife and mother, forms a obvious attempt to regain, if not the financial rewards of paid work, at least some of the psychological rewards, such as a sense of importance and usefulness.

Caroline does not realize that she and other middle-class women cannot emulate the productive, praiseworthy "virtuous woman" until she herself fails to find emotional solace and strength through sewing, the chief activity of the "old maids." After Robert's financial difficulties and Caroline's poverty force their potential marriage to be postponed indefinitely, she begins to search in earnest for something else to do. Though this something else can only be some kind of household work, most "women's work" holds little interest for Caroline. Hortense's lessons in darning are burdensome and useless, and Caroline is even less interested in busying herself with meaningless work for the "Jews'-Basket" that allows other "active-minded women, with a good trading spirit [to] enjoy exceedingly the fun of making hard-earned worsted-spinners cash up, to the tune of four or five hundred per cent above cost price, for articles useless to them."[43] The false piety and crass bargaining of the women who contribute to the Jews'-Basket is a parody of the honorable entrepreneurship of the "virtuous woman"; Caroline rejects it along with the mercenary "trading spirit" that conflates philanthropy and profiteering.

Instead of occupying herself with useless activity, Caroline apprentices herself to the neighborhood's old maids, Miss Mann and Miss Ainley, whose charitable activities include sewing. The lives of the old maids provide a socially acceptable alternative to marriage. Though they seem to live independently of men, the old maids remain within the domestic sphere and defer to patriarchal authority, as when Miss Ainley insists on consulting the clergy before she will allow her plans for poor relief to be put into action. At Caroline's request Miss Ainley gives her "some work to do for certain poor women who had many children, and who were unskilled in using the needle for themselves."[44] In this, we can see another subtle connection between Caroline and female mill workers, who, given the contemporary accounts of their inability to accomplish household tasks, are probably the "poor women" who benefited from Caroline's work. In aligning herself with the old maids and the mill women, Caroline's charitable sewing provides a potentially radical response to the economic and social forces that worked against women of all classes. Again, however, Caroline does not recognize the full implications of her actions; she does not think of herself as working for the mill women, who remain invisible to her, but for their children.

Caroline's efforts do meet with some success. At the school-feast, she is pleased to see that she "has done good in her small way" by "giving her time and her industry to sew for the children." But this satisfaction is not enough for Caroline. Earlier in the novel, we have been told that "these efforts brought her neither health of body nor continued peace of mind"; Caroline cannot thrive in what is to her mind a "vacant, weary, lonely, hopeless life" without the "recompense" of "successful labor." Unlike Robert Moore, whose work at the mill distracts him from and perhaps in part fulfills his emotional needs, Caroline finds that the career of a spinster demands an "abnegation of self" that prohibits her from finding lasting relief from the frustration, loneliness and depression which threaten her. Despite the strengthening influence of her friendship with Shirley, images of

Caroline's constant sewing highlight the stagnation and isolation of her life in the parsonage. Soon after Robert rejects her, Caroline's servant Fanny notices that she "was always in the same place, always bent industriously over a piece of work"; much later, Mrs. Pryor makes the same observation: "I never saw a more industrious girl than you: you are always at work." Caroline's industriousness cannot change the fact that, as she says, "it is scarcely *living* to measure time as I do at the Rectory." Brontë uses Caroline's sewing to signal her growing frustration by linking the two: "Her head laboured to frame projects as diligently as her hands to plait and stitch the thin texture of the muslin summer dress . . . " It is no coincidence that Caroline's monologue on men's unfair treatment of women takes place while she is sewing clothing for the poor.[45] Moreover, the image of Caroline—working unceasingly, in physical discomfort ("bent"), cramped, and kept indoors—recalls the working conditions of both mill workers and seamstresses, thus showing that women's economic exploitation could take place within the home just as readily as it did within the industrialized workplace.

We see this again when Caroline's efforts to gain some control over her situation by industrious sewing actually work against her by intensifying the association, most noticeably in the mind of her uncle, of women with and as objects or mechanisms.[46] "Let a woman ask me to give her an edible or a wearable . . . I can, at least, understand the demand; but when they pine for I know not what—sympathy—sentiment—some of these indefinite abstractions—I can't do it." The man who "thinks everything but sewing and cooking above women's comprehension"[47] cannot acknowledge that Caroline has interests, or needs, beyond the material. Although Caroline and Mrs. Pryor eventually take steps towards a redefinition of sewing as a ritual of kinship rather than a sign of oppression, for most of the novel the male-defined image of the female sewer is a confining one.

Brontë makes a stronger connection between women's work within and outside of the home in her treatment of the sewing circle. As part of her effort to destabilize the domestic ideal, Brontë shows that housework is organized according to a system of female masters and apprentices which replicates the hierarchical pattern of dominance and subordination that exists in the mill. The existence of a "mother-daughter apprenticeship system" has been documented by Carroll Smith-Rosenberg, whose examination of the correspondence and diaries of nineteenth-century American women showed that "mothers and other older women carefully trained daughters in the arts of housewifery and motherhood," and that in late adolescence, this training became more systematic.[48] For British women, Davidoff and Hall's research on eighteenth- and nineteenth-century Birmingham also shows that girls underwent "informal apprenticeships in the duties and skills of the household."[49]

Although Smith-Rosenberg found that female rituals offered opportunities to identify with other women and provided emotional support, such solidarity is rare through most of *Shirley*. In her search for a "master," Caroline is also searching for a mother, and her attempts to establish a mother-daughter connection outside of the biological family fail. Caroline cannot form an emotional bond with the old maids or with Hortense Moore, and the attitudes of sewing masters such as Hortense Moore and Hesther Yorke show that the sewing circle no longer fulfills its promise as a "classic image of female community."[50] Instead, women's sewing circles share the divisive, hierarchical power structures more commonly associated with the factory system in the mill. Thus the limited success of Caroline's apprenticeship makes a powerful argument against the conditions that keep her out of the 'real' workplace, while also allowing Brontë to show that the methods of that workplace have negative repercussions even for those women who never enter it.

Caroline approaches Hortense and the old maids as masters who can teach her useful skills. There is an important difference in the attitudes these female masters take towards their new "hand." Miss Ainley has to be specifically requested to give Caroline sewing tasks; she does not seek the role of master. On the other hand, women like Hortense Moore and Mrs. Yorke are quick to exploit their power over younger, less skilled women. It is no accident that both Hortense and Mrs. Yorke have close ties to mill owners, and Brontë takes several opportunities to compare Hortense's position as a "master" to that of Robert. Hortense herself draws an analogy between her difficulties with domestic servants and Robert's problems with his workmen, and the connection between Hortense's servants and Robert's workers is strengthened when Robert offers Hortense "her choice of an attendant amongst all the girls in his mill."[51]

Like Lucretia, Hortense defines female propriety in terms of domesticity, and is "specially skilful with her needle." What to Hortense is a valuable skill that defines womanly "duty" is a "grievous burden" to Caroline, who sees her as an embodiment of Lucretia's negative qualities:

> Lucretia, I daresay, was a most worthy sort of person, much like my cousin Hortense Moore; but she kept her servants up very late. I should not have liked to have been amongst the number of the maidens. Hortense would just work me and Sarah in that fashion, if she could, and neither of us would bear it.[52]

Caroline's comparison shows that she sees no difference between her position as Hortense's pupil in "French and fine needlework"and Sarah's position as Hortense's servant. The narrator concurs, explaining that Hortense is not motivated by a sense of duty but instead "delighted in the task [of teaching Caroline], because it gave her importance; she liked to lord it a little over a docile yet quick pupil."[53] Since Lucretia is in part less attractive than the "virtuous woman" because Lucretia does not have anything to do but spin, Brontë subtly suggests that the tendency of both Hortense and Lucretia to overwork their "maidens" is connected to their own limited opportunities. As a dependent who is on the way to becoming an old maid herself, Hortense can only achieve "importance" through serving as a taskmaster to other, more vulnerable women such as her servants and her young cousin.

A similar if less successful "master" is Mrs. Yorke, who tries to create in each of her daughters "such a woman as she is herself,—a woman of dark and dreary duties" which of course include sewing. When Rose rejects the notion that women's efforts should be limited to household work, Mrs. Yorke responds by telling her to "Sit down, and do a line of marking" on a sampler. But Mrs. Yorke finds her daughters to be every bit as rebellious as Robert Moore's insubordinate workers: though Rose pledges to remain her mother's "industrious apprentice" for four more years, she indicates that she will one day "do more." Unable to control her children through coercion, Mrs. Yorke complains to Caroline, who offers a suggestion not unlike her remarks to Robert about his workmen: "with love it need not be so very difficult."[54] Mrs. Yorke's angry response underscores just how little power she really has. Though nominally dominant over her children and over single women such as Caroline, when she employs strong-arm tactics such as those defended by Robert Moore (methods that are rejected by her own mill-owning husband), she, like Moore, provokes rebellion. Unlike Moore, however, Mrs. Yorke, a woman and a dependent, is defeated by those whom she has driven to extremes.

The Language of Clothes

In *Shirley*, middle-class women are not able to accomplish much for themselves through treating their sewing as "work," in part because this effort propels them into a divisive power struggle similar to that currently taking place within the mill. However, friendship among women, as Linda Hunt and Tess Cosslett have shown, does help Caroline, Shirley and Mrs. Pryor to strengthen themselves against male exclusion and rejection.[55] Friendship also goes far to make domestic activities meaningful rather than burdensome. The possibilities of female friendship are elaborated through clothing, the product of women's sewing. The clothing women make and choose allows them to announce their individuality and to present information about themselves in a language that is primarily understood and interpreted by other women. It also offers them one last means towards the reestablishment of a sense of community and affiliation among women in the domestic sphere.

Brontë does not ignore the fact that women's status as wearers of clothing, like their status as sewers of clothing, signifies their subordination by marking them as consumers rather than producers of cloth. This is borne out by Robert Moore's remark on the prospective marriage of David Sweeting and Dora Sykes—" 'How would he propose to keep Miss Sykes in gowns only?'"—as well as young Martin Yorke's characterization of women as "dolls" who "do nothing but dress themselves finely, and go swimming about to be admired." The negative economic ramifications of women's clothing are also emphasized at the very end of the novel: when "the two Mr. Moores" celebrate the building of their new mill, all we see of Shirley and Caroline are the "bonnie and grand"[56] dresses that represent (and perhaps encourage) conspicuous consumption of the goods their husbands produce.

Clothing can also mark women's complicity in their own economic and social oppression. It can denote women's spiritless conformity, as in the case of the Sympson daughters' "pattern attire." For Hortense Yorke, clothing is a way of proclaiming her adherence to the ideology of domesticity and propriety: she wears a "thick handkerchief" because "it was quite improper not to wear a fichu," and regards her apron as "the ensign of a good housewife." Clothing styles, like the master and apprentice system seen in women's sewing, can also allow some women to make a display of power through outrageous or deliberately unfashionable dress. Hortense's "stuff petticoat" and "striped cotton camisole" are part of her refusal to adopt English customs: "she adhered to her old Belgian modes, quite satisfied that there was a merit in so doing." Her Belgian clothes allow Hortense to cling to the "distinction" with which she was treated in her native country. Mrs. Yorke's "crimson skirts" and "cap more awful than a crown"[57] also represent the wearer's sense of her own dignity and merit. But while the clothing of these women may offer their wearers the feeling of power, they tend to lessen their real power by making them look ridiculous in the eyes of both men and women.

For the most part, however, Brontë is interested in rescuing clothing from such negative connotations. She attacks the idea of women's clothing as an indicator of powerlessness, frivolity and vanity by showing how women can use clothing to rebel against such stereotypes. Whereas Hortense Moore and Hesther Yorke frequently criticize the clothing of their servants, Brontë's narrator praises the attire of Fanny, Eliza, and the other working-class women who "vied with each other in smartness and daintiness of dress" at the school-feast, remarking that "the poverty which reduces an Irish girl to rags is impotent to rob the

English girl of the neat wardrobe she knows necessary to her self-respect."[58] For Brontë, clothing is a sign of proper pride.

Clothing also allows women a safe channel through which to voice their criticisms of men. Mrs. Pryor's clothing, like that of Hortense Moore, is deliberately unusual: when she is first introduced, we are told that ". . . in a well-cut, well-made gown, hers would have been no uncomely presence. It puzzled you to guess why a garment of handsome materials should be arranged in such scanty folds, and devised after such an obsolete mode." But although Mrs Pryor's dress appears quietly "eccentric," it differs from that of Hortense or Mrs. Yorke in that its aim seems to be to avoid drawing attention. In fact, Mrs. Pryor's "style of dress" changed after she escaped her nightmarish marriage, the continuing threat of which forced her to take measures to conceal her identity. And since Mrs. Pryor's marriage also taught her to fear "loveliness" as "the stamp of perversity,"[59] she has an additional reason to avoid attractive dress. Mrs. Pryor's clothing is thus a quiet but powerful form of rebellion against male definitions of female attractiveness, and against the right of men to subject women to physical violence.

Caroline's and Shirley's clothing contradicts the negative stereotypes associated with women's clothing by expressing several aspects of their individual personalities. Caroline's plain, inexpensive clothing may be understated, but she dresses very carefully: "her style of dress announced taste in the wearer," and is flattering both in color and "make." As the book progresses, Caroline's state of mind is subtly indicated through her dress. Having resigned herself to a celibate life, she appears at the school feast in a "muslin dress . . . fashioned modestly as a nun's robe"; and after the riot at the mill, she dresses herself "carefully, trying so to arrange her hair and attire that nothing of the forlornness she felt at heart should be visible externally."[60] For Caroline, dressing and sewing are closely connected: she sews her own clothes, and she uses the process and the product of sewing to regulate the degree to which she reveals her inner thoughts.

Shirley's sumptuous gowns and costly ornaments signal her wealth and the independence and extroversion it makes possible, but her clothing contradicts the popular identification of eye-catching attire with vanity, frivolity or impropriety. In describing Shirley's clothing and accessories, Brontë takes pains to ensure that they are not interpreted by the reader as marks of vanity or unchaste behavior. That Shirley does not take undue pride in her appearance is shown by the careless way she treats her gowns, allowing her dog Tartar to sit on one of them and deliberately spilling tea on another. Later in the novel, Shirley is frequently presented in white clothing, the symbolism of which is emphasized when Louis Moore refers to her as a "stainless virgin." Moore also notes how Shirley's gloves and purse "proclaim the lady."[61]

Brontë also uses Shirley's clothing to further enhance her characterization of Caroline. Shirley's dress is often contrasted with Caroline's, particularly when Robert is present. When he pays an unexpected visit to Fieldhead, the brilliant color of Shirley's silk dress, dyed so that it is "of tints deep and changing as the hue of a pheasant's neck," contrasts with Caroline's "modest muslin dress, colourless but for its narrow stripe of pale azure." A similar contrast is made at the school feast, where the two women resemble "a snow-white dove and gem-tinted bird of paradise."[62] If Shirley represents Caroline's repressed desires (as both Gilbert and Gubar and Tess Cosslett have suggested[63]), then her clothing is one way in which this projection is enacted.

Though the clothing styles of Caroline and Shirley illustrate the contrasts in the two women's personalities and economic status, their clothing sets both of them apart from the other women in the novel. Caroline and Shirley refuse to conform to the sartorial expectations of conventional young ladies with their "pattern attire"; they also refuse to dress to please Hortense and Hesther. The only female figure with whom the clothing of Caroline and Shirley has any connection is the "woman-titan" of Shirley's imagination. Just after the school feast, where Caroline and Shirley appeared in white and purple, Shirley presents her vision in the same colors, wearing a "robe of blue air . . . a veil white as an avalanche . . . her zone, purple like that horizon."[64] The graceful, attractive clothing of Shirley and Caroline thus identifies them with nature and with Shirley's dream of an alternative, female spirituality.

Since clothing can be such a powerful means of expression for women, instances in which women try to control or supervise the style in which other women dress, or even the act of dressing itself, are especially resonant. Mrs. Yorke and Hortense, both anxious to establish dominance over other women, have very strong opinions about what subordinate women should wear. Mrs. Yorke approves Hortense's "homely precise dress," but disapproves "elegant taste in attire"—which she is most likely to find in young women like Caroline and Shirley. Hortense's views are even more pronounced, as we see in her unsuccessful efforts to make Caroline wear her own domestic uniform of handkerchief and apron, and to make her servant Sarah wear a cap. Like Mrs. Yorke, Hortense "disapproved entirely of the piquant neatness of Caroline's costume, and the lady-like grace of her appearance."[65] Committed to a culture in which femininity is devalued, and in which female sexuality is seen both as an occasion of (male) sin and as proof of women's frivolity, Hortense and Mrs. Yorke seek to gain power for themselves by wearing unfashionable and unattractive garments that draw a visual distinction between themselves and women like Caroline and Shirley, whose clothing conforms more closely to the norm of graceful, elegant, and dependent femininity.

The only woman who does manage to control the clothing of other women is Caroline. But for Caroline, dressing other women is not a means of attaining power over them. Instead, it is a way of expressing intimacy and affiliation. Smith-Rosenberg and others have commented on the physical closeness that marked female friendship in the nineteenth century. The occasions on which Caroline dresses Shirley, like the night when they sleep together and share their secrets, signify a physical intimacy typical of Victorian women's friendships. Though Shirley might outshine Caroline at the school-feast, it is Caroline who actually dresses her, and playfully "found leisure to chide her, saying, she was very naughty to be so unpunctual." Later, when Shirley is unprepared for visitors, Caroline "smooth[s] her wavy curls, [and gives] to her attire a less artistic and more domestic grace." Caroline's supervision of the "millinery preparations" for Shirley's wedding with Louis Moore—"without much reference to the bride's opinion"[66]—also fits the pattern of female friendship. Smith-Rosenberg identifies wedding preparations as a female ritual, in which young women received "assistance in the practical preparations for their new home—sewing and quilting a trousseau and linen" as well as "emotional support and reassurance."[67] By putting off her marriage to Louis, Shirley holds on to her independence; she also prolongs the ritual of preparation that allows her to enjoy a special closeness with Caroline.

Since the act of dressing another woman also has a homo-erotic aspect, one wonders if this closeness encodes another possibility, albeit unrealized, for Shirley and Caroline. Smith-Rosenberg found much evidence to suggest that a sharp distinction between heterosexuality and homosexuality did not exist in the nineteenth century; instead, the physicality of women's friendships in the nineteenth-century indicated an environment in which "a wide latitude of emotions and sexual feelings" existed in a continuum between "committed heterosexuality" and "uncompromising homosexuality."[68] According to the research of Sara Putzell-Korab, however, Brontë was likely to have been aware of the concept of lesbianism from her reading of French literature and her interest in phrenology.[69] In any event, Brontë does not provide her characters with an escape from heterosexuality, however painful and limiting it may be. But Brontë does show that heterosexual marriage can coexist with women's kinship relationships: in marrying Caroline, Robert also agrees they share his house with Mrs. Pryor. Caroline's attempts to dress other women are almost always attempts to establish kinship with them.

In her search for sisters and mothers, Caroline ultimately finds a way to circumvent the paradigm of hierarchy that threatens women's sense of community. For middle-class nineteenth-century women, the act of dressing was complicated enough to require the aid of another woman, either a servant, or a mother or sister. Even though the high-waisted dresses of the early nineteenth century allowed women to escape from stays and tight corsets, most dresses were back-fastening, and were thus difficult to put on without assistance.[70] Therefore, by helping Shirley with her clothes, Caroline also takes on the roles of a servant or kinswoman; at the same time, by allowing

Caroline to dress her, Shirley grants her a measure of control not only over her person, but over an important way in which she presents and expresses herself to other people. Thus dressing becomes a ritual exchange of power, or rather a mutual abandonment of power, that denotes reciprocity, closeness and affection between the two women. There certainly is a power struggle evinced in the clothing arguments that take place between Caroline and Hortense, but Caroline's extensive attempts to change Hortense's clothing, which involve replacing the camisole with "a decent gown" and arranging her "collar, hair, &c."[71] also represent an attempt to claim kinship, perhaps even to recognize Hortense as a mother figure. Seen in this light, Hortense's "finishing touches" of fichu and apron not only spoil the effect, but also keep Caroline at a distance.

This is why Caroline is so pleased by her 'makeover' of Mrs. Pryor, an event made especially significant by the fact that Mrs. Pryor "usually shrank from meddling fingers and near approach." Caroline's delight in describing her role—"I am her waiting-woman, as well as her child: I like—you would laugh if you knew what pleasure I have in making dresses and sewing for her"[72]—speaks for itself. Caroline no longer sees sewing as a mark of her powerlessness, but as the means by which she establishes closeness with her mother, and creates a relationship in which the hierarchical roles can be traded back and forth: each can be either "child" or "mother," "lady" or "waiting-woman." Hierarchical relationships cannot be escaped in *Shirley*; among women, however, they can at least be rendered less destructive if women are willing to allow dominant and subservient roles to be exchanged and reversed.

Shirley is a novel in which women's losses are painfully evident. The ruined nunnery, Shirley's "woman-titan" and Caroline's "virtuous woman" all symbolize a lost golden age in which women were not excluded from positions of power, and in which women were not divided but instead worked together and sustained each other's spirits. Lucretia and Solomon's "virtuous woman" represent women's economic losses in a world where men produce and women consume. In this context, Brontë's attention to sewing as "women's work" and clothing as women's means of expression provides a complex evaluation of the ways in which nineteenth-century women attempted to use domestic activities, such as making and wearing clothing, as means of empowerment. At the conclusion of *Shirley*, sewing has stopped representing fruitless or divisive labor and instead begun to mark female affiliation and solidarity. While the act of sewing in itself provides neither a meaningful alternative to careers in the industrial workplace nor a means of overcoming the emotional effects of women's isolation, dependence and exclusion, the sewing and wearing of clothing does provide women with an important means of expression and mark of affiliation. More than this, the relationship of Caroline and Mrs. Pryor suggests ways in which the hierarchical relationships established in the male workplace may eventually be subverted. If the efforts of Caroline, Shirley and Mrs. Pryor will not change the world they inhabit, they at least allow them to reclaim their portion of it.

NOTES

1. All quotations from *Shirley* are from Herbert Rosengarten and Margaret Smith's edition of the text (New York: Oxford University Press, 1986). For the history of the separation of men's and women's spaces in Western political thought see Jean Bethke Elshtain, *Public Man, Private Woman: Women in Social and Political Thought* (Princeton: Princeton University Press, 1981).

2. Brontë, *Shirley*, 62, 63.

3. On professional embroidery in the nineteenth century, see Roszika Parker, *The Subversive Stitch: Embroidery and the Making of the Feminine* (London: Women's Press, 1984), 174–75.

4. Brontë, *Shirley*, 71.

5. Bonnie Anderson and Judith Zinsser, *A History of Their Own: Women in Europe from Prehistory to the Present*, 2 vols. (New York: Harper and Row, 1988), 1:99.

6. Anderson and Zinsser, *A History of Their Own*, 1:370.

7. Anderson and Zinsser, *A History of Their Own*, 1:410.

8. Leonore Davidoff and Catherine Hall, *Family Fortunes: Men and Women of the English Middle Class, 1780–1850* (Chicago: University of Chicago Press, 1967), 273.

9. Brontë, *Shirley*, 71, 190.

10. Brontë, *Shirley*, 325.

11. Brontë, *Shirley*, 392, 391.

12. Brontë, *Shirley*, 392.

13. On the topic of androgyny in *Shirley* see Pauline Nestor's *Female Friendships and Communities: Charlotte Brontë, George Eliot, Elizabeth Gaskell* (Oxford: Clarendon Press, 1985). Nestor finds in *Shirley* a "general movement towards a more androgynous sense of sex-roles" demonstrated in a "continual play on the duality of roles" (124) for Shirley and Louis, and even Robert and Caroline.

14. Brontë, *Shirley*, 392. The most important early accounts of Lucretia are those of Livy, Ovid and Plutarch; the story was subsequently taken up by numerous European writers including Petrarch, Chaucer, and Shakespeare. Arthur Young's *Echoes of Two Cultures* (Pittsburgh: University of Pittsburgh Press, 1964) discusses the classical versions of the story along with its most significant reappearances in literature and the visual arts. The most important recent discussions are Ian Donaldson's *The Rapes of Lucretia: A Myth and Its Transformations* (Oxford: Clarendon Press, 1982) and Stephanie Jed's *Chaste Thinking: The Rape of Lucretia and the Birth of Humanism* (Bloomington: Indiana University Press, 1989).

15. Ian Donaldson, *The Rapes of Lucretia*, 19.

16. Arthur Young, *Echoes of Two Cultures*, 89–90.

17. Rozsika Parker, *The Subversive Stitch*, 66, 67.

18. Donaldson, *The Rapes of Lucretia*, 10–11.

19. Brontë, *Shirley*, 391.

20. Brontë, *Shirley*, 30. In her introduction to the Oxford edition of *Shirley*, Margaret Smith suggests that Brontë did not want to cover the same ground as Elizabeth Gaskell's *Mary Barton*, which considers the situation of male and female workers in detail ("Introduction" xi). Terry Eagleton takes a different view in *Myths of Power: A Marxist Study of the Brontës* (New York: Barnes and Noble, 1975), where he argues that Brontë is so "preoccupied with certain structural contradictions within the ruling class" that she either ignores the working class or treats them with "panicky contempt and paternalist condescension" (49).

21. The low status and pay of Victorian working women, including female wool workers, has been described in Ivy Pinchbeck's classic *Women Workers and the Industrial Revolution 1750–1850* (New York: F.S. Crofts and Co, 1930); Wanda Neff's *Victorian Working Women* (New York: Humanities Press, 1976); and more recently in Judy Lown's *Women and Industrialization: Gender at Work in Nineteenth Century England* (Minneapolis: University of Minnesota Press, 1990) and Maxine Berg's *The Age of Manufactures: Industry, Innovation and Work in Britain 1700–1820* (New York: Oxford University Press, 1986). Berg reports that by the 1830's, worsted manufacture (the main wool industry in Brontë's West Riding) depended upon a work force that was "predominantly female and juvenile" and had "little upward mobility" (222).

22. Anderson and Zinsser, *A History of Their Own*, 2: 259.

23. John Rule, *The Labouring Classes in Early Industrial England, 1750–1850* (New York: Longman, 1986), 180.

24. In *Victorian Working Women* (See n. 21) Wanda Neff gives several illustrations of the widespread belief that "working girls wore inappropriate finery," including several passages from *Mary Barton* (52). Lynda Nead discusses visual representations of prostitutes in *Myths of Sexuality: Representations of Women in Victorian Britain* (Oxford: Basil Blackwell, 1988), especially in chapter six, "Visual Culture and Visual Myth." As Nead explains, Victorians believed prostitutes to be "pathologically vain," and thought that one of the main causes of prostitution was "love of dress" (174).

25. Cecilia Macheski, "Penelope's Daughters: Images of Needlework in Eighteenth-Century Literature," in *Fetter'd or Free? British Women Novelists, 1670–1815,* ed. Mary Anne Schofield and Cecilia Macheski (Athens, OH: Ohio University Press, 1986).

26. Laurie Lieb, "'The Works of Women are Symbolical': Needlework in the Eighteenth Century," *Eighteenth Century Life* 10 (1986): 28–44.

27. Macheski, "Penelope's Daughters," 86.

28. Lieb, "'The Works of Women are Symbolical,'" 30.

29. Neff, *Victorian Working Women*, 48.

30. Rule, *Labouring Classes*, 184.

31. Rule, *Labouring Classes*, 178, 183.

32. Brontë, *Shirley*, 81, 86, 391.

33. Brontë, *Shirley*, 255.

34. Brontë, *Shirley*, 391, 255.

35. Brontë, *Shirley*, 558, 627.

36. Brontë, *Shirley*, 229.

37. Davidoff and Hall, *Family Fortunes*, 313.

38. Lieb, "'The Works of Women are Symbolical,'" 32–33.

39. Parker, *The Subversive Stitch*, 154.

40. Brontë, *Shirley*, 81.

41. Brontë, *Shirley*, 386.

42. Brontë, *Shirley*, 400–401.

43. Brontë, *Shirley*, 112–13.

44. Brontë, *Shirley*, 183.

45. Brontë, *Shirley*, 297, 184, 229, 174, 175, 241, 375, 240, 390–93.

46. A similar pattern of objectification is mentioned by Roslyn Belkin in "Rejects of the Marketplace: Old Maids in Charlotte Brontë's *Shirley*," *International Journal of Women's Studies* 4 (1981): 50–66. Belkin claims that the male manufacturers in *Shirley* treat women and the unemployed poor as "business commodities rather than sentient beings" (56).

47. Brontë, *Shirley*, 440, 93.

48. Carroll Smith-Rosenberg, "The Female World of Love and Ritual: Relations between Women in Nineteenth-Century America," *Signs* 1 (1975): 1–29, 18.

49. Davidoff and Hall, *Family Fortunes*, 281.

50. Lieb, "'The Works of Women are Symbolical,'" 40.

51. Brontë, *Shirley*, 86.

52. Brontë, *Shirley*, 81, 82, 392.

53. Brontë, *Shirley*, 76.

54. Brontë, *Shirley*, 148, 401, 402.

55. See Linda Hunt, "Sustenance and Balm: The Question of Female Friendship in *Shirley* and *Villette*," *Tulsa Studies in Women's Literature* 1 (1982): 55–66; and Tess Cosslett, *Woman to Woman: Female Friendship in Victorian Fiction* (Brighton: Harvester, 1988), especially chapter four, "*Shirley:* Disruption and Containment" (111–37).

56. Brontë, *Shirley*, 22, 158, 646.

57. Brontë, *Shirley*, 389, 80, 63, 64, 66, 396.

58. Brontë, *Shirley*, 306, 296.

59. Brontë, *Shirley*, 195, 437.

ₒₒ. Brontë, *Shirley*, 75, 306, 351.

61. Brontë, *Shirley*, 522, 524.

62. Brontë, *Shirley*, 249, 295.

63. See Sandra Gilbert and Susan Gubar's chapter, "The Genesis of Hunger, According to *Shirley*," in *The Madwoman in the Attic: The Woman Writer and the Nineteenth-Century Literary Imagination* (New Haven: Yale University Press, 1979) and Cosslett's *Woman to Woman* (See n. 55).

64. Brontë, *Shirley*, 321.

65. Brontë, *Shirley*, 397, 81.

66. Brontë, *Shirley*, 295, 469, 637.

67. Smith-Rosenburg, "The Female World of Love and Ritual," 22.

68. Smith-Rosenburg, "The Female World of Love and Ritual," 29.

69. Sara Putzell-Korab, "Passion between Women in the Victorian Novel," in *Sexuality and Victorian Literature*, ed. Don Richard Cox (Knoxville: University of Tennessee Press, 1984), 180–95.

70. See Blanche Payne's *History of Costume: From the Ancient Egyptians to the Twentieth Century* (New York: Harper and Row, 1965): "Practically all of the dresses of this era fastened down center back with buttons, lacing, or concealed closings of hooks and eyes; the only exceptions to this rule were pelisse robes and walking dresses" (495). Dresses of the forties, when Brontë wrote the novel, were still back-fastening, but featured lower waists and close-fitting bodices that necessitated tightly corseted waists.

71. Brontë, *Shirley*, 80.

72. Brontë, *Shirley*, 448, 559.

Loss of the Domestic Idyll
Slop Workers in Victorian Fiction

Lynn M. Alexander

> Oh, men, with sisters dear!
> Oh, men, with mothers and wives!
> It is not linen you're wearing out
> But human creatures' lives!
> Stitch—stitch—stitch,
> In poverty, hunger, and dirt,
> Sewing at once, with a double thread,
> A Shroud as well as a Shirt.
>
> —Thomas Hood, "Song of the Shirt"

The concepts of domesticity and of woman as angel in the house, long considered Victorian cultural constructs, were actually well established long before Victoria's coronation in 1837 or Coventry Patmore's verse idealization in 1854. But it was during the Victorian era that the cult of domesticity came into full fruition. Fed by writers such as Sarah Lewis, whose *Woman's Mission* (1839) was in its thirteenth edition by 1849, and Sarah Stickney Ellis, a well-known author of training manuals for women emphasizing the importance of knowing the practical details of running a household as well as how to adorn it with products of craft and skill, Victorians viewed women as wives and mothers, actual or potential, and as the fulcrum upon which the quality of life, particularly family life, depended. While it is easy to recognize how these goals and ideals were internalized by the middle class, their impact on the working classes may not be as immediately obvious. What a study of Victorian literature, both fiction and nonfiction, reveals is that for much of the era the ideological constructions of women and domesticity were not structured or defined by class; thus what was held to be an ideal for middle-class women was also held to be one for working-class women: as wives and mothers, women were responsible for providing a moral center, by example and instruction, for their families.

Given this blanket responsibility for the moral guidance of England, it is not surprising that much of the blame for the malfunctioning of industrial society was placed on the working-class woman. These women were held accountable for a multitude of social problems such as criminality among the young, alcoholism, prostitution, high infant mortality, and poor education. Much of the prose literature attacked working women for displacing men in the workplace (thus disrupting the natural order of the family with man as provider and woman as nurturer), abandoning their children to fend for themselves (thus failing in the duty to teach moral responsibility and, for daughters, domestic tasks), or, worse, overdosing their infants with elixirs such as Godfrey's Cordial (thus prematurely ending their lives). Complaints about working-class women ranged from those critical of their ignorance and inexperience in housekeeping to accusations of potential moral pollution. So while Mrs. Austin might complain, "It is impossible to conceive the waste and improvidence which reigns in the lowest English household. The women buy improvidently, cook improvidently, and dress improvidently. The consequences are, want, debt, disorder, and all that can make a man's home comfortless and irritating, take from him all hope of improvement in his condition, all regard for so useless a partner, and drive him to the alehouse,"[1] Frederick Engels could attack the employment of women from a moral stance:

> The employment of the wife dissolves the family utterly and of necessity, and this dissolution, in our present society, which is based upon the family, brings the most demoralizing consequences for parents as well as children. A mother who has no time to trouble herself about her child,

to perform the most ordinary loving services for it during its first year, who scarcely indeed sees it, can be no real mother to child, must inevitably grow indifferent to it, treat it unlovingly like a stranger. The children who grow up under such conditions are utterly ruined for later family life, can never feel at home in the family which they themselves found, because they have always been accustomed to isolation, and they contribute therefore to the already general undermining of the family in the working-class.[2]

Thus for Victorian social critics, employment and domesticity seemed to be incompatible concepts for women.

It should come as no surprise then that when social protest novelists decided to deal with the issue of working-class women they began with young unmarried women, removed them from the home, yet chose an occupation closely associated with domesticity: needlework. After all, in Victorian England all women were taught to sew, regardless of their social class.[3] Thus people reading about a woman sewing could identify with the character, either as women who sewed or as men whose mothers, wives, and sisters sewed. Fiction writers also took advantage of the fact that many of the young women employed in dressmaking establishments were farmers' daughters or daughters of impoverished middle-class households. In these cases the young women were employing a skill learned at home, often with the intention of returning there after learning the trade.

Initially the focus of these writers was almost exclusively the young woman employed in a millinery house.[4] While the term "house" is frequently used to indicate some kind of business or institution, in this case there are connotations which would have been of particular interest to Victorians. The term "millinery *house* " would carry connotations which would reassure both customers and parents of workers; after all, the workers were young women in a society where women were to be associated with hearth and home, and the suggestion of employment tarnished the reputation. Yet because needlework was associated with the domestic, dressmaking was considered an acceptable employment, if a woman must be employed, and thus was used most frequently by social protest novelists who wished to arouse the sympathy of their reading audience. Therefore, if an author wanted to talk about working-class women, a seamstress would be the most sympathetic choice. As Wanda Neff notes, a writer such as Elizabeth Gaskell might create a heroine who is the offspring of factory workers, but who does not work in the factories herself, since "the factory girl lacked all the qualifications for the ideal Victorian heroine."[5] Rather, Gaskell has Mary Barton employed as a seamstress, someone to whom Victorian readers could respond without prejudice.

For many early reformers the point of early seamstress literature was to demonstrate the very lack of protection that young women in millinery houses received. Not only did they work extremely long hours, sometimes eighteen hours without a break,[6] but the working conditions were poor, leading to ill health and even death. The equation between needlework and death was not as exaggerated as it might first seem. In his *Report on the Sanitary Condition of the Labouring Population of Great Britain* (1842), Edwin Chadwick shows that of the fifty-two milliners and dressmakers who were reported to have died in the Metropolitan Unions, thirty-three died of lung diseases, twenty-eight of whom specifically died of consumption. The average age of the seamstresses who died of consumption was twenty-six[7]: And while death from consumption was common among Victorians in general, during the 1840s and 1850s approximately eight percent more women than men died from it. In fact, in mid-Victorian England approximately half, sometimes more, of all women fifteen to thirty-five years of age who died were killed by some form of consumption. Moreover, the Victorian age-specific death rates for the general population are very nearly equivalent to rates for the working classes of the period, since during the entire era no more than five to fifteen percent of the total population of England and Wales was of the middle or upper classes.[8]

The common assumption has been that the higher mortality rate among women was due to complications in childbirth. However, as Sheila Johansson explains in "Sex and Death in Victorian England," according to the general statistics of the period, the increase in female mortality actually occurs between ages ten and thirty-four and young girls aged five to nineteen were the last to achieve consistently lower death rates than their male counterparts.[9] Johansson suggests that because of the lesser

Deaths from Disease of Milliners and Dressmakers, in the Metropolitan Unions during the Year 1839, as Shown by the Mortuary Registers

Age	Number of Deaths	Average Age	Number of Deaths from Consumption	Average Age	Number of Deaths from other Lung Diseases	Average Age
under 20	6	17	4	18	—	—
20 under 30	24	24	17	23	1	23
30 under 40	11	34	6	34	1	33
40 under 50	2	45	—	—	1	40
50 under 60	4	54	1	58	2	55
60 under 70	5	64	—	—	—	—
Total	52	32	28	26	5	41

Note: Out of 52 deaths in the year, 41 of the deceased attained an age of 25. The average age of the 33 who died of lung disease was 28.

Source: Edwin Chadwick, *Report on the Sanitary Condition of the Labouring Population of Great Britain*, ed. M.W. Flinn (Edinburgh: Edinburgh University Press, 1968), 176.

value placed upon women by Victorian society, girls received poorer nourishment than boys, leaving them weaker, less able to survive harsh conditions, and more susceptible to illness. Whatever the cause, consumption was so common among women in general and seamstresses in particular that in 1845 *Punch* cautioned its readers, "The question has been mooted, whether consumption is contagious. We do not mean to assert that it is; and we would not frighten anybody, especially a sensitive young lady, or her anxious mamma, unnecessarily; but we do declare that we should not, were it consistent with our sex, at all like to be in the frocks of those whose dresses have been wrought by consumptive fingers. We shall say no more on this subject, except that we hope we have now thrown out a little hint, which may induce those for whom it is intended to interest themselves, for their sakes, in behalf of the over-worked silkworms."[10] Illustrations, such as *Punch*'s "Pin Money and Needle Money" (1843), "A Shroud as well as a Shirt" (1848), and "The Haunted Lady, or 'The Ghost' in the Looking-Glass" (1863), were used by some journals to indicate the harsh existence of the seamstresses and the almost inevitable consequences, while others relied on fiction to present the conditions of needlewomen through a representative example. It is hardly surprising, therefore, that the seamstress fiction of the 1840s and 1850s portrays both the harsh conditions faced by needlewomen and the outcome, with the heroine usually succumbing to consumption.

A common secondary feature of early novels focusing on women employed in millinery houses are those women who, for whatever reason, obtained needlework through a middleman and worked in their homes. Commonly called "slop workers,"[11] such women usually made shirts or trousers, occasionally obtaining piecework from millinery houses during the season. The slop worker had a more difficult time procuring work and worked longer hours and was paid even less than her counterpart in the millinery establishment. In fact, the wages paid to slop workers were notoriously low. While preparing his series for the *Morning Chronicle* in 1849, Henry Mayhew interviewed several slop workers. One woman of "excellent character" gave the following testimony: "Upon the average, at all kinds of work, excepting the shirts, that I make, I cannot earn more than 4s. 6d. to 5s. per week—let me sit from eight in the morning till ten every night: and out of that I shall have to pay 1s. 6d. for trimmings, and 6d. for candles every week; so that altogether I earn about 3s. in the six days. But I don't earn that, for there's the firing you must have to press the work, and that will be 9d. a week. . . . So that my clear earnings are . . . say 2s. 3d. to 2s. 6d. every week."[12] Some women chose to work as piece workers in order to stay at home, perhaps trying to remain as close as they could to the ideal of not having to work outside the house. But many women worked in their homes because they or their families could not pay the premium required for an apprenticeship.

Economic instability in the 1830s and 1840s pushed many shop owners to find the least expensive way to create their product; more and more this meant turning to slop workers. In 1852 T. Hughes, in *A Lecture on the Slop-System*, claimed that three out of every four garments sold in England were made by slop workers in London or in one of the other large towns; in London alone, in 1849, there were estimated to be 14,000 female slop workers, 11,440 of whom were under the age of twenty.[13] It should not be surprising, therefore, that the slop worker became a popular figure for social protest writers as diverse as Charles Dickens, Elizabeth Gaskell, G.W.M. Reynolds, or Eliza Meteyard during the late 1840s and 1850s.

One of the most harrowing, yet conversely most hopeful, portrayals of slop work appeared in Charles Dickens's 1844 Christmas book, *The Chimes*. As in his earlier work *A Christmas Carol*, Dickens transports his main character, in this case a messenger named Trotty, into a frightening future determined by his lack of Christmas spirit. In this phantom future Trotty, and Victorian readers, are presented with the worst conditions which could befall slop workers, in this case Trotty's daughter, Meg, and Lilian, the daughter of Will Fern, a friend:

> In a poor, mean room; working at the same kind of embroidery which he had often, often seen before her; Meg, his own dear daughter, was presented to his view. . . .

> Ah! Changed. Changed. The light of the clear eye, how dimmed. The bloom, how faded from the cheek. Beautiful she was, as she had ever been, but Hope, Hope, Hope, oh

where was the fresh Hope that had spoken to him like a voice!

She looked up from her work, at a companion. . . . [Lilian speaks:] "Such work, such work! So many hours, so many days, so many long, long nights of hopeless, cheerless, never-ending work—not to heap up riches, not to live grandly or gaily, not to live upon enough, however coarse; but to earn bare bread; to scrape together just enough to toil upon, and want upon, and keep alive in us the consciousness of hard fate! Oh Meg, Meg!" she raised her voice and twined her arms about her as she spoke, like one in pain. "How can the cruel world go round, and bear to look upon such lives!"[14]

A few pages later Trotty again sees his daughter, but now fallen on even harder times:

His daughter was again before him, seated at her work. But in a poorer, meaner garret than before; and with no Lilian by her side.

The frame at which she had worked, was put away upon a shelf and covered up. The chair in which she had sat, was turned against the wall. A history was written in these little things, and in Meg's grief-worn face. Oh! who could fail to read it!

Meg strained her eyes upon her work until it was too dark to see the threads; and when the night closed in, she lighted her feeble candle and worked on.[15]

Meg continues working until she is interrupted at half past midnight. The visitor is Lilian, who, as indicated, has fallen into prostitution but has returned to Meg one last time to tell her she is loved and to ask forgiveness before dying at Meg's feet. But Dickens saves the most horrific for last. At the end of his dream Trotty sees Meg one last time: a widow with a young child, unable to find work and thus unable to buy food or pay her rent. Finally, in despair she, with her child, jumps from the bridge into a river.[16]

Despite this series of nightmare visions, Dickens suggests that a slop worker's life does not have to be a gradual descent into despair. When Trotty awakes he has learned his lesson, that "there is a Sea of Time to rise one day, before which all who wrong us or oppress us will be swept away like leaves. . . . that we must trust and hope, and neither doubt ourselves, nor doubt the Good in one another."[17] Although we are not shown Meg and Lilian living well and happy later in life, it is implied that such will be the case if they trust in tomorrow rather than assume the worst, as they had been advised by negative forces such as Alderman Cute, who warns that he, and thus society, will "put down" anything he cannot deal with.

Perhaps less Dantesque, but equally heart rending, is the picture of slop work presented by Elizabeth Gaskell in *Mary Barton* (1848). Early on Gaskell deals with the difficulty of a working-class girl gaining employment in a millinery house. Mary Barton's father is unable to obtain her a position because the millinery houses are all requiring a higher premium than he can afford. The only way she can secure employment is by applying herself because "her beauty . . . made her desirable as a show woman."[18] But Gaskell does not abandon the working-class needleworker. Mary's character is balanced with that of Margaret, a slop worker, and it is Margaret whom Gaskell most often shows at her needle. The scenes involving needlework usually show Mary helping Margaret in the evenings, with any discussions of working or health conditions, including the inevitable blindness resulting from long hours and poor lighting, centering around those experienced by the working-class slop worker, Margaret:

> "Mary! do you know I sometimes think I'm growing a little blind, and then what would become of grandfather and me? . . . last autumn I went to a doctor; and he did not mince the matter, but said unless I sat in a darkened room, with my hands before me, my sight would not last me many years longer. But how could I do that, Mary? . . . There now, Mary," continued she, shutting one eye, "now you only look like a great black shadow, with the edges dancing and sparkling."
>
> "And can you see pretty well with th' other?"
>
> "Yes, pretty near as well as ever. Th' only difference is, that if I sew a long time together, a bright spot like th' sun comes right where I'm looking; all the rest is quite clear

> but just where I want to see. . . . I suppose I'm going dark
> as fast as may be. Plain work pays so bad, and mourning
> has been so plentiful this winter, I were tempted to take in
> any black work I could; and now I'm suffering from it."

> "And yet, Margaret, you're going on taking it in; that's
> what you'd call foolish in another."

> "It is Mary! and yet what can I do? Folk mun live . . ."

> She took up her sewing, saying her eyes were rested now,
> and for some time they sewed on in silence.[19]

Fifty pages later, Margaret is totally blind.

Although Margaret soon gains employment as a singer, and ironically is better paid than she was as a seamstress, she is now handicapped and deprived of what would be considered a normal life; if her blindness does not preclude marriage, the traveling involved in her singing career will. And so, even here, although the outcome is not total destruction, life for a slop worker is portrayed as undesirable and destructive.

In 1850 two novels—Eliza Meteyard's *Lucy Dean, the Noble Needlewoman* and G.W.M. Reynolds' *The Seamstress*—appeared which not only deal with the living and working conditions of slop workers, but also with business aspects (such as the employment of middlemen) and possible means of alleviating the suffering of these women (such as emigration). Meteyard's interest in emigration is obvious from the first installment of *Lucy Dean* in *Eliza Cook's Journal* (16 March 1850), since the novel opens with two epigraphs taken from Edward Gibbon Wakefield's *The Art of Colonization.* The first quote stresses the need to inform the working classes of the possibilities offered by emigration; the second argues the importance women play in shaping the communities formed through colonization. Through these quotations, Meteyard introduces three themes which are stressed throughout *Lucy Dean*: the need for the working classes to receive information concerning emigration, preferably from others who have emigrated; the need for emigrants to raise the fare necessary to emigrate themselves, and the need for women who are both virtuous and religious to emigrate.

Lucy Dean, like most of the seamstresses in the fiction immediately preceding and those interviewed by Henry Mayhew for *London Labour and the London Poor,* is a slop worker. And although she has work to do, she does not have the money to purchase thread or candles, let alone bread, and so cannot work. It is when she is trying to raise money by selling her deceased brother's songbird, after unsuccessfully attempting to obtain credit from her materials supplier, that Lucy first hears of emigration and Mary Austen, a character modeled after Caroline Chisholm of the Family Colonization Loan Society. For many Victorians emigration seemed an excellent way to alleviate the sufferings of needlewomen. Theoretically, it would reduce the number of women competing for jobs and allow the women to fulfill the Victorian ideal of domesticity, since these women were expected to marry shortly after their arrival in Australia.

The first time Lucy meets Mary Austen it is stressed that Lucy will need skills other than needlework. The first thing Austen asks is "'Could you wash, cook, bake, do you know how to provide a comfortable dinner, and nurse a child?'" When Lucy answers affirmatively, Austen replies: "'This is well, for these are chief points . . . in all womanly life, . . . but much more needful ones, to those who seek a new country.'"[20] Thus Meteyard uses emigration as a possible way to fulfill the readers' belief that every woman should have the opportunity to participate in the cult of domesticity: both as wife and mother, and as family moral and spiritual leader.

But not everyone was equally impressed with the emigration scheme for the relief of needleworkers. During the latter part of 1849 and early 1850 a debate was carried out in the press as to the wisdom of Sidney Herbert's Fund for Promoting Female Emigration. During the month of December *The Spectator* ran four articles on Herbert's plan which, while not attacking the idea, demonstrated that it would not solve the problem of unemployment or low wages for seamstresses. More outspoken was G.W.M. Reynolds' "A Warning to the Needlewomen and Slopworkers," which appeared in *Reynolds's Political Instructor.* In his article Reynolds emphatically rejects Herbert's program:

> A more scandalous proceeding was never initiated by that patrician class which is so heartless in its oppression and so base in its duplicity towards the sons and daughters of toil. This gilded pill which a parcel of titled and reverend

quacks are endeavouring to cram down the throats of
starving Englishwomen, is entitled a "Fund for Promoting
Female Emigration"; . . . I conjure the needlewomen and
slopworkers to put no faith in the promises held out: I
warn them—emphatically, earnestly warn them against
yielding to the representations set forth in such brilliant
colours and in such an apparently Christian spirit . . . Miserable enough ye are in your own country, poor women!—
I know it well: but ten thousand times more miserable still
would ye find yourselves on board the worthless old emi-
grant-ships in which it is proposed to pen you up like so
many sheep,—ten thousand times more miserable when
turned adrift in some colony at the end of the world, with
the harrowing conviction that you have been basely jug-
gled into accepting a change of condition only too well
calculated to prove that even in the lowest depths of
wretchedness there is lower deep still![21]

Although Reynolds levels much of his attack at the sponsors of
the plan, the aristocracy and the clergy, he also voices many of
the fears of those considering the program: the conditions of the
ships and of the land to which they would emigrate. Until this
time Australia was generally considered a wasteland, a place to
which convicts were transported. Indeed, Reynolds uses this
past transportation as part of his argument against Herbert's
program: "The Society's Prospectus shows that in the colonies
there are more males than females. . . . But of what class does a
large proportion of the male population of Australia consist? Of
the banished felony from England!" According to Reynolds, any
relief for urban needleworkers must come from "an alteration in
the laws which *make* the millions poor, and *keep* them poor too,
in order that the few may be rich now and grow richer as time
moves on."[22]

But Reynolds's attack against the emigration of needlewomen was not limited to articles in his newspapers. On 23
March 1850, Reynolds began publishing *The Seamstress* in his
miscellany; it was to be part of a larger series entitled *The Slaves
of England*. Concentrating on the plight of the seamstress, its
causes, and what could be done in England to relieve the situation, Reynolds mentions emigration only as a means of getting
rid of unsavory characters: Lovel, a forger and murderer, and his

common-law wife. He thus reminds readers that Australia originally served England as a penal colony, and reinforces any doubts about sending helpless or delicate women there.

Reynolds's story is strongly influenced by the many portrayals of seamstresses which preceded it, and is in many ways a return to the earlier seamstress narratives, such as Gaskell's *Mary Barton*. Reynolds's most important sources, however, predate most fictional portrayals. The opening of the novel is set in January 1844 and uses the imagery of Thomas Hood's "The Song of the Shirt" (December 1843) and Redgrave's *The Sempstress* (1844), for setting and characterization. The opening description of the seamstress's room—

> That back attic—for it was nothing more—was scrupulously clean as the nicest sense of female tidiness could render it. . . . Upon the floor was stretched the humble bedding—a flock mattrass [sic] and one thin blanket, with a pair of sheets as white as snow. A small deal table, a solitary chair, a basin and ewer, a candlestick, a little moveable cupboard, and a piece of broken looking-glass hanging to the window . . . [23]

—is an amalgamation of the room described in Hood's poem, with its single table, broken chair, and blank wall, and the one shown in Redgrave's painting, a small attic room with a single window, lighted by a candle, with a table holding a broken basin and pitcher, a chair, the low bed, a cupboard, an empty fireplace, and a clock showing two-thirty. Even the time correlates, for Reynolds's seamstress hears the clock strike two and calculates that another half-hour to finish her work.[24]

The influence of Redgrave's *The Sempstress* is again seen in Reynolds's creation of Virginia's saintliness. Virginia is one of the first fictional seamstresses to live alone, all others live at the millinery house or with relatives. The isolation of the seamstress was unusual in literature but common in painting. According to T.J. Edelstein, in "They Sang 'The Song of the Shirt': The Visual Iconology of the Seamstress," the use of the single figure by Redgrave and his followers was a conscious artistic choice which allowed them to create a stronger empathy with their audiences.[25] Edelstein also comments on the traditional association of the single figure with that of images of saints, which she claims is easily visible in Redgrave: "His portrayal of the seamstress as a martyr to modern urban society is heightened by the almost supernatural light of the candle, hidden by the cloth, and by the upturned gaze of the shirtmaker."[26] The influence of Redgrave's portrayal can also be seen in Reynolds's selection of illustrations. The opening sketch, drawn by Henry Anelay, is actually two pictures separated by a pair of scissors. On the right is a drawing room scene with a number of well-dressed women, while on the left a lone seamstress is shown working. To readers familiar with Redgrave's painting the similarities would be unmistakable: the lone figure in a room lighted by a single candle, a window, one chair and table, an empty fireplace, a mattress on the floor, and a broken basin and pitcher.

The blending of an in-depth study of the seamstress with that of a working-class setting allows Reynolds to cover material never before discussed at length. Of primary interest is his discussion of the securing of work through middlewomen. When Reynolds begins his series, he goes to great lengths to show the reader how the system operates. By having Virginia, the young seamstress, deliver a finished garment to the various levels of the middlewoman system, Reynolds demonstrates both how the system works and why needleworkers starve despite the cost of the garment to the customer. Virginia delivers a dress to her contact, Mrs. Jackson, and is paid three shillings and six pence. As a favor to Mrs. Jackson she then delivers the dress to Mrs. Jackson's contact, Mrs. Pembroke, who gives her the seven shillings Mrs. Jackson is to be paid for the garment. Mrs. Pembroke then requests that Virginia deliver the gown, with a bill for fourteen shillings, to the milliner who originally requested the work. The milliner also has Virginia deliver the dress, this time to the customer, with a bill for four pounds and four shillings. When Virginia questions another seamstress about the system, she, along with the reader, receives a lengthy lesson in suppression through economics:

> "Madam Duplessy employs a middle-woman, because it saves trouble in the first instance—and secondly because the result is to keep down the price of the work thus put out to be done. . . . the more hands it passes through, the better she is pleased, because the earnings of the wretched

needlewomen who do the work are diminished in proportion. By thus keeping down the wages of the needlewomen, the great houses . . . can from time to time reduce the prices paid to the middle-women. . . . The result is that your earnings, Virginia, will continue to grow less and less: but I question whether Madame Duplessy will lower her prices towards her aristocratic customers. . . . Mrs. Jackson crushes you—Mrs. Pembroke grinds Mrs. Jackson—and Madam Duplessy keeps a tight hand over Mrs. Pembroke. . . . Now, were Madame Duplessy left to fight the battle of labour's value direct with *you* who did the labour, she would be pretty well at your mercy—because you could charge her at least a guinea for the work which she charged the Duchess four guineas for: and, however discontented Madame Duplessy might be at such a charge on your part, she has not the time to run all over London to ascertain who will work cheaper for her than you."[27]

The middlewoman system was, to Reynolds, at the heart of the economic problems faced by needlewomen; therefore, when he returns to the harsh conditions faced by needleworkers at the close of the novel he also returns to the issue of middlewomen:

But why could not Virginia, who was so proficient with her needle, obtain the best and most delicate work from the mantua-makers and milliners, instead of the coarse slop-work of the delectable Messrs. Aaron and Sons?—or why, at all events, could she not procure the work direct from the establishment itself, instead of through the hands of a middle-woman? . . . the same system which in the first instance rendered Virginia the slave of Mrs. Jackson, now enchains her to the service of one of the numerous "sweaters" who farm the work of Messrs. Aaron and Sons.[28]

Thus for Reynolds, slop workers have fallen out of the social structure: they are "serviceable and valuable slave[s] " who, because of their proficiency at a skill that is at the heart of domesticity but devalued because it is taken for granted, are "enchained" to the system because the long hours of their employment locks them away from society and thus the possibility of marriage and family. Reynolds then proceeds to give an account of Virginia's wages as compared to the cost of the

garments, and the costs of necessities such as rent, food, and supplies—based on figures presented by Mayhew.

Considering the need to disprove the seeming correlation
between needlewomen and prostitution established by Mayhew,
and to encourage the support, especially financial, of the upper
classes, the portrayal of the seamstress as a martyr who sacrifices
her health and hopes of a future home and family, perhaps even
her life to urban society was a logical step. This image is particularly strong in Reynolds's *The Seamstress*. Reynolds builds the image of Virginia as suffering victim, turning her into a martyr of a
system established by the middle class in order to prey upon the
working classes. As she succumbs to consumption, Virginia is
increasingly described as saintlike: from presenting the
"resigned meekness of a saint" to displaying looks "full of the
martyrised sweetness and resignation of a saint," and finally
demonstrating, on her death bed, "the mingled meekness of an
angel and resignation of a martyr-saint."[29] Adding to the image
of Virginia as saint is her unflagging moral integrity. Reynolds
makes it clear that such virtue is unusual for a slop worker:
"And if our humble heroine remained pure and spotless in the
midst of contamination—in the midst of temptation—in the
midst of sorrow, suffering, and crushing toil,—she must be regarded on as an exception to the rule, and not as a type of her
class in this respect. With pain and indignation do we record the
fact that virtue in the poor seamstress is almost an impossibility."[30] Such a presentation suggests that, while somewhat unusual, there may be others out there who, like Virginia, are
worthy of rescue.

When presenting readers with shocking material or information which might be considered questionable, Reynolds, like
earlier novelists, uses known sources to back up his presentation,
although unlike the majority of his predecessors he merely presents the statistical data without naming the source. For example, Reynolds opens the fifteenth installment with a chapter
entitled "The Temptations of a Seamstress" in which he uses
statistics to demonstrate the seeming inevitability of the needlewoman's fall into prostitution: "Of the thirty thousand females
living in London ostensibly by the needle and slop-work, not less
than twelve thousand are *under* twenty years of age;—and nine-

tenths of those girls are plunged by stern necessity into the vortex of vice before they scarcely know what vice means! Eighty thousand daughters of crime walk the streets of London . . ."[31] But, Reynolds does not reveal the source of his statistics, Mayhew's *London Labour and the London Poor* (1849).

As a response to Meteyard's idealized portrait of emigration and the opportunities it offered needlewomen, Reynolds's picture of a slop worker's life is carefully crafted. In his novel the woman's sphere is reduced to a single, crowded room uninhabited by any family, let alone husband or child. And as the story continues, the young needlewomen are faced with the ultimate Victorian dilemma: moral purity resulting in homelessness and starvation or prostitution and a temporary respite from destitution. Reynolds actually examines both choices, but in each case the young woman is forced to abdicate the Victorian domestic ideal: forced out of the home and the hope of family either literally through homelessness or figuratively by renouncing the hope of marriage for a life of prostitution.

Although the literature concerning slop workers was aimed at spurring the middle and upper classes into some kind of reform, some aspects were misleading: virtually all the literature portrayed slop workers as young women, often displaced from the middle class, who were toiling alone, often in an attic room. This romantic vision of a struggling heroine may have occasionally been the case, but frequently the women involved were married with children, sewing to provide a second income or to replace an income lost to illness or injury of the male head of household. And rather than living in a dry, romantic garret, all too often these women and their families lived in damp, often polluted, cellar dwellings. Once again, Dickens was one of the first social protest writers to risk presenting a realistic portrait of these workers. In *The Uncommercial Traveller* (1860) he showed Victorian readers two slop workers whose near starvation and dire poverty are shocking. The first needlewoman is the wife of an unemployed boilermaker, and it is through her work that they and their four children have survived:

> She did slop-work; made pea-jackets. She produced the pea-jacket then in hand, and spread it out upon the bed,— the only piece of furniture in the room on which to spread

> it. . . . According to her calculation at the moment, deduct-
> ing what her trimming cost her, she got for making a pea-
> jacket tenpence half-penny, and she could make one in
> something less than two days. [32]

Dickens's paraphrased presentation of the woman's explanation
of why she went through a middleman for her work combines
the voice of the impartial observer, the narrator, with that of the
knowledgeable worker, lending the explanation a validity which
it would lack if explained by either voice independently. And
Dickens's insistence on the pride, the lack of "whine and mur-
mur," and the fact that the family was not relying on parish relief
creates a strong character, a woman holding her family together
even if not in the traditional way.

Dickens does not present his other slop worker; she is at
work when the Traveller visits her home. Instead the narrator
talks with her mother about their inability to meet the rent, six-
pence a week, on the daughter's salary. But Dickens first catches
the reader's attention with a detailed inventory of the room
where the seamstress, her parents, and her four brothers and
sisters live:

> She was boiling the children's clothes in a saucepan on the
> hearth. There was nothing else into which she could have
> put them. There was no crockery, or tinware, or tub, or
> bucket. There was an old gallipot or two, and there was a
> broken bottle or so, and there were some broken boxes for
> seats. The last small scraping of coals left was raked to-
> gether in a corner of the floor. In a corner of the room was
> a crazy old French bedstead. . . .

> As I stood opposite the woman boiling the children's
> clothes,—she had not even a piece of soap to wash them
> with,—and apologising for her occupation, I could take in
> all these things without appearing to notice them, and
> could even correct my inventory. I had missed, at first
> glance, some half pound of bread in the otherwise empty
> safe, an old red ragged crinoline hanging on the handle of
> the door by which I had entered, and certain fragments of
> rusty iron scattered the floor, which looked like broken
> tools and a piece of stove-pipe.[33]

Again Dickens's use of an outside observer gives the description verisimilitude, while the crippled father creates sympathy, and the independence of the family—they, too, receive no out-of-door relief—gives them dignity.

Thus Victorians were finally forced to admit that the ideal of domesticity held by the upper and middle classes was virtually impossible for working-class women, even those involved in a "domestic" occupation such as needlework. Although some, such as Dickens in *The Chimes* and Meteyard in *Lucy Dean*, held out for what would be seen as acceptable alternatives (married and working or emigrating and married with children), most writers saw little possibility of working-class families achieving the financial security necessary for women to be primarily, let alone exclusively, wives and mothers. Some writers took the impossibility of reaching the ideal to its obverse by presenting women forced to survive by prostituting themselves, thereby destroying the possibility of functioning as the moral center of the family. Others showed young women desperately clinging to their moral standards while succumbing to starvation or illness. Yet, in either case the woman is destroyed—morally, physically, or both. Thus for Victorian readers these portraits of slop workers signaled the destruction of the domestic ideal for working-class women.

NOTES

1. Mrs. Austin, *Two Letters on Girls' Schools and on the Training of Working Women* (London: Chapman and Hall, 1857), 25.

2. Frederick Engels, *The Condition of the Working Class in England* (London: Granada, 1981), 172.

3. For a discussion of needlework and women see Rozsika Parker, *The Subversive Stitch: Embroidery and the Making of the Feminine* (London: Women's Press, 1984).

4. Although technically a "dressmaker" made dresses and a "milliner" made headgear, most shops made entire outfits

encompassing both so that the terms became interchangeable. The shops were usually referred to as millinery houses.

5. Wanda Neff, *Victorian Working Women: An Historical and Literary Study of Women in British Industries and Professions, 1832–1850* (New York: Columbia University Press, 1929), 86.

6. E. Royston Pike, *Human Documents of the Victorian Golden Age (1850–1875)* (London: George Allen and Unwin, 1974), 171–73.

7. Edwin Chadwick, *Report on the Sanitary Condition of the Labouring Population of Great Britain,* ed. M.W. Flinn (Edinburgh: Edinburgh University Press, 1968), 176.

8. Shelia Ryan Johansson, "Sex and Death in Victorian England: An Examination of Age- and Sex-Specific Death Rates, 1840–1910," in *A Widening Sphere: Changing Roles of Victorian Women,* ed. Martha Vicinus (Bloomington: Indiana University Press, 1977), 169, 174.

9. Johansson, "Sex and Death," 166, 164.

10. Quoted in Christina Walkley, *The Ghost in the Looking Glass: The Victorian Seamstress* (London: Peter Owen, 1981), 32.

11. The term "slop worker" comes from the colloquial term for sailors' clothing, "slops," which were primarily made by these women.

12. Henry Mayhew, *The Unknown Mayhew: Selections from the Morning Chronicle, 1849–1850,* ed. E.P. Thompson and Eileen Yeo (New York: Shocken, 1971), 120–21.

13. T. Hughes, *A Lecture on the Slop-System, Especially as It Bears Upon the Females Engaged in It* (Exeter: W. and H. Pollard, 1852), 4–5, 8.

14. Charles Dickens, *The Chimes,* in *The Christmas Books,* vol. 1 (New York: Penguin, 1982), 208–209.

15. Dickens, *The Chimes,* 217–19.

16. Meg's attempt to drown herself and her child in the Thames is derived from an actual incident: Mary Furley and her two sons had been living in a workhouse, where the eldest child had become ill and continued to suffer from poor treatment and unsanitary conditions. After leaving the workhouse Furley made shirts, but "as they only allowed 1 3/4d. for a shirt, and by working hard she could only make three shirts a day," she decided to seek work making caps. On her way to buy materials, however, she either lost her purse or was robbed. With no money to buy materials, she could get no work. But her aversion to reentering the workhouse was so strong that she, while holding her youngest child, jumped off a bridge. A boatman witnessed the incident and pulled her out; she was alive, but her infant was dead. Furley was

tried and convicted of murder and sentenced to death (The Times, 17 April 1844: 8). Later, through the intercession of Dickens and others, the sentence was commuted to seven years' transportation (Lynn Alexander, "Following the Thread: Dickens and the Seamstress," *Victorian Newsletter* (Fall 1991), 1–7).

17. Dickens, *The Chimes*, 240.

18. Elizabeth Gaskell, *Mary Barton: A Tale of Manchester Life* (New York: Penguin, 1977), 63.

19. Gaskell, *Mary Barton*, 85–86.

20. Eliza ("Silverpen") Meteyard, *Lucy Dean, the Noble Needlewoman*, in *Eliza Cook's Journal* 2 (16 March – 20 April 1850), 329.

21. G.W.M. Reynolds, "A Warning to Needlewomen and Slopworkers," in *Reynolds's Political Instructor* 1 (1849–1850), 66.

22. Reynolds, "A Warning," 66.

23. G.W.M. Reynolds, *The Seamstress*, in *Reynolds's Miscellany* 4 (23 March 1850): 5; (10 August 1850): 129.

24. Reynolds, *The Seamstress*, 130.

25. T.J. Edelstein, "They Sang 'The Song of the Shirt': The Visual Iconology of the Seamstress," *Victorian Studies* 23 (Winter 1980), 190.

26. Edelstein, "They Sang 'The Song of the Shirt,'" 190.

27. Reynolds, *The Seamstress*, 163–64.

28. Reynolds, *The Seamstress*, 541–42.

29. Reynolds, *The Seamstress*, 369, 370, 44.

30. Reynolds, *The Seamstress*, 356.

31. Reynolds, *The Seamstress*, 356.

32. Charles Dickens, *The Uncommercial Traveller* (New York: The University Society, 1908), 314.

33. Dickens, *The Uncommercial Traveller*, 315.

Domestic Ironies
Housekeeping as Mankeeping in Conrad's The Secret Agent

Brian W. Shaffer

In the middle of Joseph Conrad's *The Secret Agent* (1907), a tale, in the author's own words, of "half a dozen anarchists, two women, and an idiot,"[1] the Assistant Commissioner of Police sums up the novel's events with an uncanny precision of which even he could not have been aware: "From a certain point of view we are in the presence of a domestic drama."[2] Indeed, despite the fact that this novel, in Eloise Knapp Hay's words, expresses Conrad's "fundamental political convictions with greater clarity and simplicity than any other novel he wrote,"[3] it is also centrally concerned with the domestic sphere and private family life in late-Victorian London. How else explain the novel's more than one hundred combined references to "domestic," "domesticated," "domicile," "home," "house[s]," and "household";[4] and how else explain Conrad's own determination that *The Secret Agent* is fundamentally "Winnie Verloc's Story"[5]—and hence that this materfamilias, and not her husband, Adolf Verloc, is the true "Secret Agent" of the novel.[6] Although it is hardly news to observe that "domestic drama" consumes *The Secret Agent*—that "all of the novel's politics are literally domestic issues, and virtually all of the domestic issues are parental"[7]—none to my knowledge has scrutinized the significant role and context of housekeeping, construed in its broadest sense as homemaking, in this novel.

Thus, beyond the familiar claim that *The Secret Agent* satirizes late-Victorian domestic life, I will argue that the novel explores the unbridgeable gap between the period's domestic ideals and domestic realities, especially for homemakers. More specifically, I will argue that this novel critiques Winnie Verloc's self-imprisoning role as housekeeper. Not only is her secret strategy to keep the house for her brother on the pretext of keeping the house for her husband a failure, but she also fails to recognize that her existence is little more than a series of humiliating situations in which she must "keep the house" in order to "keep the man": whether for her violently abusive father, for the male lodgers in her mother's "decayed" Belgravian boarding house, for her husband and brother, or, finally, for the abusive "revolutionist" Ossipon.

Indeed, from Winnie's earliest memories of life ("It was a crushing memory, an exhausting vision of countless breakfast trays carried up and down innumerable stairs . . . of the endless drudgery of sweeping, dusting, cleaning, from basement to attics") to her final moments of life (in which she promises Ossipon, "I'll work for you. I'll slave for you"),[8] Winnie must keep the house in order to keep the man, revealing not that harmonious domestic and competitive commercial values can be kept distinct and separate from one another, and that marriage is born of selfless union, as many Victorians wished to believe, but that public and private values are alarmingly interanimating and that marriage is a "trade"—an exchange of domestic labor for the means of subsistence. Finally, I will argue that Winnie, in the late chapters of the novel, stands as Conrad's attack on the Victorian New Woman as popularized in the works of Ibsen, Grant Allen, Marie Corelli, and others: the woman who earns her freedom from constraining domestic and matrimonial attachments. Indeed, rather than attaining the rewards such freedom confers, the New Woman Winnie is depicted instead as degenerating into a "savage woman" who remains as dependent on men and chained to housekeeping as the old Winnie ever was. Thus, while Ian Watt is correct to point out that "Conrad's works deal much less than those of most novelists with women, love, sex, and marriage,"[9] *The Secret Agent* nevertheless confronts these issues unflinchingly, in the spirit of a number of other *fin de siècle* works.[10] And if, as Conrad writes in an essay, "the distinctively English novelist is always at his best in denunciations of institutions, of types or of conventionalized society,"[11] then *The Secret Agent* is its author's most "distinctively English" novel, as it satirizes the institutions of middle-class homemaking and "conventionalized" marriage in ways unseen in Conrad's other fictions.

Before arguing my case, however, it will first be useful to explore briefly those *Victorian* domestic ideals to which the Verlocs aspire. For while *The Secret Agent* was actually published in *Edwardian* England, it was set in 1886[12] and was understood by Conrad to be a "Simple Tale of the XIX Century."[13] Moreover, as Patricia Stubbs correctly observes, "the death of Victoria did not mean the death of Victorianism, and the opening years of the century saw if anything an intensification of the struggles" inherent in many key Victorian debates.[14]

Whereas the precise contours of Victorian domestic ideology (and its depiction in literature) remains an open question,[15] the Victorian *ideal* of domesticity in general and of the female homemaker in particular is relatively clear. If the title of Coventry Patmore's poem "The Angel in the House" (1854–63) was superlatively influential in naming the Victorian housewife, John Ruskin's lecture *Sesame and Lilies* (1865) was superlatively influential in articulating a vision for her. In this work Ruskin writes:

> This is the true nature of home—it is the place of Peace;
> the shelter, not only from all injury, but from all terror,
> doubt, and division. In so far as it is not this, it is not
> home; so far as the anxieties of the outer life penetrate into
> it, and the inconsistently-minded, unknown, unloved, or
> hostile society of the outer world is allowed by either hus-
> band or wife to cross the threshold, it ceases to be home; it
> is then only a part of that outer world which you have
> roofed over and lighted fire in.[16]

As Jenni Calder interprets Ruskin's meaning here in her monumental study, *The Victorian Home*,

> It is the woman who must ensure that the home remains a
> 'Place of Peace'. The outside world, what we might think
> of as the 'real' world, is to be excluded. The home, and this
> means also marriage, is the salvation of modern man, be-
> cause there he can forget the pressures and strains of the

outside world, the commercial world, the competitive
world, and relax, replenish his spirit, find comfort and solace. The modern woman, of course, was not to have any
dealings with the real world. She could only preside over
man's refuge, create man's refuge, if she were unsullied by
the horrors that lay without.[17]

Indeed, virtually every Victorian articulation of this ideal viewed
the home to be a buffer from the "jungle out there," and the
female homemaker within it to be the sustainer of that buffer. In
Calder's words,

It was the wife who made the home, who cared for her
children within it, who brought her husband back to it
when work was done, who provided the hot dinners and
created the atmosphere of comfort and protection. It was
in the nineteenth century that homemaking became a major activity, an essential one for the preservation of the
standards and values of the Victorians, and a justification
for the existence of women who were denied activity beyond their protectively closed front doors.[18]

Hence, the Victorian homemaker's role was both "practical" and
"moral": to provide a place of comfort and security, a physical
and moral sanctuary, for the men and children in her keep.[19]

In *The Secret Agent*, the Verlocs clearly aspire to this domestic ideal. Whereas the city of London, replete with its political and commercial intrigues, is depicted as "a town of marvels
and mud, with its maze of streets . . . a black abyss"[20] and "a
monstrous town . . . in its man-made might as if indifferent to
heaven's frowns and smiles; a cruel devourer of the world's
light,"[21] the Verlocs view their own home as a place of light, a
"haven isolated from the trials and temptations of the 'real'
world outside."[22] We read, for example, that when Adolf Verloc
closes up his "business" for the day he assures "a solitude
around his hearth stone"; that he leaves the "slightly stuffy cosi-
ness" of his home for work[23] only "with evident reluctance," and
that Winnie represents for him "the sacredness of domestic
peace." Moreover, we read that Verloc cultivates his
"pronounced" "domestic virtues" at home. "Neither his spiritual, nor his mental, nor his physical needs were of the kind to
take him much abroad," the narrator comments. "He found at

home the ease of his body and the peace of his conscience, together with Mrs. Verloc's wifely attentions . . . " Indeed, it is indicated repeatedly that Verloc is "thoroughly domesticated" and possesses a "comfortable home" replete with "all essentials of domestic propriety and domestic comfort." Verloc is also said to possess a "steady fidelity to his own fireside" and to secure "his repose and security" at home. In addition, mutual "trust," "fondness," "appreciation," and "sympathy" reign between the Verlocs, just as their "respectable home life" and "respectable bond" confer prestige upon them both. Verloc's voice even assumes a "domestic tone" and "marital authority" when he addresses Winnie. [24]

It goes without saying that the being who makes possible Verloc's "domestic ease" is Winnie, his "angel in the house." And like any late-Victorian "angel in the house," Winnie is her husband's subordinate and personal property: "Mr. Verloc loved his wife as a wife should be loved—that is, maritally, with the regard one has for one's chief possession."[25] And it is Verloc's "chief possession" who keeps the house and keeps "the master" comfortable. This passage is typical:

> She laid two plates, got the bread, the butter, going to and fro quietly between the table and the cupboard in the peace and silence of her home. On the point of taking out the jam, she reflected practically: "He will be feeling hungry, having been away all day," and she returned to the cupboard once more to get the cold beef. [26]

Indeed, references to Winnie's "household duties" and "domestic occupation[s]" are rife in the novel. Whether she is depicted as working in the "kitchen," "dishing-up" meals, serving "tea," "cleaning up the table," washing "the cups," cleaning rooms, "sewing," or "dusting,"[27] Winnie keeps the house in order to maintain the Verloc sanctuary against a corrupting, inhospitable, taxing world.[28]

Despite the Verlocs' aspirations to maintain the Victorian ideal of a home, however, it is soon apparent that the Verloc abode is a "menaced home"[29] that shatters more than it embodies this ideal. The perceptive reader will notice—all Verloc hopes and intentions to the contrary—that the Verloc home is less a "sanctuary, a firelit circle enclosed against the hostile and dangerous external world,"[30] than it is a place of darkness, a "household, hidden in the shades of the sordid street seldom touched by the sun . . . "[31] which mirrors and replicates that hostile and dangerous external world.[32]

First, *The Secret Agent* constantly collapses the distinction between these two worlds, suggesting, as Robert L. Caserio puts it in a different context, that "family man and plotting man are synonymous with what they are supposed to be defenses against: aggression and violence, disruption and anarchy."[33] Indeed, rather than being "an area quite distinct from the public sphere, a private world upholding different values,"[34] the Verloc home is depicted instead as "nestling in a shady street behind a shop where the sun never shone." In other words, Conrad collapses the absolute Victorian distinction between home and world, private and public domains, and familial and commercial values by situating Winnie's past and present abodes *in places of business.* Whether it is her mother's Belgravian boarding house (which at one point is called a "business house"[35] or her present domicile with Verloc on Brett Street (which also houses her husband's porn "business"), Winnie's two homes cannot help but be penetrated and corrupted by the menacing public spheres of commercial and political competition.

Second, *The Secret Agent* reveals the homemaker to be motivated not by love but by the commercial spirit; and marriage to be understood not as a selfless union of souls but as a "trade." While many Victorians would have wanted to agree with Ferdinand Tonnies' sentimental conception of the household—

> The house constitutes the realm and . . . body of kinship.
> Here people live together under one protecting roof. Here
> they share their possessions and their pleasures; they feed
> from the same supply, they sit at the same table[36]—

and hence would have wanted to believe that the housekeeper remains untouched by "the cash nexus" and the "dishonesties" of commercial "competition,"[37] Conrad's novel suggests otherwise. Indeed, this novel at many points reveals marriage to be a trade, in the sense that Cicely Hamilton speaks of it in her *Marriage as a Trade* (1910). There, Hamilton argues that "marriage is . . . essentially a trade on the part of woman—the exchange of her person for the means of subsistence." Specifically, Hamilton insists that the "rough manual work of most households" that constitutes housekeeping—the "ordering of a man's house, the bearing and rearing of his children"—distorts what would be "the real, natural and unbiased attitude of women towards love and marriage." This attitude, Hamilton continues, "is perfectly impossible for even a woman to guess at under present conditions, and it will continue to be impossible for just so long as the natural instincts of her sex are inextricably interwoven with, thwarted and deflected by, commercial considerations."[38] While Conrad in no way would have countenanced Hamilton's feminism, and while *Marriage as a Trade* emerged three years after *The Secret Agent*, Conrad nevertheless betrays a critique of the turn-of-the-century English homemaker that is uncannily similar to Hamilton's.

For example, rather than Winnie keeping the house for love of Verloc, as he believes she does,[39] she is shown to keep it for "commercial considerations" and socioeconomic expedience: to keep her brother Stevie out of the "workhouse infirmary."[40] The great irony, of course, is that while Winnie uses (and is used by) Verloc to protect her brother Stevie from the world, she falls victim to a self-imprisoning role of housekeeper. Not only does her secret strategy to keep Verloc's house in order to keep Stevie "safe" backfire with a vengeance, but she perpetuates her own victimization as a woman who blindly serves—and sacrifices everything for—the men in her life.[41]

That Winnie sacrifices herself in significant ways to "keep the house" in order to "keep the man" is made clear repeatedly. References to her "self-sacrifice," to her battling for Stevie— "even against herself"—and to her secret strategy of keeping Stevie on the pretext of keeping Verloc are rife. Because Winnie's "only real concern" is "Stevie's welfare," she earlier in life sacrifices herself by slamming "the door" on the one man with whom she is genuinely in love ("The memory of the early romance with the young butcher survived, tenacious, like the image of a glimpsed ideal . . ."), and presently sacrifices her marital existence to a man otherwise too old for her. Moreover, not only does Winnie forgo children with Verloc on Stevie's behalf ("And with peaceful pride she congratulated herself on a certain resolution she had taken a few years before. It had cost her some effort, and even a few tears"), but she treats Stevie not only as if she were his "sister, guardian, and protector," but as if she were his mother ("He was much more mine than mother's," she explains).[42] Of course, her final sacrifice is the ultimate sacrifice of all: she murders Verloc and commits suicide on Stevie's account—or, rather, because Stevie in death is of no more account.

It is worth pointing out that of the four dwellers in the Verloc home, the two men, Verloc and Stevie, are murdered, whereas the two women, Winnie and her doubly unnamed mother ("Mrs. Verloc's mother") are suicides (Winnie literally; and her self-sacrificing mother figuratively, for when this older woman voluntarily departs for a retirement home she is said to have "departed this life." It is also worth noting that Winnie's sacrificial position as keeper of the house for the sake of keeping the man is inherited from her mother, who also exercised this strategy— and also on behalf of the marginally demented Stevie. Intentionally wishing to keep Stevie forever "destitute and dependent," and hence under the protecting charge of his sister, Winnie's mother views her own"act of abandonment" as really "an arrangement for settling her son permanently in life." That Winnie's mother willingly sacrifices Winnie in the process ("Girls frequently get sacrificed to the welfare of the boys. In this case she was sacrificing Winnie.")[43] goes a long way toward explaining Winnie's own eagerness to housekeep for the sake of mankeeping. Indeed, she knows no other way.

One other reason for Winnie's bizarrely selfless behavior is discoverable: she wishes to protect Stevie from the memory of his father's beatings.[44] Yet this strategy also backfires when Winnie inadvertently gives Verloc the idea of using Stevie to deliver the bomb. As Jenni Calder would explain this characteristically Victorian situation: "Like the wife, the child was to be protected within the home from possible threats without," even if "There were no means of protection from the threats within."[45] Indeed, *The Secret Agent*'s greatest irony of all may be that harm comes to the Verloc household less because of external than because of internal intriguing and plotting. In this sense the question that Conrad's mocking novel seems to be asking is not whether the Verloc home can be a safe haven from the nefarious world but whether the world can ever be safe from such nefarious, intriguing domestic situations. Aaron Fogel is correct to claim that "The Verlocs have a 'political' marriage: each has entered into it partly out of unstated politic motives,"[46] yet it should also be pointed out that the Verlocs' "married estate" is inherently vulnerable. While Verloc at one point calls his home a "doomed ship," Winnie at another muses that the "abode of her married life appeared to her as lonely and unsafe as though it had been situated in the midst of a forest."[47] In this way Conrad's novel depicts marriage and housekeeping to be superlatively cynical acts, and the home to be a place of extreme potential danger—the very opposite of the Victorian domestic ideal. If anything, the Verloc *mariage de convenance* turns out to be a deadly and duplicitous marriage of inconvenience, a Victorian nightmare union that can end only in tragedy.

Despite the fact that Winnie, by the late chapters of *The Secret Agent*, has been revealed to fail in and be victimized by her own secret strategy of keeping the house in order to keep the man, Conrad is not through with her yet, just as he is not through with satirizing Victorian domestic ideals. For in these late chapters of the novel Winnie stands as Conrad's parody of the late-Victorian New Woman as celebrated in the period's feminist thought, and as represented in such works as Ibsen's *A Doll's House* (1879) and, more crudely and popularly, Grant Allen's *The Woman Who Did* (1895) and Marie Corelli's novels— works that Conrad is known to have read and detested.[48] Indeed, instead of renouncing her marital and domestic attachments in order to secure her freedom from and equality with men, Conrad's New Woman Winnie degenerates into a nihilistic, adulterous, homicidal, "savage woman"—and still cannot free herself from the role of housekeeper and mankeeper. In fact, when she finally sees through her constraining domestic attachments with males, she can only see through to nothing—and kills herself in an ultimate and paradoxical act of freedom in imprisonment.

While there is no evidence to suggest that Conrad studied the "woman question" in any detail, there can be little doubt that he was familiar with much of the literature of the New Woman to emerge in the 1890's. This woman was commonly characterized as "in revolt against her legal and social bondage,"[49] and as

concerned with her overall role in society—with "Higher education, the growth of the female labour market, the campaign for
the vote and . . . birth control."[50] Wishing to shed her image as a
"domestic animal," the New Woman of late-Victorian times re-
belled openly and forcefully against the patriarchal world in
which she lived.[51]

In the closing chapters of the novel Winnie at first appears
to be such a New Woman. Believing herself to be a "betrayed
woman," and finding herself in possession of "her husband's
capital," Winnie wishes only to free herself from all domestic
and marital attachments to Adolf, "the master of a house, the
husband of a woman, and the murderer of her Stevie." Indeed, it
is certainly no coincidence that Winnie and Verloc have been
married for seven years, and that this, their jubilee year, is the
year in which Winnie is to realize her freedom from wifely
servitude. Not only are Winnie's ties with her mother at an end
("Now that Stevie was dead the bond seemed to be broken"), but
her bond with her husband is also severed (no longer is she "a
loyal woman bound to [Verloc] by an unbroken contract"). Possessing a "sentiment of regained freedom," Winnie is obsessed
with the notion that

> There was no need for her now to stay there, in that
> kitchen, in that house, with that man—since the boy was
> gone for ever. No need whatever . . . She had her freedom.
> Her contract with existence, as represented by [Verloc],
> was at an end. She was a free woman.[52]

Repeatedly referred to by the narrator as "Mrs. Verloc" the "free
woman," Winnie wishes only to get "outside the door" of her
home "for ever." At one point she even imagines that "she could
slip by [Verloc], open the door, run out." But then he "would
dash out after her," Winnie worries, "seize her round the body,
drag her back into the shop."[53]

That Conrad satirically attacks rather than sympathetically
portrays the plight of the New Woman is easy to see: rather than
capitalizing on her newfound freedom, Winnie, we read, does
"not exactly know what use to make of her freedom." Rather
than evolving into the New Woman she imagines herself destined to become, Winnie instead devolves into a "savage
woman"—an "armed lunatic"[54] who will murder, commit sui-

cide, prostitute herself, and succumb to nihilism. Most ironic of all, Winnie at this point even seeks to reattach herself to a man, offering to housekeep for Ossipon "for ever." No character in any of Conrad's works contradicts as much as does Winnie Cicely Hamilton's prophecy in *Marriage as a Trade*:

> When ... the day of woman's complete social and economic independence dawns upon her, when she finds herself free and upright in a new world where no artificial pressure is brought to bear upon her natural inclinations or disinclinations, then ... will it be possible to untwist a tangled skein and judge to what extent ... she is swayed by those impulses, sexual and maternal, which are now ... presumed to dominate her existence.[55]

Not only does the "free woman" Winnie appropriately use the "domestic carving knife"[56] to slay her husband as he reposes on the sofa,[57] but she then absurdly wishes "to commit suicide because she fears death."[58] She even succumbs to nihilism, the very opposite impulse one would expect from the hopeful New Woman:

> She had become a free woman with a perfection of freedom which left her nothing to desire and absolutely nothing to do, since Stevie's urgent claim on her devotion no longer existed. . . . She was a woman enjoying her complete irresponsibility and endless leisure, almost in the manner of a corpse. She did not move, she did not think.[59]

So much for the New Woman, *The Secret Agent* seems to be suggesting.[60]

Finally, the New Woman Winnie despairs of her own freedom enough to prostitute and reattach herself to a man—and even to keep a house for him. As Aaron Fogel puts it, "Winnie, traumatized from the outset by her childhood, is not educated but only retraumatized by the main action. She learns nothing by the end of the book ... and then, having learned nothing, she goes on to try to push Ossipon into a similar union."[61] Promising Ossipon that she will "slave" and "work" for him but never ask him to marry her, Winnie even offers to become his mistress and once again take up domestic servitude. "Tom, you can't throw me off now," Winnie tells Ossipon; "not unless you crush my head under your heel. I won't leave you." She later adds: "I will live all my days for you, Tom." The narrator satirically concludes, "Mrs. Verloc was no longer a free woman,"[62] suggesting that even this New Woman must keep the house in order to keep the man until the end of her days. And, to be sure, Winnie only frees herself of the "endless drudgery" of housekeeping in death.

In his letters and in his "Author's Note" to *The Secret Agent* Conrad defends himself against the charge that in writing this novel he intended "to commit a gratuitous outrage on the feelings of mankind,"[63] and insists instead that his goal in writing *The Secret Agent* was to perfect his "ironic method" and the "ironic treatment" of his "sensational" materials.[64] Nevertheless, there can be little doubt that Conrad intentionally attacked those late-Victorian ideals of domestic life that he found pretentious or untenable, and that he fully expected that many would be offended by the novel. As Thomas Mann correctly observes, Conrad wrote *The Secret Agent* in a "grotesque" and "anti-bourgeois style."[65] And Conrad himself even privately admitted that the public might not "be amused by me at all": "I should not be surprised if [the novel] were violently attacked."[66]

To the extent that Mann and Conrad are correct, the ironic, grotesque, "anti-bourgeois" *The Secret Agent* represents the Victorian home to be less a safe haven than a place of intrigue, and the Victorian homemaker to be less an "angel in the house" than a calculating and potentially murderous "savage" woman. "The cult of the home was partly an effort at compensation," Jenni Calder observes of Victorians; "The home was idealized partly as a form of escapism . . . and partly because they could hardly fail to see how unsatisfactory the home and the family could very easily be. That "the Victorians were troubled by their version of the home at the same time as they reverenced it there is little doubt," she adds. Yet "the full impact of this realization did not emerge until towards the end of the century."[67] Whether or not Robert Caserio is correct to conclude that Conrad "seems to convince himself that authentic domestic order . . . has never yet existed, that such order remains an ideal, a possibility for the *future*,"[68] it is clear that no such ideal order exists in *The Secret Agent*, however much the Verlocs and their society would like to pretend that it does. For in reality Winnie can only lament "aloud her love of life, that life without grace or charm, and almost without decency, but of an exalted faithfulness of purpose,"[69] and keep the house in order to keep the man, "from the days of her childhood to the end."[70]

NOTES

1. Frederick R. Karl and Laurence Davies, eds., *The Collected Letters of Joseph Conrad* (Cambridge: Cambridge University Press, 1983–), 3:372.

2. Joseph Conrad, *The Secret Agent* (Garden City, NY: Anchor Books, 1953), 184. Herbert N. Schneidau more accurately refers to the novel as a "domestic tragedy" in his *Waking Giants: The Presence of the Past in Modernism* (New York: Oxford University Press, 1991), 113.

3. Eloise Knapp Hay, *The Political Novels of Joseph Conrad* (Chicago: University of Chicago Press, 1963), 241. Hay's and Schneidau's readings of *The Secret Agent* have been particularly influential in my understanding of this text.

4. See Todd K. Bender, *A Concordance to Conrad's "The Secret Agent"* (New York: Garland, 1979).

5. Joseph Conrad, "Author's Note" to *The Secret Agent*, in Conrad, *The Secret Agent*, 13.

6. As Robert L. Caserio puts it in *Plot, Story, and the Novel: From Dickens and Poe to the Modern Period* (Princeton: Princeton University Press, 1979), 267: Winnie "is the secret agent of the death of three persons: Stevie, Verloc, and herself."

7. Caserio, *Plot, Story, and the Novel*, 265. And Aaron Fogel writes in *Coercion to Speak: Conrad's Poetics of Dialogue* (Cambridge: Harvard University Press, 1985), 157: "The tale's themes are in fact the basic sympathetic themes of nineteenth-century domestic fiction, drastically altered." Also see Ruth Nadelhaft, *Joseph Conrad* (Atlantic Highlands, NJ: Humanities Press International, 1991), 100.

8. Conrad, *Secret Agent*, 200, 236.

9. Ian Watt, *Conrad in the Nineteenth Century* (Berkeley: University of California Press, 1979), 69.

10. As Anthea Trodd observes in *Domestic Crime in the Victorian Novel* (New York: St. Martin's Press, 1989), 157: "The end of the nineteenth century and the beginning of the twentieth saw a massive assault in fiction on the concept of the Victorian family."

11. Joseph Conrad, "A Glance at Two Books," in *Last Essays* (Garden City, NY: Doubleday, 1926), 132.

12. Avrom Fleishman, *Conrad's Politics: Community and Anarchy in the Fiction of Joseph Conrad* (Baltimore: Johns Hopkins University Press, 1967), 205.

13. See the dedication page of *The Secret Agent*.

14. Patricia Stubbs, *Women and Fiction: Feminism and the Novel, 1880–1920* (New York: Barnes and Noble, 1979), 175.

15. See, for example, Elizabeth Langland, "Nobody's Angels: Domestic Ideology and Middle-Class Women in the Victorian Novel," *PMLA* 107 (1992): 290–304. Also see Judith Lowder Newton, *Women, Power, and Subversion: Social Strategies in British Fiction, 1778–1860* (Athens: University of Georgia Press, 1981), and Jeanne Peterson, *Family, Love, and Work in the Lives of Victorian Gentlewomen* (Bloomington: Indiana University Press, 1989).

16. John Ruskin, *Sesame and Lilies,* quoted in Jenni Calder, *The Victorian Home* (London: B. T. Batsford, 1977), 10.

17. Calder, *Victorian Home,* 10.

18. Calder, *Victorian Home,* 27

19. Calder, *Victorian Home,* 105, 119.

20. Conrad, *Secret Agent,* 222.

21. Conrad, "Author's Note," 11.

22. Jenni Calder, *Women and Marriage in Victorian Fiction* (New York: Oxford University Press, 1976), 13.

23. Verloc's "work" may be defined as follows: he is a porn shop owner and a triple agent in the employ of the Czarist Russian Embassy, the English Police, and a group of revolutionary anarchists opposed both to Russia and England.

24. Conrad, *Secret Agent,* 196, 20, 152, 19, 209, 163–64, 149, 54; "trust," "fondness," "appreciation," "sympathy": 60, 148, 157, 160, 162, 195, 205, 208; "home life," "marital relation": 217, 184; "domestic tone," "marital authority": 164, 212, 215.

25. Conrad, *Secret Agent,* 152.

26. Conrad, *Secret Agent,* 162.

27. Conrad, *Secret Agent*, 22, 131, 160, 44, 160, 164, 165, 154, 160, 132.

28. Of course, Winnie employs Mrs. Neale, a charwoman, to do the heavy work in the Verloc home. Of this charwoman we read: "Victim of her marriage with a debauched joiner, she was oppressed by the needs of many infant children. Red-armed, and aproned in coarse sacking up to the arm pits, she exhaled the anguish of the poor in a breath of soap-suds and rum, in the uproar of scrubbing, in the clatter of pails" (153). As Aaron Fogel argues in *Coercion to Speak*, 165–67: "Mrs. Neale becomes one of the key figures of the novel." Noting the "pun *kneel* in the amphibious working woman's name," Fogel points out the novel's "forceful identification" between Winnie and "'Mrs. Kneel,' the enslaved wife," of which Winnie remains unaware. Winnie is "like Mrs. Neale, or rather, she is forced to be like her," Fogel observes. "Constrained into a horrible marriage, she plays similar beggarly tricks." For more on the role of household servants and on the mistress-servant relationship in Victorian England, see Patricia Branca, *Silent Sisterhood: Middle Class Women in the Victorian Home* (Pittsburgh: Carnegie-Mellon University Press, 1975), 22; Calder, *Victorian Home*, 23; and Marion Lochhead, *The Victorian House* (London: John Murray, 1964), 30–44.

29. Conrad, *Secret Agent*, 150.

30. Trodd, *Domestic Crime*, 1.

31. Conrad, *Secret Agent*, 44.

32. Elsewhere in the novel we read that "shadows gathered about the humble abode of Mr. Verloc's domestic happiness" (130).

33. Caserio, *Plot, Story, and the Novel*, 267. And Ossipon at one point correctly relates the "Greenwich Park affair" (the bombing) with the "unhappy circumstances of the Verloc's married life" (*Secret Agent*, 227).

34. Trodd, *Domestic Crime*, 2.

35. Conrad, *Secret Agent*, 212, 200.

36. Ferdinand Tonnies, *Community and Society* (1887), quoted in Leonore Davidoff, et al., "Landscape with Figures: Home and Community in English Society," in *The Rights and Wrongs of Women*, ed. Juliet Mitchell and Ann Oakley (New York: Penguin, 1976), 139.

37. Calder, *Victorian Home*, 126.

38. Cecily Hamilton, *Marriage as a Trade* (London: Chapman and Hall, 1910), 38, 101, 39, 26–27. In *The Victorian Frame of Mind, 1830–1870*

(New Haven: Yale University Press, 1957), 381, Walter E. Houghton puts this same point differently: "In a society so permeated by the commercial spirit, love could be blatantly thrust aside if it interfered with more important values."

39. Conrad, *Secret Agent*, 196, 207, 211.

40. Conrad, *Secret Agent*, 140.

41. Thus, while David Daiches in *The Novel and the Modern World* (Chicago: University of Chicago Press, 1960), 57, long ago noted that the Verloc's marital intimacy is "both illusory and squalid," and while Schneidau, *Waking Giants*, 113, recently claimed that Conrad "holds out the prospect of an abyss of meaninglessness at the base" of marriage, none has explored Winnie's role as a housekeeper in this equation.

42. Conrad, *Secret Agent*, 148, 203; "keeping Verloc": 45, 150, 152, 157, 193, 194, 201; 164, 225–26, 157; "protector": 159, 215; 225.

43. Conrad, *Secret Agent*, "Mrs. Verloc's mother": 132, 139; 144, 133, 139, 138.

44. Conrad, *Secret Agent*, 21, 44–45, 59, 146, 200.

45. Calder, *Victorian Home*, 157.

46. Aaron Fogel, "Coerced Speech and the Oedipus Dialogue Complex," in *Rethinking Bakhtin: Extensions and Challenges*, ed. Gary Saul Morson and Caryl Emerson (Evanston, IL: Northwestern University Press, 1989), 191. For this reason, as Houghton would put it, 352, Winnie, the Verloc's "angel in the house," does not really stand a chance of preserving and quickening "the moral idealism so badly needed in an age of selfish greed and fierce competition."

47. Conrad, *Secret Agent*, 226, 151, 168.

48. We know that Conrad read the "middle plays of Ibsen," including *A Doll's House* (See *Collected Letters of Joseph Conrad* 4:218), and that he read and hated Allen's *The Women Who Did* and Corelli's romances. As Conrad puts it of Allen in a letter (2:137): "En somme - un imbecile." "Grant Allen's *Woman Who Did*, c'est un livre mort. Gr. Allen is a man of inferior intelligence and his work is not art in any sense. *The Woman Who Did* had a kind of success, of curiosity mostly and that only among the philistines—the sort of people who read Marie Corelli and Hall Caine. Neither of these writers belongs to literature." Whereas Allen's novel treats "a woman who is not only against marriage in principle but who condemns the whole idea of setting up in domestic union with a man" (Calder, *Women and Marriage*, 169), Corelli's novels attack "what she called 'the modern marriage market,' the selling-off of daughters to the highest bidder" (Calder, *Victorian Home*, 124).

49. Houghton, *Victorian Frame of Mind*, 348.

50. Merryn Williams, *Women in the English Novel, 1800–1900* (New York: St. Martin's Press, 1984), 40.

51. For more on the New Woman and the backlash against her, see Calder, *Victorian Home*, 132, 141, 143, 149–50; and Williams, *Women in the English Novel*, 40–43.

52. Conrad, *Secret Agent*, 200, 169, 219, 221, 215, 213, 207.

53. Conrad, *Secret Agent*, 209, 210, 211.

54. Conrad, *Secret Agent*, 209, 233, 236, 216.

55. Hamilton, *Marriage as a Trade*, 27.

56. Conrad, *Secret Agent*, 217.

57. As Schneidau argues of this moment in *Waking Giants*, 116: "He is the passive victim, she the penetrator: the killing reverses the complicit rape of which their sex life has consisted."

58. Schneidau, *Waking Giants*, 119.

59. Conrad, *Secret Agent*, 216.

60. Winnie's nihilism may be connected to her wish not to "look too deeply into things," an aspect of her personality emphasized throughout the novel. However, this may have less to do with her constitutional shallowness than with her detrimental proclivity to censor from her own scrutiny painful truths about sensitive subjects.

61. Fogel, *Coercion*, 155.

62. Conrad, *Secret Agent*, 236, 237, 243, 238.

63. Conrad, "Author's Note," 13.

64. Conrad, *Collected Letters*, 4:9.

65. Thomas Mann, "Conrad's *The Secret Agent*," in *Past Masters and Others Papers* (New York: Knopf, 1933), 241.

66. Conrad, *Collected Letters*, 3:454, 371.

67. Calder, *Victorian Home*, 137.

68. Caserio, *Plot, Story, and the Novel*, 274. For the manifold ways in which *The Secret Agent* approximates a Victorian sensation novel of domestic crime, see Trodd, *Domestic Crime*, 1–11.

69. Conrad, *Secret Agent*, 243.

70. Conrad, "Author's Note," 11.

Select Bibliography

Adams, Samuel and Sarah Adams. *The Complete Servant*. London: Knight and Lacey, 1825.

Adorno, Theodor. "Veblen's Attack on Culture." In *Prisms*, translated by Samuel and Shierry Weber, 73–94. Cambridge: MIT Press, 1967.

Agress, Lynne. *The Feminine Irony: Women on Women in Early-Nineteenth Century English Literature*. Rutherford, NJ: Fairleigh Dickinson University Press, 1978.

Alexander, Lynn. "Following the Thread: Dickens and the Seamstress." *The Victorian Newsletter* 80 (Fall 1991): 1–7.

Allchin, A.M. *The Silent Rebellion: Anglican Religious Communities 1845–1900*. London: SCM Press, 1958.

Anderson, Bonnie S. and Judith P. Zinsser, eds., *A History of Their Own: Women in Europe from Prehistory to the Present*, 2 vols. New York: Harper and Row, 1988.

Anderson, Donald and Peter Beauclerk Dewar. *The House of Nell Gwynn: The Fortunes of the Beauclerk Family 1670–1974*. London: William Kimber, 1974.

Anson, Clodagh, Lady. *Book: Discreet Memoirs*. London: G. Bateman Blackshaw, 1931.

Anson, Peter F. *The Call of the Cloister: Religious Communities and Kindred Bodies in the Anglican Communion*. London: SPCK, 1955.

Ardener, Shirley. "Ground Rules and Social Maps for Women: An Introduction." In *Women and Space: Ground Rules and Social Maps*, edited by Shirley Ardener. New York: St. Martin's Press, 1981.

Arkwright, Lucy. MS letters to John Hungerford Arkwright 1869–1900. Herefordshire Records Office. Herefordshire, England.

Armstrong, Frances. *Dickens and the Concept of Home*. Ann Arbor: UMI Research Press, 1990.

Armstong, Nancy. *Desire and Domestic Fiction: A Political History of the Novel.* New York: Oxford University Press, 1987.

Armstrong, Nancy and Leonard Tennenhouse. "Gender and the Work of Words." *Cultural Critique* 13 (Fall 1989): 229–78.

Askwith, Betty. *The Lyttletons: A Family Chronicle of the Nineteenth Century.* London: Chatto and Windus, 1975.

Asquith, Cynthia. *Remember and Be Glad.* London: James Barrie, 1952.

Atwood, Margaret. *The Handmaid's Tale.* New York: Fawcett Crest, 1985.

Auerbach, Nina. *Communities of Women: An Idea in Fiction.* Cambridge: Harvard University Press, 1978.

———. *Woman and the Demon: The Life of a Victorian Myth.* Cambridge: Harvard University Press, 1982.

Austin, Mrs. *Two Letters on Girls' Schools and on the Training of Working Women.* London: Chapman and Hall, 1857.

Axton, William. "The Trouble with Esther." *Modern Language Quarterly* 26, no. 4 (1965): 545–57.

Bachelard, Gaston. *The Poetics of Space.* Translated by Maria Jolas. Boston: Beacon Press, 1969.

Baker, Joseph. *The Novel and the Oxford Movement.* New York: Russell and Russell, 1965.

Balsan, Consuelo. *The Glitter and the Gold.* London: Heinemann, 1953.

Barret, Michele and Mary MacIntosh. *The Anti-Social Family.* Norfolk: Thetford Press, 1982.

Battiscombe, Georgina. *Mrs. Gladstone: The Portrait of a Marriage.* London: Constable, 1965.

Battiscombe, Georgina and Marghanita Laski, eds. *A Chaplet for Charlotte Yonge.* London: Cresset, 1965.

Baudrillard, Jean. *For a Critique of the Political Economy of the Sign.* Translated by Charles Levin. St. Louis, MO: Telos Press, 1981.

Baym, Nina. "Fleda Vetch and the Plot of *The Spoils of Poynton*." *PMLA* 84 (1969): 102–111.

Beales, H.L. "The Victorian Family." In *Ideas and Beliefs of the Victorians: An Historic Revaluation of the Victorian Age.* Series of Talks Broadcast by the British Broadcasting Company. London: Sylvan, 1949.

Beard, Daniel C. *The American Boy's Handybook; Or, What to Do and How to Do It.* New York: Scribner's, 1888.

Beard, Lina and Adelia B. *The American Girl's Handybook; Or, How to Amuse Yourself and Others.* New York: Scribner's, 1888.

Beeton, Isabella. *How to Manage House and Servants.* London: Ward, Locke and Tyler, 1871.

Belkin, Roslyn. "Rejects of the Marketplace: Old Maids in Charlotte Brontë's *Shirley.*" *International Journal of Women's Studies* 4 (1981): 50–66.

Bender, Todd K. *A Concordance to Conrad's "The Secret Agent."* New York: Garland Publishing, 1979.

Berg, Maxine. *The Age of Manufactures: Industry, Innovation and Work in Britain 1700–1820.* New York: Oxford University Press, 1986.

Bersani, Leo. "The Subject of Power." *Diacritics* 7, no. 3 (Sept. 1977): 2–21.

Betterton, Rosemary. *Looking On.* New York: Pandora's Press, 1987.

Bixler, Phyllis. (See also Koppes, Phyllis Bixler.) "The Oral Formulaic Training of a Popular Fiction Writer: Frances Hodgson Burnett." *Journal of Popular Culture* 15, no. 4 (1982): 42–52.

Blackwell, Patricia. "The Landed Elite in Decline: A Case Study of Five Sussex Country Houses." Master's thesis, University of Sussex, 1978.

Blain, Virginia. "Double Vision and the Double Standard in *Bleak House:* A Feminist Perspective." In *Charles Dickens' "Bleak House,"* edited by Harold Bloom. New York: Chelsea House, 1987.

Bodenheimer, Rosemarie. *The Politics of Story in Victorian Social Fiction.* Ithaca, NY: Cornell University Press, 1988.

Bonaparte, Felicia. *The Gypsy-Bachelor of Manchester: The Life of Mrs. Gaskell's Demon.* Charlottesville: University Press of Virginia, 1992.

Booth, P.H.W. *Burton Manor: The Biography of a House.* Cheshire, England: Burton Manor Residential College for Adult Education, 1978.

Bradley, Harriet. *Men's Work, Women's Work: A Sociological History of the Sexual Division of Labour in Employment.* Cambridge: Polity Press, 1989.

Branca, Patricia. *Silent Sisterhood: Middle-Class Women in the Victorian Home.* Pittsburgh: Carnegie Mellon University Press, 1975.

Brillat-Savarin, Jean Authelme. *The Physiology of Taste.* Translated by Arthur Mechen. New York: Doubleday, 1926.

Brontë, Anne. *The Tenant of Wildfell Hall.* Edited by G.D. Hargreaves. New York: Penguin, 1979.

Brontë, Charlotte. *Jane Eyre.* Edited by Jane Jack and Margaret Smith. Oxford: Clarendon Press, 1969.

———. *Shirley.* Edited by Herbert Rosengarten and Margaret Smith. Oxford: Clarendon Press, 1979.

———. *Villette.* Edited by Herbert Rosengarten and Margaret Smith. Oxford: Clarendon Press, 1984.

Brontë, Emily. *Wuthering Heights.* Edited by David Daiches. New York: Penguin, 1965.

Brown, Marion E. "Three Versions of *A Little Princess:* How the Story Developed." *Children's Literature in Education* 19, no. 4 (1988): 199–210.

Brownell, David. "The Two Worlds of Charlotte Yonge." In *The Worlds of Victorian Fiction,* edited by Jerome Buckley, 165–78. Cambridge: Harvard University Press, 1975.

Burke, Kenneth. *A Grammar of Motives.* New York: Prentice Hall, 1945.

Burnett, Frances Hodgson. *A Little Princess.* New York: Scribner's, 1905.

———. *Little Lord Fauntleroy.* New York: Scribner's, 1914.

———. *Sara Crewe, Or What Happened at Miss Minchin's?* New York: Scribner's, 1888.

Calder, Jenni. *The Victorian Home.* London: B. T. Batsford, 1977.

———. *Women and Marriage in Victorian Fiction.* New York: Oxford University Press, 1976.

Carlyle, Jane Welsh. *I Too Am Here: Selections from the Letters of Jane Welsh Carlyle.* Edited by Alan Simpson and Mary McQueen Simpson. Cambridge: Cambridge University Press, 1977.

Carter, Ann A. "Food, Feasting, and Fasting in the Nineteenth-Century British Novel." Ph. D. diss., University of Wisconsin, 1979.

Cartwright, Julia, ed. *The Journals of Lady Knightley of Fawsley.* London: John Murray, 1915.

Caserio, Robert L. *Plot, Story, and the Novel: From Dickens and Poe to the Modern Period.* Princeton: Princeton University Press, 1979.

Casteras, Susan P. "Down the Garden Path: Courtship Culture and Its Imagery in Victorian Painting." Ph. D. diss., Yale, 1977.

———. "Virgin Vows: The Early Victorian Artists' Portrayal of Nuns and Novices." In *Religion in the Lives of English Women, 1760–1930,* edited by Gail Malmgreen. Bloomington: Indiana University Press, 1986.

Chadwick, Edwin. *Report on the Sanitary Condition of the Labouring Population of Great Britain.* Edited by M.W. Flinn. Edinburgh: Edinburgh University Press, 1968.

Chamberlain, Mary. *Fenwomen: A Portrait of Women in an English Village.* London: Virago Press, 1975.

Chapman, Raymond. *Faith and Revolt: Studies in the Literary Influence of the Oxford Movement.* London: Weidenfeld and Nicholson, 1970.

Charlton, L.E.O. *The Recollections of a Northumbrian Lady.* London: Jonathan Cape, 1949.

Chernin, Kim. *Reinventing Eve: Modern Woman in Search of Herself.* New York: Random House, 1987.

Child-Villiers, Margaret, Dowager Countess of Jersey. *Fifty-One Years of Victorian Life.* London: John Murray, 1922.

Cixous, Hélène and Catherine Clément. *The Newly Born Woman.* Minneapolis: University of Minnesota Press, 1986.

Clifford, James. "Objects and Selves: An Afterword." In *Objects and Others: Essays on Museums and Material Culture,* edited by George W. Stocking, Jr. History of Anthropology, vol. 3. Madison: University of Wisconsin Press, 1985.

Cobbe, Frances Power. "Celibacy v. Marriage." *Fraser's* 65 (1862): 228–235.

———. "Female Charity—Lay and Monastic." *Fraser's* 66 (1862).

———. "What Shall We Do With Our Old Maids?" *Fraser's* 66 (1862): 594–610.

Collins, Wilkie. *No Name.* Edited by Virginia Blain. New York: Oxford University Press, 1986.

Colvin, Howard. *Calke Abbey Derbyshire: A Hidden House Revealed.* London: The National Trust/George Philip, 1985.

Conrad, Joseph. "A Glance at Two Books." In *Last Essays.* Garden City, NY: Doubleday, 1926.

———. *The Collected Letters of Joseph Conrad.* Edited by Frederick R. Karl and Laurence Davies. Cambridge: Cambridge University Press, 1983.

———. *The Secret Agent.* Garden City, NY: Anchor Books, 1953.

Conrad, Peter. *The Victorian Treasure House.* London: Collins, 1973.

Conroy, Michael P. *Backcloth to Gawthorpe.* Nelson: Hendon Publishing, 1971.

Coon, Lynda L., Katherine J. Haldane and Elisabeth W. Sommers, eds., *That Gentle Strength: Historical Perspectives on Women in Christianity.* Charlottesville: University Press of Virginia, 1990.

Cornwallis, Laura. MS notes for the housekeeper, n.d. Kent Archives Office. Kent, England.

Cosslett, Tess. *Woman to Woman: Female Friendship in Victorian Fiction.* Brighton: Harvester, 1988.

Craik, Dinah Mulock. *A Woman's Thoughts About Women.* Philadelphia: T. B. Peterson and Brothers, 1861.

———. "Miss Tommy: A Mediaeval Romance." In *Miss Tommy: A Mediaeval Romance and In a House Boat: A Journal.* New York: Harper, n.d.

———. *Olive,* 3 vols. New York: Garland, 1975.

———. "On Sisterhoods." In *About Money and Other Things: A Gift Book.* London: Macmillan, 1886.

Cripps, Elizabeth A. Introduction to *Alton Locke: Tailor and Poet,* by Charles Kingsley. Oxford: Oxford University Press, 1983.

Csikszentmihalyi, Mihaly and Eugene Rochberg-Halton. *The Meaning of Things: Domestic Symbols and the Self.* New York: Cambridge University Press, 1981.

Cust, Elizabeth and Evelyn Georgiana Pelham, eds. *Edward, Fifth Earl of Darnley and Emma Parnell His Wife.* Leeds: Richard Jackson, 1913.

Daiches, David. *The Novel and the Modern World.* Chicago: University of Chicago Press, 1960.

Daly, Mary. *Pure Lust: Elemental Feminist Philosophy.* Boston: Beacon Press, 1984.

Davidoff, Leonore. *The Best Circles: Society Etiquette and the Season.* London: Century Hutchinson, 1986.

Davidoff, Leonore and Catherine Hall. *Family Fortunes: Men and Women of the English Middle Class, 1780–1850.* Chicago: University of Chicago Press, 1987.

Davidoff, Leonore, et al., "Landscape with Figures: Home and Community in English Society." In *The Rights and Wrongs of Women,* edited by Juliet Mitchell and Ann Oakley. New York: Penguin, 1976.

Day, Alice Catharine. *Glimpses of Rural Life in Sussex During the Last Hundred Years.* Idbury: The Countryman Press, 1927.

Dennis, Barbara. "The Two Voices of Charlotte Yonge." *Durham University Journal* 34 (1973): 181–88.

———. "The Victorian Crisis: A Contemporary View." *Durham University Journal* 42 (1980): 27–36.

Dickens, Charles. *Bleak House.* Edited by Morton Dauwen. Boston: Riverside Press, 1956.

———. *The Chimes.* In *The Christmas Books,* vol. 1. New York: Penguin, 1982.

———. *Oliver Twist.* London: Nonesuch Press, 1937.

———. *Our Mutual Friend.* New York: Penguin, 1971.

———. *The Uncommercial Traveller.* New York: The University Society, 1908.

Dickerson, Vanessa. "The Ghost of a Self: Female Identity in Mary Shelley's *Frankenstein.*" *Journal of Popular Culture* 27 (Winter 1993): 79–92.

Dixon, Mary Ann. Diaries: 1838–62. Lincolnshire Archives Office. Lincolnshire, England.

Dodsworth, Martin. "Women Without Men at Cranford." *Essays in Criticism* 13 (1963): 132–45.

Donajgrodzki, A.P. "Social Police and the Bureaucratic Elite: A Vision of Order in the Age of Reform." In *Social Control in Nineteenth-Century Britain,* edited by A. P. Donajgrazki. London: Croom Helm, 1977.

Donaldson, Ian. *The Rapes of Lucretia: A Myth and Its Transformations.* Oxford: Clarendon Press, 1982.

Donzelot, Jacques. *The Policing of Families.* Translated by Robert Hurley. New York: Random House, 1979.

Douglas, Mary and Baron Isherwood. *The World of Goods.* New York: Basic Books, 1979.

Dow, Mrs. *Hints to Mistresses.* London: Bosworth and Harrison, 1856.

Dutton, Ralph. *Hinton Ampner, A Hampshire Manor.* London: Country Book Club, 1969.

Dyhouse, Carol. *Girls Growing Up in Late Victorian and Edwardian England.* London: Routledge and Kegan Paul, 1981.

Eagleton, Terry. *Myths of Power: A Marxist Study of the Brontës.* New York: Barnes and Noble, 1975.

Edelstein, T.J. "'They Sang the Song of the Shirt': The Visual Iconology of the Seamstress." *Victorian Studies* 23, no. 2 (Winter 1980): 183–211.

Eliot, George. *Adam Bede.* Edited by F.R. Leavis. New York: New American Library, 1961.

———. *Daniel Deronda.* Edited by Barbara Hardy. New York: Penguin, 1967.

———. *Felix Holt.* Edited by Fred C. Thomson. Oxford: Clarendon Press, 1980.

———. *Middlemarch.* Edited by David Carroll. Oxford: Clarendon Press, 1986.

———. *The Mill on the Floss.* Edited by George S. Haight. Oxford: Clarendon Press, 1980.

Ellis, Sarah Stickney. *The Wives of England, Their Relative Duties, Domestic Influence, and Social Obligations.* New York: n.p., 1844.

Elshtain, Jean Bethke. *Public Man, Private Woman: Women in Social and Political Thought.* Princeton: Princeton University Press, 1981.

Elwes, Winefride. *The Fielding Album.* London: Geoffrey Bles, 1950.

Engel, Elliot. "The Heir of the Oxford Movement: Charlotte Mary Yonge's *The Heir of Redclyffe.*" *Études Anglaises* 33 (1980): 132–41.

Engels, Friedrich. *The Condition of the Working Class in England.* Edited and translated by W.O. Henderson and W.H. Chaloner. Stanford: Stanford University Press, 1968.

Ferichs, Sarah C. "Elizabeth Missing Sewell: Concealment and Revelation in a Victorian Everywoman." In *Approaches to Victorian Autobiography,* edited by George Landow. Athens: Ohio University Press, 1979.

Figes, Eva. *Sex and Subterfuge: Women Writers to 1850.* New York: Persea Press, 1982.

Fleishman, Avrom. *Conrad's Politics: Community and Anarchy in the Fiction of Joseph Conrad.* Baltimore: Johns Hopkins University Press, 1967.

Fogel, Aaron. *Coercion to Speak: Conrad's Poetics of Dialogue.* Cambridge: Harvard University Press, 1985.

———. "Coerced Speech and the Oedipus Dialogue Complex." In *Rethinking Bakhtin: Extensions and Challenges,* edited by Gary Saul Morson and Caryl Emerson. Evanston, IL: Northwestern University Press, 1989.

Foster, Shirley. *Victorian Women's Fiction: Marriage, Freedom and the Individual.* London: Croom Helm, 1985.

Foucault, Michel. *Discipline and Punish: The Birth of the Prison.* Translated by Alan Sheridan. New York: Pantheon Books, 1977.

Frazee, John P. *"The Character of Esther and the Narrative Structure of Bleak House." Studies in the Novel* 17, no. 3 (Fall 1985): 227–40.

Fryckstedt, Monica Correa. "Defining the Domestic Genre: English Women Novelists of the 1850's." *Tulsa Studies in Women's Literature* 6, no. 1 (1987): 9–23.

[G. S.] *The Governess.* Houlston's Industrial Library no. 18. London: Houlston and Stoneman, 186–?.

Gagnier, Regenia. "The Literary Standard, Working-Class Lifewriting, and Gender." *Textual Practice* 3, no. 1 (Spring 1989): 36–55.

Gallagher, Catherine. *The Industrial Reformation of English Fiction: Social Discourse and Narrative Form 1832–1867.* Chicago: University of Chicago Press, 1985.

Gardner, Judith Kegan. "Mind Mother: Psychoanalysis and Feminism." In *Making a Difference,* edited by Gayle Greene and Coppélia Kahn. London: Routledge, 1985.

Garfinkel, P.E. and D.M. Garner. "Accepting the Symptom: A Feminist Psychoanalytic Treatment of Anorexia Nervosa." In *A Handbook of Psychotherapy for Anorexia and Bulimia,* edited by David M. Garner and Paul E. Garfinkel. New York: Guilford Press, 1985.

Gaskell, Catherine Milnes. "Women of To-Day." *The Nineteenth Century* 24 (Nov. 1889).

Gaskell, Elizabeth. *Cranford.* London: Macmillan, 1903.

———. *Elizabeth Gaskell: Four Short Stories.* London: Pandora Press, 1983.

———. *The Life of Charlotte Brontë.* New York: Penguin, 1985.

———. *Lizzie Leigh and Other Tales.* Freeport, New York: Books for Libraries Press, 1972.

———. *Mary Barton: A Tale of Manchester Life.* Edited by Stephen Gill. New York: Penguin, 1988.

———. *Ruth.* Oxford: Oxford University Press, 1987.

Gathorne-Hardy, Jonathan. *The Public School Phenomenon.* London: Hodder and Stoughton, 1977.

Gay, Peter. *The Bourgeois Experience: Victoria to Freud,* 2 vols. New York: Oxford University Press, 1984, 1986.

Gearhart, Sally. "Womanpower: Energy Re-Sourcement." In *The Politics of Women's Spirituality: Essays on the Rise of Spiritual Power Within the Feminist Movement*, edited by Charlene Spretnak. New York: Anchor Books, 1982.

Gell, Edith Mary. *Under Three Reigns 1860–1920*. London: Kegan Paul, Trench, Trubner and Co., 1927.

Gérin, Winifred. *Charlotte Brontë: The Evolution of Genius*. Oxford: Clarendon Press, 1967.

——. *Elizabeth Gaskell*. Oxford: Oxford University Press, 1980.

Gilbert, Sanda M. and Susan Gubar. *The Madwoman in the Attic: The Woman Writer and the Nineteenth-Century Imagination*. New Haven: Yale University Press, 1979.

Gilman, Charlotte Perkins. *Women and Economics: A Study of the Economic Relation Between Men and Women as a Factor in Social Evolution*. Boston: Small, Maynard, 1898.

Girouard, Mark. "Introduction" to *Victorians at Home*, edited by Susan Lasdun. New York: Viking, 1981.

——. *The Victorian Country House*. New Haven: Yale University Press, 1979.

Goldsmith, Arnold. "The Maltese Cross as Sign in *The Spoils of Poynton*." *Renascence* 16, no. 1 (Fall 1963): 73–77.

Gombrich, E.H. *Art and Illusion*. Princeton: Princeton University Press, 1961.

Gorham, Deborah. *The Victorian Girl and the Feminine Ideal*. Bloomington: Indiana University Press, 1982.

Gorsky, Susan. "Old Maids and New Women: Alternatives to Marriage in Englishwomen's Novels, 1847–1915." *Journal of Popular Culture* 7 (1973): 68–85.

Graver, Suzanne. "Writing in a 'Womanly Way' and the Double Vision of *Bleak House*." *Dickens Quarterly* 4, no. 1 (March 1987): 3–15.

Greg, W.R. "Why Are Women Redundant?" *National Review* 14 (1862): 434-460.

Greville, Violet. *The Gentlewoman in Society*. London: Henry and Co., 1892.

——. *Vignettes of Memory*. London: Hutchinson and Co., 1927.

Grimm, Jacob and Wilhelm. *The Complete Fairy Tales of the Brothers Grimm*. Translated by Jack Zipes. Toronto: Bantam, 1987.

Guiliani, Maria Vittoria. "Naming the Rooms: Implications of a Change in the Home Model." *Environment and Behavior* 19, no. 2 (March 1987).

Habegger, Alfred. *Henry James and the "Woman Business."* Cambridge: Cambridge University Press, 1989.

Haight, Gordon S. *George Eliot: A Biography.* Oxford: Oxford University Press, 1968.

Hall, Catherine. "The History of the Housewife." In *The Politics of Housework,* edited by Ellen Malos. London: Allison and Busby, 1980.

Halttunen, Karen. "From Parlor to Living Room: Domestic Space, Interior Decoration, and the Cult of Personality." In *Consuming Visions: Accumulation and Display of Goods in America, 1880–1920,* edited by Simon J. Bronner. New York: Norton, 1989.

Hamilton, Cecily. *Marriage as a Trade.* London: Chapman and Hall, 1910.

Hamley, W.G. "Old Maids." *Blackwood's Edinburgh Magazine* 112 (1872): 94–108.

Hanrahan, Meaghan. "'A Transitory Splendour': Portrayals of the Fallen Woman in the Mid-Century Victorian Novel." Honors thesis, College of William and Mary, 1991.

Hansen, William and Irwin Altman. "Decorating Personal Places: A Descriptive Analysis." *Environment and Behavior* 8, no. 4 (Dec. 1976).

Hare, Augustus. *The Story of My Life,* 6 vols. London: George Allen, 1896–1900.

Hay, Eloise Knapp. *The Political Novels of Joseph Conrad.* Chicago: University of Chicago Press, 1963.

Heeney, Brian. *The Women's Movement in the Church of England 1850–1930 .* Oxford: Clarendon Press, 1988.

Helsinger, Elizabeth, Robin Sheets, and William Veeder. *The Woman Question.* 2 vols. Chicago: University of Chicago Press, 1986.

Henderson, Mrs. *The Young Wife's Own Book: Her Domestic Duties and Social Habits.* Glasgow: W. R. M'Phun, 1857.

Henley, Dorothy. *Rosalind Howard, Countess of Carlisle.* London: The Hogarth Press, 1959.

Hickok, Kathleen. "The Spinster in Victoria's England: Changing Attitudes in Poetry by Women." *Journal of Popular Culture* 15 (1981): 119–20.

Hiley, Michael. *Victorian Working Women: Portraits from Life*. London: Gordon Fraser, 1988.

Hill, Michael. *The Religious Order: A Study of Virtuoso Religion and Its Legitimization in the Nineteenth-Century Church of England*. London: Heinemann, 1973.

Himmelfarb, Gertrude. *The Idea of Poverty: England in the Early Industrial Age*. New York: Knopf, 1984.

Hinton, Denys. "High Victorian 1840–80." In *Great Interiors*, edited by Ian Grant. New York: Dutton, 1967.

Hobhouse, Stephen. *Margaret Hobhouse and Her Family*. Rochester: Stanhope Press (privately printed), 1934.

Holcombe, Lee. *Victorian Ladies at Work: Middle-Class Working Women in England and Wales 1850–1914*. Hamden, CT: Archon Books, 1973.

———. *Wives and Property: Reform of the Married Women's Property Law in Nineteenth-Century England*. Toronto: University of Toronto Press, 1983.

Homans, Margaret. *Bearing the Word: Language and Female Experience in Nineteenth-Century Women's Writing*. Chicago: University of Chicago Press, 1986.

hooks, bell. *Feminist Theory: from margin to center*. Boston: South End Press, 1984.

Horn, Pamela. *Labouring Life in the Victorian Countryside*. Dublin: Gill and Macmillan, 1976.

———. *Ladies of the Manor: Wives and Daughters in Country-House Society 1830–1918*. Wolfeboro Falls: Alan Sutton, 1992.

———. *The Rise and Fall of the Victorian Servant*. Dublin: Gill and Macmillan, 1975.

Horne, Eric. *More Winks*. London: T. Werner Laurie, 1932.

Houghton, Walter E. *The Victorian Frame of Mind, 1830–1870*. New Haven: Yale University Press, 1957.

Hughs, T. *A Lecture on the Slop System, Especially as It Bears Upon the Females Engaged in It*. Exeter: W. and H. Pollard, 1852.

Hunt, Linda C. "Sustenance and Balm: The Question of Female Friendship in *Shirley* and *Villette*." *Tulsa Studies in Women's Literature* 1 (1982): 55–66.

———. *A Woman's Portion: Ideology, Culture, and the British Female Novel Tradition*. New York: Garland, 1988.

Huxley, Gervas. *Lady Elizabeth and the Grosvenors: Life in a Whig Family, 1822–1839.* London: Oxford University Press, 1965.

Hyde, H. Montgomery. *The Londonberrys: A Family Portrait.* London: Hamish Hamilton, 1979.

Irigaray, Lucy. *This Sex Which Is Not One.* Translated by Catherine Porter. Ithaca, NY: Cornell University Press, 1985.

Irwin, Michael. *Picturing: Description and Illusion in the Nineteenth-Century Novel.* London: George Allen and Unwin, 1979.

Jalland, Pat. *Women, Marriage and Politics 1860–1914.* Oxford: Clarendon Press, 1986.

James, Henry. *The Complete Notebooks of Henry James.* Edited by Leon Edel and Lyall H. Powers. New York: Oxford University Press, 1987.

———. "Preface to *The Spoils of Poynton.*" In *The Art of the Novel*, edited by R.P. Blackmur. New York: Scribner's, 1962.

———. *The Spoils of Poynton.* New York: Penguin, 1978.

———. *The Wings of the Dove.* New York: New American Library, 1964.

James, Mrs. Eliot. *Our Servants: Their Duties to Us and Ours to Them.* London: Ward, Lock and Co., 1883.

Jed, Stephanie. *Chaste Thinking: The Rape of Lucretia and the Birth of Humanism.* Bloomington: Indiana University Press, 1989.

Johansson, Shelia Ryan. "Sex and Death in Victorian England: An Examination of Age- and Sex-Specific Death Rates, 1840–1910." In *A Widening Sphere: Changing Roles of Victorian Women*, edited by Martha Vicinus. Bloomington: Indiana University Press, 1977.

Kanner, Barbara. *Women in English Social History, 1800–1914*, 3 vols. New York: Garland, 1987, 1988, 1990.

Kennard, Jean E. *Victims of Convention.* Camden, CT: Shoestring Press, 1978.

Kestner, Joseph. *Protest and Reform: The British Social Narrative by Women.* Madison: University of Wisconsin Press, 1985.

Kingsley, Charles. "The Poetry of Sacred and Legendary Art." *Fraser's* 39 (1849).

———. *Yeast: A Problem, The Life and Works of Charles Kingsley in Nineteen Volumes.* London: Macmillan, 1902.

Knoepflmacher, U.C. "Thoughts on the Aggression of Daughters." In *The Endurance of Frankenstein: Essays on Mary Shelley's Novel*, 88–

119, edited by George Levine and U.C. Knoepflmacher. Berkeley: University of California Press, 1974.

Koppes, Phyllis Bixler. "Tradition and the Individual Talent of Frances Hodgson Burnett: A Generic Analysis of *Little Lord Fauntleroy, A Little Princess,* and *The Secret Garden.*" *Children's Literature* 7 (1979): 191–207.

Krueger, Christine. *The Reader's Repentance: Women Preachers, Women Writers, and Nineteenth-Century Social Discourse.* Chicago: University of Chicago Press, 1992.

Lancaster, Osbert. *Home, Sweet Homes.* London: John Murray, 1948.

Langland, Elizabeth. "Nobody's Angels: Domestic Ideology and Middle-Class Women in the Victorian Novel." *PMLA* 107 (1992): 290–304.

Lansbury, Coral. *Elizabeth Gaskell.* Boston: G.K. Hall, 1984.

Lawrence, Roderick. "What Makes a House a Home?" *Environment and Behavior* 19, no. 2 (March 1987): 154–68.

Leacock, Eleanor and Helen I. Safa, eds. *Women's Work: Development and the Division of Labor by Gender.* South Hadley, MA: Bergin and Garvey, 1986.

Lears, Jackson. "Beyond Veblen: Re-thinking Consumer Culture in America." In *Consuming Visions: Accumulation and Display of Goods in America, 1880–1920,* edited by Simon J. Bronner. New York: Norton, 1989.

Leslie, Anita. *The Marlborough House Set.* New York: Dell, 1977.

Levine, George and U.C. Knoepflmacher, eds., *The Endurance of Frankenstein: Essays on Mary Shelley's Novel.* Berkeley: University of California Press, 1974.

Lichten, Frances. *Decorative Art of Victoria's Era.* New York: Scribner's, 1950.

Lieb, Laurie. "'The Works of Women Are Symbolical': Needlework in the Eighteenth Century." *Eighteenth Century Life* 10 (1986): 28–44.

Linehan, Thomas. "Parallel Lives: The Past and Self-Retribution in *Bleak House.*" *Studies in the Novel* 20, no. 2 (Summer 1988): 131–50.

Lister, Raymond. *Victorian Narrative Paintings.* London: London Museum Press, 1966.

Lochhead, Marion. *The Victorian House.* London: John Murray, 1964.

Louis, S.L. *Decorum: A Practical Treatise on Etiquette and Dress of the Best American Society.* New York: Union Publishing House, 1881.

Lown, Judy. *Women and Industrialization: Gender at Work in Nineteenth-Century England*. Minneapolis: University of Minnesota Press, 1990.

Lubbock, Percy. *Earlham*. London: Jonathan Cape, 1926.

Lyons, Richard S. "The Social Vision of *The Spoils of Poynton*." *American Literature* 61, no. 1 (March 1989): 59–77.

[M. S., An Old Servant]. *Domestic Service*. Boston: Houghton Mifflin, 1917.

McBride, Theresa. *The Domestic Revolution: The Modernisation of Household Service in England and France 1820–1920*. London: Croom Helm, 1976.

Maccoll, Gail and Carol McD. Wallance. *To Marry an English Lord: The Victorian and Edwardian Experience*. London: Sidgwick and Jackson, 1989.

McCormack, Peggy. "The Semiotics of Economic Language in James's Fiction." *American Literature* 58, no. 4 (Dec. 1986): 540–56.

McGregor, O.R. *Divorce in England: A Centenary Study*. London: Heinemann, 1957.

Macheski, Cecilia. "Penelope's Daughters: Images of Needlework in Eighteenth-Century Literature." In *Fetter'd or Free? British Women Novelists, 1670–1815*, edited by Mary Anne Schofield and Cecilia Macheski. Athens, OH: Ohio University Press, 1986.

Maison, Margaret. *The Victorian Vision: Studies in the Religious Novel*. New York: Sheed and Ward, 1961.

Mann, Thomas. "Conrad's *The Secret Agent*." In *Past Masters and Other Papers*. New York: Knopf, 1933.

Mare, Margaret and Alicia C. Percival. *Victorian Bestseller: The World of Charlotte M. Yonge*. London: Harrap, 1948.

Margetson, Stella. *Victorian High Society*. New York: Holmes and Meier, 1980.

Mauchline, Mary. *Harewood House*. Newton Abbot: David and Charles, 1974.

Mayhew, Henry. London Labour and the London Poor, 4 vols. New York: Dover Publications, 1968.

———. *The Unknown Mayhew: Selections from the Morning Chronicle, 1849–1850*. Edited by E.P. Thompson and Eileen Yeo. New York: Shocken, 1971.

Meade-Fetherstonehaugh, Margaret and Oliver Warner. *Uppark and Its People*. London: George Allen Unwin, 1964.

Mellor, Anne K., ed., *Romanticism and Feminism*. Bloomington: Indiana University Press, 1988.

Meteyard, Eliza ["Silverpen"]. *Lucy Dean, the Noble Needlewoman*. In *Eliza Cook's Journal* 2 (16 March–20 April 1850).

Michie, Helena. *The Flesh Made Word: Female Figures and Women's Bodies*. Oxford: Oxford University Press, 1987.

Mill, John Stuart. *The Subjection of Women*. Cambridge: MIT Press, 1970.

Miller, D.A. *The Novel and the Police*. Berkeley: University of California Press, 1988.

Mingle, Wanda. "The Industrial Revolution and the European Family: 'Childhood' as a Market for Family Labor." In *Women's Work: Development and the Division of Labor by Gender*, edited by Eleanor Leacock and Helen I. Safa. South Hadley, MA: Bergin and Garvey, 1986.

Mitchell, Sally. *Dinah Mulock Craik*. Twayne's English Authors' Series, 364. Boston: Twayne, 1983.

———. "Sentiment, and Suffering: Women's Recreational Reading in the 1860's."*Victorian Studies* 21 (1977): 29–45.

Mitford, Nancy. *The Stanleys of Alderley: Their Letters between the Years 1815–1865*. London: Chapman and Hall, 1973.

Moers, Ellen. *Literary Women*. New York: Doubleday, 1976.

Morey, Jenn. "Subtle Subversion: Gaskell's Use of Scripture in Her Social Purpose Novels." Master's thesis, College of William and Mary, 1990.

Morgan, Joan and Alison Richards. *A Paradise Out of a Common Field: The Pleasures and Plenty of the Victorian Garden*. New York: Harper and Row, 1990.

Morgan, Susan. *Sisters in Time: Imagining Gender in Nineteenth-Century British Fiction*. New York: Oxford University Press, 1989.

Mull, Donald L. *Henry James's "Sublime Economy": Money as Symbolic Center in the Fiction*. Middleton, CT: Wesleyan University Press, 1973.

Nadelhaft, Ruth. *Joseph Conrad*. Atlantic Highlands, NJ: Humanities Press International, 1991.

Nead, Lynda. *Myths of Sexuality: Representations of Women in Victorian Britain*. Oxford: Basil Blackwell, 1988.

Neff, Wanda. *Victorian Working Women: An Historical and Literary Study of Women in British Industries and Professions, 1832–1850*. New York: Humanities Press, 1967.

Nelson, Claudia. *Boys Will Be Girls: The Feminine Ethic in British Children's Fiction, 1857–1917*. New Brunswick: Rutgers University Press, 1991.

Nestor, Pauline. *Female Friendships and Communities: Charlotte Brontë, George Eliot, Elizabeth Gaskell*. Oxford: Clarendon Press, 1985.

Nevill, Ralph. *Reminiscences of Lady Dorothy Nevill*. London: Edward Arnold, 1907.

Newton, Judith Lowder. *Women, Power, and Subversion: Social Stategies in British Fiction, 1778–1860*. Athens, GA: University of Georgia Press, 1981.

Nightingale, Florence. "Cassandra." In *"The Cause": A Short History of the Women's Movement in Great Britain*, edited by Ray Strachey. Port Washington, NY: Kennikat Press, 1969.

Northwick MSS, 1859–68. Worcestershire Record Office. Worcestershire, England.

Oakley, Ann. *Woman's Work: The Housewife Past and Present*. New York: Pantheon Books, 1974.

Olivier, Edith. *Four Victorian Ladies of Wiltshire*. London: Faber and Faber, 1945.

Olsen, Tillie. *Silences*. New York: Delacorte, 1978.

Opie, Peter and Iona Opie. *The Classic Fairy Tales*. London: Oxford University Press, 1974.

Packe, Alice, Lady. MS letters of reference sent to, 1875–1883. Leicestershire Record Office. Leicestershire, England.

Papishvilly, Helen. *All the Happy Endings*. New York: Harper's, 1966.

Parker, Roszika. *The Subversive Stitch: Embroidery and the Making of the Feminine*. London: Women's Press, 1984.

Patmore, Coventry. *The Angel in the House*. In *Poems*, edited by Basil Channeys. London: Bell, 1921.

Payne, Blanch. *History of Costume: From the Ancient Egyptians to the Twentieth Century*. New York: Harper and Row, 1965.

Pearsall, Ronald. *The Worm in the Bud: The World of Victorian Sexuality*. New York: Penguin, 1983.

Peterson, M. Jeanne. *Family, Love, and Work in the Lives of Victorian Gentlewomen*. Bloomington: Indiana University Press, 1989.

Pike, E. Royston. *Human Documents of the Victorian Golden Age (1850–1875)*. London: George Allen and Unwin, 1974.

Pinchbeck, Ivy. *Women Workers and the Industrial Revolution 1750–1850.* New York: F.S. Crofts and Co., 1930.

Pollock, Griselda. *Vision and Difference: Femininity, Feminism, and Histories of Art.* New York: Routledge, 1988.

Poovey, Mary. *Uneven Developments: The Ideological Work of Gender in Mid-Victorian England.* Chicago: University of Chicago Press, 1988.

Putzell-Korab, Sara. "Passion Between Women in the Victorian Novel." In *Sexuality and Victorian Literature,* 180–95, edited by Don Richard Cox. Knoxville: University of Tennessee Press, 1984.

Randall, Rona. *The Model Wife, Nineteenth-Century Style.* London: Herbert, 1989.

Reynolds, G.M.W. *The Seamstress.* In *Reynold's Miscellany* 4 (23 March 1850) and 5 (10 Aug. 1850).

———. "A Warning to Needlewomen and Slopworkers." In *Reynold's Political Instructor* 1 (1849–1850): 66–67.

Ridley, Cecilia. MS, letter to Lady Parke, Oct. 1844. Northumberland Record Office. Northumberland, England.

———. *The Life and Letters of Cecilia Ridley.* Edited by Ursula Ridley. London: Rupert Hart Davis, 1958.

Roberts, Elizabeth. *Women's Work: 1840–1940.* London: Macmillan Studies in Economic and Social History, 1988.

Roberts, Helene E. "Marriage, Redundancy or Sin: The Painter's View of Women in the First Twenty-Five Years of Victoria's Reign." In *Suffer and Be Still: Women in the Victorian Age,* edited by Martha Vicinus. Bloomington: Indiana University Press, 1972.

Rose, Hilary. "Women's Work: Women's Knowledge." In *What Is Feminism?* edited by Juliet Mitchell and Ann Oakley. New York: Pantheon Books, 1986.

Rosenberg, Charles E. *No Other Gods: On Science and American Social Thought.* Baltimore: Johns Hopkins University Press, 1976.

Rubenius, Aina. *The Woman Question in Mrs. Gaskell's Life and Works.* Cambridge: Harvard University Press, 1950.

Rule, John. *The Labouring Classes in Early Industrial England 1750–1850.* New York: Longman, 1986.

Ruskin, John. "The Ethics of the Dust." In *Works,* vol. 18, edited by E.T. Cook and Alexander Wedderburn. London: Allen, 1905.

———. "Lilies: Of Queens' Gardens." In *Essays English and American.* New York: Collier, 1910.

————. "On Domestic Art." In *The Lamp of Beauty: Writing on Art by John Ruskin*, edited by Joan Evans. Ithaca, NY: Cornell University Press, 1959.

————. "Sesame and Lilies." In *Sesame and Lilies, The Two Paths, The King of the Golden River*. London: Dent, 1965.

Said, Edward. *Orientalism*. New York. Pantheon Books. 1978.

Sandbach-Dahlstrom, Catherine. *Be Good Sweet Maid: Charlotte Yonge's Domestic Fiction: A Study in Dogmatic Purpose and Fictional Form*. Stockholm Studies in English, no. 59. Stockholm: Almquist and Wiksell, 1984.

————. "Perceiving the Single Woman: Elizabeth Sewell's *The Experience of Life*." In *Proceedings from the Second Nordic Conference for English Studies* , edited by Haan Ringbom and Matti Rissanen, 497–504. Åbo, Finland: Åbo Akademi, 1984.

Saunders, Valerie. "Absolutely an Act of Duty: Choice of Profession in Autobiographies of Victorian Women." *Prose Studies* 9, no. 3 (1986): 54–70.

Sawicki, Joseph. "'The Mere Truth won't do': Esther as Narrator in *Bleak House*." *Journal of Narrative Technique* 17, no. 2 (Spring 1987): 211–28.

Schneidau, Herbert N. *Waking Giants: The Presence of the Past in Modernism*. New York: Oxford University Press, 1991.

Schonfield, Zuzanna. *The Precariously Privileged: A Professional Family in Victorian London*. New York: Oxford University Press, 1987.

Scott, Patrick. "Genre and Perspective in the Study of Victorian Women Writers: The Case of Elizabeth Missing Sewell." *Victorian Newsletter* 66 (1984): 5–10.

See, Fred G. "Henry James and the Art of Possession." In *American Realism*, edited by Eric J. Sundquist. Baltimore: Johns Hopkins University Press, 1982.

Senf, Carol A. "Bleak House: Dickens, Esther, and the Androgynous Mind." *Victorian Newsletter* 64 (Fall 1983): 21–27.

Sewell, Elizabeth. *The Autobiography of Elizabeth M. Sewell*. New York: Longmans, Green, and Co., 1907.

————. *The Experience of Life; Margaret Percival: The Experience of Life*. In *A Garland Series: Victorian Fiction: Novels of Faith and Doubt*. New York: Garland, 1977.

Sewell, William. *Hawkstone*. In *A Garland Series: Victorian Fiction: Novels of Faith and Doubt*. New York: Garland, 1976.

Shakespeare, William. *The Taming of the Shrew.* In *The Riverside Shakespeare,* edited by G. Blakemore Evans. Boston: Houghton Mifflin, 1974.

Shanley, Mary Lyndon. "One Must Ride Behind: Married Women's Rights and the Divorce Act of 1857." *Victorian Studies* 25 (1982).

Shelley, Mary. *Frankenstein, or The Modern Prometheus.* New York: Signet, 1965.

Shor, Naomi. *Reading in Detail: Aesthetics and the Feminine.* New York: Methuen, 1987.

Showalter, Elaine. *A Literature of Their Own.* Princeton: Princeton University Press, 1977.

———. "Dinah Mulock Craik and the Tactics of Sentiment: A Case Study in Victorian Female Authorship." *Feminist Studies* 2. 2/3, (1975): 5–23.

Siefert, Susan. *The Dilemma of the Talented Heroine: A Study in Nineteenth-Century Fiction.* St. Albans, VT: Edens, 1979.

Sitwell, Edith. *Taken Care Of.* London: Hutchinson and Co., 1965.

Smith-Rosenberg, Carroll. *Disorderly Conduct: Visions of Gender in Victorian America.* New York: Oxford University Press, 1985.

———. "The Female World of Love and Ritual: Relations Between Women in Nineteenth-Century America." *Signs* 1 (1975): 1–29.

———. "In Search of Woman's Nature, 1850–1920." *Feminist Studies* 3 (1975): 141–54.

Spacks, Patricia Meyer. *The Female Imagination.* New York: Knopf, 1975.

Spain, Daphne. *Gendered Spaces.* Chapel Hill, NC: University of North Carolina Press, 1992.

Springer, Marlene. "Angels and Other Women in Victorian Literature." In *What Manner of Woman: Essays in English and American Life and Literature,* edited by Marlene Springer. New York: New York University Press, 1977.

St. Helier, Susan, Lady Jeune. *Lesser Questions.* London: Remington and Co., 1895.

Stanley, Liz, ed. *The Diaries of Hannah Cullwick, Victorian Maidservant.* New Brunswick: Rutgers University Press, 1984.

Steele, Richard. "The Tatler: No. 126." In *The Tatler,* edited by George A. Aitken. London: Duckworth, 1899.

Stewart, Susan. *On Longing: Narratives of the Miniature, the Gigantic, the Souvenir, the Collection.* Baltimore: Johns Hopkins University Press, 1984.

Stirling, A.M.W. *Life's Little Day.* London: Thornton Butterworth, 1924.

Stone, Lawrence. *The Family, Sex and Marriage, 1500–1800.* London: Weidenfeld and Nicholson, 1977.

Stoneman, Patsy. *Elizabeth Gaskell.* Bloomington: Indiana University Press, 1987.

Storr, Catherine. "Parents." In *A Chaplet for Charlotte Yonge,* edited by Georgina Battiscombe and Margharita Laski. London: Cresset, 1965.

Streatfield, Noel, ed. *The Day before Yesterday: Firsthand Stories of Fifty Years Ago.* London: Collins, 1956.

Stubbs, Patricia. *Women and Fiction: Feminism and the Novel, 1880–1920.* New York: Barnes and Noble, 1979.

Sutherland, George, 5th Duke of Sutherland. *Looking Back.* London: Oldhams Press, 1957.

Swindells, Julia. *Victorian Writing and Working Women.* Minneapolis: University of Minnesota Press, 1985.

Tartar, Maria. *Off With Their Heads!: Fairy Tales and the Culture of Childhood.* Princeton: Princeton University Press, 1992.

Thackeray, William Makepeace. *The History of Pendennis.* New York: Scribner's, 1917.

Thompson, E.P. *The Making of the English Working Class.* New York: Vintage, 1966.

Thomson, Ethel. *Clifton Lodge.* London: Hutchinson, 1955.

Thwaite, Ann. *Waiting for the Party: The Life of Frances Hodgson Burnett, 1849–1924.* London: Secker and Warburg, 1974.

Todorov, Tzvetan. *The Poetics of Prose.* Translated by Richard Howard. Ithaca, NY: Cornell University Press, 1977.

Tristram, Phillipa. *Living Space in Fact and Fiction.* London: Routledge, 1989.

Trodd, Anthea. *Domestic Crime in the Victorian Novel.* New York: St. Martin's Press, 1989.

Tweedsmuir, Susan. *The Lilac and the Rose.* London: Gerald Duckworth and Co., 1952.

Van Boheemen, Christine. *The Novel as Family Romance: Language, Gender and Authority from Fielding to Joyce.* Ithaca, NY: Cornell University Press, 1987.

Vance, Norman. *The Sinews of the Spirit: The Ideal of Christian Manliness in Victorian Literature and Religious Thought.* Cambridge: Cambridge University Press, 1985.

Vanden Bossche, Chris. "Cookery, Not Rookery: Family and Class in *David Copperfield.*" *Dickens Studies Annual* 15 (1986): 87–109.

Veblen, Thorstein. *Theory of the Leisure Class.* New York: Macmillan, 1899.

Verey, David, ed. *The Diary of a Victorian Squire: Extracts from the Diaries and Letters of Dearman & Emily Birchall.* Gloucester: Alan Sutton, 1983.

Vicinus, Martha. *Independent Women: Work and Community for Single Women, 1850–1920.* London: Virago, 1985.

———, ed. *A Widening Sphere: Changing Roles for Victorian Women.* Bloomington: Indiana University Press, 1977.

———, ed. *Suffer and Be Still: Women in the Victorian Age.* Bloomington: Indiana University Press, 1972.

Walker, Alice. *In Search of Our Mothers' Gardens: Womanist Prose.* San Diego: Harcourt, Brace, Jovanovich, 1983.

Walkley, Christina. *The Ghost in the Looking Glass: The Victorian Seamstress.* London: Peter Owen, 1981.

Walkowitz, Judith. "The Making of an Outcast Group: Prostitutes and Working Women in Nineteenth-Century Plymouth and Southampton." In *A Widening Sphere: Changing Roles of Victorian Women,* 72–93, edited by Martha Vicinus. Bloomington: Indiana University Press, 1977.

Warhol, Robyn. *Gendered Interventions: Narrative Discourse in the Victorian Novel.* New Brunswick: Rutgers University Press, 1989.

Watt, Ian. *Conrad in the Nineteenth Century.* Berkeley: University of California Press, 1979.

Welter, Barbara. "The Cult of True Womanhood: 1800–1860." In *Dimity Convictions: The American Woman in the Nineteenth Century,* edited by Barbara Welter. Athens: Ohio University Press, 1976.

Wemyss, Countess of. *A Family Record.* London: privately printed, 1932.

Wharton, Edith and Ogden Codman, Jr. *The Decoration of Houses.* New York: Scribner's, 1907.

Wheeler, Michael. *The Art of Allusion in Victorian Fiction*. London: Macmillan, 1979.

White, Cynthia L. *Women's Magazines: 1693–1968*. London: Michael Joseph, 1970.

Williams, Jan, Hazel Twort and Ann Bachelli. "Women and the Family." In *The Politics of Housework*, edited by Ellen Malos. London: Allison and Busby, 1980.

Williams, Merryn. *Women in the English Novel, 1800–1900*. New York: St. Martin's Press, 1984.

Wilson, Francesca. *Rebel Daughter of a Country House: The Life of Eglantyne Jebb, Founder of the Save the Children Fund*. London: George Allen Unwin, 1967.

Winn, Sharon A. and Lynn M. Alexander, eds. *The Slaughter-House of Mammon: An Anthology of Victorian Social Protest Literature*. West Cornwall, CT: Locust Hill Press, 1992.

Wittner, Judith. "Domestic Labor as Work Discipline." In *Women and Household Labor*, edited by Sarah Fenstermaker. Beverly Hills: Sage, 1980.

Wolff, Janet. *Feminine Sentences: Essays on Women and Culture*. Berkeley: University of California Press, 1990.

Woodham-Smith, Cecil. *Florence Nightingale*. London: Reprint Society, 1952.

Woolf, Robert Lee. *Gains and Losses: Novels of Faith and Doubt in Victorian England*. London: Garland, 1977.

Woolf, Virginia. *A Room of One's Own*. New York: Harcourt, Brace and World, 1957.

Yonge, Charlotte. *Heartsease; or The Brother's Wife*. London: Parker, 1854.

———. *Hopes and Fears; or Scenes from the Life of a Spinster*. London: Parker, 1860.

———. *Womankind*. London: Mozley and Smith, 1876.

Young, Arthur. *Echoes of Two Cultures*. Pittsburgh: University of Pittsburgh Press, 1964.

Zwerdling, Alex. "Esther Summerson Rehabilitated." *PMLA* 88 (1973): 429–39.

Contributors

Lynn M. Alexander is an associate professor of English at the University of Tennessee at Martin. She is co-editor of *The Slaughter-House of Mammon: An Anthology of Victorian Working-Class Literature.* She has published articles in *Victorian Newsletter* and *Studies in the Humanities* on working women in nineteenth-century literature.

Eileen Connell is a graduate student instructor at the University of Virginia. She will soon complete her dissertation, *The Age of Experience: Edith Wharton and the 'Divorce Question' in Early Twentieth-Century America.*

Martin A. Danahay is an assistant professor of English at Emory University. His publications include a book on nineteenth-century autobiography, *A Community of One: Masculine Autobiography and Autonomy in Nineteenth-Century Britain,* and articles on Victorian literature and contemporary ethnic autobiographies. He not only studies housework, but also occasionally performs domestic labors himself.

Vanessa D. Dickerson is an assistant professor of English at Rhodes College. She has published articles on both Victorian women and on contemporary African-American women writers. She has recently completed a manuscript on Victorian women and supernaturalism and has begun work on her next project—a study of the black Victorian.

Laura Fasick is an assistant professor of English at Moorhead State University in Minnesota. She has published articles in

Nineteenth-Century Literature, Victorian Newsletter, and other journals. Her current project focuses on representations of women's bodies in selected eighteenth- and nineteenth-century British novels.

Francis L. Fennell is professor of English at Loyola University Chicago. He is the author of numerous articles on Victorian literature, especially on Ruskin, Newman, Hopkins, and Rossetti. He is also author or editor of five books, the most recent of which is *The Fine Delight: Centenary Essays on the Poetry of Gerard Manley Hopkins.*

Monica A. Fennell, formerly managing editor of *Lawyer's Alert,* is the author of numerous articles in legal publications, most recently "Hunger and Homelessness" in the *Fordham Urban Law Journal* (1994). Currently she is an attorney with the firm of Michael, Best, and Friedrich in Milwaukee, Wisconsin.

Jessica Gerard teaches in the history department at Southwest Missouri State University. She has had several articles published, and her book, *Country House Life: Family and Servants, 1815–1914,* is forthcoming.

Julia M. Gergits is an assistant professor at Youngstown State University. She has articles in *Written Communication, Journal of Advanced Composition,* and *Victorian Britain: An Encyclopedia.* Her most recent project is co-editing three volumes of *British Travel Writers,* which will form a part of the *Dictionary of Literary Biography.*

Maura Ives is an assistant professor of English at Texas A & M University. In addition to Victorian and twentieth-century women's writing, her research interests include bibliographies, textual criticism, and the history of the book. She has presented several papers on these topics and is currently completing a critical edition of George Meredith's publications in the *New Quarterly Magazine.*

Thad Logan is a lecturer in the English Department at Rice University. She has recently published "Foreign Object: Souvenirs and Exotic in the Victorian Parlor" in *Nineteenth-Century Contexts* and "Victorian Treasure Houses: The Novel and the Parlor" in *The Journal of Narrative and Life History*. She is currently completing an interdisciplinary study which investigates feminine practices of collection and display in middle-class Victorian homes.

Deborah Denenholz Morse is an assistant professor at the College of William and Mary, where she teaches Victorian literature. Her publications include a book, *Women in Trollope's Palliser Novels*, and articles on Trollope, Elizabeth Gaskell, Kay Boyle, Mona Simpson, and Maxine Hong Kingston. Morse is currently writing a book on Gaskell and a long article on feminist consciousness in the novel of manners tradition.

Brian W. Shaffer is an assistant professor of English at Rhodes College and the author of *The Blinding Torch: Modern British Fiction and the Discourse of Civilization*. He is also the author of essays in *PMLA, Journal of Modern Literature, James Joyce Quarterly*, and *Joyce in Context*, and the guest editor of a special issue of *Conradiana* devoted to teaching *Heart of Darkness*. He is presently at work on a study of politics and sexuality in the modern British Novel.

Sandra Kumamoto Stanley is an assistant professor of English at California State University, Northridge. Her book *Louis Zukofsky and the Transformation of a Modern American Poetics* has recently been published by University of California Press. She is currently focusing her research activities on issues of gender and ethnicity.

Index